Film Studies

D0472210

Film Studies
Critical Approaches

Edited by

JOHN HILL and **PAMELA CHURCH GIBSON**

Consultant Editors

Richard Dyer   E. Ann Kaplan   Paul Willemen

OXFORD
UNIVERSITY PRESS
2000

OXFORD

UNIVERSITY PRESS

Great Clarendon Street, Oxford OX2 6DP

Oxford University Press is a department of the University of Oxford.
It furthers the University's objective of excellence in research, scholarship,
and education by publishing worldwide in

Oxford New York
Auckland Cape Town Dar es Salaam Hong Kong Karachi Kuala Lumpur
Madrid Melbourne Mexico City Nairobi New Delhi Taipei Toronto
Shanghai

With offices in
Argentina Austria Brazil Chile Czech Republic France Greece
Guatemala Hungary Italy Japan South Korea Poland Portugal
Singapore Switzerland Thailand Turkey Ukraine Vietnam

Oxford is a registered trade mark of Oxford University Press
in the UK and in certain other countries

Published in the United States
by Oxford University Press Inc., New York

British Library Cataloguing in Publication Data
Data available

Library of Congress Cataloging in Publication Data
Data available

ISBN-13: 978-0-19-874280-7
ISBN-10: 0-19-874280-0

10 9 8

Typeset by J&L Composition Ltd, Filey, North Yorkshire
Printed in Great Britain by
Antony Rowe Ltd., Chippenham, Wiltshire

Acknowledgements

We would like to thank a number of people who have helped in the preparation of this book. We are, of course, grateful to all our contributors, some of whom worked to particularly tight deadlines. We would also like to thank our consultant editors—Richard Dyer, Ann Kaplan, and Paul Willemen—for their assistance and advice. Geoffrey Nowell-Smith also provided good advice and suggestions at an early stage.

At Oxford University Press, we would particularly like to thank our editor Andrew Lockett for his constant support and enthusiasm for the book, Tania Pickering for her invaluable assistance, and Mick Belson and Ruth Marshall for their help and efficiency in preparing the manuscript for publication.

We are also grateful to Roma Gibson, Celia Britton, Stella Bruzzi, and Teresa de Lauretis for their help. John Hill is also indebted to his colleagues David Butler, Dan Fleming, and Martin McLoone at the University of Ulster for their support for the project and to the Faculty of Humanities for a well-timed period of leave of absence. Thanks also to the staff at BFI Stills.

J. H. and P. C. G.

Contents

Contributors

EDITORS

John Hill is Professor of Media Studies at the University of Ulster at Coleraine. He is the author of *Sex, Class and Realism: British Cinema 1956–63* (1986) and *British Cinema in the 1980s* (1999), co-author of *Cinema and Ireland* (1987), and co-editor of *Border Crossing: Film in Ireland, Britain and Europe* (1994), and *Big Picture, Small Screen: The Relations Between Film and Television* (1996).

Pamela Church Gibson is a Senior Lecturer in Contextual and Cultural Studies at the London College of Fashion, a constituent college of the London Institute. She is the co-editor of *Dirty Looks: Women, Pornography, Power* (1993) and has written on heritage film both for *British Cinema in the Nineties* (ed. Murphy, 1999) and for the French journal *1895*. She has a chapter on the *Alien* cycle of films in *Popular Film and Cultural Studies* (forthcoming) and is currently working with Stella Bruzzi on a collection of essays tentatively entitled *Fashion and Culture: Theories and Explorations*.

CONSULTANT EDITORS

Richard Dyer is Professor of Film Studies at the University of Warwick. He is the author of a number of books including *Stars* (1979), *Heavenly Bodies* (1986), *The Matter of Images* (1993), *Now You See It* (1990) and *White: Essays on Race and Culture* (1997).

E. Ann Kaplan teaches at the Department of English at the Humanities Institute at Stony Brook, New York. She is the author of a number of books including *Women and Film: Both Sides of the Camera* (1983), *Motherhood and Representation: The Mother in Popular Culture and Melodrama* (1992), and *Looking For The Other: Feminism, Film, and the Imperial Gaze* (1997).

Paul Willemen is Professor of Critical Studies at Napier University, Edinburgh. He has published widely on film theory and is the author of a number of books, including *Looks and Frictions: Essays in Cultural Studies and Film Theory* (1994) and co-editor of *Questions of Third Cinema* (1989) and the *Encyclopaedia of Indian Cinema* (1994).

CONTRIBUTORS

Dudley Andrew is a Professor at the Institute for Cinema and Culture at the University of Iowa and is the author of *The Major Film Theories* (1976), *Concepts in Film Theory* (1984), and *Mists of Regret: Culture and Sensibility in Classic French Film* (1995).

Peter Brunette teaches in the Department of English at George Mason University, Fairfax, Virginia, and is author of *Roberto Rossellini* (1987) and co-author of *Screen/Play: Derrida and Film Theory* (1989).

Rey Chow is Andrew W. Mellon Professor of the Humanities and Professor of Modern Culture and Media and Comparative Literature at Brown University. Her publications in English include *Women and Chinese Modernity: The Politics of Reading Between East and West* (1990), *Writing Diaspora: Tactics of Intervention in Contemporary Cultural Studies* (1993), *Primitive Passions: Visuality, Sexuality, Ethnography, and Contemporary Chinese Cinema* (1995), and *Ethics after Idealism: Theory–Culture–Ethnicity–Reading* (1998).

Ian Christie is Professor of Film and Media History at Birkbeck College, University of London. He has published widely on Russian and British Cinema, on early film, and on the avant-garde, and is author of *Arrows of Desire: The Films of Michael Powell and the Emeric Pressburger* (1994).

Barbara Creed is Associate Professor in the Department of Fine Arts at Melbourne University,

Australia. She has published widely on feminism, psychoanalysis, and the horror film and is author of *The Monstrous-Feminine* (1993).

Alexander Doty is an Associate Professor in the English Department at Lehigh University, Bethlehem, USA. He is the author of *Making Things Perfectly Queer: Interpreting Mass Culture* (1993) and co-editor of *Out in Culture: Gay, Lesbian and Queer Essays on Popular Culture* (1995). His latest book is *Flaming Classics: Queering the Film Canon* (2000).

Anthony Easthope is Professor of English and Cultural Studies at the Metropolitan University, Manchester, and author of a number of books including *Poetry as Discourse* (1983), *British Post-Structuralism* (1988), *What a Man's Gotta Do: Masculine Myth in Popular Culture* (1986) and *Literary into Cultural Studies* (1991).

Claudia Gorbman is a Professor of Liberal Studies at the University of Washington, Tacoma, USA where she teaches film, media studies, and literature. Her work on film music includes *Unheard Melodies: Narrative Film Music* (1987). Among her translations are Michel Chion's *Audio-Vision: Sound on Screen* (1994).

Jostein Gripsrud is a Professor in the Department of Media Studies at the University of Bergen, Norway. He is author of *The Dynasty Years: Hollywood Television and Critical Media Studies* (1995). He was on the Board of the Moving Images in Norway Project 1990–93, and co-authored a book in Norwegian on the recent history of film in Norway (1996).

Noel King teaches in the School of Humanities at the University of Technology, Sydney, and has written widely on film theory.

Laura Kipnis is an Associate Professor of Radio/Television/Film at Northwestern University, Evanston. She is the author of *Ecstasy Unlimited: On Sex, Capital, Gender and Aesthetics* (1993) and *Bound and Gagged: Pornography and the Politics of Fantasy in America* (1999), and is an independent video-maker whose work is exhibited and broadcast internationally.

Chuck Kleinhans teaches at the Department of Radio/Television/Film at Northwestern University, Evanston, and is co-editor of *Jump Cut: A Review of Contemporary Media*.

Robert P. Kolker teaches in the Department of English at the University of Maryland and is the author of *The Altering Eye: Contemporary International Cinema* (1983), *A Cinema of Loneliness* (1988) and *Film, Form, and Culture* (1999), an introductory text and CD-ROM.

Paul McDonald is a Senior Lecturer in Film and Television Studies at the University of Surrey, Roehampton where he lectures on screen acting. He trained and worked as a professional actor and has written on screen performance for a number of published collections.

Robert B. Ray is Professor of English and the Director of Film and Media Studies at the University of Florida, Gainesville, and author of *A Certain Tendency of the Hollywood Cinema 1930–1980* (1985) and *The Avant-Garde Finds Andy Hardy* (1995).

Anneke Smelik is a lecturer in film studies at the University of Nijmegen, the Netherlands. She is the author of *And the Mirror Cracked: Feminist Cinema and Film Theory* (1998) and co-editor of *Women's Studies: A Feminist Introduction* (1995).

Andrew Tudor is a Reader in Sociology at the University of York. He was the film critic of *New Society* for several years and is the author of *Theories of Film* (1974), *Image and Influence: Studies in the Sociology of Film* (1974) and *Monsters and Mad Scientists: A Cultural History of the Horror Movie* (1989).

Graeme Turner is Professor of Cultural Studies in the Department of English at the University of Queensland, Australia. He has published widely on topics in cultural studies and film, and on Australian media and popular culture. He is currently researching the function of celebrity in Australian television news and current affairs programming. He is author of *Film as Social Practice* (1990) and *British Cultural Studies* (1990).

Patricia White teaches at Swarthmore College and is the author of *Uninvited: Classical Hollywood Cinema and Lesbian Representability* (1999).

Robyn Wiegman is Director of Women's Studies at the University of California, Irvine. She is author of *American Anatomies: Theorizing Race and Gender* (1995) and editor of *Feminism Beside Itself* (1995) and *Who Can Speak? Authority and Critical Identity* (1995).

List of illustrations

LIST OF ILLUSTRATIONS

General Introduction

John Hill

In 1995 the cinema celebrated its centenary. Since 1895, the cinema has grown and spread globally and, despite an actual decline in cinema attendances worldwide, the watching of films is now more popular than ever thanks to television and video. Although new communication technologies and forms of entertainment have undoubtedly affected the social and cultural role of cinema, the cinema nonetheless retains a huge importance as an economic, cultural and artistic activity. As such, film continues to attract enormous critical attention and commentary in both popular discourses and academic fields of study and it is the critical study of film which is the central concern of this book.

The aim of *Film Studies: Critical Approaches* is to provide the reader with an overview and assessment of the main ways in which film has been understood, explained and made sense of by critics, writers and academics. In doing so, it looks at the main disciplinary approaches and theoretical frameworks which have been employed in the study of film, the main concepts and methods involved in film analysis, and some of the key issues and debates that have characterized the field. As such, the emphasis of the book is on *critical approaches* to the study of film rather than on the provision of detailed information.

In doing so, the book aims to look at film 'in the round'. A distinction that is sometimes drawn is that between 'film' (the actual 'film texts' shown in cinemas or on television and video) and 'cinema' (the array of activities involved in the production and reception of films). While it is the film text which is central to the book (and which provides film studies with much of its distinctive focus), there is also a clear concern on the part of the book to address the variety of ways in which the film text is intermeshed with a whole set of economic, technological, social, and cultural practices. As such, *Film Studies: Critical Approaches* not only examines the ways in which the techniques and conventions specific to film have been analysed and interpreted by film scholars, but also looks at the critical issues involved in explaining how films come to be made and distributed, how they are responded to by audiences, and how the meanings 'spoken' by films—and the various 'readings' which audiences make of them—may be seen to connect to larger patterns of social and cultural meanings and identities.

An additional aim of the book is to represent the diversity and range of theoretical and critical perspectives which have been a feature of the study of film. Since the 1960s, the study of film has been an especially fertile one. During this time, film studies has borrowed heavily from other areas (importing ideas from semiotics, structuralism, psychoanalysis, marxism, feminism, post-structuralism and deconstruction and, more recently, cultural studies and postmodernism) but has also fed back into more general debates within the humanities and social sciences where the insights of film theory have often been particularly influential. At the same time, the study of film has been characterized by intense debate so that while certain theoretical frameworks may have achieved pre-eminence at certain junctures—such as authorship study in the early 1960s or 'psycho-semiotic' approaches in the 1970s—there have always been alternative traditions which have sought to challenge these perspectives and provide alternative means for explaining the workings of film. So while *Film Studies* clearly reflects that certain traditions (such as psychoanalytic feminism) have been especially influential in shaping the study of film, it is also intended that the book should acknowledge less well-known perspectives (such as those of impressionism or hermeneutics) and address issues which dominant strands of film study may often have neglected (such as the sociology of audiences or debates around cultural identity).

The structure of the book is as follows. The book begins with a discussion of why we should study film and the value in doing so. The following section—'Studying the film text'—focuses on the specific techniques, formal devices and aesthetic materials employed in filmmaking. This section introduces the critical vocabulary necessary to understand the operations of film texts as well as some of the critical debates surrounding the analysis of cinematography, composition, editing, acting, costume, and music. The following section—'The film text: theoretical frameworks'—maintains the emphasis upon the film text but assesses a range of theoretical paradigms—such as semiotics and formalism—that have shaped the ways in which films have been analysed and interpreted by film scholars.

The next two sections -'Film text and context: gender, ideology, and identities' and 'Film text and context: culture, history and reception'—examine theoretical frameworks and critical approaches that have looked at film in relation to various social, historical and ideological contexts. The first of these sections looks at how different theoretical and critical traditions (including marxism, feminism, queer theory and ethnic studies) have addressed the relationship of films to ideologies and cultural identities associated with social class, gender, sexual orientation, race, and ethnicity. The second of the sections addresses the range of social and historical circumstances in which films are made and consumed, placing a particular emphasis on how 'readings' of films are authorized and may vary according to social and cultural circumstances.

In all cases, each chapter is intended to lay out and assess the history and meaning(s) of key critical terms, issues and debates in film studies in relation to a particular approach or topic. In some chapters, there are also additional 'readings' of individual films which are intended to illustrate how different theories or critical perspectives have been applied to particular examples. In this respect, the chapters (and extracts) are also intended as a guide to further reading and viewing, identifying those books, articles, and films which have figured most prominently in discussions and debates. The bibliographies which accompany each chapter not only include full details of the material referred to in each chapter but also certain texts which may not actually be cited but are nonetheless significant texts of relevance to the area. Particularly useful texts, especially recommended for further reading, are accompanied by an asterisk.

The structure of the book is such that chapters are intended to follow on from one another and provide a cumulative sense of the field. However, chapters are also self-contained and may be read separately. There are, nonetheless, some cross-reference across chapters to indicate which chapters have the strongest connections. Thus, in the case of the chapter of 'feminism', it would clearly be an advantage to read it alongside the chapter on 'psychoanalysis' earlier in the book. In the same way, the chapter on 'feminism' provides a useful opening onto the chapter on 'gay and lesbian criticism'.

In all cases, the authors of individual chapters have been asked not only to survey their particular area but also to identify some of the questions that still remain unresolved in relation to it. In this way, it is planned that the reader should gain some sense of the field (and individual areas within it) not simply as a body of agreed knowledge but as a site of continuing debate and discussion concerning critical approaches and methods. In this respect, the book does not adopt one 'line' or advocate one critical approach above others (even though individual authors may often argue for particular theoretical frameworks or critical preferences). What it seeks to do instead is to suggest the issues which have been a feature of film study and what is at stake in them.

It is ultimately in this spirit that the book is presented: to provoke thought, to encourage debate and stimulate further reading and research. The excitement of film studies is that, despite a growing institutionalization, it nonetheless remains a field in which a variety of approaches coalesce and compete and in which basic questions remain 'unsettled'. If this volume can communicate some of that excitement amongst its readers (be they students, teachers, or those with a general interest in the serious study of film) then it may be judged a success.

Introduction to film studies

Richard Dyer

Anything that exists can be studied, and in these last years of the twentieth century it may well seem that virtually everything is. Yet only some things become organized into disciplines and institutionalized into departments and conferences; if everything has its web site, only some things have their boards of examiners, refereed journals, and employed enthusiasts, or possess the (often insecure) cultural capital of being understood to be 'studies'. Nor is the form that studies take wholly determined by the object of study—the history of film studies, as of any other discipline, makes clear that there are many different ways of deciding what it is you attend to, and how you attend to it, when you 'study' something.

All manner of factors, including chance, determine why something gets taken up as worthy of 'study' and what form that takes, but cutting across them all is the conviction, one that must be or be made widespread, that the object of study is important, that it matters. It is the terms of such mattering that then characterize the changing forms of study.

In principle, there could be film studies based upon the science and techniques of film, its physics and chemistry, the practices and possibilities of the camera and the other apparatuses of filmmaking. Yet these have not constituted a discrete branch of film studies, nor even very often been seen as indispensable to the study of film. This is despite not only a handful of academic studies, but also the in fact rather wide-spread discourse of film science and technique in the culture at large, from the journals of professional cine-matography all the way through to the lively market in special effects (how they are done) fandom.

> **All manner of factors, including chance, determine why something gets taken up as worthy of 'study' and what form that takes, but cutting across them all is the conviction, one that must be or be made widespread, that the object of study is important, that it matters.**

An interest in the physics and chemistry of film has made some impact within film studies in work on what are seen as the three decisive innovations in the history of film: its very invention and the introductions of sound and colour. (To these we might add wide screen—though this is generally seen as less transfor-mative of the medium—and television, video, and digitization, which sometimes seem to open out onto the vista of the end, or at any rate acute marginalization, of our object of study, film.) Here such matters as the phenomenon of persistence of vision, the chemistry of photographic stock and celluloid, or the subtractive versus additive methods for colour production do form part of many curricula, reference books, and histories. Yet the study of such things, the very basic means and possibility of film, for their own sake, as central to the discipline, is not established. Similarly, although students of film do sometimes know something about technique—know, for instance, what a fresnel does, or the merits of one Eastman Kodak stock over another—such knowledge has remained at best an optional extra to the constitution of film studies.

This has in part to do with the scientific illiteracy of most of those who constructed the field. It has also to do with a divide in conceptions of science and technology, between what I shall call—and polarize as—objectivists and historicists. The former see the truths of science as facts discovered in the natural world and technical practices as things imposed upon practitioners by apparatuses; the latter, the historicists, see scientific knowledge constructed according to cultural paradigms and see practices as routinized uses of apparatuses, apparatuses that were themselves constructed according to cultural norms and could be used differently. Though many scientists and technicians are much more profoundly aware of the relative nature of their knowledge and practices than film scholars are ever likely to be, the wider scientific, technical culture remains wedded to objectivism. Film scholars are far more likely to be on the historicist side, sometimes to the point of refusing altogether to acknowledge—and therefore to know anything about—the stubborn resistance of matter, of apparatuses, of physical and chemical givens.

Yet the reason for the absence, or at any rate extreme marginalization, of scientific and technical discourses in film studies is not so much this epistemological mismatch as those discourses' perceived value in relation to what matters about film. On the one hand, to pure science, film is not important enough of itself to constitute a field of study, but is only an instance in a wider field, optics and acoustics, say, or even physics and chemistry *tout court*. Meanwhile, technical discourse has not yet established for itself the place in scholarship that would enable it to found a field (even though, probably, more people teach and want to learn technical discourse than film studies). On the other hand, scientific and technical discourses don't tell film scholars what they want to know about film or films, that is, why they are fascinating or valuable. Knowledge of the chemistry of Kodak stocks in given periods, or of how a fresnel affects the focus and fall of lighting, tells us how

a given image or characteristic filmic quality takes the form it does, and probably enables us to refine our description of it, but it still doesn't tell us why, or even if, it matters.

Mattering has tended to be affirmed in one of two ways: the formal–aesthetic and the social–ideological. The first argues for, or assumes, the importance of film in terms of its intrinsic worth, whereas the latter focuses on film's position as symptom or influence in social processes.

The formal–aesthetic value of film study

For formal and aesthetic discourse, film matters for its artistic merits. In this, it shares a concern with newspaper and magazine film reviewing, even if this common cause is sometimes obscured by antagonism of both journalists and academics towards one another. Both groups are concerned with championing film in general and with debating the merits of particular films. Film journalism long anticipated and made possible academic film study, and it has continued rather more whole-heartedly to concern itself with the questions that won't go away (is this film any good? is film in general any good?). At its best, journalism's readiness to mix a well-expressed, honest response with a fine, accurate, and evocative description of a film is of great methodological importance. There is value in the freshness and immediacy of the reviewer's response, just as there is in the distance and mulled-over character of academic work. And if academics may be rightly wary of the implications of the pressure on journalists to entertain (not least by imposing their personality between the reader and the film), it is regrettable that more film academics do not seem to share the journalistic concern with communication.

> **For formal and aesthetic discourse, film matters for its artistic merits.**

Both reviewing and film studies concern themselves with film as art. The notion of art is notoriously loaded—it carries an inextinguishable overtone of value, so that we may say that the term 'art' in practice designates art that is approved of. For much of its brief life film studies has mobilized just this overtone in its defence, usually quite explicitly. The most famous instance of this—and in terms of widespread, long-term influence, probably film studies' greatest hit—is the auteur theory. This made the case for taking film seriously by seeking to show that a film could be just as profound, beautiful, or important as any other kind of art, provided, following a dominant model of value in art, it was demonstrably the work of a highly individual artist. Especially audacious in this argument was the move to identify such artistry in Hollywood, which figured as the last word in non-individualized creativity (in other words, non-art) in wider cultural discourses in the period. The power of auteurism resided in its ability to mobilize a familiar argument about artistic worth and, importantly, to show that this could be used to discriminate between films. Thus, at a stroke, it both proclaimed that film could be an art (with all the cultural capital that this implies) and that there could be a form of criticism—indeed, study—of it.

Auteurism is the particular form that the argument from art took in the 1960s, the crucial moment for the establishment of film as a discipline. But film scholarship long before this had concerned itself with film as art, including, but not only, in terms of individual creativity. The terms may differ, but the form of the argument remains the same: film is worth studying because art itself is worth studying and film is art. Why art itself should be deemed to have worth, leave alone to merit study, are not matters to be gone into here: suffice it to say that film as art discourse leans on this wider art-as-a-good discourse, or rather, its many variations (e.g. individual creativity, formal coherence, moral depth, sublime or dionysiac experience).

One particularly productive strand of such discourse can be linked back at least to the German philosopher Lessing and his insistence (in *Laokoon*, 1766) on the importance of establishing what is intrinsic and essential to each artistic medium: only by being true to this can real art emerge. Thus painting should not try to be like sculpture, and much less should either try to be like music or literature. It is some such conviction, whether explicitly acknowledged or not, that informs work that has sought to specify the particularity of film. What is it about the medium itself that makes it distinctive and that therefore properly forms the basis for an account of what is potentially best about it?

Many answers have been proposed. One is film's particular relationship to reality, the fact that it is reality itself that makes an impression on film stock—a sunset is put on a canvas by means of a hand applying paint, but it gets onto film by the chemical reaction of film stock to a real sunset. Theorists and practitioners alike have not naïvely supposed that film unproblematically captures or reflects reality, but they have argued that the fundamental way in which the film image is produced is in some sense by means of reality itself, that this process is unique to the photographic arts and that it is in maximizing the formal implications of this (e.g. shooting on location with available light, using long takes) that the art of film is realized. A second tradition takes film's temporal combination of shots in the act of editing (or 'montage') as most characteristic of it and thus, again, the foundation of film art. Realism and/versus montage long held sway as paradigms in film studies, but more recently there has been a renewed interest in other, obscured conceptualizations: 'photogénie', for instance, the particular *transformation* of recorded reality effected by the camera and its auxiliaries (lighting, movement, editing), or 'Zerstreuung', the delirious, dazzling, profoundly irrational quality of the film experience (bright light flickering on a huge surface in a darkened room, with vertiginous illusions of impossible realities).

The argument from essence remains an argument for film as (approvable) art, but there have developed formalist approaches more equivocal with regard to value. These have sought to establish the forms in practice of cinema—not what they must or should be, as in essentialist arguments, but what, as a matter of fact, they are. Most notoriously, these were developed under the sign of the 'language of cinema'. This is an often unhelpful term. Language is a sign system characterized by arbitrary signs (there is no reason for the word 'cow' to designate the animal 'cow'), discrete elements (the sounds are clearly distinguished from one another, the written elements even more so), and constraining grammar (with only some latitude, you have to follow the rules of grammar if you wish to be understood). Film's signs, on the other hand, are motivated (by the 'special relation' to reality or by virtue of resemblance—an image of a cow looks like a cow), cannot be neatly separated out (for instance, how long does a take have to be to be long?), and their combination knows only the rather particular rules of certain traditions (notably 'classical cinema'). Yet the ambition of linguistics, or more broadly semiotics, to be an objective description, a 'science', of the forms and procedures of a medium of signing has continued to haunt film studies (see Easthope, Part 1, Chapter 6).

The strongest such work has sought to overcome the weaknesses of the language model by identifying formal elements of film which correspond to norms of human perception. Among such work we may note—despite the huge divergence in the paradigms at work—three tendencies. Phenomenological work, which has come and gone and re-emerged as a presence in the field, focuses on the experience of the film image, drawing explicitly upon philosophical understandings of the nature of perception and consciousness. Here the unfolding of the film, the succession of images, and the image repertoire itself are all understood to work, probably in an unusually immediate way, with the habitual processes of the human mind. Psychoanalytic work, developing in the 1970s, links formal elements to unconscious psychic processes, most influentially in the feminist treatment of the point-of-view shot, whose organization is seen to privilege the male look at women in ways which either sadistically punish or satisfyingly fetishize the always threatening image of women to the male psyche (see Creed, Chapter 9). Thirdly, most recently, what we might call the Wisconsin School, building on its highly influential work on 'classical Hollywood cinema', has started working on correspondences between film form and norms of perception posited in cognitive psychology, notably those between the film forms and mental processes required in order that a film may be 'followed' (see Christie, Chapter 7).

By this stage, though, the need for there to be a point to studying film is in danger of being lost. In part, the yearning for science includes the shibboleth that things are studied because they are there and that there should be no tendentious point. In part, the very success of film studies in establishing itself as a discipline may mean that the reasons for establishing it no longer need asserting or even addressing. This may be short-sighted—funding realities mean that disciplines still have to be defended in terms of why they should be pursued. (The popular-with-students argument is not enough: for one thing, film studies is only popular with students relative to classics or chemistry, not to media or business studies, and for another, those who fund study may be more interested in what government and business want than in what students want.) The scientific stance may also be self-deluding, since in practice a sense of what matters is always present in scholarship at the level of the choice of what instances and aspects get studied and what don't. In any event, it should be stressed that there is a risk of loss of point, not that this has occurred. The study of filmic language or formal–perceptual correspondences consistently provides a ground for understanding how film and films work, even if leaving out of account why we should want to know about this.

The social–ideological value of film

Film-as-art discourses argue, or assume, that film is intrinsically worth studying. If they lean on wider discourses of art, of aesthetics or sometimes erotics, then this is only because film itself is an art and therefore valuable in the terms of art. There is no appeal to something outside film art. Social–ideological arguments, on the other hand, do make such an appeal.

One kind of social argument sees film as the exemplary or symptomatic art form of the category 'modernity'. This itself is conceived of as a structure of feeling characterizing an epoch in Western (and subsequently world) society from, say, the late eighteenth century onwards, based in capitalism, industrialism, urban and large-scale, centralized, 'mass' societies. To what extent we are still in this epoch, or whether there has been a qualitative change so profound that a new epoch must be recognized, one that may be designated 'postmodern', is part of this debate (see Hill, Chapter 11). One consequence of considering that we are in transition out of modernity, or perhaps are already in postmodernity, is that film may come to be seen as an archaic and marginal cultural form. Postmodernity may rob film's modernity of the sense of the new and the now.

Film's modernity may be located first in its industrial character. Cameras and projectors are machines. Films are endlessly reproducible, as in all mass commodity production. They are made, for the most part, in conditions akin to factory production, which involves large numbers of people, a highly differentiated division of labour, and a temporally linear organization (e.g., at its most rudimentary, scriptwriting followed by filming, then processing, then editing). The numerical and geographical scale of distribution and marketing are comparable with other major commodities in modern societies. Production and distribution are centralized, a relatively small number of people putting out products consumed by millions upon millions (and, in the case of Hollywood, throughout the world).

The director confronts the studio logo in Guru Dutt's *Kaagaz Ke Phool/Paper Flowers* (1959)

The modernity of film at the level of production and consumption has been seen as of a piece with film form. The camera's mechanical reproduction creates a new, perhaps rather strange relationship between image and reality, just as the experience of modernity is said to distance people from nature and an immediately graspable, localized social reality. Editing is founded in fragments, a characteristic which has produced a variety of analyses in terms of modernity. One is that an art of fragments is analogous to the common experience of fragmentation in modernity, as rapid mobility, mechanical and long-distance communications, the mixing of classes and other social groups in cities, as all these break up the fixed, holistic bonds of traditional communities. A second view of the modernity of editing sees combining fragments as akin to the dynamic of Marxist dialectical thought, itself understood as the mode of thinking and feeling appropriate to modernity and to what modernity makes possible, the construction of a new, post-capitalist society. A third view sees continuity editing as an attempt to cover over the cracks between film fragments in just the same way that mass culture seeks to weld a unity out of the fragmentation of modern societies.

Other aspects of film form have also been seen as distinctly modern. Both editing and the flicker of film (to say nothing of the importance of action and suspense genres in popular cinema) may be of a piece with the restless, febrile quality of modern life, or may, in another version, provide the intensity and excitement lacking in lives essentially drab and anomic. Camera movement, elaborate lighting, and special effects all display the advanced technology at film's disposal. Finally, the conditions under which film is viewed— vast assemblies of strangers gathered together in the dark to see flickering, rapidly changing, fabulous images that they know are being seen in identical form across the world—locate both film's industrial mode of production and its formal properties in the actual experience of being at the movies.

Accounts of film's modernity have in principle simply been attempts to characterize and understand what contemporary life is about, what it feels like; but they have also usually been fuelled by an anxiety about this (see Gripsrud, Chapter 22). Is not fragmentation a bad thing for human kind, and does not film either exacerbate it or seek to disguise the reality of it (and thus put it beyond critique and change)? Is there not a danger in the hypnotic quality of the film image, an inherent danger because it is a lure to passivity? Is not passivity dangerous, partly because, *quelle horreur*, it is feminine, partly because passivity at the movies is coterminous with political passivity in life (a wholly dubious assumption)? Hasn't film demonstrably been used to manipulate people to acquiesce in totalitarian regimes? In short, is not film inherently political?

It is a concern with the politics of film that has underpinned the emergence of what we may call a cultural studies perspective in recent years. Its central proposition is that culture of all kinds and brows produces, reproduces, and/or legitimizes forms of thought and feeling in society and that the well-being of people in society is crucially affected and shaped by this. Who we think we are, how we feel about this, who we believe others to be, how we think society works, all of this is seen to be shaped, decisively, perhaps exclusively, by culture and to have the most profound social, physical, and individual consequences. Importantly, cultural studies has a differentiated model of society. Rather than treating cultural products as part of a mass, uniform, and homogeneously modern society, it has focused on the particularities of cultures founded on social divisions of class, gender, race, nation, sexuality, and so on. Within this perspective, cultural studies stresses the importance of power, the different statuses of different kinds of social group and cultural product, the significance of control over the means of cultural production. Equally, cultural studies does not assume that cultural products are unified expressions of sections of society, but may often treat them as products of contestation within such sections or else of struggles of such sections against other social groups.

Film is something of a minor player in this. Cultural studies emerged with television and has gone on to privilege popular music and new technologies among the media it analyses. None the less, the cultural studies perspective is widespread in film studies. Its most familiar form is ideological textual analysis. At worst this can be a reductive seeking out of politically incorrect narrative structures and stereotypical characters or an impossibly elusive, wordplaying, obfuscatory 'deconstruction' (a word often used to mean little more than taking something to bits as brilliantly as possible). At best it seeks to show the way that the textual facts of a film itself, its narrative organization, its address to the viewer, its visual and aural rhetoric, construct, not necessarily coherently or without contradiction, a perception of social reality (even and especially in films not apparently about social reality at all).

The chief problem for ideological analysis is the methodological weakness of the claims it seems to want to make about the social significance of the ideological operations it uncovers. Wary of claims of the effects of the media, claims associated with rightwing moral panics and unimaginative social-scientific empirical investigation, ideological analysis still assumes that it matters what ideology a film carries. Yet it only matters if it can be shown that the ideology is believed, or acted upon as if believed—in other words, if it cannot be shown to be effective. This is a move cultural studies has often been reluctant to make. Awareness of the problem has, however, led to an opening out of interest in cultural studies into areas that had hitherto been largely left to the social scientists but are now beginning to be more centrally discussed within film studies: production and consumption.

At a level of relative abstraction, modes of produc-

It is a concern with the politics of film that has underpinned the emergence of what we may call a cultural studies perspective in recent years. Its central proposition is that culture of all kinds and brows produces, reproduces, and/ or legitimizes forms of thought and feeling in society and that the wellbeing of people in society is crucially affected and shaped by this.

tion have been talked about in film studies in the past. There have been moments too of guilty conscience, when it has been felt that students of film 'ought to talk about the industry', often resulting in surprisingly unsophisticated empirical accounts—surprising both because being given house room beside the most arcane textual discussions and because there was no lack of theoretical sophistication about the study of industry and business available in social science. Recently, however, film studies has woken up to the unanticipated impact that cultural studies has had in management, business, and other 'hard' social sciences, where talk of the culture of an enterprise is widely accepted as a key explanatory concept. We are now seeing the beginnings of work on the culture of the production of film. At the other end of the process, and even more developed, we may note the influence in cultural studies of conceptualizations of consumption in terms of active, interpreting, differentiated audiences and an interest in what kinds of sense social groupings make of films, genres, stars, and so on.

At times, films may get rather lost in this process, dissolved into the cultures of producers or the multiplicity of audience readings. This seems a pity, since without a sense of film itself, producers and audiences alike become just one instance of production and consumption among thousands. If this is the case, there is no particular reason to study them any more than producers or users of wheat or cars—perfectly good and important subjects, but neither seems set to define a discrete discipline. Moreover, there remains the problem of how one understands the relation between the culture of producers and the culture they actually produce, or the relation between readings and the detail of what is being read. Why does a given set of personnel, organized like this, with this set of shared and contested understandings of what they are doing, why does all this produce this kind of film? What exactly is it that this given set of readers is latching onto in a film to make this interpretation, to have this feeling about it? And in either case, so what? Why does it matter what kind of film is produced, what kind of reading is made, unless the film itself matters? Cultural studies approaches to production and consumption may show us why films matter to producers and readers, which is good for them but not in itself reason to pursue and fund a discipline. We have to go back to considering the aesthetic or social reasons for thinking why film matters, reasons not themselves entirely vouchsafed by the cultures of production and consumption.

Films studies should include physics and chemistry, technology, aesthetics, psychology (of some sort), the sociology of organizations and consumption, empirical study of producers and audiences, textual study of films themselves, and no doubt much else that we cannot yet envisage. On the other hand, it is never possible to do everything. Most of the time one has to put on hold crucial aspects of a phenomenon that one has not time (or perhaps inclination) to address. This means that one has to operate with a 'closed system, open mind' mental orientation, focusing on a particular neck of the woods but being ready to take on board findings and perceptions from those labouring away in other parts. (The phrase is borrowed from the title of a collection of essays by Max Gluckman published in 1964.) I do not say this in a spirit of tolerating everything—there are substantial intellectual reasons for wishing to dispute particular paradigms at work within all the many modes of film study I have tried to characterize. Rather, I want to insist that in particular, the aesthetic and the cultural cannot stand in opposition. The aesthetic dimension of a film never exists apart from how it is conceptualized, how it is socially practised, how it is received; it never exists floating free of historical and cultural particularity. Equally, the cultural study of film must always understand that it is studying film, which has its own specificity, its own pleasures, its own way of doing things that cannot be reduced to ideological formulations or what people (producers,

> **The aesthetic and the cultural cannot stand in opposition. The aesthetic dimension of a film never exists apart from how it is conceptualized, how it is socially practised, how it is received; it never exists floating free of historical and cultural particularity. Equally, the cultural study of film must always understand that it is studying film, which has its own specificity, its own pleasures, its own way of doing things that cannot be reduced to ideological formulations or what people (producers, audiences) think and feel about it.**

audiences) think and feel about it. The first cultural fact about film is that it is film. Quite what 'film' then is we must go on debating, but that debate must always be at the heart of a cultural understanding, just as any conclusions we come to will always be cultural as well as aesthetic ones.

BIBLIOGRAPHY

Gluckman, Max (1964), *Closed Systems and Open Minds* (Chicago: Aldine).

2

The film text and film form

Robert P. Kolker

Defining the film text

What do we mean when we talk about a film? The answers to this apparently straightforward question are not simple, not at all based in common sense, and go to the heart of the complexities of the institutions, the practices, and the viewing of movies.

The terms themselves suggest our uncertainties. Cinema, as Christian Metz (1977/1982: 5–9) suggests, implies the entire institution of filmmaking, film distribution, film exhibition, and film viewing. In England, the cinema usually refers to the place where a film is shown. In the United States, 'movies' replaces 'cinema', and the word 'film' is reserved for serious intent. In Hollywood, the people who make films sometimes call them 'pictures', and once referred to them (some still do) as 'shows'.

Is everyone talking about the same thing? And what is the 'thing'? As we try to untangle a definition of the film text, I will use 'film' instead of 'movie' (reserving my right to be serious) and will try to restrict the term

'cinema' to Metz's definition of the encompassing institution of production, distribution, exhibition, and reception. But that will be the easiest part of the untangling process. Film and the cinema are such a regular part of our lives, that defining, differentiating, and analysing them are not only difficult, but also difficult for many people to accept. Indeed, there are some things we would rather were left alone, and the movies are one of them. The preference to think of a film as a kind of self-constructed presence, full of story, characters, and emotion, is strong. A film is there, complete, full, and waiting for our gaze. Why make it more difficult than it appears? Precisely because it appears so simple and because the influence of film on our lives is so great.

Our first response to the question 'What is a film?' might be: 'A film is what we see when we go to the cinema (or the movies) or watch a videocassette or a television broadcast of a film'. A direct enough response, but one that actually responds to different things. Or, more appropriately, different, but closely related, texts. We can define a text as a coherent, delimited, comprehensible structure of meaning. A text is something that contains a complex of events (images, words, sounds) that are related to each other within a context, which can be a story or narrative. All of the parts of a text cohere, work together towards a common goal of telling us something. In ordinary parlance, a text is also something physical, like a novel or a book of poems. We all know about a textbook. But a painting is also a text. So is a television show, and the entire process of watching television. In fact, any event that makes meaning can be called a text if we can isolate and define its outside boundaries and its internal structure—and our responses to it (for a text to be completed, it must be seen, read, heard by someone). If we think of this in relation to a film, we begin to see how hard it is to define the film text—or texts—which are physical, narrative, economic, and cultural, and which include production, distribution, exhibition, and viewing.

The physical presence of a film constitutes one aspect of film's textuality: the five or six reels of 35mm plastic ribbon containing photographic images that are projected onto the screen in the theatre, or the videocassette we rent from the video store with its hundreds of feet of magnetized plastic coating contained in the cassette. A videocassette shown on a television set is not the same as the theatrical screening of a 35mm print. On the most obvious level, the conditions of its viewing are not the same. The kind of concentration made possible in a darkened cinema where a high-resolution image is projected on the screen is not the same as the bright busy living-room, or the comfort of the bedroom, where a small, low-resolution image is projected from behind onto a cathode ray tube. The image and the ways in which we attend to it are different. The television or videotaped image are not only smaller, but also more square. The sides of the image are lost on most transfers of film to video (almost two-thirds of the image if the original was filmed in anamorphic wide screen and then 'pan and scanned' for videotape). The difference in size, resolution, and response creates a different textual construction for televisual as opposed to theatrical viewing.

We can extend these differences further. In theatrical exhibition the size, proportion, and resolution of the film image are no longer under the control of the filmmakers or the audience. They are controlled by the physical circumstances, resources, and commitment of the exhibitor. For a number of years the size of the screen in any given theatre has been determined by the size of the theatre, not by a standard ratio for recording and projecting the image. While a standard ratio did exist from the early 1930s to the early 1950s, the advent of different widescreen formats, the small shopping-mall theatre, the need to compose the image ultimately to fit on television, makes image size and composition inexact and undependable for any given film. The film text, in its physical, visible sense, is therefore subject to architecture, to theatre management, to the exigencies of broadcast and videotape conventions. Almost every videotape released in the United States comes with two warnings: one from the FBI, warning us about copyright restrictions; the other telling us that 'this film has been formatted to fit your television'. Physical textuality, like so much else in the creation and reception of film, is subject to external forces that make it difficult for us to define it as some essential, unchanging thing.

Ultimately, the physicality of film, even the forms of its projection, are less important than the effect it has when we view it. Watching a film is more than any of its physical parts: it is an event that occurs when the physical thing becomes activated by human perception through some kind of projection or broadcast. As soon as a thinking, feeling person is present—viewing the film—that person's experience is brought to bear on the film's images, sounds, and narrative. The viewer's experience is itself informed by the culture in which he or she lives. A person's beliefs, understandings, and values are all activated within the context of film viewing. That is true for the people who created the film as well. They, too, are a major part of the text. Their beliefs, their understanding of what a film should or should not be, the economic constraints that allow them to say and do only so much in any given film—these become textualized.

Is this any different from our contact with other works of the imagination? The German critic Walter Benjamin, wrote in his 1936 essay 'The Work of Art in the Age of Mechanical Reproduction' that film is unique among the arts because of the fact that it is not unique. Of all the arts, Benjamin wrote, film is without 'aura', without the singularity of the immediate experience of an artefact uniquely connected with a singular human creative imagination. Film seems to have no origin; it is there, whole and complete, ready for our enjoyment or the enjoyment of anyone else with the price of admission, a monthly cable fee, or money for rental. For Benjamin, film's lack of aura, lack of forbidding uniqueness, and its ease of access makes it the most social and communal of the arts. Film addresses the world, pierces through the realities of daily life like a surgeon's knife (1936/1969: 233) and, by opening perceptions of the ordinary to the many, holds the possibility of engaging an audience in a social and cultural discourse, a mass engagement of the imagination unlike any other art form. (Benjamin also made it clear that film runs the risk of forging an authoritarian assent to the dominant ideology.)

The textuality of film is therefore different from a novel or a painting. Less personal, but more accessible. Neither unique nor intimate, yet closer to the world most of us live in, engaged in its dailiness, and powerfully in touch with the social. The text without aura becomes the text that resonates across many fields and many consciousnesses. In any film we are witness to a rich and often conflicting structure of imaginative, cultural, economic, and ideological events. Because most films are made for profit, they attempt to speak to the largest number of people, and by so doing have to appeal to what their makers believe are the most common and acceptable beliefs of a potential audience. But audiences often respond in ways the filmmakers don't expect. The result is that the film text often lies at a nexus of expectation and response, of cultural belief and individual resistance. It is available and legible to many interpreters, whose responses are themselves part of its very textuality and form.

The film text and authenticity

Textuality and form include questions about 'authenticity'. Benjamin's concept of the work without aura suggests that film removes authenticity from its text. However, despite Benjamin's argument about the loss of aura, actual people do make films. But given the collaborative and commercial basis of filmmaking—so different from the individual creativity attributed to the traditional arts—the creative authority of the filmic text has been at the core of theoretical and historical debate.

One part of the debate involves the ability to find and identify authoritative texts for early cinema that would enable us to create a reliable history of early film. It is estimated that almost 75 per cent of the films made before and just after the turn of the century no longer exist. Those that do exist, from the early twentieth century up to the teens, are in questionable, often inauthentic forms. For example, Edward S. Porter's *The Life of an American Fireman* (1903) has been regarded as one of the earliest films to intercut different scenes for the sake of narrative complexity.

One of the first films to intercut different scenes— Porter's *The Life of an American Fireman* (1903)

Recently, it was discovered that the print with the inter-cut scenes (we will discuss intercutting and cross-cutting a bit further on) may have been put together years later by distributors. The speculation is that the original version of *The Life of an American Fireman* may have been constructed with less cross-cutting, depending more on a succession of shots, which was the norm of the period (Gaudreault 1990). We do know that Porter's other famous film, *The Great Train Robbery* (1903), went out to distributors with a shot that showed one of the train robbers pointing his gun at the camera and firing. The film exhibitor was given the choice whether to put that shot at the beginning or the end of the film. This ability of the distributor and exhibitor to alter a film parallels the contemporary problem we spoke of earlier, in which the size of the theatre or television screen determines the look of the film.

As we move forward in film history, the authenticity of the early film text becomes closely related to the personality of the filmmaker. Eric von Stroheim's *Greed* (1925) was brutally cut by MGM. Stroheim's authority over his production was compromised when Irving Thalberg, head of production at MGM, refused to distribute Stroheim's original ten-hour cut. Thalberg caused *Greed* to be trimmed to two hours and destroyed the rest. Stroheim's film, and his career as director, were all but destroyed as well. Orson Welles's *The Magnificent Ambersons* (1942), perhaps the most infamous example of an inauthentic text, was removed from Welles's control before it was edited. The studio, RKO, reshot portions of it, changed the ending, and—as MGM did with *Greed*—destroyed the deleted footage. In both cases studio policy, personal dissension, and economic determinants conflicted sharply with the artistic endeavours of the filmmaker.

What is the authoritative text of *Greed* or *The Magnificent Ambersons*: the films Stroheim and Welles made, or the films released by their studios? These are egregious examples of a perpetual problem, which is intimately connected to the question of authorship. The assumption of auteur theory, for example, has been that we can identify the text with a person—the director. In doing so, it is argued, we can not only discover the authoritative boundaries that give a personal, textual legitimacy to a film, but authorize our reading of the film as well. But the auteur theory—especially as applied to American film—has been based more on desire than fact. The reality is that the texts of classical American studio cinema were and are only rarely the products of an individual imagination,

and the director's job was primarily to transfer the script to film: to make the shots and to coach the actors. In the end, the producer and studio head had the final say on how the film looked.

Because it is so intensely a public, commercial art, film is authorized—or textualized—from a number of directions. No one person or event determines it. During the studio period, a film emerged from the collective work of a large staff under contract. Today a film is often conceived by a scriptwriter who, with the help of an agent, sells his or her idea to a studio. The agent plays a key role, brokering actors and director. During these initial periods of conception and selling, many decisions about narrative, characterization, and commercial appeal are made. Also during this period intense economic negotiations are carried on in an attempt to sell the film to a studio. The shooting of the film by the director may involve some cinematic experiment, but, more often than not, because of budgetary and scheduling restrictions, standard, conventional storytelling techniques predominate, as they will have during the scriptwriting process.

A film is made for an audience and will survive only as far as an audience finds it acceptable. Therefore, the creation of a film is, in part, a structure of educated guesswork and creative repetition. If audiences responded well to certain structures, stories, and characters in the past, they should be (most filmmakers believe) repeated, with some variation, in the new work. When that work is finished, the audience is put into negotiation with it. (During the studio days that negotiation process was fairly immediate, as studio executives and the filmmakers went to suburban Los Angeles theatres to watch a pre-release screening of their current film, and would then make changes to it, depending upon the audience's response.) The negotiation process includes film reviews, familiarity with and responsiveness to the film's stars, resonance with the narrative content of the film, willingness to accept the inevitable exploitation of sexuality and violence that are the major components of most films.

The textuality of a film therefore becomes part of a resonant field of creation and response. It is a field that radiates from the film or videotape back to its making and forward into the environs of movie theatre or living-room. It confuses the safe categories of authentic and inauthentic versions, and calls upon the entire cultural surround of the viewer and its creators. It is encapsulated within other textual forms: the forms of production that drive the economy of a given culture which is as responsible for the way a film is made, marketed, and received as is the work of any individual. In short, the ribbon of plastic that holds the images is only a part of a large structure of imagination, economics, politics, and ideology and of individuals and the culture as a whole.

Analysing the film text: the shot and the cut

The diverse critical approaches to the study of film reflect this complexity. But, no matter what the approach, it is now generally accepted that the film text is a plural, complex, simultaneously static and changing event, produced by the filmmakers who put it together and the audience members who view it. It is unified by certain established ways in which shots are made and edited together. These structures are as conventionalized as the stories they create. By examining the internal structure of film narrative, the way images are made and put together in order to tell us stories, we can discover a great deal of information about what films expect of us and we of them.

Analysis of the form of the cinematic text concentrates on the two basic building-blocks of film, the shot and the cut, and on the structure that comes into being when the film is assembled, the combination of shot and cut that is the finished film. The first element, the shot, is the photographic record made when film is exposed to light. The second comes into being when the shot is interrupted, when the camera is shut off, or when one piece of film is cut and then fastened to another piece of film during the editing process. The third element is the completed structure of image and editing that communicates the narrative (or overall shape of the film). It is the initializing constituent of the text as we have defined it: the complex interaction of film and audience, structure, content, context, and culture.

None of these formal elements are simple or uncontested. Controversy over the structure and importance of the shot and the cut, of the shot versus the cut, forms the bedrock of film theory. In the writings of Sergei Eisenstein and André Bazin, especially, and the work of a variety of filmmakers, belief in the priority of one element over the other has determined the way films are made and understood, at least outside of Hollywood.

Sergei Eisenstein was the great Soviet director of films such as *Battleship Potemkin* (1925), *October* (1928), and *Ivan the Terrible* (1943). He theorized that the shot was only the raw material that the filmmaker used to construct the edifice of his film. For Eisenstein, a shot has no meaning until it is put in contention with another shot in a montage structure. Montage—a specific kind of editing—is constructed out of shots that affect one another in particular ways. One shot takes on meaning in relation to the shot that precedes and follows it. Spatial dynamics of the shot's composition, the length of the shot, the rhythm achieved when different shots of varying visual and thematic content are juxtaposed, all contribute to a carefully calculated 'montage of attractions'. For Eisenstein, montage was not merely the filmmaker's most important tool, but the sign of his aesthetic and political control. The shot, by itself, is inert, he believed. Making the shot (and, with the help of his cinematographer Edward Tisse, Eisenstein filmed powerful and dynamic compositions) was only craft. Turning the shot into a temporal structure of rhythmic, conflicting, kinetic montage was the director's art.

For Eisenstein, editing not only created a visual dynamism of conflicting forms, but it had the potential of being a cinematic equivalent of Karl Marx's theory of dialectical materialism. Through the interaction of form and content between shots, by the way one shot determined the meaning of the preceding or following shot, Eisenstein believed he could create a third thing, a dialectical synthesis of idea, emotion, perception, that would, in turn, create an intellectual perception of revolutionary history for the viewer. Montage, in short, was a tool that allowed the filmmaker to address history, as well as art, in a dialectical way.

Eisenstein believed so profoundly in the basic, driving aesthetic and ideological force of montage that he saw it developing in literature and the arts before film. Montage was an aesthetic event waiting to be politicized with the invention of cinema.

> **Analysis of the form of the cinematic text concentrates on the two basic building-blocks of film, the shot and the cut, and on the structure that comes into being when the film is assembled, the combination of shot and cut that is the finished film.**

André Bazin was not a filmmaker. A critic and film theorist who was active from the end of the Second World War until his death in 1958, he influenced a generation of directors and is considered to be the father of the French New Wave. Bazin's film aesthetic is directly opposed to Eisenstein's. For Bazin, editing was the destruction of cinematic form, indeed the destruction of the essence of cinema. For him, it is the shot, the unedited gaze of the camera onto the world before its lens, that constitutes cinema's aesthetic core. If Eisenstein's aesthetic was political at its root, Bazin's was religious and founded in the faith that the cinematic image could reveal the world in fact and spirit and confirm the temporal and spatial thereness of the world with the camera's meditative eye.

Editing, according to Bazin, denies that faith, because it cuts off the filmmaker's and the film viewer's opportunity to see into the wholeness and continuity of time and space. Editing is manipulative; it forces us to see what the filmmaker wants us to see. The shot is reverential. Political, too. An uninterrupted shot, preferably in deep focus (an effect of lens and lighting that makes everything in the composition, from the closest object in the frame to the farthest, appear to be equally clear) might create a kind of democracy of perception. The viewer would be free to pick and choose what to look at within the frame, rather than have the filmmaker pick out what he or she considers important by cutting and foregrounding specific faces or objects.

Bazin's cinema is painterly. It depends upon composition, lighting, and the profound revelatory effect of the camera's gaze. The construction of mise-en-scène—the complex articulation of space through composition, light, and movement—is pre-eminent

Does 'the long take reveal the world to the viewer', as Bazin suggests? Wyler's *The Best Years of our Lives* (1946)

in Bazin's theory. In fact, Bazin uses the example of painting to describe the prehistory of cinema, the early and ongoing urge of the imagination to preserve images of the world. In a sense, Eisenstein's is a painterly cinema too, a dynamic kinetic form analogous to Cubism and Russian Constructivism (an art movement contemporary with Eisenstein's filmmaking). The difference is that, for Bazin, the image and its complex construction is primary; so is the spectator's gaze, liberated to roam the image and connect its internal parts. Bazin asks the spectator to look and put the parts of the image together, to achieve understanding through contemplation. For Eisenstein, the viewer must respond to the invisible space that is created by images in conflict. The spectator responds to the dialectic of montage and the revolutionary history it articulates.

Eisenstein's concept of montage dominated film theory and some film practice for a brief period (the French avant-garde movement of the 1920s and the American documentarists of the 1930s) and then waned. Its only appearance in Hollywood cinema was through the work of an editor named Slavko Vorkapich, who created 'montage sequences' for such 1930s films as *San Francisco* (1936) and *Mr Smith Goes to Washington* (1939). The Bazinian aesthetic of the long take had a broader history and a powerful influence. Bazin looked to the work of Erich von Stroheim, F. W. Murnau, Jean Renoir, Orson Welles, William Wyler, and the films of the post-war Italian Neo-Realists (Roberto Rossellini, Vittorio De Sica, especially) as examples of the cinema of the long take. The followers of Bazin, from Jean-Luc Godard and François Truffaut to Michelangelo Antonioni, Bernardo Bertolucci, the Greek director Theo Angelopoulos, and the British filmmaker Terence Davies (to name only a few), depend upon the complex gaze of the camera rather than editing to construct their mise-en-scène and, from it, their narrative. It can be said, with strong empirical evidence, that any filmmaker who sets out to make a film that is counter to the structure of the dominant Hollywood cinema turns not to Eisenstein, but to the cinema that Bazin applauded and championed, the cinema of the long take, of coherent mise-en-scène.

The concept of mise-en-scène attracted the attention of critics as well. *Cahiers du cinéma* (the French journal Bazin helped found), as well as the British journal *Movie*, along with writers such as V. F. Perkins and Raymond Durgnat, pursued the idea of the shot and its constituent parts as the defining elements of a film. In France, England, and the United States, study of mise-

en-scène, hand in hand with the auteur theory, helped to found the field of cinema studies. A focus on mise-en-scène permitted an emphasis upon the elements of film that made it distinct from other narrative forms and was used to explain how images, through composition, camera movement, lighting, focus, and colour, generate narrative event and guide our perception through a film. Mise-en-scène analysis was also a way to connect personality, style, and meaning.

Mise-en-scène and auteur criticism were closely intertwined within the analysis of style, and style was often implicitly defined as the personal expression of mise-en-scène. When V. F. Perkins (1972: 84–5) for example, analyses the use of colour in Nicholas Ray's *Bigger than Life* (1956), or Terry Comito (1971) talks about the vertiginous horizon in Welles's *Touch of Evil* (1958); when any number of critics define F. W. Murnau's use of moving camera, Otto Preminger's long takes, or Hitchcock's use of framing to describe his characters' states of mind, they are speaking of the ways in which the imagination of the auteur visualized their world in distinctly cinematic ways. Mise-en-scène criticism served many purposes: it helped concentrate the critical gaze on the formal structures of film; it explored the significance of style in a medium that few had ever considered capable of manifesting style; and it helped to determine a field—cinema studies—by proving that both artistic personality and style could exist in a mass art.

Like auteurism, mise-en-scène criticism was a useful construct, a way of building a critical discourse. Even as it helped define film form and structure, it was something of an evasion, for it tended to repress the realities of the dominant Hollywood cinema, whose forms construct most of the films we see. Because of its place of origin, this form has come to be known as the classical form of Hollywood cinema or, more simply, the continuity style. It is a remarkable form because of its persistence, its invisibility, and because we learn how to read it easily and without any more instruction than seeing the films themselves.

The continuity style

Eisensteinian montage and the long-take–deep-focus aesthetic advocated by Bazin are attention-drawing forms. They foreground cinematic structure and make them part of the narrative movement. They are intrusive in the sense that they make the viewer aware of the meaning-making apparatus; they ask the viewer to look at the way the world is being observed and constructed cinematically. Despite Bazin's insistence that the long take reveals the world to the viewer, what more often happens is that it reveals the cinematic apparatus and its ways of looking. Montage, of course, is dynamic, intrusive: Eisenstein meant his moviemaking to have a shock effect, to raise the blood pressure and the intellectual temperature. He called it the 'kino fist'. The classical Hollywood style, on the other hand, asks that form be rendered invisible; that the viewer see only the presence of actors in an unfolding story that seems to be existing on its own; that the audience be embraced by that story, identify with it and its participants. Unlike montage and the long take, the continuity style was neither theorized nor analysed (not by the people who developed and used it, at least); its rules were developed intuitively and pragmatically through the early years of filmmaking. The continuity style developed because it worked, and its working was measured by the fact that it allowed filmmakers to make stories that audiences responded to with ease and with desire. They liked what they saw and wanted more. We want more still.

On the level of ideology, the classical Hollywood style is a capitalist version of Eisensteinian montage and a secular version of Bazin's deep-focus, long-take style. (Eisenstein recognized this, and in his essay 'Dickens, Griffith, and the Film Today', wrote about how the Hollywood style spoke the ideology of Western capitalism.) It is the form that placates its audience, foregrounds story and characters, satisfies and creates a desire in the audience to see (and pay for) more of the same. It is also a form that is economical to reproduce. Once the basic methodology of shooting and editing a film became institutionalized—quite early in the twentieth century—it was easy to keep doing it that way. Although every studio during the classical period of Hollywood production (roughly between the late 1910s to the early 1950s) performed slight variations on the continuity style, its basics were constant and used by everyone. What this means is, when we talk about the classical style of Hollywood filmmaking, we are talking about more than aesthetics, but about a larger text of economics, politics, ideology, and stories—an economics of narrative. The Hollywood studio system, which was the central manufacturing arm of the continuity style, developed as many other manufacturing institutions did by rationalizing production, creating a division of labour, and discovering methods by means of which all production parts and personnel would be on hand and easily put into place in order to create a product attractive to the greatest number of people.

> **Eisensteinian montage and the long-take–deep-focus aesthetic advocated by Bazin are attention-drawing forms. They are intrusive in the sense that they make the viewer aware of the meaning-making apparatus.**

Given the fact that the classical style developed prior to the studio system, we can speculate that the structures of narrative may have contributed to the rise of the economies of studio production. In other words, the development of a means to deliver narrative meaning through an economical visual construction created templates for the formation of an industrial mass production of narratives (Burch 1990). Early film consisted of a presentation of shots in series, each one of which showed something happening (as in the Lumière brothers' early film in which a train pulls into the station, or Edison's first efforts in which a shot showed a man sneezing or a couple kissing). Within a few years, during the turn of the century, such shots became edited together in the service of expressing stories. Georges Méliès made primitive narratives of a trip to the moon or a voyage under the sea in which different shots succeeded one another. Porter's *The Great Train Robbery* reflects a more complex process in which parts of the narrative that are occurring simultaneously, but in different spatial locations, are placed one after the other (Gaudreault 1983). One site where the process of establishing the continuity style can be observed is the series of films made by D. W. Griffith for the Biograph Company from 1908 to 1913. Griffith made more than 400 short films during that period, and in them we can see the development of what would become the basic principles of continuity: an apparent seamlessness of storytelling; the movement of characters and story that appear to be flowing in an orderly, logical, linear progression, with the camera positioned in just the right place to capture the action without being obtrusive; and, perhaps most important of all, an authority of presentation and expression that elicits precisely the correct emotional response at precisely the right moment, without showing the means by which the response is elicited.

The key to the continuity style is its self-effacement, its ability to show without showing itself, tell a story and make the storytelling disappear so that the story seems to be telling itself. This legerdemain was not a natural occurrence. The elements that came together to make it possible began as arbitrary, imaginative, and usually intuitive choices. In early cinema there were no rules and no groups that set the standards that would develop into the classical style. The only arbiters were directors like Porter and Griffith who tried things out, and audiences, who responded favourably to the experiments and their refinements.

> **The key to the continuity style is its self-effacement, its ability to show without showing itself, tell a story and make the storytelling disappear so that the story seems to be telling itself.**

There are a few basic formal components that were developed by Griffith and others in the early 1910s that established the classical style. Narrative flow is pieced together out of small fragments of action in such a way that the piecing together goes unnoticed and the action appears continuous. Sequences that occur at the same time but in different places are intercut to create narrative tension. Dialogue sequences are constructed by a series of over-the-shoulder shots from one participant in the dialogue to the other. The gaze of the viewer is linked to the gaze of the main characters through a series of shots that show a character and then show what the character is looking at. The result of these constructions is that narrative proceeds in a straight trajectory through time. Any transitions that break linearity (flashbacks, for example) are carefully prepared for and all narrative threads are sewn together at the end. The spectator is called into the narrative and becomes part of the story's space (cf. Althusser 1977).

Griffith was instrumental in establishing cross- or intercutting as a primary narrative device. The literary equivalent of this device is the simple narrative transition—'meanwhile' or 'in another part of town' or 'later the same day'—and some films borrow these verbal clues through intertitles or voice-over narration. But

implying such transitions visually is more difficult. In early cinema there lurked the continual concern that such things would be misunderstood. Too much cutting would confuse or trouble the viewer. But these fears were rarely realized, and filmmakers as early as Edward Porter found that, as long as they contained some kind of narrative glue, scenes placed side by side would be understood as occurring either simultaneously, earlier, or later than one another. Shots of a woman held captive by a menacing male (or caught in some other dangerous situation) are intercut with shots of an heroic male figure purposively moving in a direction that has been established as that of the menaced woman. The result is quite legible: the man is coming to save the threatened woman. The pattern comes from nineteenth-century stage melodrama, but Griffith was imaginative enough to realize that film could stretch its spatial and temporal boundaries (Fell 1974). His audience was imaginative enough to accept the illusion and substitute the emotional reality (suspenseful expectation that the hero will conquer space and reach the heroine in time) for the formal reality (two sequences actually occurring one after the other on the film strip, each sequence constructed in the studio at different times). The pattern stretches out time and narrows space, providing the viewer with a way to enter the narrative and be affected by it. Gender is clearly marked as the woman—like the viewer—becomes the passive figure, waiting for salvation, and the male the active figure, redeemed by his heroism. (Griffith did reverse the roles in contemporary sequences of *Intolerance* (1916), in which a mother moves to save her imprisoned son awaiting execution.) Even less complicated *manœuvres* than the traversal of large areas of physical and narrative space required thought and practice. Take something as simple as getting a character out of a chair, on her feet, and out of the door. In the Biograph films, Griffith worked through the structuring of this movement until it became invisible.

What was the drive to develop such constructions? For one thing, they allow for a great manipulation of space and narrative rhythm. Much of very early cinema consisted of a kind of proscenium arch shot, the camera located at a point at which an imaginary spectator in an imaginary theatre would best see an overall gaze at the space in which events were taking place. This is a restrictive, monocular perspective, static and inflexible. But why create complex editing only to generate the illusion of a continuous movement? Eisenstein didn't. He cut into temporal linearity and restructured it. He would return to a shot of a person falling, for example, at a slighty earlier point than when he left it, so that the inevitable action is retarded, time manipulated. In the famous plate-smashing sequence in *Potemkin*, the single act of an enraged sailor is broken into eight separate shots, each less than a second long, which extends the act and emphasizes the fury behind it. Even Griffith wasn't absolute in his own construction of linearity. In films during the Biograph period, and sometimes later, there are occasional sequences of people rising from chairs in which the second shot is earlier in the trajectory of action than the first, and the person appears as if he were getting up twice.

Despite Griffith's 'lapses' in the continuity cutting he helped develop, the development of continuity in the early 1910s continued to privilege an illusion of linearity and of unbroken movement across a series of edits. We can, finally, only speculate on the reasons after the fact. The continuity style developed as a way to present a story in forward progression, not as a way to look at how the story was created. It generated its own economy, in narrative as well as physical production. Filmmakers developed formal methods that made shooting relatively quick and easy: shoot whatever scenes are most economical to shoot at a given time (shoot out of sequence when necessary); cover any given sequence from as many different angles as possible and with multiple takes of each angle to give the producer and editor a lot of material to choose from; edit the material to create linear continuity, cut on movement, keep eyelines matched (maintaining the direction a person is gazing from one shot to the other). Make the story appear to tell itself as inexpensively and quickly as possible.

No more interesting and enduring examples of the continuity style can be found than in the cutting of basic dialogue sequences. Even before dialogue could be recorded on a soundtrack, the following pattern emerged: the dialogue begins with a two-shot of the participants in the scene. The cutting pattern then starts as a series of over-the-shoulder shots from one participant to the other. The pattern may be slightly altered. For example, shots of just one of the participants listening or talking may appear in the course of the sequence. But the main series of shots are over-the-shoulder cuts, back and forth, that conclude with a return to the original two-shot. A simple dialogue has, therefore, to be filmed many different times with numerous takes of the two-shot and the over-the-shoulder set-ups. It sounds complicated, but the economies are clear. As a normative process, everyone concerned with the making of a film knows how to do it with dispatch. The use of over-the-shoulder shots means that one of the high-priced actors in the sequence does not have to be present all the time. A shot from behind the shoulder of a stand-in can be made to look just like a shot from behind the shoulder of the primary actor. The reverse shots of the over-the-shoulder sequence do not even have to be done in the same place! Cut together, keeping the eyelines matched, two spaces will look the same as one. The process results in many shots—many choices—available for the producer and the film editor to work with in a much less expensive environment than the studio floor. The result is standard patterns of narrative information, comprehensible to everyone from a technician in the studio to a member of the audience in the theatre.

And the process provides a unifying structure. This is its great paradox. The fragments of over-the-shoulder dialogue cutting, or any other part of the continuity style, create unity out of plurality, focus our gaze, suture us into the narrative flow and the space between the glances of the characters. Theories have been set forth that the constant cutting across the gazes of the characters slips us into their narrative space because we are continually asked by the cutting to expect something more. Someone looks, and we are primed to respond, 'What is the character looking at?' And the next shot inevitably tells us, by showing the person (or object) being looked at. This play of intercut gazes creates an irresistible imaginary world that seems to surround us with character and actions. It is as if the viewer becomes part of the text, reading the film and being read into it (Dayan 1992). It is this element of the irresistible, of desire and its satisfaction, that most clearly demonstrates the staying-power of the classical continuity style.

Alfred Hitchcock—to take one example—can create overwhelming emotions simply by cutting between a character looking and what the character is looking at. Early in *Vertigo* (1958), James Stewart's Scottie drives through the streets of San Francisco, following a woman he has been told is obsessed by someone long dead. The sequence is made up by a relatively simple series of shots and reverse shots. We see Scottie in his car driving, we see from his car window, as if from his point of view, Madeleine's car. She arrives at a museum. Scottie looks at her, Hitchcock cuts to a point-of-view shot of her, looking at a painting, and being looked at by Scottie. She goes into a dark alley. Scottie follows, his gaze pursuing her to a door. As the door opens, and Scottie's gaze penetrates it, the darkness changes to a riot of colourful flowers in a flower shop. Throughout the sequence we see with Scottie, but see (as he does) only a mystery, which, we learn later, is not a mystery but a lie. The woman he follows is not the person he thinks she is: both he and the audience are fooled. The director uses elements of the classical style to manipulate our responses, to place us close to the gaze of the central character, which turns out to be seriously compromised. We identify with an illusion.

And as we identify with it, some of us want to discover how it has been constructed and perpetuated. Some of the most important work in recent film criticism has developed in the process of discovering the working of the classical Hollywood style. Bordwell, Staiger, and Thompson's *The Classical Hollywood Cinema* (1985) is a massively detailed catalogue of the attributes of what its authors call 'an excessively obvious cinema'. Other writers have discovered that beneath or within this obviousness lies a complex form and structure, and a rich interplay between a film and the culture that spawns and nurtures it with its attention. Films speak to us and we respond with the price of admission or the rental of a video. Its articulateness is created through a narrative economy in which narrative, gesture, composition, lighting, and cutting are tightly coded so that we understand the intended meaning immediately.

But immediate comprehension often means simple assenting to the reproduction of gender and racial stereotypes. It is necessary, therefore, to analyse why we assent, to what we assent, and why we keep coming back for more. Theories of subject placement—how the viewer is fashioned by a film into a kind of ideal spectator who desires to see what is shown him or her on the screen—attempt to answer questions of how form creates attention, and attention fashions perception. Critics such as Dana Polan (1986) have investigated the tight links between culture and film, indicating how history and our responses to it make of film an ideological mirror and an engine of affirmation. Others, like Mary Ann Doane (1987), have probed in detail the interplay between the American style and our given ideas of gender; or they have read against the grain to point out how films can question the con-

ventional wisdom if we look carefully and decode them with a knowing eye.

Much has been done and much remains. Attention needs to be paid to the minute particulars of the classical Hollywood style; more needs to be said about the way a gesture with a coffee cup, how a cut between two characters glancing at or away from each other, generate meaning. The economy of style of the classical form may present apparent obviousnesses, but it is in fact a structural shorthand, a code book that keeps critics and viewers attentive and attracted. In its very invisibility lie the structures of desire that make us want to see more and more.

Contesting the Hollywood style

The Hollywood style was and is the dominant style the world over. But there have been periods when some filmmakers consciously worked against its structures, rethinking its structural and semantic codes. These filmmakers favoured long takes (in the Bazinian manner), atemporal or non-linear narratives, and subject-matter that differed from the usual Hollywood stories of violence and melodrama. They called attention to their methods, exploited the possibilities of mise-en-scène, and asked viewers to become aware that form creates content; that stories don't exist without the telling of them.

One great period of such experimentation occurred during the 1960s and 1970s. Spawned by the French New Wave, extending to Italy, England, the United States, and then, in the 1970s, to Germany, the movement produced a body of work, and a series of imaginative filmmakers who, briefly, changed some basic assumptions of cinematic form. The results were a series of films that reconsidered American genre films in a form that stressed the long take and oblique cutting, an avoidance of classical continuity rules, and, in the case of French director Jean-Luc Godard, a cinema that questioned the form and content of the cinematic image itself. Godard and his contemporaries and followers—Alain Resnais in France; Michelangelo Antonioni, Pier Paolo Pasolini, the early Bertolucci in Italy; Rainer Werner Fassbinder and the early Wim Wenders in Germany; Glauber Rocha in Brazil; the filmmakers of ICAIC (the Cuban film Institute) (to name only a few)—made films that took their own textuality as one of their subjects. They asked their viewers to think about the images they produced, the stories they told. Their films questioned whether other images might be used, other stories be told. Many of these filmmakers worked in the tradition of the German playwright and theorist Bertolt Brecht, who demanded that a work of art put the spectator in a speculative position, reveal its internal mechanisms, and show how the power of the imagination can work with or against the power of a culture's dominant ideology. Many of their films were passionately political, speaking the inquisitive and corrective voice of the left.

> **The Hollywood style was and is the dominant style the world over. But there have been periods when some filmmakers consciously worked against its structures, rethinking its structural and semantic codes.**

The structural principle of this modernist, reflexive movement was complexity and mediation, a recognition that the film image and its editorial structure are not givens, certainly not natural, but the constructions of convention. And what is made by convention can be questioned and altered. The over-the-shoulder cutting pattern, naturalized in the classical American style, is not necessary; and most of the filmmakers of this movement avoided it, using instead the Bazinian long take, which permitted the image to be interrogated, found false or adequate, but always only a representation. 'This is not a just image,' Godard says. 'It is just an image.'

Yet, no matter how much they used film as medium of exploration, these filmmakers kept referring to their base of American cinema. Alain Resnais's *Last Year at Marienbad* (1961) is a radical meditation on the conventions of past and present tense in film editing, and a remake of Hitchcock's *Vertigo*. Antonioni, whose *L'avventura* (1960), *La notte* (1961), *L'Éclisse* (1962), *Red Desert* (1964), and *Blow-up* (1966) show an extraordinary commitment to the idea that filmic composition is an architectural form obeying its own rules of narrative logic, keeps playing his work off against the conventions of 1940s American melodrama. Rainer Werner Fassbinder, the most Brechtian filmmaker after Godard, and the one director most committed to exploring the

working class, bases his interrogations of form on the 1950s American melodrama of Douglas Sirk. Through these approaches they take the classical style into account, respond to it, and, finally, honour it by recognizing it as their base. For better or for worse, the classical style has survived, and absorbed, all of the responses to it. Everything else stands, finally, in dialectical relationship to it. This static, dynamic, dominant, and absorptive textuality embraces the cultural surround and articulates the complexities of ideology. The film text becomes a rich and a complex event, reticent and boisterous, asking passivity from its viewers while provoking their desire, hiding itself while announcing its power in film after film.

BIBLIOGRAPHY

Althusser, Louis (1977), 'Ideology and the Ideological State Apparatuses', in *Lenin and Philosophy*, trans. Ben Brewster (New York: Monthly Review Press).

*****Bazin, André** (1967), *What is Cinema?*, 2 vols., trans. Hugh Gray, i (Berkeley and Los Angeles: University of California Press).

Benjamin, Walter (1936/1969), 'The Work of Art in the Age of Mechanical Reproduction', in *Illuminations*, ed. Hannah Arendt and trans. Harry Zohn (New York: Schocken Books).

Bordwell, David, Janet Staiger, and **Kristin Thompson** (1985), *The Classical Hollywood Cinema: Film Style and Mode of Production to 1960* (New York: Columbia University Press).

*****Burch, Noël** (1990), *Life to those Shadows* (Berkeley: University of California Press).

*****Cameron, Ian** (1972), *Movie Reader* (New York: Praeger).

Comito, Terry (1971), 'Touch of Evil', *Film Comment*, 7/2 (Summer), *Three Masters of Mise-en-Scène: Murnau, Welles, Ophuls*.

Dayan, Daniel (1992), 'The Tudor-Code of Classical Cinema', in Gerald Mast, Marshall Cohen, and Leo Braudy (eds.), *Film theory and Criticism* (New York: Oxford University Press).

Doane, Mary Anne (1987), *The Desire to Desire* (Bloomington: Indiana University Press).

*****Eisenstein, Sergei** (1949), 'Dickens, Griffith, and Film Today', in *Film Form: Essays in Film Theory*, ed. and trans. Jay Leyda (New York: Harcourt, Brace, & World).

—— (1943), *The Film Sense*, ed. and trans. Jay Leyda (London: Faber & Faber).

Fell, John (1974), *Film and the Narrative Tradition* (Norman: University of Oklahoma Press).

Gaudreault, André (1983), 'Temporality and Narrativity in Early Cinema 1895–1908', in John Fell (ed.), *Film before Griffith* (Berkeley: University of California Press).

—— (1990), 'Detours in Film Narrative: The Development of Cross-Cutting', in Thomas Elsaesser and Adam Barker (eds.), *Early Cinema: Space, Frame, Narrative* (London: British Film Institute).

*****Kolker, Robert Phillip** (1983), *The Altering Eye* (New York: Oxford University Press).

—— (1988), *A Cinema of Loneliness*, 2nd edn. (New York: Oxford University Press).

Metz, Christian (1977/1982), *The Imaginary Signifier*, trans. Celia Britton, Annwyl Williams, Ben Brewster, and Alfred Guzzetti (Bloomington: Indiana University Press).

*****Perkins, V. F.** (1972), *Film as Film: Understanding and Judging Movies* (Harmondsworth: Penguin).

Polan, Dana (1986), *Power and Paranoia* (New York: Columbia University Press).

Written on the Wind

Robin Wood from Robin Wood: Film Studies at Warwick University Vision, 12 (Dec. 1974), 27–36.

One might talk about *Written on the Wind* (1957) in terms of fundamental American myth, the myth of lost innocence and purity: the characters of the film repeatedly look back to their collective childhood. Universal myth, perhaps, but deriving a particular meaning from the Virgin Land that has so rapidly become one of the most technologically advanced countries of the world. The nostalgic yearning for innocence has a markedly pastoral flavour: the characters, among their oil pumps and scarlet sports cars, long to return to 'the river', where they were happy (or think they were). The same myth, in the form of 'Rosebud', animates *Citizen Kane* (1941).

This might prove a useful starting-point for an exploration of more than *Written on the Wind*. One might develop an investigation of the film itself further by considering the genre within which it is situated: the Hollywood melodrama. Melodrama has proved a very difficult word to define (like so many such shifting, complex, dangerous terms— 'tragedy', 'sentimentality', 'classical', 'Romantic', etc.). It implies in this context, I take it, characters divided fairly markedly into 'good' and 'bad'; simplified issues; violent or extreme emotions; a reliance on rhetoric. '*Crude* melodrama': the words often go together. One can ask— *Written on the Wind* might well prompt one to ask— whether crudeness is a necessary feature of melodrama. Certainly the forceful projection of violent feelings is, though that is also a feature common to many tragedies. One can see the simplification of issues and the powerful projection of emotion as a matter of cliché or vulgarity; one might also see it, in certain cases, as a reduction of things to essentials, the stripping away of the intricacies of personal psychology (though Sirk's film is not exactly lacking in that quarter) to reveal fundamental human drives in the most intense way possible.

Which set of terms should be applied to *Written on the Wind* can only be argued, I would claim, through close attention to the level of realization, or of style: the level at which the personal artist supervenes, the level at which, for the critic, considerations of national myth and genre must give place to a consideration of personal authorship. Certain elementary features of style belong more to the studio than to Sirk: notably the set design. Connoisseurs of Universal films will, for example, probably find the hallway and staircase somewhat familiar: they will have seen them in *Marnie* (1964), and perhaps in other Universal movies. But the extract we have seen contains striking stylistic features which can't be explained in this way; features that are not just functional, like the staircase, but determine our response and aspire to the creation of the film's meaning. Certain of these features some might again want to label 'crude', though again they are capable of another description. Douglas Sirk was originally Danish, but settled for a time in Germany and made films there before he went to Hollywood. It can be argued that he inherited something of the tradition of German Expressionism (a tradition that other directors also— Lang, Hitchcock, Murnau—have found readily compatible with the Hollywood melodrama in one form or another), of which the central aim was the projection of emotional states by means of imagery: the use of the colour scarlet in *Written on the Wind* might be seen as having Expressionist derivation. Sirk also admired, and collaborated with, Bertolt Brecht, a writer who seems at first sight very far removed from the Hollywood melodrama. There is no room in the Hollywood genre movie for Brechtian alienation devices: the central aims are obviously incompatible, the tendency of the genre movie being to enclose the spectator in an emotional experience, the function of alienation devices being to detach him by means of interruptions. Alienation effects, one might say, can be sneaked into Hollywood movies only on condition that they cease to alienate (unless we bring to the films prior expectations of being 'alienated'). One can, however, see the extremeness of some of Sirk's effects as the result of a desire to break the audience's absorption in the narrative and force it to conscious awareness. In the drugstore at the start of the extract, there are not just one or two signs saying 'Drugs', they are suspended all over the shop to an extent that *almost* oversteps the bounds of the Hollywood demand for plausibility. How does one see this?—as part of the excesses of Hollywood melodrama?—as the legacy of Expressionism?—as derived from Brechtian alienation? The idea of a society drowning its awareness in alcohol (like the Stack character) or in drugs is central to the film.

Then there is the very loaded, obtrusive shot with the camera tracking out of the drugstore in front of Stack to reveal the boy on the wooden horse in the foreground. One can say many things about that: the decision to do it as a tracking shot instead of cutting to a close-up of the boy—the effect is to stress the connection (both psychological and symbolic) between Stack and the boy by uniting them in the frame, without loss of impact. There is then the question of what the boy signifies; and a device that may at first sight seem crude takes on surprising complexity. First, most obviously, the boy represents the son Stack has just learnt he will probably never have; second, the violent rocking–riding motion carries strong sexual overtones, and in Stack's mind the idea of sterility is clearly not distinct from that of impotence;

Written on the Wind continued

third, the child takes up the recurrent idea of the characters' yearning for lost innocence—and for the unreflecting spontaneity and vitality that went with it—a central theme in the film. The child's expression and actions are very precisely judged: we see him as enjoying himself, yet we also see how, to Stack, his smile appears malicious, taunting. The obtrusiveness of the device is perhaps justifiable in terms of density of meaning.

It is impossible to leave this topic without reference to the use of colour. The film is built partly on colour contrasts: the strident scarlet associated with Dorothy Malone against the 'natural' greens and browns of Lauren Bacall. The use of scarlet is a beautiful example of the integration of 'Expressionist' effect within Hollywood's 'psychological realism': the glaring red of Dorothy Malone's phone, toenails, flowers, and car is explainable in psychological

terms as her rebellious assertion of herself in a drab world. The effect is again not simple: the red carries the simple traditional sense of the 'scarlet woman', certainly, but it also expresses vitality and powerful, if perverted, drives; it has positive as well as negative connotations within the world the film creates. I should like to single out two moments where colour is used particularly forcefully and expressively. One is the moment when the camera tracks forward towards Dorothy Malone's car, the whole screen fills with red, and the image dissolves to the *green* car in which Lauren Bacall is arriving for the arranged meeting with her already drunken husband. The use of the colour contrast combines with the technical device of the dissolve to create a complex significance (a significance *felt*, perhaps, rather than consciously apprehended, as we might experience effects in music): it contrasts the two women through the colours with which they are associated; it evokes the idea of

The curved staircase forms an integral part of the mise-en-scène in Douglas Sirk's *Written on the Wind* (1957)

Written on the Wind continued

simultaneity, suggesting the convergence of forces (which will culminate in the father's death); hence it links Dorothy Malone with her brother, underlining the parallels between them—his alcoholism, her nymphomania, the common cause (or complex of causes, at the centre of which is the Rock Hudson character, the film's apparent 'hero'). The second example is the dance, which employs not only scarlet but a particularly strident colour clash involving Dorothy Malone's cerise negligée. The dance itself is an extraordinary device for suggesting all those things that couldn't be shown on the screen in 1956, and which perhaps gain greater force from the partial suppression: sexual exhibitionism and masturbation (the use of Rock Hudson's photograph as a substitute for his physical presence being crucial to this scene and an indication of themes central to Sirk's cinema).

From the use of colour (and with this photograph still in mind), we might pass to another feature of Sirk's style that has elicited the word 'baroque': the use of mirrors and other glass surfaces. One might argue that this is merely decorative, but not that it is accidental: there are three striking shots involving mirrors. First, at the bar, when the camera swings left to show the characters reflected in the bar mirror. Second, when Robert Stack is brought home. Third, when Dorothy Malone is brought home (the parallel between her and her brother again 'musically' underlined), and, as she

passes, Rock Hudson is shown reflected in the hall mirror, watching her. There is also, related to this, the use of windows: repeatedly, Sirk shows characters as seen through glass. One can see this in various ways: the 'framing' of people who are trapped; the inability of people to help each other, each reduced to a glass surface that can't be penetrated; the unreality of the characters, who, trapped in their own fantasies, have become mere 'reflections' of human beings (Sirk's last film was called *Imitation of Life*, 1959).

Finally, I should talk briefly about what is the most difficult aspect of film to analyse. I suggested earlier an analogy with poetry; I hope to make this clearer rather than more obscure by adding to it the analogy with music. Sirk himself has said that his conscious model for *Written on the Wind* was Bach fugue. He talked about the acting as pared down to clean intersecting lines, like counterpoint. If *Written on the Wind* is a fugue for four voices, the sequence of the father's death is clearly the *stretto*. What I want to indicate is the obvious fact that film, like music, has a fixed duration. Hence the appropriateness to it of musical terms like 'tempo' and 'rhythm'. We still haven't found a way of talking satisfactorily about this 'musical' dimension, the direct effect of the *movement* of film on the senses, except in dangerously impressionistic terms. There is a lot of work to be done.

Citizen Kane

Peter Wollen from 'Introduction to *Citizen Kane*', *Film Reader*, no. 1 (1975), 9–15.

To write about *Citizen Kane* (1941) is to write about the cinema. It is impossible to think about this film without thinking about its place in film history. Most critics, despite Welles's own unhappy relations with Hollywood, have seen him primarily, implicitly within the framework of the American narrative cinema. Pauline Kael talks about the 1930s newspaper picture and builds up the role of Mankiewicz, a hard-core Hollywood scribe if ever there was one. Charles Higham talks of a 'wholly American work', Andrew Sarris of 'the American baroque', and they leave no doubt, I think, that, where the cinema is concerned, for them America = Hollywood. And, from the other side, an enemy

of Hollywood such as Noël Burch puts Welles in relation to Elia Kazan, Robert Aldrich, Joseph Losey, and Arthur Penn, and condemns *Kane* for simply displaying an amplification of traditional narrative codes which it does nothing to subvert.

Against this mainstream trend, of course, we have to set the massive influence of André Bazin. For Bazin, *Kane* and *The Magnificent Ambersons* (1942) were crucial moments in the unfolding of the cinema's vocation of realism. Together with the work of Jean Renoir and William Wyler, *Kane* represented a rediscovery of the tradition of realism, lost since the

Citizen Kane continued

silent epoch (Louis Feuillade, Erich von Stroheim, F. W. Murnau). *Kane* looked forward to Italian Neo-Realism and, had Bazin lived longer, his interest would surely have turned to cinéma verité and the new developments in documentary which followed the invention of magnetic tape, lightweight recorder and camera, and the tape join. (Indeed the strain of 'technological messianism' in Bazin's thought must surely have taken him in this direction).

For Bazin, of course, the crucial feature of *Citizen Kane* was its use of deep focus and the sequence shot. Yet one senses all the time, in Bazin's writings on Welles, an uneasy feeling that Welles was far from sharing the spiritual humility and self-effacement, or even the democratic mentality, which marked for Bazin the 'style without style', the abnegation of the artist before a reality whose meaning outruns that of any artefact. It is easy to forget that, on occasion, Bazin talked about the 'sadism' of Welles, of his *rubbery* space, stretched and distended, rebounding like a catapult in the face of the spectator. He compared Welles to El Greco (as well as the Flemish masters of deep focus) and commented on his 'infernal vision' and 'tyrannical objectivity'. But this awareness of Welles the stylist and manipulator did not deflect Bazin from his main point. Fundamentally, his enthusiasm was for the deep-focus cinematography which Welles and Gregg Toland introduced with such virtuosity. It was on this that Welles's place in film history would depend.

Yet a third current has been felt recently, again often more implicit than explicit. Putting together some remarks of Alain Robbe-Grillet, the article by Marie-Claire Ropars-Wuilleumier in *Poétique* and that by William van Wert in *Sub-Stance*, we can see how it is possible to place *Kane* as a forerunner of *Last Year at Marienbad* (1961), a film which pointed the way towards the breakdown of unilinear narration and a Nietzschean denial of truth. It is in this sense too that we can understand Borges's praise of *Kane* as a 'labyrinth without a centre'. *Kane's* perspectivism (leading so easily to nihilism), its complex pattern of nesting, overlapping, and conflicting narratives, put it in a particular tendency within the modern movement, which has its origins perhaps in Conrad or Faulkner and its most radical exponents in Pirandello and the further reaches of the French new novel.

And of course, this tendency, whose origins are in literature, has begun to spread into the cinema, especially in France, through the influence of writers—Marguerite Duras, Jean Cayrol, Robbe-Grillet—who have worked on films, even become filmmakers.

The oddest of these three versions of *Kane* is undoubtedly

Bazin's. So flexible, so generous in many respects, Bazin was nevertheless able at times to restrict and concentrate his vision to an amazing degree. Obviously he felt the influence of Expressionism (which he hated) on *Kane*, but he simply discounted it—or tried to justify it by pointing to the exaggeration and tension in the character of Kane, a kind of psychological realism, similar to the way in which he defended the expressionist style of a film about concentration camps. (In the same vein, Christian Metz remarks how the formal flamboyance of *Kane*, the film, parallels the flamboyant personality of Kane, the man.) In general, however, Bazin simply hurried on to his favourite theme—the importance of deep focus and the sequence shot.

The key concepts here for Bazin were those of spatial and temporal homogeneity and dramatic unity. It is almost as if the theatrical scene was the model for Bazin's theory of the cinema. Of course, he believed that filmed theatre should respect the scene and the stage. Beyond that, it seems he believed in a *theatrum mundi*, which it was the calling of the cinema to capture and record—there is a sense in which all cinema was for him filmed theatre, only in Neo-Realism, for instance, the world was a stage, the players were living their lives, and the dramatist, who gave meaning to the action, was God himself. No wonder then that, for him, the artist, in Annette Michelson's phrase, was 'artist as witness' and the whole of reality the offering of an 'Ultimate Spectacle'. Indeed, Bazin writes that in Italy daily life was a perpetual *commedia dell'arte* and describes the architecture of Italian towns and cities as being like a theatre set.

Bazin always laid great stress on the theatricality of Orson Welles. He saw Welles as a man of the theatre and talked about the sequence shot as a device for maintaining the primacy of the actor. 'An actor's performance loses its meaning, is drained of its dramatic blood like a severed limb, if it ceases to be kept in living, sensory contact with the other characters, and the setting. Moreover, as it lasts, the scene charges itself like a battery . . .'.

Basically Bazin justifies the sequence shot and deep focus for three reasons: it maintains the dramatic unity of a scene, it permits objects to have a residual being beyond the pure instrumentality demanded of them by the plot, and it allows the spectator a certain freedom of choice following the action. In *Kane* it was the first which was uppermost. The second was important to Bazin—he talks about the door-handle of Susan Alexander's bedroom, in the sequence after the suicide attempt, and goes on to describe the cold feel of copper, the copper or indented enamel of a door-handle,

Citizen Kane continued

yet we must feel that this is his own projection, reverie almost (in the Bachelardian sense), which has little relevance to *Kane*. As for the third reason, Bazin recognizes that Welles directs the spectator's attention through lighting and movement as imperiously as any editor at times, but he remains aware of the potential ambiguity of the sequence shot and, of course, links this to the ambiguous portrayal of Kane's character.

Yet, with the advantage of hindsight, we can see that Bazin's love of the sequence shot has been strangely betrayed by the filmmakers who have subsequently used it. Who do we think of? Andy Warhol, Michael Snow, Jean-Luc Godard, Jean-Marie Straub, Miklós Jancsó. There are links of course—Straub reveres Bazin's hero, Bresson; Godard was deeply marked by Roberto Rossellini—but clearly the sequence shot has been used for purposes quite different from those which Bazin foresaw. Some of these filmmakers have stressed the autonomy of the camera and its own movement, rather than the primacy of the actors or the drama (Jancsó, Snow), others have used the sense of duration to de-realize the imaginary world of the film (Godard), others have been interested in duration as a formal feature in itself (Warhol). Straub, probably the closest to Bazin in his insistence on authenticity, on a refusal of guidance for the spectator's eye, has none the less put his Bazinian style to purposes very different from those Bazin himself could have envisaged.

It is worth noting that most of the sequence shots in *Citizen Kane* are, in fact, used in the framing story rather than the flashbacks, in the scenes in which Thompson talks to each of the interior narrators. The average length of a shot in *Citizen Kane* is not particularly long because of the number of short shots that exist both in the newsreel sequence and in the numerous montage sequences which Welles uses, mostly as transitions. The decision to use sequence shots in the framing story is clearly a decision not to use classical field reverse-field cutting, and thus to de-emphasize the role of Thompson, the narratee. Thompson only appears as a shadowy figure with his back to the camera. It is hard to separate decisions on length of shot and editing from decisions on narrative structure. By shooting Thompson in this way Welles precludes any spectator identification with the character who, from the point of view of information and focalization, is the spectator's representative in the film.

In the last analysis, what concerned Bazin was dramaturgy (even if, as with the Neo-Realists, he could speak of a 'dramaturgy of everyday life'), and he tended to assume the need for characters and a continuous narrative line. He simply thought that psychological truth and dramatic configurations would reveal themselves more fully if there was a minimum of artistic intervention. He remained hostile throughout to experimental film (for him Stroheim was the great experimentalist and Welles, of course, can easily be perceived as an avatar of Stroheim) and thought of theatre and the novel as the models with which cinema should be compared. There too he tended to have conventional tastes—he aligns himself with Sartre's condemnation of Mauriac, but seems also to accept without question Sartre's positive tastes—Dos Passos, Faulkner, Hemingway—and clearly was not interested in the literary revolution inaugurated by Gertrude Stein and James Joyce.

Yet the example of contemporary filmmakers has shown that the long take and the sequence shot tend to undermine the primacy of the dramaturgy: duration becomes a stylistic feature in itself and, far from suppressing the filmmaking process, the sequence shot tends to foreground it. At most, the sequence shot can be associated with a Brechtian type of dramaturgy, based on tableaux. In fact this tendency can be seen even in *Citizen Kane*, where it is disguised by the movement in and out of the framing story and the complex character of the transition. Bazin thought that the principal function of the cut should be that of ellipsis, but, within the kind of rhythm built up by a series of long sequence shots, the cut automatically takes on a role as caesura rather than ellipsis alone.

Truffaut, always fundamentally a conservative critic—as he has shown himself to be a conservative filmmaker—has said that 'if *Citizen Kane* has aged, it is in its experimental aspects'. It seems to me that it is precisely the opposite which is true. All Welles's 'tricks', as they are often contemptuously called—the lightning mixes, the stills which come to life, the complex montages, the elasticity of perspective, the protracted dissolves, the low-angle camera movements, etc.—are what still gives the film any interest. Nobody, after all, has ever made high claims for its 'novelistic' content, its portrayal of Kane's psychology, its depiction of American society and politics in the first half of the twentieth century, its anatomy of love or power or wealth. Or, at any rate, there is no need to take such claims very seriously. It seems quite disproportionate for Noël Burch to submit them to his acute dissection and attack, as he himself seems to half-acknowledge.

Indeed, the 'pro-Hollywood' defence of *Kane* is quite pathetic in its lack of ambition (*Kane* after all, is widely held to be the greatest film ever made). Pauline Kael begins with hyperbole 'the one American talking picture that seems as

Citizen Kane continued

fresh now as the day it opened', but soon descends to dub *Kane*, in a famous phrase, 'a shallow work, a *shallow* masterpiece'. The shallowness does not worry her, however, because it is what makes *Kane* 'such an American triumph', and then we discover its triumph lies in 'the way it gets its laughs and makes its points'. Basically, she assimilates *Kane* to the tradition of the well-made Broadway play, translated into the 1930s comedy film, with all its astringency and sense of pace and fun. Other critics do not really claim much more: Charles Higham talks of a 'masterpiece', but also 'epic journalism'; once again, we get the insistence on the 'American' quality of Welles and *Kane*, ironic in the light of the original intention to call the film *The American*. Energy, grandeur, and emptiness.

The truth is that the 'content' of *Citizen Kane* cannot be taken too seriously. Yet it had an enormous impact—largely because of its virtuosity, its variety of formal devices and technical innovations and inventions. In themselves, of course, these are purely ornamental, and the dominant aesthetic of our age is one that rejects the concept of ornament—the ruling aesthetic of our day is one of expressionism or functionalism or symbolism or formalism, seen as a complex process of problem-solving rather than wit or decoration. Welles is usually described in terms of baroque or expressionism, sometimes the Gothic, but this seems to reflect the ponderousness of his themes. His interest in formal devices and technical ingenuity puts him closer to mannerism, to a conscious appreciation of virtuosity and the desire to astonish.

It is this 'mannerist' aspect of Welles which still lives—not the dramatic unity which deep focus and the long take make possible, but the long take and deep focus as formal features in themselves. Similarly, it is not the theme of time, youth, memory, age, etc. which is of any interest, but the devices used to organize time within the film. Many of these point the way towards a quite different kind of use—contemporary filmmakers' variations on the long take, Robbe-Grillet's variations on the freeze frame–still. *Kane* remains an important film historically, not within the terms it set itself, or those within which it has been mainly seen by critics, but because, by a kind of retroactive causality, it is now possible to read there an entirely different film, one which Welles probably never intended. *Citizen Kane*, we can now say, was a milestone along the road which led, not to a reinvigoration of Hollywood, or a novelistic complication of narrative, or the unfolding of the realistic essence of film, but towards the expansion and elaboration of a formal poetic which would transform our concept of cinema entirely, towards film as a text which is a play with meaning rather than a vehicle for it.

3

Film acting

Paul McDonald

Acting is the form of performance specifically involved with the construction of dramatic character. Actors construct characters by using their voices and bodies. For an audience, the activity of reading a performance involves the bringing together of actor and character, and the interpretation and evaluation of acting has tended to assess whether or not the actor has 'become' the character. This has produced a familiar language of interpretation, in which judgements about acting are articulated in terms of whether a performance is more or less 'believable', 'truthful', or 'realistic'.

Although acting remains a major component of narrative cinema, film studies has yet to provide any sustained inquiry into film acting. If it is to examine acting further, it should not discard such terms as 'believable', 'truthful', and 'realistic', but rather question what they mean and how those meanings are constructed as the effects of film acting. Part of the agenda of film studies has been to develop critical frameworks for analysing and contesting how film reproduces ideological beliefs and 'truths'. Questions of the believable, the truthful, and the realistic in film acting may therefore provide the basis for assessing how, and with what effect, screen performance is a socially meaningful act.

Any study of film acting needs first and foremost to be aware of the medium. Film acting is as much a product of camera angles, camera movements, lighting, editing, and music as it is of the actor's voice and body. Barry King (1985: 28) has discussed how, for actors working both on stage and screen, film presents a problem of professional power, for the actor loses part of his or her creative control to the camera and the cutting-room. Conversely, in a labour market where work is scarce, some actors criticize film and television because camera-work and editing can made 'bad' actors appear 'good' (1985: 33). What is at stake in this conflict between the film actor and film technology is a debate concerning whether it is the actor or the film technology which is the primary source of meaning. In a famous case of experimentation, the Soviet film-maker Lev Kuleshov took shots of an open prison door and a bowl of soup, along with two reaction shots of an actor longing for freedom and feeling hunger. Although the reaction shots showed different expressions on the actor's face, Kuleshov (1929: 54) reported that, when the shots were juxtaposed, their meaning changed, and concluded that it was the editing and not the actor that determined the meaning of the performance.

Walter Benjamin (1936) saw the impact of film technology on the actor as part of a wider cultural change. For Benjamin, reproduction defined a new phase in cultural production, as the technology of reproduction had the effect of separating the art object from its creator. Benjamin believed this diminished the 'aura' attached to works of art, as the object no longer carried with it the mystical 'presence' of the person who made them. In this context 'presence' should be taken to mean both that the creator was present at the making of the object and that this original contact with the creator left the object with a special 'charisma'. It was this effect of reproduction which led Benjamin to argue that, in contrast to acting for the stage, film acting loses the presence of the performer and, in doing so, diminishes the aura, or charisma, of the individual.

In John Ellis's (1982) view, the overall effect of film reproduction lies in how it forms an illusion of presence in absence. In other words, film constructs the illusion that there is something or somebody present, when that spectacle is in fact recorded, reproduced, and absent. The separation of actor and image is then part of this effect. Using psychoanalytic concepts, Ellis argues that the film actor is placed in relation to the narcissistic, voyeuristic, and fetishistic looks of movie-goers. Through the construction of point of view, moviegoers will adopt various narcissistic identifications with the actors playing characters who control the narrative. By the convention of not looking at the camera, actors become part of the voyeuristic spectacle which the audience spies on. And, as the presence in absence of the film actor divides the moviegoer between relief and disbelief, actors also become part of the fetishistic attraction of cinema (see Creed, Chapter 9).

Benjamin and Ellis emphasize the film apparatus as more meaningful than the work of the actor. Both discuss what film does, and what film does to actors, but they do not address what film actors are doing. This type of approach has led to the tendency for film studies to discuss 'performance' as the performance of the medium rather than of the actor (e.g. Heath 1977). This neglect of actors in film studies has left them, instead of a presence in absence, simply absent. Any critical study of film acting would benefit from not merely dismissing 'aura' or 'presence' as metaphysical and mystical qualities, but from asking how such effects are constructed from the material elements of the film actor's voice and body. Benjamin's conclusion that reproduction removes the aura of presence from film acting is debatable, not just because the film image still makes the actor appear to be present, but also because the work and signification of acting may at one level be read as constructing the performer as a special focus of attention. While it is always the case that the film actor is absent, it should not be ignored that the use of camera, lighting, and editing, but more importantly the actor's voice and body, also work at trying to construct a charismatic spectacle. Rather, it should be asked how film acting constructs presence to compensate for the actual absence of the actor?

One way of understanding the film actor's position in the play of presence and absence is suggested by what James Naremore (1988) calls the 'performance frame'. At one level, this frame is to be understood as the limits of the film frame. When projected in the cinema, this frame is equivalent to the proscenium arch in theatre, marking the boundary between the world of the audience and the dramatic world of the actors. As any observation of film acting makes immediately clear, the realistic in acting does not arise from exact imitation of everyday behaviour. This difference between film acting and the everyday world is further distinguished by the performance frame. Whatever appears in the frame may be more or less similar to everyday life, but simply by appearing on screen the actor is immediately framed as apart from the everyday. When turned into public spectacle, the contents of the frame become more significant and meaningful than the experiences of everyday life. At this further level, the frame therefore constructs a context for meaning. Although the film actor only appears as a recorded image, that actor may still have a presence entirely because his or her actions are contextualized as meaningful. This effect is described by Barry King (1985: 41) as the 'hypersemiotisation' of the film actor. The film actor obtains an aura because the frame invests every action of the voice and body with meaning.

> **Any critical study of film acting would benefit from not merely dismissing 'aura' or 'presence' as metaphysical and mystical qualities, but from asking how such effects are constructed from the material elements of the film actor's voice and body.**

The performance frame only provides a context for the meaning of film acting; it does not account for how the acting voice and body actually construct meanings. Stephen Heath (1979: 179–82) proposes that film acting combines different sources or forms of meaning. The role played by the actor can be divided between the 'agent', or narrative function, and the 'character' formed from a set of individuating traits and peculiarities. The 'person' or actor may already be a source of meanings known from previous performances. Each of these sources is visualized in the 'image', but at some points the image may also stand apart from these other forms to present the performer only as spectacle. For Heath, these sources are never integrated to form a closed, coherent construction, but are various points of meaning which remain in continuous circulation to form what he calls a 'figure'.

Heath's model would suggest that the actor never 'disappears' into a role. From this view, believability in film acting is never the effect of how an actor has 'become' a role, but is the effect of how the actor is involved with becoming the role. Therefore, believable acting can in part be understood as the effect of making something which is absent and does not exist, i.e. the dramatic role, into something which is present and which appears to exist. The separation of actor and role makes the voice and body of the actor particularly significant, for these are the means for bringing together agent, character, actor, and image in a believable configuration. The actor's voice and body provide hypersemiotized fragments burdened with meaning. Heath's description of such fragments as 'intensities' (1979: 183) usefully identifies that it is through the small details of the actor's speech and movement that interpretations and judgements about film acting are formed.

Different effects are produced in acting depending on the extent to which the actor or the role is foregrounded. Barry King (1985: 41) describes as 'impersonation' acting in which the actor undergoes significant transformations to 'become' his or her role. Where actors do not impersonate their role but appear across a series of performances always to 'be themselves', acting is described by King as 'personification' (42). Impersonation, constructed through significant transformations, is based on difference, while personification connects similarities between performances. While some actors will produce performances that are more different than similar, and some the reverse, the two categories are not exclusive, and any performance should be seen for how it combines impersonation and personification.

Critical judgements about 'good' or 'bad' film acting can also be understood in terms of impersonation versus personification. Respected performers are often evaluated for what is read as their ability to transform themselves into different roles. This critical judgement

is premissed on a realist aesthetic which values the actor's skills employed in attempting to close the gap between actor and role in order to form a figure integrated into the narrative fiction. Personification disrupts this closure, emphasizing the actor's identity against the single role. The importance given to the actor's identity carries distinctive meanings between films, and personification has tended to be integral to the acting of film stars. It is because star acting is usually based on personification rather than impersonation that stars are so often criticized for not 'really' acting but for always 'playing themselves'.

While Heath and King offer terms for understanding the levels at which the relationship of actor to role is formed, they do not provide the means for understanding the detail in how the voices and bodies of film actors construct characters. Richard Dyer (1979: 121) identifies the appearance, speech, gestures, and actions of actors as elements in the construction of character in film. By their physical appearance, actors already represent a set of meanings. The use of costume, make-up, hairstyle, or posture becomes the means for impersonatory transformations. With speech, it is necessary to distinguish what is said from how it is said. Apart from cases where actors improvise, dialogue is usually produced by the writer. It is in how the writer's dialogue is spoken that the work of the actor is identified. The 'paralinguistic' features of volume, tone, and rhythm are the elements by which the actor's voice inflects the script. Dyer divides the signification of the body between gestures, which indicate the personality and temperament of the character, and actions, which are movements produced for the purpose of effecting a change in the narrative (1979: 126–8). In their various ways, it is these 'bits' of voices and bodies from which the relationship between actor, agent, character, and image is constructed.

Both the vocal and bodily significations of acting present a difficulty for the detailed analysis of film acting. Despite references to body language, physical movements and the paralinguistic dimensions of speech do not divide up into units similar to the letters and words of written and spoken language. It is difficult therefore to break down film acting performances into component signs. For this reason, Roberta Pearson (1992) employs the semiotic concept of 'code' as an alternative to the study of discrete acting signs. A code is formed when a set of signs, or signifying features, are deployed in familiar ways to signify a conventionalized set of meanings. Using codes, the analysis of acting

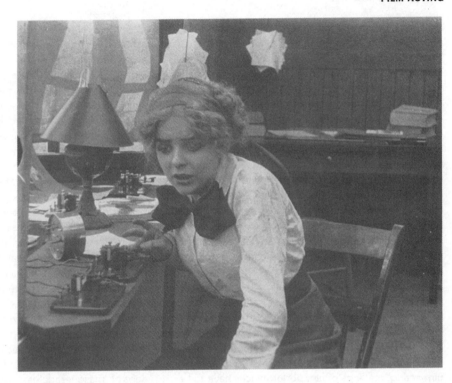

Towards verisimilitude— Blanche Sweet in an early Griffith film for Biograph/ *The Lonedale Operator* (1911)

shifts from the sign to questions of style. In her analysis of film acting in the early Biograph films of D. W. Griffith, Pearson traces a transformation between 1907 and 1912 from what she calls the 'histrionic code' to the 'verisimilar code'. In the former, the actor represented emotions through large gestures, and Pearson refers to this style as 'histrionic' because of the way in which it used conventions which did not imitate a sense of the everyday but belonged to the stage or screen drama only. In contrast, the verisimilar code was judged to be more 'realistic' because it was not so clearly conventionalized and gave more of a sense of everyday behaviour.

Despite the dominance of the verisimilar in screen acting, it should be noted that the histrionic component of screen acting never entirely disappears. Film acting remains distinguishable from everyday behaviour and so is always to a degree obviously acting. This difference between acting and everyday behaviour indicates that the 'realistic' in film acting has to be examined as a set of coded conventions. Where film acting is closer to approximating to the everyday, then a critical difficulty arises as it becomes less obvious that the actor is acting. This is an important problem, for it is precisely in this 'invisible' acting that the con-

struction of believability, truthfulness, or the realistic is most active. Judgements about 'bad' acting are often formed on the basis that the performer 'was obviously acting' and was therefore unbelievable. Analysis of film acting therefore has to make acting obvious if it is to examine the basis on which such judgements are made.

> **Film acting remains distinguishable from everyday behaviour and so is always to a degree obviously acting. This difference between acting and everyday behaviour indicates that the 'realistic' in film acting has to be examined as a set of coded conventions.**

One way of making acting obvious is suggested by John O. Thompson's (1978) use of the semiotic exercise the 'commutation test'. This test works by substituting actors to see what effect the substitution has on the meaning of a performance. Changes in meaning can then be analysed for the significant features which produced that difference. While the problems of breaking acting down into its constitutive signs prevent this method of analysis from being scientifically precise, it can draw attention to how a change of meaning is read from impressions formed about the colour of the eyes, the length of the nose, or the angle of the fingers, for example. Additionally, the test does not need to work just by substituting actors but can substitute ways of acting, so that the movement of the body becomes evident from substituting fast for slow, or the tone of the voice by changing high for low.

While Pearson's category of the verisimilar is useful, because the realistic in acting has taken several forms it is necessary to appreciate the many styles that the verisimilar has taken. Readings of acting style can be directed at different levels, looking at changes in style across historical periods, the relation of genre to performance style (de Cordova 1986), schools of acting such as the Method (Vineburg 1991), and how actors combine codes to form a personal style, or idiolect. As different ways of acting have served to define at particular times what is believable, truthful, or realistic in film acting, readings of film performances have to be seen in their historical contexts. Grahame F. Thompson (1985) has suggested that acting performances form a discourse which is only meaningful in a context of other discourses. From such a perspective, it is necessary to see how other forms of knowledge will influence what will be regarded as believable or truthful in acting. At the same time, it should be recognized that acting does not just reflect those other discourses, but that it is necessary to examine how an actor's voice and body construct believability and truth in their own terms.

The question of believability in acting is only at issue where film performers are placed in the formal conventions of realist narrative cinema. Alternative or oppositional cinema cultures have often developed through the transformation or rejection of realist and narrative conventions. In such movements the role of the film actor has been used in various ways to counter the illusion of narrative cinema, precisely in order that the actor's work will cease to be believable. The influence of Brechtian theories of acting (Brecht 1940) on filmmakers such as Jean-Luc Godard has resulted in some acting strategies where the film actor works at signifying their distance from a character (Higson 1986). Acting in this way attempts to make the fiction unbelievable as a means of questioning how believ-

ability in representation reproduces familiar and accepted truths. The distance between actor and character therefore opens up a perspective on how meaning is constructed. Other experimentations in film acting occurred as part of the post-revolution Soviet avant-garde. Vsevolod Meyerhold developed a system of training actors called 'bio-mechanics', in which actors used the body in ways which imitated the regular and repetitive actions of machines. Lez Cooke (1986) reads the use of this technique by the director Dziga Vertov as constructing, not a believable character, but a metaphor between the machine and the human body, which, in its historical context, produced a symbol of hope for the future. As these counter-strategies begin to problematize or depart from the actor–character relationship which is fundamental to acting, it could be questioned whether 'acting' is a suitable way of describing these ways of performing.

A considerable amount of current work in film studies is concerned with how cinematic forms produce and reproduce social categories of gender, race, and sexuality. As yet, these critical concerns have not significantly influenced the study of film acting. The concept of 'masquerade' is a useful point from which to establish such connections (see White, Chapter 13). According to this concept, social identities such as 'masculinity' or 'femininity' are not the effect of internal and ahistorical essences. Instead, these categories have to be continually constructed and reproduced, so that gender categories are understood as ways of 'acting' or 'performance'. In film studies, some uses of this concept (e.g. Holmlund 1993) have discussed how costuming and narrative situations construct gender. There is a problem with this view though, for it suspends the performance at the level of an artificial 'surface' behind which a 'real' identity is hidden. The fuller implications of the concept of masquerade will only become apparent when gendered, racial, and sexual meanings are seen to be acted in the uses of speaking voices and moving bodies.

BIBLIOGRAPHY

Benjamin, Walter (1936/1977), 'The Work of Art in the Age of Mechanical Reproduction', in J. Curran, M. Gurevitch, and J. Woollacott (eds.), Mass Communication and Society (London: Edward Arnold and the Open University).

Brecht, Bertolt (1940/1978), 'Short Description of a New Technique of Acting which Produces an Alienation

Effect', in J. Willet (ed.), *Brecht on Theatre* (London: Methuen).

*Butler, J. (ed.) (1991), *Star Texts: Image and Performance in Film and Television* (Detroit: Wayne State University Press).

Clark, D. (1990), 'Acting in Hollywood's Best Interest: Representations of Actors' Labour during the National Recovery Administration', *Journal of Film and Video*, 42/4.

Comolli, J. (1978), 'Historical Fiction—A Body too Much', *Screen*, 19/2: 41–53.

Cooke, Lez (1986), *Acting in the Cinema: Notes on the 'Acting Tapes'* (London: British Film Institute Education).

de Cordova, R. (1986), 'Genre and Performance: An Overview', in B. K. Grant (ed.), *Film Genre Reader* (Austin: University of Texas Press).

—— (1990), *Picture Personalities: The Emergence of the Star System in America* (Urbana: University of Illinois Press).

Dyer, Richard (1979), *Stars* (London: British Film Institute).

Ellis, John (1982), *Visible Fictions: Cinema, Television, Video* (London: Routledge & Kegan Paul).

Heath, Stephen (1977/1981), 'Film Performance', in *Questions of Cinema* (London: Macmillan).

—— (1979), 'Body, Voice', in *Questions of Cinema* (London: Macmillan).

Higson, A. (1986), 'Film Acting and Independent Cinema', *Screen*, 27/3–4: 110–32.

Holmlund, C. (1993), 'Masculinity as Multiple Masquerade: The "Mature" Stallone and the Stallone Clone', in S. Cohan and I. Hark (eds.), *Screening the Male: Exploring Masculinities in Hollywood Cinema* (London: Routledge).

King, Barry (1985), 'Articulating Stardom', *Screen* 26/5: 27–50.

Kuleshov, Lev (1929/1974), 'Art of the Cinema', in R. Levaco (ed.), *Kuleshov on Film: Writings of Lev Kuleshov* (Berkeley: University of California Press).

*Naremore, James (1988), *Acting in the Cinema* (Berkeley: University of California Press).

Nash, M., and J. Swinson (1985), 'Acting Tapes', *Framework*, 29: 76–85.

Pearson, Roberta (1992), *Eloquent Gestures: The Transformation of Performance Style in the Griffith Biograph Films* (Berkeley: University of California Press).

Peters, A., and M. Cantor (1982), 'Screen Acting as Work', in J. Ettema and D. Whitney (eds.), *Individuals in Mass Communication Organisations* (Beverly Hills: Sage).

Prindle, D. (1988), *The Politics of Glamour: Ideology and Democracy in the Screen Actors Guild* (Madison: University of Wisconsin Press).

Pudovkin, V. (1958), *Film Technique and Film Acting* (London: Vision Press).

Thompson, Grahame F. (1985), 'Approaches to "Performance"', *Screen*, 26/5: 78–90.

Thompson, John O. (1978), 'Screen Acting and the Commutation Test', *Screen*, 19/2: 55–69.

—— (1985), 'Beyond Commutation: A Reconsideration of Screen Acting', *Screen*, 26/5: 64–76.

Vineburg, S. (1991), *Method Actors: Three Generations of an American Acting Style* (New York: Schirmer).

Wexman, V. (1993), *Creating the Couple: Love, Marriage and Hollywood Performance* (Princeton: Princeton University Press).

Zucker, C. (ed.) (1990), *Making Visible the Invisible: An Anthology of Original Essays on Film Acting* (Metuchen, NJ: Scarecrow Press).

4

Film costume

Pamela Church Gibson

Most students of film and media will probably complete their course without having studied film costume in any detail, if at all. Why this should be the case, when it is arguably such an important component of the way in which a film or television programme functions, needs consideration. It is, after all, one of the aspects of film most frequently mentioned by 'the audience', particularly by women, as is evident from *Star Gazing*, Jackie Stacey's (1994) work on the female spectator. Costume is undeniably an important site of filmic pleasure, and why this source should be so often disregarded as an area of serious academic study must be addressed. This is not to say that there is no literature on the subject—in fact there are a number of books and articles, anecdotal, factual, descriptive, and sometimes lavishly illustrated. What has been missing until quite recently is a body of work which attempts to provide some theoretical framework for the study of film costume. However, things are changing, and it is to be hoped that in five years time an overview such as this will begin by acknowledging the existence of a large number of significant texts and a plurality of critical approaches.

Here some contextualization might seem appropriate. Film costume—and for the purposes of this chapter, 'costume' will be used to mean, quite simply, the clothes worn in films, whether period or contemporary dress—has been slighted in the same way as fashion itself. Only in the last decade or so has fashion really established itself as a serious academic discipline and as an important area of theoretical debate. The reasons, of course, are well documented: the centuries-old belief in the inherent frivolity of fashion, reinforced by the puritanism of many on the left, for whom fashion is the most obvious and the most objectionable form of commodity fetishism, and the conviction of the majority of second-wave feminists that fashion is an arena in which women present and display themselves in order to gratify male desire. As anyone following the progress of Anglo-American feminism over the past thirty years will know, opposition to fashion in the 1970s was both a rallying-point and a seeming consensus. This intransigent attitude to personal adornment persisted until sustained critical interest in consumer culture, particularly within cultural studies, opened up different perspectives. The publication of Elizabeth Wilson's radical text *Adorned in Dreams* (1985) was perhaps the most significant move in a feminist reclamation of fashion. Now, with recent developments in third-wave feminism, all this hostility might yet become history. As Valerie Steele writes in her introduction to the first issue of *Fashion Theory*:

Several years ago I wrote an article entitled 'The F-Word', which described the place of fashion within academia. It was not a pretty picture: Fashion was regarded as frivolous, sexist, bourgeois, 'material' [not intellectual] and, therefore, beneath contempt. Today, it is said, fashion is no longer the 'F-word' in intellectual circles. Certainly, scholars across the disciplines have begun to explore the relationship between body, clothing and cultural identity. . . . The trend began, as many fashions do, in Paris. Thanks to the influence of French theorists, intellectuals around the world recognized the importance of studying the body as a site for the deployment of discourses. Eventually, the subject of clothing also began to receive attention from artists and intellectuals alike. (1997: 1)

If fashion is now a legitimate area of study, what are the implications, if any, for the student of film? Students of fashion design have been denied until recently a body of informing theory other than that specifically concerned with their area of expertise, such as the work of Veblen, Flugel, and Laver (which, unfortunately, *can* be utilized to reinforce the notion of fashion as the provenance of the feeble-minded) and that of later fashion historians, such as Hollander and McDowell. Now there is a proliferation of cultural studies work focused on the field and, following Elizabeth Wilson, concerted efforts to open up specifically feminist studies of fashion (Ash, Craik, Thornton, and Evans, to cite but a few).

It is students of fashion who have traditionally been most interested in, and enthusiastic about, film costume. Many of them can write with authority on the designs of Adrian and Edith Head, can list and describe each outfit worn by Audrey Hepburn in *Sabrina Fair* (1954) (and most, if not all, of her other films) and can make informed observations about mass market spin-offs and tie-ins from the 1930s onwards. Does this devalue costume in the eyes of some 'film scholars'? Is there some sort of élitism at work which suggests that this sort of interest is, indeed, the proper concern of the fashion student or historian? The fact that fashion journalists frequently fill their pages with photographs of their favourite cinematic icons, often accompanied by text that verges on the hagiographic, does not help to establish the study of film costume as a legitimate field of academic discourse.

Charles Eckert's seminal article on the close links between cinema and merchandising in the late 1920s and 1930s, 'The Carole Lombard in Macy's Window' (1978), provoked much debate. Eckert concludes 'Hollywood gave consumerism a distinctive bent . . .'. It 'did as much or more than any other force in capitalist culture to smooth the operation of the production-consumption cycle' (1978/1990: 120–1). Further investigations of the processes he described followed, including articles by Jane Gaines and Mary Ann Doane in a special issue of the *Quarterly Review of*

Film and Video (1989) on 'Female Representation and Consumer Culture'. Gaines's article is a fascinating account of the way in which *Queen Christina* (1933)—of all films—was used by retailers across the United States to promote everything from hostess gowns to flatware. However, mass market response to, and use of, cinematic influence is perceived by many involved within the field of film study as of little interest, and more suited to those involved in retail studies, marketing, and visual merchandising.

A final barrier to the study of film costume is the lack of homogeneity within the subject-area itself. It is difficult to write about film costume as a unified subject in the way that acting and music are discussed elsewhere in this volume, given the variety of ways in which costuming is effected within different categories of film. There is, for example, the classic Hollywood film with its studio designer. There are those films where a designer from the world of *haute couture* is involved—an increasingly complex phenomenon in recent years with the on- and off-screen involvement of designers such as Cerruti. There are films set in period—and latterly the European heritage film—where the clothes are of paramount importance in establishing visual style and overall effect. There are European independent, low-budget films where the clothes will probably be sourced, rather than designed and made, so that they do not obtrude and have the appearance of 'authenticity'. There are films, *Orlando* (1992) and *The Sheltering Sky* (1990) for example, where the clothes *do* obtrude, to the extent that they not only dominate the film but interfere in some way with its operation. There are, finally, non-Western cinemas where the semiotics of dress may be impenetrable to Western critics and where costume, in consequence, has not been given the attention it merits. After this contextualization and these observations, it is now time to look at the literature that does exist to date, to attempt some categorization of the texts available, and to ask, where there are omissions, what directions future studies might take.

References to costume are found, firstly, within discussions of mise-en-scène—the visual organization or composition of what is in front of the camera (the 'profilmic' event). Traditionally a concern with mise-en-scène has focused upon a film's use of setting, props, lighting, colour, positioning of figures, and, of course, costume. Mise-en-scène analysis has conventionally been associated with the study of the narrative film and how mise-en-scène may be seen to reinforce,

Updated gangster chic—*Reservoir Dogs* (1993)

complement, or, in some cases, subvert the meanings suggested by plot, dialogue, and character. Costume, in this respect, is read as a signifying element which carries meanings or creates emotional effects, particularly in relation to character. However, although traditional mise-en-scène analysis encourages attention to costume, it is not interested in dress or costume *per se*. Costume is seen as the vehicle for meanings about narrative or character and thus simply as one of a number of signifying elements within a film. Thus, David Bordwell and Kristin Thompson link the analysis of costume to that of props and argue that 'In cinema any portion of a costume may become a prop; a pince-nez (*Battleship Potemkin*), a pair of shoes (*Strangers on a Train*, *The Wizard of Oz*), a cross pendant (*Ivan the Terrible*), a jacket (*Le Million*)' (1980: 81). Similarly, in his article 'Costuming and the Color System of *Leave Her to Heaven*', Marshall Deutelbaum provides an intricate analysis of the way in which 'the film constructs a system of relational meaning through consistent oppositions encoded in the colors of the

characters' costumes' (1987: 17). The colours of the women's clothes in the film, he argues, are selected in order to structure and segment the complexities of the narrative. This is in contrast to the more usual narrative readings of colour in costume where the colours are seen to possess symbolic functions seemingly drawn from those that operate within a dominant Western cultural tradition and, in particular, from the language of painting (e.g. Victor Perkins on *Elmer Gantry*, 1960).

An interest in costume as a part of mise-en-scène analysis may be linked to an interest in genres where costuming is often regarded as a defining element. In the 1960s genre theorists turned to the idea of iconography as a way of distinguishing different genres in visual terms. Iconography—recurring patterns of images associated with different genres—is usually subdivided into settings, objects, and dress (McArthur 1972). Thus, in the case of the gangster film, specific settings (the city, saloons), specific objects (cars, machine-guns), and specific kinds of dress (the dark topcoat, the sharp suit, the white shirt and obtrusive tie, the fedora and gloves) have become characteristic icons of the genre, which are used to cue many of the audience's responses. Conventional genre analysis has examined dress in the western, the gangster film, and the horror film; but it is seen only as one of a number of defining elements together with plot, characterization, and setting. The relevant clothes—or 'costume props', to quote again from Bordwell and Thompson (1980)—are nevertheless a vital part of genre recognition.

However, in the case of costume drama, it is costume and setting which are the key generic features. 'Costume drama' is not, of course, an entirely straightforward term, but here it is used to refer to films set in a perceived 'historical' past and includes 'heritage' films. The particular interest of this genre is the emphasis it gives to costume and the way it is linked to traditional 'feminine' genres, such as the 'woman's film'. Thus, whereas feminist film criticism has often read costume in classical cinema, if at all, in terms of a reinforcement of the 'male gaze', feminist analysis of costume drama focuses upon the pleasures of dress for a female audience (and the different kinds of pleasure, other than voyeurism, which it provides). Thus, Richard Dyer identifies the particular appeal of the heritage film for a female audience in terms of the 'sensuousness' of the 'fixtures and fittings', which, he argues, require 'the skilled reading of the female spectator' (1995: 205). Sue Harper, in her comprehensive book *Picturing the Past*, adopts a similar position with regard to costuming in the Gainsborough melodramas: 'The Gainsborough film-makers and their publicists clearly intended that their films would usher women into a realm of pleasure where the female stars would function as the source of the female gaze, and where the males, gorgeously arrayed, would be the unabashed objects of female desire' (1994: 122). She suggests that Elizabeth Haffenden, the costume designer, created in these films a 'costume narrative' working against the moralistic drives within the main narrative 'whose provenance was sexual desire' (30), and she describes in some detail the clothes worn by Margaret Lockwood in *The Wicked Lady* (1944), and the 'vulval symbolism' of some. She contrasts the sumptuous garments Lockwood wears throughout the film with the 'severe tailored blouse, similar to severe 1940s fashion' (like those doubtless worn by many sitting in the audience) seen in her adulterous tryst with James Mason on the moonlit riverbank. This suggests quite graphically the way in which these films give free rein to female desires.

Harper also discusses the way in which Haffenden's designs can be seen as prefiguring the New Look; her costumes, she argues, 'could be seen as a debate, on a symbolic level, on female sexuality and the contemporary crisis of permission'. Pam Cook continues the scrutiny of Gainsborough films—and of their contribution to discourses on national identity—in *Fashioning the Nation* (1996). In the third chapter she explicitly addresses the 'marginalisation of costume design by film theorists', which she argues is 'marked enough to be diagnosed as a symptom' (1996: 41). She examines the links between fashion and fetishism, and the place of fetishism in feminist film theory following the debates initiated by Laura Mulvey's (1975) article 'Visual Pleasure in Narrative Cinema' (see Creed, Chapter 9, and White, Chapter 13). She continues: 'the concept of fetishism . . . traditionally used to condemn fashion and costume for their impurity . . . can instead be employed to illuminate the ways in which our erotic obsessions with clothes are also transgressive in their play with identity and identification. Identification is another area which has been perceived in a limiting manner by film theory, with consequences for discussion of screen costume' (Cook 1996: 46).

Three of the essays discussed by Cook in this chapter are to be found in *Fabrications: Costume and the Female Body*, edited by Jane Gaines and Charlotte Herzog. Published in 1990, this book arguably made it possible for film costume finally to be recognized as an area for serious and sustained feminist analysis. It includes an account of the conditions under which those clothes were made and another of the ways in which similar garments, and other products featured in films, were widely and successfully marketed. The main thrust of the book, however, is to examine—and reassess—the function of costume in classical Hollywood narrative, and its place within theories of voyeurism, fetishism, and masquerade. These theories, again, are discussed elsewhere in this book, but it is important to understand the way in which they are dependent upon dress. Gaylyn Studlar points out in her article 'Masochism, Masquerade, and the Erotic Metamorphoses of Marlene Dietrich' that 'the role of costuming in forming the pleasures of viewing remain undertheorised within current psychoanalytic discourse on film' (1990: 229). Jane Gaines's essay 'Costume and Narrative: How Dress Tells the Woman's Story' suggests that within melodrama, where 'the work on costume . . . lags behind the work on musical scoring', the 'vestural code' and costume plot can organize an 'idiolect with

Copies of this fringed dress
designed by Givenchy for
Audrey Hepburn (*Breakfast
at Tiffany's*, 1961) soon
appeared in the high street

its own motifs . . . which unfold in a temporality which does not correspond with key developments' (1990: 205).

She also mentions costume design and its use in the creation of the 'star persona'—which is where this survey of costume might have started. The collaborations between top Hollywood designers and certain female stars have been extensively documented, as have their visual solutions to the perceived physical shortcomings of these stars. The famous full-sleeved dress that Adrian designed for Joan Crawford in *Letty Lynton* (1932) was his first obvious gambit to shift the viewer's

gaze upwards, and so away from her wide hips. (Later he was to use the padded shoulders and the narrow skirts now synonymous with 1980s power-dressing to create a similar illusion—that of an inverted triangle.) Gaines and Herzog, in their article 'Puffed Sleeves before Tea-Time', show how the Letty Lynton dress acqired 'far more significance than the film in which it was showcased', introducing 'a fashion that lingered until the end of the Thirties' (1985: 25).

Perhaps there is a tendency to devalue the contribution of the stars themselves. Mae West's control over her own image is well known—but other stars were not merely passive mannequins, to be draped, disguised, and accoutred. Edith Head describes her work, throughout her career, as involving close collaboration between designer and star. For instance, when starting to work with Dietrich on *Witness for the Prosecution* (1957), she found that the actress had already decided that, for a particular flashback scene, the character should have 'some platform shoes with ankle straps, very hussy, red'. Since no such shoes were to be found in any studio wardrobe in her size, Dietrich arranged a shopping-trip to Main Street the following morning: 'Tomorrow, Edith, you and I will go into town early . . . we'll wear scarfs over our heads' (Head and Ardmore 1959/1960: 15). In the same book, *The Dress Doctor*, Head tells how Cary Grant planned the colour scheme for his clothes in *To Catch a Thief* (1955), asking her exactly what Grace Kelly would be wearing in each scene and then selecting his own outfits in order to complement hers (156).

This might remind the reader of this piece that, so far, men have not been discussed, except by implication as directors, designers, and potential voyeurs. Men as consumers of their own, masculine, dress are not included in the texts discussed—nor are films that have a contemporary setting, or, indeed, a woman director. These last two categories form the basis of an article by Renée Béart, 'Skirting the Issue' (1994), where she examines three films by feminist directors and the ways in which they use clothing. She wishes 'to draw attention to a further approach to costume in women's film, one which also shifts the denotative dimensions of feminine dress onto a second register, doubled over the first', thus establishing 'two interacting positions, feminine and feminist' (1994: 360).

But what of the masculine? Some male film stars are now involved within the world of high fashion in a way reminiscent of the female stars in the heyday of Hollywood. They feature in fashion spreads and designer advertising, they sit in privileged positions at couture shows—some even make it onto the catwalk—and they consort with supermodels. Couturiers fight to dress them, on screen, off screen, and on the night of the Oscars. But critical studies have largely ignored the contemporary and the masculine. Stella Bruzzi's book *Undressing Cinema: Clothing and Identities in the Movies* (1997) seeks to address this particular omission, among others; her intention is 'to reassess and challenge some of the assumptions and truisms that have dominated the study of dress, gender and sexuality, and to recontextualise others by applying them to

cinema' (xvi). She discusses not only masculine attire but subcultural style, usually ignored, and argues that in all cinema 'clothing can be seen to construct an independent discursive strategy' (xvii). Finally, and significantly, she refutes the assumption that fashion is produced for consumption by the opposite sex. This suggests a programme for the study of film costume which attends to the specificities of the 'language' of dress and the variety of pleasures which costuming affords.

This indicates the way forward, and should widen the debates around costume still further. More interdisciplinary approaches of the type here deployed by Stella Bruzzi are needed, as is more investigation of the relationship between costume, fashion, and industry. Lynn Spigel and Denise Mann have provided a bibliography of texts on 'Women and Consumer Culture' taken, as they explain, 'from what have traditionally been disparate academic fields and interests in order to facilitate research into areas relatively unexplored by film studies' (1989: 85). More in-depth case-studies of fashion 'spin-offs' from film—rather than the intentional tie-ins—would be helpful. Lastly, it is to be hoped that this work will not remain forever focused on Western cultural production. Given critical interest in the re-creation of a recognizable and supposedly 'authentic' past in the heritage film, an interesting comparison could potentially be made with Indian historical films, where the costumes are used to create an ahistorical past, a conglomeration of periods and consequently a mythological realm. A close scrutiny of dress in non-Western cinemas is long overdue.

To conclude: clothing is a part of our daily discourse—and a source of personal pleasures—in a way that, say, camera angles and cinematography are not. Yet, for too long film costume has been granted only grudging attention and there has been little informed discussion. While it is pleasant to think that things are finally changing, a current news item seems ominous. In January 1997, exactly fifty years after the unveiling of Dior's New Look and the outraged response it provoked from members of the British government, Labour MP Tony Banks sponsored a motion in the House of Commons to deplore the publicity given to two Paris couture collections. Both were created by British designers—John Galliano for the house of Dior, though Banks seemed unaware of the irony, and Alexander McQueen for Givenchy. 'It is vulgar and obscene', the motion proposed, 'that so much significance should be attached to overpriced and grotesque flights of fancy for hanging on the limbs of the super-rich.' *Plus ça change* . . .

BIBLIOGRAPHY

Ash, Juliet, and Lee Wright (1987), *Components of Dress* (London: Routledge).

Beart, Renée (1994), 'Skirting the Issue', *Screen*, 35/4 (Winter), 354–73.

Bordwell, David, and Kristin Thompson (1980), *Film Art: An Introduction* (Reading, Mass.: Addison-Wesley).

*Bruzzi, Stella (1997), *Undressing Cinema: Clothing and Identity in the Movies* (London: Routledge).

*Cook, Pam (1996), *Fashioning the Nation: Costume and Identity in British Cinema* (London: British Film Institute).

Craik, Jennifer (1994), *The Face of Fashion: Cultural Studies in Fashion* (London: Routledge).

Deutelbaum, Marshall (1987), 'Costuming and the Color System of *Leave her to Heaven*', *Film Criticism*, 11/3 (Spring), 11–20.

Doane, Mary Ann (1989a), 'The Economy of Desire: The Commodity Form in/of the Cinema', *Quarterly Review of Film and Video*, 11/1: 23–35.

—— (1989b) 'Female Representation and Consumer Culture', *Quarterly Review of Film and Video*, 1/11.

Dyer, Richard (1995), 'Heritage Cinema in Europe', in Ginette Vincendeau (ed.) *Encyclopedia of European Cinema* (London: Cassell and British Film Institute).

*Eckert, Charles (1978/1990), 'The Carole Lombard in Macy's Window', in Gaines and Herzog (1990).

Evans, Caroline, and Minna Thornton (1989), *Women and Fashion: A New Look* (London: Quartet Books).

Flugel, J. C. (1930), *The Psychology of Clothes* (London: Hogarth Press).

*Gaines, Jane (1989), 'The *Queen Christina* Tie-Ups: Convergence of Show Window and Screen', *Quarterly Review of Film and Video* 11/1: 35–60.

*—— (1990), 'Costume and Narrative: How Dress Tells the Woman's Story', in Gaines and Herzog (1990).

*—— and Charlotte Herzog (1985), 'Puffed Sleeves before Tea-Time: Joan Crawford and Women Audiences', *Wide Angle*, 6/4: 24–33.

*—— —— (eds.) (1990), *Fabrications: Costume and the Female Body* (London: Routledge).

*Harper, Sue (1994), *Picturing the Past: The Rise and Fall of the Costume Film* (London: British Film Institute).

Head, Edith, and Jane Kesner Ardmore (1959/60), *The Dress Doctor* (Kingswood: World's Work).

Hollander, Anne (1975), *Seeing through Clothes* (New York: Avon Books).

Laver, James (1969), *Modesty in Dress: An Enquiry into the Fundamentals of Fashion* (London: Heinemann).

McArthur, Colin (1972), *Underworld USA* (London: Secker & Warburg).

McDowell, Colin (1991), *Dressed to Kill: Sex, Power and Clothes* (London: Hutchinson).

Perkins, V. F. (1972), *Film as Film: Understanding and Judging Movies* (Harmondsworth: Penguin).

Spigal, Lynn, and Denise Mann (1989), 'Women and Consumer Culture: A Selective Bibliography', *Quarterly Review of Film and Video*, 11/1: 85–105.

Stacey, Jackie (1994), *Star Gazing: Hollywood Cinema and Female Spectatorship* (London: Routledge).

Steele, Valerie (1997), Letter from the Editor, *Fashion Theory: The Journal of Dress, Body and Culture*, 1/1: 1–2.

*Studlar, Gaylyn (1990), 'Masochism, Masquerade, and the Erotic Metamorphoses of Marlene Dietrich', in Gaines and Herzog (1990).

Veblen, Thorstein (1899/1957), *The Theory of the Leisure Class* (London: Allen & Unwin).

Wilson, Elizabeth (1985), *Adorned in Dreams: Fashion and Modernity* (London: Virago).

5 | Film music

Claudia Gorbman

Any attentive filmgoer is aware of the enormous power music holds in shaping the film experience, manipulating emotions and point of view, and guiding perceptions of characters, moods, and narrative events. It therefore comes as something of a surprise that, aside from a smattering of isolated writings since the 1940s, the serious, theoretically informed study of film music has come of age only in the last ten years. Film scholars, hailing chiefly from literature and communications backgrounds, have lacked the training and/or interest, while music departments inherit a high-art prejudice; although the latter may have incorporated ethnomusicology and even popular music, they apparently relegate film music to the ranks of the middle-brow, that least worthy category of all. Even now that disciplinary brakes to the academic study of film music have eased, members of the two fields have come to film music with such widely divergent training and scholarly goals that substantial dialogue between them has proven rare. For those trained as musicologists, the music itself, with the film as its context, invariably emerges as the focus of attention. Film scholars tend to examine film music and the conditions of its production primarily in order to understand films and the economic and psychic institution of cinema.

Some framing questions in the current study of film music are as follows. Why do films have music? What constitutes good film music? How should the evolution of film music be historicized, and what can a theoreti-

cally informed history of film music reveal? What are the narrative functions of music in films? To what extent is music in films explicitly heard by the moviegoer, and what are the implications of the spectator attending or not attending to a film's music? What formal and aesthetic relations obtain between film and music? What are the aesthetic and ideological consequences of the foregrounding of popular music on film soundtracks of the last twenty years? How does music work in television, and in film genres such as animated, documentary, and experimental film? How have musical idioms other than those of the European orchestral tradition functioned in Hollywood cinema and other cinemas?

Aesthetics

Auteurism

Within the general field of film studies, the study of film music might well represent the last bastion of film aesthetics. A number of factors help to explain why discussion of film music remains immersed in aesthetic discourses, even when, in film studies at large, aesthetics has been jettisoned in the tidal waves of psychoanalysis, Marxism, and cultural studies over the last twenty years. What might be considered a felt lack of musical competency among many film scholars has created a vacuum; and this vacuum has been filled not only by musicologists, influenced to a much lesser extent by post-structuralism, but also by film music fans and by composers themselves.

Since movie music is now routinely marketed as a commodity apart from the films for which it is composed or compiled, it has its own thriving ancillary audience. Film scores have taken on a musical life of their own especially since the proliferation of the compact disc in the early 1980s. Concerned relatively little with the narrative, visual, or ideological intricacies of the films from which favourite soundtrack discs come, fans and collectors focus rather on canon-formation for film composers. Serious fans have held an unusually prominent place in discussions of film music, often contributing insightful criticism, original research, and analysis.

Another unusually strong presence is the composers themselves. Successful film composers spend their lives analysing the dramatic workings of films in order to score them, and their special knowledge of music and dramatic structure gives them a well-deserved authority. Such articulate individuals as David Raskin and Elmer Bernstein have provided bridges from the classical Hollywood era to the present for students and scholars of film. A number of composers have written important texts on film music, of which Hanns Eisler's book *Composing for the Films* is a classic. More recently Fred Karlin has written two illuminating volumes: *On the Track* (1989), co-authored with Rayburn Wright, for aspiring film composers; and *Listening to Movies* (1994), for film music appreciation. George Burt, both a composer and an academic, offers an insightful examination of the practical and aesthetic aspects of film scoring in his book *The Art of Film Music* (1994).

One conspicuous result of these developments is an auteurism of the Romantic sort. Post-structuralism's dethronement of the individual artist has simply not occurred for film composers, since much academic discussion of film music occurs in contexts such as film music festivals of the Society for the Preservation of Film Music in Los Angeles, where there is a certain pressure to see and appreciate the music through the composer's eye and ear. The canon of film composers is a subject of lively debate. There has developed a virtual industry of Bernard Herrmann criticisms, for example, in the form of a stream of books and articles, and passionate partisanship in Internet forums, fed by new CD releases of Herrmann scores, new concert editions and performances, and an hour-long documentary film

about Herrmann (directed by Joshua Waletzky, 1994) shown on public television across the United States.

Aesthetic theory

Among the newest in a long tradition of theorizing relations among the arts and 'compound' arts, scholars of cinema have examined the marriage between the representational art of cinema and the generally non-representational art of music (see e.g. Brown 1994: 12–37; Gorbman 1987: 11–33; Kassabian 1993: 1–23). Thus far they have shown a predilection for studying non-diegetic orchestral film music in its interaction with images and narrative structures in narrative feature films. (Diegetic music, or source music, is music whose apparent source is the narrative world of the film. Non-diegetic music, or 'scoring', is music on the soundtrack which could presumably not be heard by characters in the film.) Areas of concern are the ways in which music inflects scenes with emotional and dramatic resonance, suggests character, setting, and mood, influences perceptions of narrative time and space, creates formal unity and a sense of continuity, interacts with human speech and other sounds, and compensates for the loss of 'liveness' and spatial depth that characterize the cinema's elder sibling, the theatre.

Most recently, Royal Brown (1994) has attempted to elucidate the effects of music as a non-iconic and non-representational medium when it is co-present with the narrative, iconic, representational system of feature films. He argues that music can *generalize* a film event—that is, it encourages the spectator to receive the event not in its particularity but on a mythic level. Thus, when the Western hero rides over a ridge and looks out on the vast landscape before him, or when the heroine of a melodrama embraces her child for the last time, the almost certain presence of orchestral music on the soundtrack in each case—music that is virtually assured to channel a certain field of readings—helps to foster emotional identification.

Brown attempts to account for the very marriage of film and music—why they got together at all. He suggests that because of the cinema's iconicity and its essentially prosaic realism, it 'needed something . . . to justify its very existence as an art form . . . to escape from the trap of referentiality in order to impose perception of its artistic structure and content' (1994: 19–20). Though he cites such artists as Abel Gance and Sergei Eisenstein for support, this position curiously endows the cinema with intention, and hardly explains the ubiquity of pianos in the nickelodeons, where music and the movies enjoyed their mass audience from the beginning.

Brown offers another formulation that is indisputable: music provides a foundation in affect for narrative cinema. To describe how music provides affect, he cites Suzanne Langer to claim that a given piece of music carries no *specific* inherent emotional signification; it is rather that the dialectical interaction of music and images–sounds produces a specific affect (Brown 1994: 26–7). (Philip Tagg (1989) provides an important counterpoint to this idea. Drawing on years of empirical research on musical connotation, he demonstrates that aspects of musical style and melody, as deployed in television and film, carry a surprising degree of semantic precision even when heard outside their audiovisual context.)

An issue central to film music aesthetics is the question of the music's place in the hierarchy of the spectator's attention. Critics and composers in the classical studio era maintained that film music should be unobtrusive. The French composer Maurice Jaubert's dictum that people do not go to the movies to hear music (with obvious exceptions for musical films) is emblematic of this aesthetic position, which dominated theory and practice of film music throughout the period. Kalinak (1992) and Gorbman (1987) cite numerous examples of the principle of inaudibility at work in classical scoring. Conventions of both composition and placement of non-diegetic music prioritize narrative exposition (Kalinak 1992: 79). The classical score features a high degree of synchronization between music and narrative action, and thus commonly relies on such devices as *ostinati*, 'stingers', and mickey-mousing. (An *ostinato* is a repeated melodic or rhythmic figure, to propel scenes which lack dynamic visual action; a stinger is a musical sforzando to emphasize dramatically an action or a character's sudden strong emotion; mickey-mousing is the musical 'imitation', through pitch and/or rhythm, of visual action.) Practices of composing, mixing, and editing privilege dialogue over music, and dictate the entrances and exits of musical cues so as not to distract attention from the narrative action. George Burt (1994) demonstrates that this aesthetic is alive and well in contemporary orchestral scoring.

The breakdown of the studio sytem began to modify the aesthetic (an aesthetic which, it must be said, was always flexible, for music routinely moved from background to foreground in the case of diegetic produc-

tion numbers, narrative moments of spectacle, comedy, beginning and end credits, and so forth). Popular idioms such as jazz and rock 'n' roll, and occasionally even atonal and electronic experiments, joined film music's stylistic arsenal. Many of the newer composers were trained in television or popular music rather than in the European late Romantic tradition.

Now, two generations later, two developments demonstrate that unobtrusiveness is no longer the rule, but rather remains as one among a number of possibilities. Brown identifies the first development as 'postmodern' scoring. This is a tendency toward prominent and self-conscious use of music, such that the music seems to occupy a 'parallel universe' to the film's visual narrative rather than function illustratively and subordinately in the manner of the classical score (Brown 1994: 235–63). To be sure, one may find isolated examples of scoring techniques and effects of this kind in scores of decades past. But in such films as *Diva* (Jean-Jacques Beineix, 1982), *The Hunger* (Tony Scott, 1983), and *Heavenly Creatures* (Peter Jackson, 1994), one senses that the focused deployment of music for irony and excess, using music to disturb rather than contain the hierarchies of subjectivity, high and low musical culture, and diegetic and non-diegetic narration, has resulted in a genuinely new paradigm of interaction between music and film.

The second development shattering the aesthetic of unobtrusiveness is pop scoring, the use of recorded popular songs on the non-diegetic soundtrack. As with 'postmodern' scoring, pop scoring has a considerable history. But the massive cross-marketing of recorded music and films which has become the rule since the 1980s has made at least some pop scoring commonplace in virtually all commercial feature films. Film music scholarship is beginning to address the aesthetic dimensions of non-diegetic songs accompanying film narrative. The stanzaic form of popular song, the presence of lyrics to 'compete' with the viewer's reception of film narrative and dialogue, and the cultural weight and significance of the stars performing the songs all work directly against classical Hollywood's conception of film music as an 'inaudible' accompaniment, relying on the anonymous yet familiar idioms of symphonic Romanticism, its elastic form dictated by the film's narrative form.

The new pop aesthetic scandalizes film music auteurists. Many critics point accusing fingers at the crass commercialism that drives decisions to insert pop songs into soundtracks and thereby spoil the integrity

'Focused deployment of music for irony and excess'—*Heavenly Creatures* (1994)

of composed scores. Others, primarily critics grounded in film and cultural studies, and also those in the growing field of popular music studies, are enthusiastically investigating the range of possibilities inherent in this new paradigm.

Critics have investigated to a lesser extent the forms and functions of music in animation, documentary, and experimental film—genres which often give music pre-eminence. Eliminating realist fictional narrative from the equation, however, allows one to focus more purely on certain relationships between music and the moving image. Serious study of the virtuousic cartoon music of Carl Stallings, and analyses of work by Virgil Thompson and Philip Glass for documentaries, for example, shed new light on music–film relationships.

Psychology

The psychological dimensions of film music have subtended much writing in the field. What effects does music have on the film's spectator-auditor? What psychological factors motivate the presence of music in movies?

In my book *Unheard Melodies* (1987), I begin to address these questions by summarizing historical,

psychological, and aesthetic arguments explaining the presence of music to accompany the silent film. For one thing, music had accompanied a number of nineteenth-century theatrical forms, and it persisted for numerous practical reasons in the evolution of film exhibition. For another, music covered the distracting noise of the movie projector. It served to explicate and advance the narrative; it provided historical, geographical, and atmospheric setting; it identified characters and qualified actions. Along with intertitles, its semiotic functions compensated for the characters' lack of speech. It provided a rhythmic 'beat' to complement, or impel, the rhythms of editing and movement on the screen. It served as an antidote to the technologically derived 'ghostliness' of the images. And, as music, it bonded spectators together in the three-dimensional space of the theatre.

The book then explores reasons why music persisted in films after the coming of sound—when the movies' new realism would seem to make music an unwelcome guest. One compelling line of thought, which has elicited considerable elaboration and debate, draws on psychoanalytic theory to explain the psychic 'pay-off' of having music on the soundtrack. Psychoanalysis was a dominant discourse of film studies in the 1970s, providing a way to understand the cinema's mechanisms of pleasure and spectator identification (see

Creed, Part 1, Chapter 9). It was particularly well suited to describing the workings of classical Hollywood cinema; in film music studies a decade later, the primary testing ground for the psychoanalytic perspective has also been the classical cinema.

According to French psychoanalytic theorists Guy Rosolato (1974) and Didier Anzieu (1976), sound plays a crucial role in the constitution of the subject. The infant exists in a 'sonorous envelope' consisting of the sounds of the child's body and maternal environment; in this primordial sonic space the child is as yet unaware of distinctions between self and other, inside and outside the body. Rosolato suggests that the pleasure of listening to music—organized, wordless sound—inheres in its invocation of the subject's auditory imaginary in conjunction with the pre-Oedipal language of sounds.

In applying this idea to cinema, critics argue that background music recaptures the pleasure of the sonorous envelope, evoking the psychic traces of the subject's bodily fusion with the mother. Classical cinema capitalizes on music's special relation to the spectator's psyche to lower the threshold of belief in the fiction. Thus film music works in the perceptual background to attack the subject's resistance to being absorbed in the narrative.

Like Muzak, which acts to make consumers into untroublesome social subjects (relieving anxiety in airports and medical waiting-rooms, greasing the wheels of consumer desire in shopping-malls), film music lulls the spectator into being an untroublesome (less critical, less wary) viewing subject. Music aids the process of turning enunciation into fiction. In doing so, film music helps fend off two potential displeasures which threaten the spectator's experience. The first is the threat of ambiguity: film music deploys its cultural codes to anchor the image in meaning. Second, film music fends off the potential displeasure of the spectator's awareness of the technological basis of cinematic discourse—the frame, editing, and so on. Like the sonorous envelope, music's bath of affect can smooth over discontinuities and rough spots, and mask the recognition of the apparatus through its own melodic and harmonic continuity. Film music thereby acts as a hypnotist inducing a trance: it focuses and binds the spectator into the narrative world.

Jeff Smith (1996) has challenged psychoanalytic film music theory by problematizing the basic premise of film music's inaudibility. He quotes my formulation:

'were the subject to be aware (fully conscious) of [music's] presence as part of the film's discourse, the game would be all over' (Gorbman 1987: 64). Although many of the questions Smith raises about my writing on soundtrack audibility are already answered in my book, his critique points aptly to further areas of investigation. If music is crucial to the creation of a 'subject-effect' but also has more foregrounded functions of narrative cueing (such as establishing historical and geographical setting, and conveying information through leitmotifs), then the spectator must be aware of the music at least some of the time. The spectator must be slipping in and out of the trance created by the music-as-hypnotist. There must be a complex fluctuation between the state of unawareness crucial to the psychoanalytic account, and levels that permit cognition of musical cues.

Smith counters the psychoanalytic model with perspectives from cognitive theory, drawing from the work of David Bordwell (1985: 29–47) and Noël Carroll (1988: 213–25) as well as from psychologists of music such as McAdams (1987) and Sloboda (1985). He argues that, like other music, film music is apprehended through a variety of different listening modes and competencies. He calls for an account of film-musical cognition that directly addresses the spectator's mental activities in processing film music's narrative cues. This focus on the competencies of film spectator-auditors is promising.

Kassabian (1993) also emphasizes the issue of competence: 'like any other language, [music] is acquired, learned, in a specific sociohistorical context' (36). Focusing on such categories of filmgoers gender and ethnicity, she lays the groundwork for an understanding of ways in which individuals identify with films. Depending on 'differences in perceivers' relations to the music', they will 'interpret cues' differently in the cues' filmic settings (69).

History

The question of how film music is perceived eludes definitive answers because of its enormous historical variation. Not only is film music more explicitly foregrounded in many scores of the 1990s than it used to be, but today's filmgoers have different competencies and 'reading formations' than those of, say, 1950. Although it seems difficult *not* to notice pop scoring

At the foreground of perception: Max Steiner's score for *Gone with the Wind* (1939)

in contemporary soundtracks, we may imagine that for some moviegoers pop scoring has become so customary that it recedes into the background of perception. Likewise, Erich Korngold's score for *Robin Hood* (USA, 1939), or Max Steiner's for *Gone with the Wind* (USA, 1939), can hardly be termed unobtrusive to today's ears.

The theoretically informed writing of film music history is quite young. Martin Mark's revealing new book *Music in the Silent Film* (1996) documents practices of composing or fitting pre-existing music to films, as well as performance practices, at various stages from the early cinema into the 1920s. (The sheer variety of such practices suggests that the current pop compilation score may have more in common with silent film music than with its more immediate predecessor, the classical film score.) Another musicologist, David Neumeyer (1996), has elucidated scoring practices of Hollywood in the 1930s through often brilliant, methodical research and close readings of film scores. His study of diegetic tunes heard in a scene in *Casablanca* (Michael Curtiz, 1943) reveals the care with which popular music was chosen for the film, and the semantic richness made available to 'competent' listeners. The study of *Casablanca*'s score receives further treatment in an essay by Marks (1996), which demonstrates the wide range of variation in classical scoring by contrasting Max Steiner's scoring techniques in *Casablanca* with Adolph Deutsch's in *The Maltese Falcon*. Krin Gabbard (1996) draws on contemporary theories of culture not so much to outline a history of jazz in the movies as to gain a historical understanding of its significations.

Finally, Jeff Smith's pathfinding dissertation 'The Sounds of Commerce' (1995) brings careful musical analysis and archival research to a study of the economic and institutional factors that led to the pop sounds of such composers as Mancini and Morricone in the 1960s. Smith chronicles the studios' financial restructuring following the 1948 Paramount decree, focusing on the decision of several major studios to acquire recording companies and to cross-market films and film music. His work forcefully demonstrates the intimate relationships among finance, marketing, and ultimately film music style itself in a key historical period. The scholarship of these and other historians bodes well for the study of film music both as art and as mass culture.

BIBLIOGRAPHY

Anzieu, Didier (1976), 'L'enveloppe sonore du soi', *Nouvelle revue de psychanalyse*, 13: 161–79.

Bordwell, David (1985), *Narration in the Fiction Film* (Madison: University of Wisconsin Press).

*Brown, Royal S. (1994), *Overtones and Undertones: Reading Film Music* (Berkeley: University of California Press).

Buhler, James, and **David Neumeyer** (1994), 'Film Studies/Film Music', *Journal of the American Musicological Society*, 47/2: 364–85.

Burt, George (1994), *The Art of Film Music* (Boston: Northeastern University Press).

Carroll, Noël (1988), *Mystifying Movies: Fads and Fallacies in Contemporary Film Theory* (New York: Columbia University Press).

Eisler, Hanns (1947), *Comparing for the Films* (New York: Oxford University Press).

Gabbard, Krin (1996), *Jammin' at the Margins: Jazz and the American Cinema* (Chicago: University of Chicago Press).

*Gorbman, Claudia (1987), *Unheard Melodies: Narrative Film Music* (Bloomington: Indiana University Press; London: British Film Institute).

*Kalinak, Kathryn (1992), *Settling the Score: Music and the Classical Hollywood Film* (Madison: University of Wisconsin Press).

Karlin, Fred (1994) *Listening to Movies: The Film Lover's Guide to Film Music* (New York: Schirmer).

—— and **Rayburn Wright** (1989), *On the Track: A Guide to Contemporary Film Scoring* (New York: Schirmer).

Kassabian, Anahid (1993), 'Songs of Subjectivities: Theorizing Hollywood Film Music of the 1980s and 1990s', dissertation, Stanford University.

McAdams, Stephen (1987), 'Music: A Science of the Mind', *Contemporary Music Review*, 2: 1–61.

Marks, Martin (1996), 'Music, Drama, Warner Brothers: The Cases of *Casablanca* and *The Maltese Falcon*', *Michigan Quarterly Review*, 35/1: 112–42.

—— (1997), *Music and the Silent Film: Contexts and Case Stuies 1895–1924* (New York: Oxford University Press).

Neumeyer, David (1996), 'Performances in Early Hollywood Sound Films: Source Music, Background Music, and the Integrated Sound Track', *Contemporary Music Review*.

Romney, Jonathan, and **Adrian Wootton** (eds.) (1995), *Celluloid Jukebox: Popular Music and the Movies since the Fifties* (London: British Film Institute).

Rosolato, Guy (1974) 'La Voix: entre corps et langage', *Revue fraçaise de psychanalyse*, 38/1: 75–94.

Sloboda, J. (1985), *The Cognitive Psychology of Music* (Oxford: Clarendon Press).

Smith, Jeff (1995), 'The Sounds of Commerce: Popular Film Music 1960–1973', dissertation, University of Wisconsin.

Smith, Jeff (1996), 'Unheard Melodies? A Critique of Psychoanalytic Theories of Film Music', in David Bordwell and Noel Carroll (eds.), *Post-Theory* (Madison: University of Wisconsin Press).

Tagg, Philip (1989), 'An Anthropology of Stereotypes in TV Music?', *Svensk Tidskrift för Musikvetenskap*, 19–39.

The film text: theoretical frameworks

6

Classic film theory and semiotics

Anthony Easthope

Film theory had to struggle a surprisingly long time before it could become a proper theory of film. Difficulty arose from the very feature which ensured cinema its universality: ever since the earliest audiences flung themselves out of the way of an oncoming screen locomotive, film has stunned us by its seeming capacity to reproduce reality transparently, immediately, directly. Because of this realism, serious analysis of film was confronted from the first by antagonism from the smothering inheritance of Kantian aesthetics.

In *The Critique of Judgement* (1790) Kant contrasts sensation and contemplation, singular and universal, interested and disinterested (useful and useless). Aesthetic experience is opposed to merely sensuous gratification (eating, for example) because it combines sensation—through hearing and vision—with contemplation. The aesthetic object is focused on as a singularity, not as an instance of a general concept, for its own sake and not for any kind of usefulness or social purpose. All this kicks against what cinema appears to do best; its rendering of the real seems just too obviously contaminated with unprocessed sensation, too liable to documentary appropriation, too easily turned to useful social purposes.

Classic film theory

As Aaron Scharf (1969) shows in convincing detail, the early impact of photography on painting and notions of art was enormous. Although encouraging some artists into innovation and experiment, photography also served to strengthen and substantiate the opposition between art and craft, the aesthetic and the useful. As 'moving pictures', produced when light is projected through strips of celluloid onto a screen, cinematic images have a double intimacy with reality since they are both caused by it (light from these objects marked photosensitive film) and also resemble it. It was only too tempting to deny cinema a status as art.

In the face of a seemingly incontestable naturalism, the labour of classic film theory was to designate the specific value of cinema—what has allowed it to provide such a compelling representation of modernity. For this two main strategies emerged. The creationists (or formalists), including Rudolf Arnheim, Sergei Eisenstein, and Béla Balázs, defend cinema as an art form which goes beyond realism, while the realists, particularly Siegfried Kracauer and André Bazin, appreciate cinema just because it does provide such an exact representation of reality.

Creationism is well represented by Rudolf Arnheim's book *Film* (1933), which sets out 'to refute the assertion that film is nothing but the feeble mechanical reproduction of real life' (1958: 37). Arnheim points out first of all how the experience of sitting in the cinema differs from our empirical perception of the everyday world. In everyday experience the world is three-dimensional, while in the cinema all we get is a flat screen; our life is lived colour with sound, while cinema is black and white, and silent (or was, up to 1929); in our ordinary world we can look wherever we want within our field of vision, while cinema limits what we see within the masked frame of the screen.

> **Formalist theory (Arnheim) and realist theory (Bazin) appear to oppose each other. But *both* positions suppose that cinema, based as it is in the photographic process, must be assessed as in part a mechanical reproduction, whether feeble or convincing.**

Arnheim celebrates the many effects through which cinema transforms and constructs a reality, including camera angles and movement, focus, lighting effects, framing, altered motion, superimposition, special lenses. And, in addition to these features pertaining mainly to the single shot, cinema works through sequences of shots edited together, producing dazzling and significant effects of contrast and repetition, metonymy and metaphor. Editing makes something available to someone in the cinema that could never be seen by any empirical viewer of what was originally filmed.

Arnheim is one of the first to codify the specific resources of cinema and the many ways it produces meanings beyond anything present in the reality from which the photographed image originates. Yet though he argues that film exceeds reality, Arnheim does not challenge the view that film is powerfully influenced by its photographic resemblance to reality. The realists, led by André Bazin, make that relation the essential virtue of the medium, as, for example, in this passage:

> The objective nature of photography confers on it a quality of credibility absent from all other picture-making. In spite of any objections our critical spirit may offer, we are forced to accept as real the existence of the object reproduced, actually *re*-presented, set before us, that is to say, in time and space. Photography enjoys a certain advantage in virtue of this transference of reality from the thing to its reproduction. (Bazin 1967: 13–14)

This passage makes it clear that Bazin is aware that in cinema filmed objects are not presented but '*re*-presented'. And elsewhere he explains how he values cinematic reality because it has an almost Brechtian effect in leaving the viewer free to criticize, when more obviously constructed cinema (Eisenstein, for instance) aims to manipulate the viewer's understanding.

Formalist theory (Arnheim) and realist theory (Bazin) appear to oppose each other. But what is crucial, and what marks off classic film theory, is the assumption they share. Formalist theory values cinema to the extent that it is, in Arnheim's phrase, more than 'the feeble mechanical reproduction of real life': realist theory values cinema to the extent that it adheres to 'a mechanical reproduction in the making of which man plays no part', as Bazin says (1967: 12). *Both* positions suppose that cinema, based as it is in the photographic process, must be assessed as in part a mechanical reproduction, whether feeble or convincing. It was not until the 1960s that this view—the naturalist, or reflectionist, fallacy—began to be finally overthrown in film theory.

1968 and after

Film theory was able to develop into a fully fledged account of cinema because it staged what Stephen Heath refers to as 'the encounter of Marxism and psychoanalysis on the terrain of semiotics' (1976: 11). Of these three theoretical interventions, semiotics (or semiology) arrived first. In a posthumous work, *Course in General Linguistics*, published in 1916, Saussure introduced into the study of language a number of theoretical distinctions, of which two in particular proved fruitful when carried over into film theory.

From ancient rhetoric, Saussure revived the distinction between signifier and signified to analyse the naïve concept of 'words'. In any utterance the level of the signifier is made up from the sounds (phonemes) selected for use by a particular language, arranged in a temporal order, while that of the signified consists of the meanings assigned to any group of signifiers. Signifiers consist of entirely arbitrary sounds related only to each other in an internally self-consistent system, and it is purely a matter of convention what set of signifiers give rise to a certain meaning. In modern English, for example, the sounds represented by 'mare' can open onto the meaning 'female horse' or possibly 'municipal leader' (mayor), while a very similar group of signifiers in French ('mer'/'mère') open onto the meanings 'sea' and 'mother'.

A principle is implied by Saussure's distinction, that the material organization of a language is ontologically prior to any meaning it produces. During the 1960s semiotics had a decisive impact upon film theory by concentrating attention on the question what were the specific properties of film, its *specifica differentia*, distinguishing it from other forms of signification (novels and drama, for example).

There are certain problems in detail, however. For while Saussure's distinction between signifier and signified applies perfectly to a language, it is much harder to get it to work for a visual medium such as film. In any famous sequence, such as that at the end of Ford's *The Searchers* (USA, 1956) when the John Wayne figure is left outside the door, what exactly takes the place of the signifier and the signified? This is a question addressed by the work of Christian Metz, as we shall see.

A second distinction put forward by Saussure was also expanded in film semiotics. Language works by moving forward in time so that in English (as in Chinese) syntax can draw simply on word order to make 'Dog bites man' mean something different from 'Man bites dog'. Naming this linear axis of discourse as 'syntagmatic', Saussure pointed out that at every point along this horizontal axis terms were selected and rejected from a potential corpus lying in a vertical dimension (the 'associative' or 'paradigmatic'). Thus, 'Snake' is a possible paradigmatic substitution for 'Dog' or 'Man' in either of the previous examples but 'Yesterday' is not, since 'Yesterday bites man' is not a meaningful sentence.

In other words, it was possible to think of the syntagmatic axis as a consistent structure which would remain the same even when different paradigmatic terms were substituted along it. In 1928 Vladimir Propp applied this principle to the analysis of narrative, discerning across 115 Russian folk stories a common structure consisting of thirty-one 'functions'. Thus, function (Propp 1968: 11), 'The hero leaves home', can be realized as easily by 'Ivan is sent to kill the dragon' as by 'Dmitri goes in search of the princess'.

A semiotic analysis of film narrative was initiated with enthusiasm and some effect, notably by Raymond Bellour (1972) in his study of *The Birds* (USA, 1963) and by Peter Wollen (1982), also discussing Hitchcock, in his account of *North by Northwest* (USA, 1959). Bellour discusses the Bodega Bay sequence shot by shot, while Wollen aims for a Proppian analysis of the whole movie. Both examinations, plausible as they are in detail, suffer from what are now recognized as the inevitable assumptions of formal narrative analysis—that there is only a single narrative and not a number of simultaneous narrative meanings, that the narrative is fixed once and for all 'out there' in the text and not constructed in a relation between text and reader.

Narrative analysis of film on the precedent of Propp had the definite benefit of shifting argument away from any question of the relation or correspondence between a film and some real it might be supposed to reflect. It focused on film as *text* but did so only by incurring a concomitant limitation. Narrative is an effect which runs across many different kinds of text, so detailing it in films does not advance understanding of what is specific to film. Nevertheless, the overall consequence of semiotic attention to cinema was to weaken concern with the issue of realism and strengthen attention to the cinema as a particular kind of textuality. After 1968 these tendencies were reinforced from a somewhat unanticipated quarter.

Classic Marxism theorized that the economic base and mode of production determines the political and ideological 'superstructure'. However, during the 1960s the French Marxist thinker Louis Althusser had argued that notions of base and superstructure should be rethought in terms of practices—economic, political, ideological—each of which was 'relatively autonomous', each with its own 'specific effectivity'. Carried over to the analysis of cinema after the revolutionary events of 1968 (by, for example, the journal *Cahiers du cinéma*), Althusserian Marxism was as rigorous in excluding apparently non-political approaches to cinema as it was in rejecting film theory which began from literary or theatrical models. As Jean-Louis Comolli and Jean Narboni assert in *Cahiers du cinéma* in 1969, it is the case that 'every film is political' and that 'cinema is one of the languages through which the world communicates itself to itself' (1993: 45, 46). To understand cinema is to understand film as film, not something else.

Christian Metz

The intervention of both semiotics and Althusserian film criticism brought the narrative of the developing discussion of film to a point where it was ready for the cavalry to ride over the hill with a more or less complete theory. This role was taken by someone whose work is characterized less by brilliant insights than by a dogged willingness in a series of essays written over nearly twenty years to try, fail, and try again: Christian Metz (1974*a*, *b*, 1982). Although the conscientious, overlapping, and exploratory nature of his project is thus compromised, it is convenient to divide Metz's writings into three main attempts.

The first, today perhaps better known through refutations than in the original (see Cook 1985: 229–31; Lapsley and Westlake 1988: 38–46), was the theory of the *grande syntagmatique*. In the search for a notion of film language, it became obvious that cinema had no equivalent to the unit of sound (phoneme) which combined to make up the particular signifiers of a language. Images in the cinema are as infinite as photographable reality. Metz therefore decided to concentrate on the single shot and treat it as a primitive sentence, a statement, on this basis considering how effects were built up syntagmatically by organizing segments, beginning with the autonomous shot, into a hierarchy (he discriminates eight levels within this hierarchy) (Metz 1974*a*: 108–46).

To some extent Metz Mark I was following Arnheim, because he looked for the specificity of cinema in its narrativization of what is photographed—the fact that 'reality does not tell stories'. But objections pile up against his account—not only the difficulties faced by semiotic narratology in general (its formalism, its belief that there is always only one narrative), but crucially the problem of deciding in the first place what constituted an autonomous shot or segment.

From the wreckage of the *grande syntagmatique*, Metz Mark II turned to the concept of codes, describing some as shared between cinema and other kinds of representation (characterization and dialogue, for example) and others as specific to cinema (editing, framing, lighting, and so on). Metz Mark III is already partly anticipated in his previous projects, for he had made the point, a little enigmatically and without properly developing it, that in a film 'the image of a house does not signify "house", but rather "Here is a house"' (1974*a*: 116).

The radical implications of this distinction do not become apparent until Metz Mark III pulls Lacanian psychoanalysis into the orbit of his effort to theorize cinema, notably in his essay 'The Imaginary Signifier', first published in 1975. Lacan distinguishes between the orders of the Imaginary and of the Symbolic, the Imaginary being the world as the individual ego envisages it, the Symbolic being the organization of signifiers which makes this possible (for this, see especially Lacan's 1964 account of vision; 1977: 67–119). Lacan's account enables Metz to argue that imaginary presence in the cinematic image must be thought of as resulting from a signifier that stands for something which is absent. Cinema provides 'unaccustomed perceptual wealth, but unusually profoundly stamped with unreality': the more vividly present the cinematic image appears to make its object, the more it insists that object is actually lacking, was once there but is there no more, 'made present', as Metz says, 'in the mode of absence' (1982: 44).

That the cinematic image is an active making-present clarifies retrospectively the view that in the cinema 'the image of a house does not signify "house", but rather "Here is a house"'. What this affirms, of course, is the ontological disjunction between perceived reality and *anything* that is supposed to be a representation of it. Representation, regardless of whether that representation derives by a photographic process from reality, is an intervention, an act of signifying which reality itself can never make. Although obviously you have to know about houses in order to recognize a shot as a shot of a house (just as you have to know about houses to follow a poem about a house), photographic derivation is neither here nor there in relation to the status of the cinematic image as utterance, statement, a meaning introduced in a semantic context in which it is always saying 'Here is a . . .'.

> Representation, regardless of whether that representation derives by a photographic process from reality, is an intervention, an act of signifying which reality itself can never make.

At the end of his famous 'Concluding Statement: Linguistics and Poetics' (1960), Roman Jakobson tells the story of a missionary complaining about nakedness among his flock, who in turn asked him why he did not wear clothes on his face and then told him they were face everywhere. Similarly, Jakobson argues, 'in poetry any verbal element is converted into a figure of poetic speech' (1960: 377). On a comparable basis, breaking with reflectionism, the achievement of film theory to Metz is to establish the principle that in cinema any visual element may be turned to expressive purpose, converted into 'poetic speech'. This renders the whole visual, aural, and narrative effect of cinema available to inspection for its significance, the meaning it produces.

The critique of realism

An immediate consequence of this theoretical breakthrough was to reopen in a much more suggestive and radical way the whole question of realism in the cinema. While film theory was committed to a reflectionist view that the text was to be assessed against some prior notion of the real, comprehensive analysis of realism was blocked. The moment reflectionism goes, the way is open to consider cinematic realism essentially as an effect produced by certain kinds of the text.

Roland Barthes had already pointed in this direction. And so also, back in the 1930s, had Bertolt Brecht. Dismissing conventional naturalist or realist theatre as Aristotelian, as finished, easily consumed commodity, Brecht promoted his own version of modernist, antiillusionist 'epic' drama, on the grounds that this form was politically radical because it forced the audience to confront the text and think for itself.

Drawing on both Barthes and Brecht, Colin MacCabe, in a wonderfully compact essay, 'Realism and the Cinema: Notes on Some Brechtian Theses' (1974), put forward an analysis of realism which was wholly 'internal': realism was explained not with reference to

external reality but as an effect the text produced through a specific signifying organization. MacCabe's first move is to concentrate on classic realism, excluding from his account such texts as the novels of Dickens or the Hollywood musical. His next two moves specify realism in terms of a discursive hierarchy and empiricism: 'A classic realist text may be defined as one in which there is a hierarchy amongst the discourses which compose the text and this hierarchy is defined in terms of an empirical notion of truth' (1993: 54).

All texts consist of a bundle of different kinds of discourse: realism, MacCabe argues, arranges these into two categories corresponding to the relation between metalanguage and object language. Introduced by Alfred Tarski, this philosophical distinction refers to what happens when one language discusses another, as, for example, in a book written in modern English called *Teach yourself Japanese*. Japanese is placed as the object language and modern English as the metalanguage, situated outside, as it were, and able to take Japanese as an object of study. In the classic realist text, the words held in inverted commas (what the characters say to each other) become an object language which the narrative prose (what is not marked off as cited) promises to explain as it cannot explain itself.

> 'A classic realist text may be defined as one in which there is a hierarchy amongst the discourses which compose the text and this hierarchy is defined in terms of an empirical notion of truth'

The relation between the two modes of discourse is said to be empiricist because while the object language is seen to be rhetorically constructed—the partiality of the points of view of the represented characters is all too apparent—the metalanguage can pass itself off as though it were simply transparent, the voice of Truth: 'The unquestioned nature of the narrative discourse entails that the only problem that reality poses is to go and see what *Things* are there' (1993: 58). In realist cinema, MacCabe concludes, dialogue becomes the object language, and what we see via the camera takes the place of the metalanguage by showing what 'really' happened. This effect invited the spectator to overlook the fact that film is constructed (through script, photography, editing, sets, and so on) and treat the visual narrative as though it revealed what was inevitably *there*. Realism for MacCabe (as for Brecht) is conservative in that this givenness necessarily cannot deal with contradiction, which contains the possibility of change.

Stephen Heath's (1976) discussion of realism as 'narrative space' follows on from MacCabe's theory. Heath begins with the system of visual representation on which cinema, as photography, depends, that is, the Quattrocentro tradition developed to depict three-dimensional objects on a flat surface in such a way that the image affects the viewer much as the natural objects would have done (for a brilliant development of this thesis, see Bryson 1983). Quattrocento space relies not only on linear perspective but on various strategies for placing the viewer at the centre of an apparently all-embracing view.

Cinema, however, is 'moving pictures', a process which constantly threatens the fixity and centring aimed for by the Western tradition of the still image. Figures and objects constantly move, moving in and out of frame, likely therefore to remind the spectator of the blank absence which actually surrounds the screen. Mainstream cinema seeks to make good this dangerous instability through narrative, a narrativization which 'contains the mobility that could threaten the clarity of vision' (1993: 76) by constantly renewing a centred perspective for the spectator. Heath cites in detail the procedures advised by the film manuals—use of master shot, the 180-degree rule, matching on action, eyeline matching, avoidance of 'impossible angles', and so on—and affirms that all of this is designed to ensure that 'the spectator's illusion of seeing a continuous piece of action is not interrupted' (Heath 1993: 80, quoting Reisz and Millar 1968: 216).

A perfect example is the beginning of *Jaws* (USA, 1975): 'a beach party with the camera tracking slowly right along the line of faces of the participants until it stops on a young man looking off; eyeline cut to a young woman who is thus revealed as the object of his gaze; cut to a high-angle shot onto the party that shows its general space, its situation before the start of the action with the run down to the ocean and the first shark attack' (1993: 80). Through such narrativization, Heath maintains, conventional cinema seeks to transform fixity into process and absence into presence by promoting (in Lacanian terms) the Imaginary over the Symbolic. An alternative or radical cinema would refuse this kind of coherence; it would open its textuality, compelling the viewer to experience the process

they are always part of, a process implying change and which is the condition for any sense of coherence and stability.

In these ways MacCabe and Heath intend to fulfil the promise of bringing together semiology and ideology, a close analysis of the fundamental operation of cinema as a signifying effect with an understanding that cinema is always political. There is, however, one important difference between the two accounts.

Heath's argument is that realism and the effect of narrative space try to *contain* the process of signification, while for MacCabe realism effaces the signifier to achieve *transparency*. It is arguable that MacCabe is still writing from an essentially structuralist conception in which realism is an organization of the signifier which necessarily produces certain effects on the viewer. Heath, in contrast, asserts that transparency is 'impossible' (1993: 82) and assumes from the start a conception of process as a process of the *subject*. Subjectivity does appear in MacCabe's account but is not integral to it as it is to Heath's. Heath, then, looks beyond structuralism to a post-structuralism which draws on psychoanalysis to discuss cinema in relation to subjectivity, including, in the work of Laura Mulvey, *gendered* subjectivity. After Metz, after the redefinition of realism as a textual effect, that is where film theory goes next.

BIBLIOGRAPHY

Arnheim, Rudolf (1933/1958), *Film*; repr. corr. as *Film as Art* (London: Faber).

Barthes, Roland (1953/1968), *Writing Degree Zero*, trans. Annette Lavers and Colin Smith (New York: Hill & Wong).

*****Bazin, André** (1967), *What is Cinema?*, 2 vols., trans. Hugh Gray, i (Berkeley: University of California Press).

Bellour, Raymond (1969/1972), 'The Birds: Analysis of a Sequence, trans. Ben Brewster (London: British Film Institute).

Brecht, Bertolt (1964), *Brecht on Theatre*, ed. and trans. John Willett (London: Eyre Methuen).

Bryson, Norman (1983), *Vision and Painting: the Logic of the Gaze* (London: Macmillan).

Comolli, Jean-Louis, and **Jean Narboni** (1969/1993), 'Cinema/Ideology/Criticism (1)', trans. Susan Bennett, in Antony Easthope (ed.), *Contemporary Film Theory* (London: Longman).

Cook, Pam (ed.) (1985), *The Cinema Book* (London: British Film Institute).

Heath, Stephen (1976a), 'Jaws, Ideology and Film Theory', *Times Higher Education Supplement*, 26 Mar.

—— (1976b, 1993), 'Narrative Space', in Antony Easthope (ed.), *Contemporary Film Theory* (London: Longman).

Jakobson, Roman (1960), 'Concluding Statement: Linguistics and Poetics', in T. A. Sebeok (ed.), *Style in Language* (Cambridge: Mass.: MIT Press).

Kant, Immanuel (1790/1952), *The Critique of Judgement*, trans. James Meredith (Oxford: Oxford University Press).

Lacan, Jacques (1964/1977), *The Four Fundamental Concepts of Psycho-Analysis*, trans. Alan Sheridan (London: Hogarth).

*Lapsley, Rob, and Mike Westlake (1988), *Film Theory: An Introduction* (Manchester: Manchester University Press).

*MacCabe, Colin (1974/1993), 'Realism and the Cinema: Notes on Some Brechtian Theses', in Antony Easthope (ed.), *Contemporary Film Theory* (London: Longman).

*Metz, Christian (1971a/1974a), *Film Language: A Semiotics of Cinema*, trans. Michael Taylor (New York: Oxford University Press).

—— (1971a/1974b), *Language and Cinema*, trans. D. J. Umiker-Sebeok (The Hague: Mouton).

—— (1977/1982), *Psychoanalysis and Cinema: The Imaginary Signifier*, trans. Celia Britton (London: Macmillan).

Propp, Vladimir (1928/1968), *The Morphology of the Folktale*, trans. Laurence Scott (Austin: University of Texas Press).

Reisz, Karel, and Gavin Millar (1968), *The Technique of Film Editing* (New York: Hastings House).

Saussure, Ferdinand de (1916/1959), *Course in General Linguistics*, trans. Wade Baskin (New York: Philosophical Library).

Scharf, Aaron (1968), *Art and Photography* (London: Allen Lane).

Wollen, Peter (1976/1982), '*North by North-West*: A Morphological Analysis', *Film Form*, 1/1: 19–34; repr. in *Readings and Writings* (London: Verso).

7

Formalism and neo-formalism

Ian Christie

Formalism is the usual, if somewhat misleading, name of a critical tendency which has survived for over eighty years, despite misunderstanding and even persecution. First used by opponents, the label was reluctantly adopted by Russian exponents of 'the formal method'—although they protested that it was neither a single method, nor confined to what is normally considered 'form'. But aside from these local disputes, the tradition of Formalism could well be considered the twentieth century's distinctive contribution to aesthetics. For it was born, historically, of the desire to find an objective or scientific basis for literary criticism, partly in order to respond to the novelty of modern art—specifically Futurist poetry—and at the same time to revitalize appreciation of the classics. In short, it was a critical position which uniquely responded to the peculiar challenge of the modern era; and one that would later be echoed by the American 'new critics' of the 1930s, as well as by structuralists and semioticians.

But if its focus was literature, how did Formalism first become involved with film? This is largely explained by the peculiar status that cinema acquired during the early years of the Soviet regime in Russia. With film-makers like Dziga Vertov and Sergei Eisenstein making large ideological claims for their work, film aesthetics became a subject of intense public debate, and eventually a political issue. In this heady climate of polemic and innovation, leading Formalist critics such as Viktor

Shklovsky and Yuri Tynyanov found themselves not only theorizing the new forms of Soviet cinema, but acutally working as scriptwriters and advisers. The scene had been set for a dangerous slippage between critical and political disagreement. When the Soviet leadership began to regiment cultural life at the end of the 1920s, 'Formalism'—now meaning any commitment to artistic experiment, or resistance to an authoritarian 'socialist realism'—became an all-purpose term of abuse, and during the purges of the 1930s it could carry a death sentence.

Unsurprisingly, surviving Russian Formalists fell silent or recanted, and it was not unlike the 1960s, amid renewed Western interest in the early Soviet era, that many key Formalist texts were translated for the first time and began to exert a wide cultural influence. Once again, the links between Formalist criticism and cinema were revived, as semiotics became the basis for a new theorization of film—and for a revival of avant-garde filmmaking, which partly drew on Soviet Formalist models. The Russian structural or cultural semiotic movement which emerged in the late 1960s counted the Formalist school as one of the influences on its wide-ranging analysis of different cultural and artistic texts; and this continues to produce valuable work on cinema. Formalist critical tools are also still used, under the banner of 'Neo-Formalism', by film theorists concerned with analysing the structure of narration and by critics wishing to sharpen our percep-

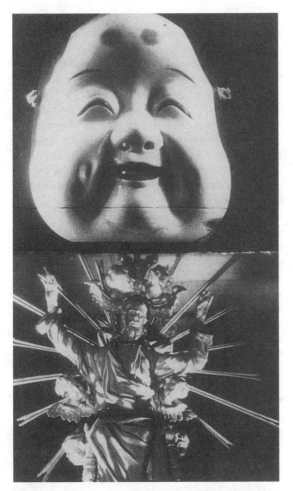

October (1928) undermines the Tsarist invocation of 'God and country' by showing an otherwise unmotivated montage sequence of increasingly bizarre folk-gods

tion of—or in Formalist terms 'defamiliarize'—mainstream cinema.

The birth of a poetics

Formalist poetics developed rapidly in the highly charged atmosphere of Russian avant-garde art in the years immediately before and after the revolutions of 1917. Futurist poets were experimenting with invented language in an effort to return to the very roots of speech in sound and gesture, and Viktor Shklovsky took this as a particularly vivid example of how artists play a vital part in sharpening our habitual

perception by a deliberate 'roughening' of normal language. For Shklovsky and his fellow members of the St Petersburg Society for the Study of Poetic Language (OPOYAZ), the poetic use of language involved a whole range of techniques or 'devices' which are not confined to poetry as such, but may also be found in literary prose. He traces an inexorable movement from poetry to prose, from novelty to routine, as language becomes automatic, and compares this with the way old art is 'covered with the glassy armour of familiarity' as we cease to experience it in a truly artistic way.

What is lost in this transition is art's characteristic purpose of making the familiar screen strange (*ostranenie*), or of 'defamiliarizing' what is normally taken for granted—an influential idea which would later be echoed in Bertolt Brecht's 'alienation effect' in theatre. For the Formalists, art is less an object or a body of work than a *process* by which perception is slowed down, or even obstructed. Hence what the critic studies are the forms and devices which achieve this effect. As Shklovsky put it, provocatively; 'I know how a car is made; I know how *Don Quixote* is made.'

> **For the Formalists, art is less an object or a body of work than a *process* by which perception is slowed down, or even obstructed. Hence what the critic studies are the forms and devices which achieve this effect.**

Although the Formalists drew much of their inspiration from the contemporary energy of Russian Futurist art, which they saw as typically 'laying bare the device' in its radical new forms, many of their most influential analyses were of the classics seen from a revealing new angle. Shklovsky, in particular, delighted in drawing examples from a wide range of sources, and his 1925 essays on Sterne's *Tristram Shandy* and Cervantes' *Don Quixote* (Shklovsky 1990) established the basic formalist approach to fictional narrative. The crucial distinction to be made in narrative is between what Formalists call *fabula* and *syuzhet*, usually translated as 'story' and 'plot' (Bordwell 1985: 49–50 provides the clearest modern definition of these as applicable to cinema). However, these translations can be misleading (and indeed contradict some uses of these terms in English). For *fabula*, in the Formalist sense, is an imaginary sequence of events narrated by the *syuzhet*, which provides the actual narrative pattern of the work, or 'story-as-told'. Thus, in literature, Cervantes' and Sterne's numerous digressions, abrupt shifts forward and backward in time, repetitions, and withholding of information are all *devices* which constitute the *syuzhet*, or plot; and the Formalists regarded the relationship between the *syuzhet* and *fabula*, rather than one or the other, as the essence of literary art.

Such an analysis of the 'literariness' of literature clearly could be developed for other arts, and Shklovsky led the way in applying formalist analysis to cinema (Shklovsky 1923). His discussion of Chaplin noted that the same basic character, 'Charlie', appears in many films, and that these all use similar cinematic devices, which are 'stunts' such as the fall, the chase, and the fight. In each film some of these devices are 'motivated', in that they appear to arise plausibly from the specific plot's characters or props, while others are 'unmotivated'—the typical 'Charlie' gestures and actions whose familiarity had made Chaplin a star. The critical issue for Shklovsky was whether Chaplin would succeed in going beyond the self-referential parody that was already evident by 1921–2; and he predicted that Chaplin might move toward the 'heroic comic' genre—which, in fact, he did in later films such as *The Gold Rush* (1925) and *The Great Dictator* (1940).

The Formalist insistence that poetic and prosaic language are not confined to the literary genres of poetry and prose could also be applied to cinema, with interesting consequences. Amid the passionate debates of the early Soviet era between advocates of polemical fiction and those who opposed all film drama as intrinsically false, Formalists were able to argue that the use of 'factual' documentary material by Dziga Vertov did not in itself make his films factual. Having rejected the fictional structures of the novel and drama, he had effectively fallen into those of poetry, the lyric, and the epic: 'red verse with the rhythms of cinema'. Similarly, a Formalist comparison between Chaplin's drama *A Woman of Paris* (1923), Vertov's *One Sixth of the World* (1926), and Pudovkin's *The Mother* (1926), based on the idea that poetry uses more arbitrary formal devices than the semantic ones of prose, suggests that Chaplin is here working in cinematic 'prose' and Vertov in poetry, but that Pudovkin had created a hybrid form which moves between prose and poetry (Shklovsky 1927).

This hybrid quality, making full use of the 'poetic' devices that appeared in early cinema, was also what

attracted the Leningrad Formalist critic Yuri Tynyanov to the irreverent Factory of the Eccentric Actor (FEKS) group. Having already worked on the use of parody by such writers as Gogol and Dostoevsky, he adapted Gogol's *The Overcoat* for FEKS in 1926 as a polemical intervention, to pose 'anew the question of "the classics" in cinema'. The film functions as a radical commentary on the original text and its conventional accretions. And in the FEKS's subsequent historical films, *SVD* and *New Babylon* (1929), Tynyanov saw a welcome challenge to the merely picturesque in the elaborate use of metaphorical devices to produce irony and pathos.

The culmination of Russian Formalist engagement with cinema came in 1927, with the publication of an anthology, *The Poetics of the Cinema*, which included Boris Eikhenbaum's major essay 'Problems of Film Stylistics' (Taylor 1982). Amid many shrewd observations which make this one of the most sophisticated early texts in film aesthetics, Eikhenbaum focuses on two key features which can perhaps be considered the filmic equivalents of *fabula* and *syuzhet*. From the French critic Louis Delluc he borrowed the concept of 'photogeny' to describe the photographic raw material of cinema—what makes filmed images of people and things intrinsically attractive—and from the Soviet avant-garde he takes 'montage' as the fundamental principle of syntax for combining these images (plot construction). Filmic utterance then depends on the creation of film phrases, which require the construction of an illusory, yet convincing, impression of continuity in space and time.

Eikhenbaum's most original contribution is his answer to the question: what links film phrases? Or, in Formalist terms, how do transitions appear motivated, rather than arbitrary? He suggests that the viewer is prompted to supply links through internal speech, by completing or articulating what is implied by the sequence of (silent) screen images. This idea is most easily illustrated by examples of visual metaphor. Eikhenbaum quotes the sailor in *The Devil's Wheel* (Chërtovo koleso', FEKS, 1926), who has decided to stay on shore with his girl and enters a tavern, where we see a billiard-ball *fall* into a pocket, thus triggering the idea of his *fall* from duty. Another example would be the famous 'gods' montage sequence in Eisenstein's *October* (1928), in which a series of images of increasingly bizarre statues of folk-gods are intended to undermine the Tsarist invocation of 'God' by showing this to be a heterogeneous concept.

Boris Eikhenbaum linked the fall of a billiard-ball in the tavern scene in *The Devil's Wheel* (1926) with the sailor's 'fall' from duty as an example of 'inner speech' reinforcing filmic metaphor

Appearing as it did on the even of the sound revolution in cinema, Eikhenbaum's concept of internal speech attracted little interest until the 1970s. In the wake of Christian Metz's (1982) combination of semiology and psychoanalysis, it was then taken up again, notably by Paul Willemen (1974–5, 1994*a*), who argued that it need not be confined to silent cinema or to examples of 'literalizing' metaphor as in the *Devil's Wheel* example. Might not this discourse of 'thought work' accompany *all* filmmaking and viewing, he asked, and be subject to the same processes of abbreviation, condensation, distortion, and the like that Freud identified in dreams, so that it could function as both a constituent and a product of the filmic text—a kind of unconscious of the filmic system?

Another branch of Russian Formalist research also had to wait nearly forty years before it began to be applied to cinema, although Vladimir Propp's (1968) *Morphology of the Folktale* was already becoming known in the early 1960s through the anthropologist

Claude Lévi-Strauss's use of it in his study of myth, and consequently became a corner-stone of the emergent structuralist movement. In line with the Formalists' ahistorical, scientific spirit, Propp's analysis of a body of Russian fairy-tales took as its model the biological idea of morphology, or the study of a plant's component parts in relation to the whole. By identifying the full range of fairy-tale characters and their narrative functions, and determining the 'moves' which constitute each story, Propp was able to show how these could all be reduced to variations on a single basic formula.

In adapting this structural approach to the study of a filmmaker's body of work, Peter Wollen (1972: 93) noted that there is a danger in mapping resemblances of reducing all the texts in question 'to one, abstract and impoverished'. He draws a distinction between this result, as 'formalist', and the 'truly structuralist' aim of comprehending 'a system of differences and oppositions'. Thus, for Wollen and other structuralist film critics, a measure of success is to bring works which may at first seem eccentric or deviant within an enlarged system of recurrent motifs or 'oppositions'.

Despite this rejection of morphology as a goal, the terms of Propp's narrative analysis have proved valuable in other ways too. Laura Mulvey (1981) recalls the function of marriage as a means of narrative closure in all the tales studied by Propp in her discussion of Oedipal patterns in the western. But unlike the Russian folk-hero who *must* marry to conclude the tale satisfactorily, the western hero may choose not to marry for a different, though no less common, closure. Mulvey's exploration of these alternatives, discussed in terms of *The Man who Shot Liberty Valance* (1962) and *Duel in the Sun* (1947), again points away from Propp's essentially descriptive enterprise, but none the less draws upon its characteristic Formalist clarity.

Neo-formalism

The most substantial and influential modern use of Formalism in the film study has been that of David Bordwell and Kristin Thompson, notably in the former's *Narration in the Fiction Film* (Bordwell 1985) and the latter's 'essays in neoformalist film analysis', *Breaking the Glass Armour* (Thompson 1988). In defending Formalism against claims that it is 'merely' formal, seeking to isolate theory from either detailed textual criticism or social and historical interpretation, Bordwell and Thompson argue that, on the contrary, only its basic tools can contribute to building an adequate historical poetics of cinema.

Formalism, they believe, unlike some structuralist and psychoanalytic methodologies, crucially implies an active spectator, and to supply this important subject Bordwell proposes a 'constructivist' theory which links perception and cognition. Drawing on cognitive psychology, he identifies a hierarchy of schemata by which the individual's perception is organized. Thus, following a film—like many other everyday yet complex activities—routinely involves the use of already learned prototype and template schemata to identify basic situations, characters, and events. Individual films then involve mobilizing (or learning) procedural schemata, at the level of narrative, and stylistic schemata. These art- or film-specific schemata correspond in part to the Formalists' concept of motivations as compositional, realistic, or

artistic (this last expanded to cover 'transtextual' allusion to other texts).

Bordwell's many detailed examples of this enhanced and systematized Formalism at work show how, for example, the typical operations of film noir and melodrama can be distinguished in terms of different patterns of *syuzhet* and stylistic construction—gaps and retardation, the deliberate withholding of information, different motivations—and how a broad sampling of films made within certain production regimes can lead towards a 'formalist' historical classification. Thus 'classical Hollywood' (the subject of Bordwell *et al.* 1985) can be described in more dynamic terms than usual, as having 'normalised options for representing the fabula and for manipulating the possibilities of syuzhet and style'. Art cinema, by contrast, can be defined by a particular set of procedural schemata which underlie widely differing narrational strategies.

Both Thompson and Bordwell make use of the term 'parametric cinema', adapted from Burch (1973) to take their neo-formalist analyses into more challenging terrain. This is defined as the foregrounding of an artistic motivation in a systematic, structuring fashion. Examples discussed range from Jacques Tati's *Play Time* (1968), and Michael Snow's *Wavelength* (1967) (where style completely dominates *syuzhet* as the film's vestigial narrative is subordinated to an overriding continuous zoom structure), and also include films by Robert Bresson and Jean-Luc Godard.

Like Shklovsky's famous comparison of literary history to the knight's move in chess, Formalism's influence outside its Slavic homeland has largely depended on the erratic progress of translation and, indeed, fashion. Thus, it was not until the 1980s that translations began to appear of the long-neglected work of Mikhail Bakhtin and his colleagues, who were critical of the Formalists in the late 1920s but can now perhaps be seen as extending Formalism's range through their critique of its ahistoricism and dogmatism.

Bakhtin's most influential concept is probably that of 'dialogism', which emerged particularly from his study of Dostoevsky's novels. Put at its simplest, in a 1929 paper (Matejka and Pomorska 1978), this involves distinguishing between an author's direct speech and that of his characters, which can 'approach the relationship between two sides in a dialogue'. Bakhtin's wideranging analysis of novels from many periods and cultures reveals degrees of 'polyphony' among the discourses present and, by implication, validates such dialogism for its complexity and richness. From his work on Rabelais comes another key concept, 'carnivalism', denoting the persistence of a 'folk tradition of laughter' and parody characteristic of the carnival.

If 'dialogism' and 'carnivalistic' have become quite widely used terms of critical approbation in film as well as literary and cultural criticism, two of Bakhtin's other contributions seem even more pertinent to cinema. In tackling the variety of 'speech genres' encountered in everyday as well as artistic discourse, Bakhtin showed how these interact with literary genres to define a 'genre memory' which sets limits to each genre. Ivanov (1981) suggest that this is directly applicable to cinema, as is Bakhtin's concept of the 'chronotype'. This term, taken from mathematics, is used by Bakhtin (1981) to refer to the specific interrelationship of time and space in differnt forms of narrative. Thus, he identifies 'adventure time' and 'romance time' in the Greek novel, with their characteristic elisions and transitions; and Ivanov proposes that similar distinctions may be made within the main film genres.

Despite the promise of Bakhtin's ideas, it must be admitted that relatively little has been done by non-Russian critics to apply them widely or systematically. Exceptions, however, are Robert Stam's (1989) survey of the tradition of reflexive, carnivalesque works from a specifically Bakhtinian perspective, and the use Paul Willemen (1994) makes of Bakhtin's concepts of dialogue, otherness, and genre as 'a fragment of collective memory' in his work on Third Cinema. Within the Russian tradition, Maya Turovskaya (1989) has used the concept of the chronotope to illuminate Andrei Tarkovsky's idea of cinema as 'imprinted time', and a Bakhtinian influence is discernible in the work of Yuri Lotman and his circle in cultural semiotics (Lotman and Uspenskij 1984).

One of Lotman's followers, Yuri Tsivian (1994), defines cultural semiotics as studying 'texts as they are processed "through" people', so that faulty transmission is as much its focus as 'successful' communication without interference. Tsivian's pioneering study of the early reception of cinema in Russia ranges from consideration of the architecture of cinemas and the practice of projection (including mishaps), to the social reception of films as coloured by prevailing cultural assumptions. Most radically, he argues that the boundary of the 'cinema text' is inherently unstable, since non-filmic elements could, and often did, prove culturally more significant for spectators than the films themselves.

Tsivian's evidence is drawn from journalism, literature, and memoirs, and its extent shows how widely the forms and devices of cinema had permeated Russian culture by the 1920s. Although this was also the culture that produced Formalism, his work has wider methodological implications. And together with that of other contemporary cultural semioticians, Neo-Formalists, and assorted fellow travellers, it proves that the Formalist impulse continues to provide sharp, versatile tools for both critical and historical analysis.

BIBLIOGRAPHY

Bakhtin, Mikhail (1929/1978), 'Discourse Typology in Prose', in *Problems of Dostoevsky's Art* (Leningrad); trans. Richard Balthazar and I. R. Titunik in Ladislav Matejka and Krystyna Pomorska (eds.), *Readings in Russian Poetics* (Ann Arbor: Michigan Slavic Publications).

—— (1981), *The Dialogic Imagination* (Austin: University of Texas Press).

—— (1986), *Speech Genres and Other Late Essays* (Austin: University of Texas Press).

*Bordwell, David (1985), *Narration in the Fiction Film* (London: Methuen).

—— **Janet Staiger,** and **Kristin Thompson** (1985), *The Classical Hollywood Cinema: Film Style and Mode of Production to 1960* (London: Routledge).

Burch, Noël (1973), *Theory of Film Practice* (London: Secker & Warburg).

Ivanov, Vyacheslav (1981), 'Functions and Categories of Film Language', in L. M. O'Toole and Ann Shukman (eds.), *Russian Poetics in Translation*, viii (Oxford 1976).

Lotman, Yuri (1976), *Semiotics of Cinema* (Ann Arbor: Michigan Slavic Contributions).

—— and **Boris Uspenskij** (1984), *The Semiotics of Russian Culture* (Ann Arbor: Michigan Slavic Contributions).

Metz, Christian (1977/1982), *Psychoanalysis and Cinema: The Imaginary Signifier*, trans. Celia Britton (Bloomington Indiana University Press).

Mulvey, Laura (1981/1989), 'Afterthoughts on "Visual Pleasure and Narrative Cinema"', in *Visual and Other Pleasures* (London: Macmillan).

Propp, Vladimir (1968), *Morphology of the Folktale* (Austin: University of Texas Press).

Shklovsky, Viktor (1923/1988), 'Literature and Cinema', extracts in Taylor and Christie 1988.

—— (1925/1990), *Theory of Prose* (Elmwood Park, Ill: Dalkey Archive Press).

—— (1927), 'Poetry and Prose in the Cinema', in Taylor and Christie 1988.

Stam, Robert (1989), *Subversive Pleasures: Bakhtin, Cultural Criticism and Film* (Baltimore: Johns Hopkins University Press).

CRITICAL APPROACHES

*Taylor, Richard (ed.) (1927/1982), *The Poetics of Cinema, Russian Poetics in Translation*, ix (Oxford Complete trans. of the original Russian anthology, with essays by Eikhenbaum, Shklovsky, Tynyanov, and other Formalists).

—— and **Ian Christie** (eds.) (1994), *The Film Factory: Russian and Soviet Cinema in Documents 1896–1939* (2nd edn. London: Routledge).

Thompson, Kristin (1988), *Breaking the Glass Armor: Neoformalist Film Analysis* (Princeton, NJ: Princeton University Press).

Tsivian, Yuri (1994) *Early Cinema in Russia and its Cultural Reception* (London: Routledge).

Turovskaya, Maya (1989), *Tarkovsky: Cinema as Poetry* (London: Faber).

Willemen, Paul (1974–5), 'Reflections on Eikhenbaum's Concept of Inner Speech in the Cinema', in *Screen*, 15/4 (Winter), 59–70.

—— (1994a), 'Cinematic Discourse: The Problem of Inner Speech', in *Looks and Frictions* (London: British Film Institute).

—— (1994b), 'The Third Cinema Question', in *Looks and Frictions* (London: British Film Institute).

Wollen, Peter (1972), *Signs and Meaning in the Cinema* (3rd edn. London: Secker & Warburg).

Poetry and prose in cinema

Viktor Shklovsky from Viktor Shklovsky, 'Poetry and Prose in Cinema', in Richard Taylor and Ian Christie (eds.), *The Film Factory: Russian and Soviet Cinema in Documents* (revised edition London and New York, Routledge 1994).

In literary art poetry and prose are not sharply differentiated from one another. On more than one occasion students of prose language have discovered rhythmic segments, the recurrence of the same phrase construction, in a prose work. Tadeusz Zieliński has produced interesting studies of rhythm in oratorical speech and Boris Eichenbaum has done a great deal of work on rhythm in pure prose that is intended to be read rather than recited, although it is true that he has not pursued this work systematically. But, as problems of rhythm have been analysed, the boundary between poetry and prose has, it seems been confused rather than clarified. It is possible that the distinction between poetry and prose does not lie in rhythm alone. The more we study a work of art, the more deeply we penetrate the fundamental unity of its laws. The individual constructional aspects of an artistic phenomenon are distinguished qualitatively, but this qualitativeness rests on a quantiative base, and we can pass imperceptibly from one level to another. The basic construction of plot is reduced to a schema of semantic constants. We take two contrasting everyday situations and resolve them with a third; or we take two semantic constants and create a parallel between them; or, lastly, we take several semantic constants and arrange them in ranking order. But the usual basis of plot (*syuzhet*) is story (*fabula*), i.e. an everyday situation. Yet this everyday situation is merely a particular instance of semantic construction and we can create from one novel a 'mystery novel', not by changing the story but simply by transposing the constituent parts: by putting the ending at the beginning or by a more complex rearrangement of the parts. This is how Pushkin's *The Blizzard* and *The Shot* were produced. Hence what we may call everyday constants, the semantic constants, the situational constants, and the purely formal features may be interchanged with, and merge into, one another.

A prose work is, in its plot construction and its semantic composition, based principally on a combination of everyday situations. This means that we resolve a given situation in the following way: a man must speak, but he cannot, and so a third person speaks on his behalf. In *The Captain's Daughter*, for instance, Grinev cannot speak and yet he must in order to clear his name from Shvabrin's slanders. He cannot speak because he would compromise the captain's daughter, so she herself offers Ekaterina an explanation on his behalf. In another example a man must vindicate himself, but he cannot do so because he has taken a vow of silence: the solution lies in the fact that he manages to extend the deadline of his vow. This is the basis

for one of Grimm's fairy-tales, *The Twelve Swans*, and the story *The Seven Viziers*. But there may be another way to resolve a work, and this resolution is brought about not by semantic means but by purely compositional ones whereby the effect of the compositional constant compares with that of the semantic.

We find this kind of resolution to a work in Fet's verse: after four stanzas in a particular metre with caesura (a constant word division in the middle of each line), the poem is resolved not by its plot but by the fact that the fifth stanza, although in the same metre, has no caesura, and this produces a sense of closure.

The fundamental distinction between poetry and prose lies possibly in a greater geometricality of devices, in the fact that a whole series of arbitrary semantic resolutions is replaced by a formal geometric resolution. It is as if a geometricization of devices is taking place. Thus the stanza in *Eugene Onegin* is resolved by the fact that the final rhyming couplet provides formal compositional resolution while disrupting the rhyme system. Pushkin supports this semantically by altering the vocabulary in these last two lines and giving them a slightly parodic character.

I am writing here in very generalized terms because I want to point out the most common landmarks, particularly in cinema. I have more than once heard film professionals express the curious view that, as far as literature is concerned, verse is closer to film than is prose. All sorts of people say this and large numbers of films strive towards a resolution which, by distant analogy, we may call poetic. There is no doubt that Dziga Vertov's *A Sixth Part of the World* (USSR, 1926) is constructed on the principle of poetic formal resolution: it has a pronounced parallelism and a recurrence of images at the end of the film where they convey a different meaning and thus vaguely recall the form of a triolet.

When we examine Vsevolod Pudovkin's film *The Mother* (USSR, 1926), in which the director has taken great pains to create a rhythmical construction, we observe a gradual displacement of everyday situations by purely formal elements. The parallelism of the nature scenes at the beginning prepares us for the acceleration of movements, the montage, and the departure from everyday life that intensifies towards the end. The ambiguity of the poetic image and its characteristically indistinct aura, together with the capacity for simultaneous generation of meaning by

Poetry and prose in cinema continued

different methods, are achieved by a rapid change of frames that never manage to become real. The very device that resolves the film—the double-exposure angle shot of the Kremlin walls moving—exploits the formal rather than the semantic features: it is a poetic device.

In cinema at present we are children. We have barely begun to consider the subjects of our work, but already we can speak of the existence of two poles of cinema, each of which will have its own laws.

Charlie Chaplin's *A Woman of Paris* (USA, 1923), is obviously prose based on semantic constants, on things that are accepted.

A Sixth Part of the World, in spite of its government sponsorship, is a poem of pathos.

The Mother is a unique centaur, an altogether strange beast. The film starts out as prose, using emphatic intertitles which fit the frame rather badly, and ends up as purely formal poetry. Recurring frames and images and the transformation of images into symbols support my conviction that this film is poetic by nature.

I repeat once more: there exist both prose and poetry in cinema, and this is the basic division between the genres: they are distinguished from one another not by rhythm, or not by rhythm alone, but by the prevalence in poetic cinema of technical and formal over semantic features, where formal features displace semantic and resolve the composition. Plotless cinema is 'verse' cinema.

8

Impressionism, surrealism, and film theory: path dependence, or how a tradition in film theory gets lost

Robert B. Ray

Film theory's two traditions

In the fall of 1938, when the movies were only 40 years old, Walter Benjamin received a rejection letter. Inspired by Louis Aragon's Surrealist narrative *Le Paysan de Paris* (1927) and by Soviet experiments with cinematic montage, Benjamin had conceived what has come to be known as *The Arcades Project*, a history of nineteenth-century Paris constructed primarily from found material—texts, documents, images—whose juxtaposition would reveal the buried origins of modern life. Benjamin had been receiving financial support from Frankfurt's Institute for Social Research, relocated in New York, and he had submitted three chapters of a book on Baudelaire, designed as a prologue to the more experimental work ahead. But speaking for the Institute, Benjamin's friend Theodor Adorno said no. 'Your study', Adorno wrote, in the now famous passage, 'is located at the crossroads of magic and positivism. That spot is bewitched. Only theory could break the spell' (Adorno 1938/1980: 129).

Although Adorno came to regret this decision, his formulation of it defines the history of film theory. For what could be a more exact definition of the cinema than 'the crossroads of magic and positivism'? Or a more succinct definition of film theory's traditional project than to 'break the spell'?

> **What could be a more exact definition of the cinema than 'the crossroads of magic and positivism'?**

As a technologically based, capital-intensive medium, the movies quickly developed into an industry keenly attracted by positivism's applications: the Taylorist–Fordist models of rationalized production. Indeed, as Thomas Schatz (1988) has described, the Hollywood studios set the tone by explicitly imitating the organizational system developed in large-scale manufacturing. Mass production, standardized designs, concentration of the whole production cycle in a single place, a radical division of labour, the routinizing of workers' tasks, even the after-hours surveillance of employees—all of these Fordist practices became Hollywood's own. Thus, at the peak of its early 1930s power, MGM could produce one feature film per week, a quota enabled by its standardized genres, enormous physical plant, strict definition of roles, and a star system whose performers remained as alienated from their tasks as any factory worker. And to guarantee this system's reliability, L. B. Mayer kept watch on his personnel's every move.

And yet, for all of its commitment to the positivism which Taylor and Ford had perfected, Hollywood was not making Model Ts. That ascetic vehicle, a triumph of functionalism, had succeeded by avoiding any traces of the irrational decoration that Ford portrayed as wasteful, inefficient, 'feminine'. Strikingly, however, the Model T's decline (Ford abandoned the car in 1927) coincided with Hollywood's ascendancy, as Ford's increasingly successful rival General Motors' Alfred Sloan began to demonstrate the enormous seductive power of style (Wollen 1993; Batchelor 1994). In doing so, Sloan was deriving an explicit business practice from the crucial discovery intuited by Hollywood's moguls: the movies succeeded commercially to the extent that they *enchanted*.

Hence the inevitable question: could enchantment be mass-produced? The movies' most influential form, Hollywood cinema (what Noël Burch (1990) calls the Institutional Mode of Representation), arose as an attempt to address this problem. The calculus has always been a delicate one: the temptations of rationalization on the one hand, the requirements of seduction on the other. As a result, any commercial filmmaking represents a site of negotiation between these conflicting positions. 'The cinema', Jean-Luc Godard once told Colin MacCabe, 'is all money' (MacCabe 1980: 27), but at any moment it can also become, as Godard once wrote of Renoir's *La Nuit du carrefour* (France, 1932) 'the air of confusion . . . the smell of rain and of fields bathed in mist' (Godard 1972: 63).

Developed as the means for balancing filmmaking's competing demands, Hollywood's protocols became the norm of cinema. Increasingly, film history has suggested that the key figure in their development was less D. W. Griffith than MGM's Irving Thalberg. Far more than the independent Griffith, Thalberg spent his days negotiating between L. B. Mayer's insistence on thrift and the popular audience's demand for glamour. In effect, he occupied Adorno's crossroads, embracing both positivism and magic. Working at the origins of the cinema's dominant mode, a rationalist longing to be enthralled by his own productions, Thalberg, in fact, embodied the two tendencies of all subsequent film theory.

Film history's conceptual neatness depends on its dual provenance in those great opposites, Lumière and Méliès, documentary and fiction. 'Cinema', Godard famously summed up, 'is spectacle—Méliès—and research—Lumière,' adding (impatient with the forced choice) that 'I have always wanted, basically, to do research in the form of a spectacle' (Godard 1972: 181). Inevitably, film theory took longer to appear, but after the First World War it quickly developed into two analogous positions, only one of which was attached so neatly to a single name.

That name, of course, was Eisenstein. With his insistence that filmmaking-as-an-art depended on repudiating the camera's automatic recording capacity, Eisenstein aligned himself not only with Méliès, but also with pictoralism, the movement that sought to legitimize photography by disguising its images as paintings. Eisenstein avoided that retrograde move while nevertheless sharing its fundamental premise: that a medium's aesthetic value is a direct function of its ability to transform the reality serving as its raw material. For Eisenstein, the means of such transformation was montage, the ideal tool for deriving significance (chiefly political) from the real details swarming in his footage (see Kolker, Chapter 2).

As his theoretical essays appeared in the 1920s, Eisenstein assumed the role simultaneously perfected by T. S. Eliot—the artist-critic whose writings create the taste by which his own aesthetic practice is judged. Eisenstein's sensational films enhanced the prestige of his theoretical positions, which quickly triumphed over the alternative proposed by the French Impressionists and Surrealists. If Eisenstein saw the cinema as a means of argument, the French regarded it as the vehicle of revelation, and the knowledge revealed was not always expressible in words. 'Explanations here are out of place,' Louis Delluc wrote about the 'phenomenon' of Sessue Hayakawa's screen presence, an example of what the Impressionists called *photogénie*. 'I wish there to be no words,' Jean Epstein declared, refusing to translate the concept that he posited as 'the purest expression of cinema' (Abel 1988: 138–9, 243, 315).

The concept of *photogénie*, especially in the Surrealists' hands, emphasized precisely what Eisenstein wished to escape: the cinema's automatism. 'For the first time', André Bazin would later elaborate, 'an image of the world is formed automatically, without the creative invention of man' (Bazin 1967: 13). Moreover, for reasons which the French could not define, the camera rendered some otherwise ordinary objects, landscapes, and even people luminous and spellbinding. Lumière's simple, mesmerizing films had proved that fact. Eisenstein anticipated Brecht's proposition that 'less than ever does the mere reflection of reality reveal anything about reality . . . something must in fact be *built up*, something artificial, posed' (Benjamin 1979: 255). The French who followed Lumière, however, insisted that just turning on the camera would do the trick: in René Clair's words, 'There is no detail of reality which is not immediately extended here [the cinema] into the domain of the wondrous' (Willemen 1994: 125). And in his first published essay, Louis Aragon suggested that this effect did not result from 'art' films alone:

All our emotion exists for those dear old American adventure films that speak of daily life and manage to raise to a dramatic level a banknote on which our attention is riveted, a table with a revolver on it, a bottle that on occasion becomes a weapon, a handkerchief that reveals a crime, a typewriter that's the horizon of a desk, the terrible unfolding telegraphic tape with magic ciphers that enrich or ruin bankers. (Hammond 1978: 29)

This response seems, in retrospect, an acute description of the way movies are often experienced—as intermittent intensities (a face, a landscape, the fall of light across a room) that break free from the sometimes indifferent narratives which contain them. Why, then, was the Impressionist–Surrealist approach so rapidly eclipsed by Eisenstein's? First, its emphasis on fragmentation poorly suited the rapidly consolidating commercial cinema whose hard-earned basis lay precisely in its continuity system. Both the Impressionists and the Surrealists, in fact, often regarded narrative as an obstacle to be overcome. ('The telephone rings,' Epstein complained, pointing to the event that so often initiates a plot. 'All is lost'; Abel 1988: 242.) urrealist filmwatching tactics, for example, were designed to reassert the autonomy and ambiguity of images: think, for example, of Man Ray's habit of watching the screen through his fingers, spread to isolate certain parts of the screen. Lyrical, contemplative, enraptured by the camera's automatism, the Impressionist attitude derived more from Lumière's way of working than from that of Méliès. The latter's commitment to fiction, and his willingness to construct a narrative world out of discontinuous fragments, proved

the premise of all subsequent commercial filmmaking, including Eisenstein's which quickly attracted the attention of the Hollywood studios. (Samuel Goldwyn: 'I've seen your film *Potemkin* and admire it very much. What I would like is for you to do something of the same kind, but a little cheaper, for Ronald Colman.') Although Méliès had begun as a magician, the filmmaking tradition he inspired lent itself readily to the Taylorist procedures adopted by the American moguls. It was Lumière who had discovered the cinema's alchemy.

> **Surrealist filmwatching tactics, for example, were designed to reassert the autonomy and ambiguity of images: think, for example, of Man Ray's habit of watching the screen through his fingers, spread to isolate certain parts of the screen.**

Second, by insisting that film's essence lay beyond words, the *photogénie* movement left even its would-be followers with nowhere to go. As Paul Willemen (1994: 131) has suggested, 'mysticism was indeed the swamp in which most of the theoretical statements of the Impressionists eventually drowned'. By contrast, Eisenstein had a thoroughly linguistic view of filmmaking, with shots amounting to ideograms, which, when artfully combined, could communicate the equivalent of sentences. As the hedonistic 1920s yielded to the intensely politicized 1930s, Eisenstein's propositions seemed a far more useful way of thinking about the cinema.

In fact, however, while *photogénie*'s elusiveness caused the term to disappear gradually from film theory, other people were thinking about it—people like Irving Thalberg. Having perfected its continuity system by the mid-1920s, the Hollywood studios turned to the great remaining problem. MGM's constant screen tests; its commitment to having the best cameramen, costume designers, and lighting technicians; its regular resort to previews—these practices indicated Thalberg's obsessive quest for the photogenic actor, location, or moment. MGM's pre-eminence during this period suggests that Thalberg achieved, however intuitively, what the Impressionist theoreticians did not: a formula for *photogénie*.

Current film theory has often discredited Impressionist–Surrealist film theory by pointing to *photogénie*'s obvious connection to fetishism. Aragon's own explanation of the cinematic marvellous, amounting to a precise definition of the fetishist's gaze, confirms this diagnosis: 'To endow with a poetic value that which does not yet possess it, to wilfully restrict the field of vision so as to intensify expression: these are two properties that help make cinematic *décor* the adequate expression of modern beauty' (Hammond 1978: 29).

In its history, fetishism has appeared most prominently as knowledge's opposite, as a means of false consciousness and disavowal. Marx, for example, argued that the 'fetishism of commodities' encourages us to ignore the exploitative social relations that such objects simultaneously embody and conceal. The commodity is a 'hieroglyph', all right, but not one meant to be read. It substitutes the lure of things for a curiosity about their production. Similarly, Freud posited fetishism as the result of an investigation's *arrest*. Fearing the sight of the mother's genitals, misunderstood as 'castrated', the male infant stops at another place (a foot, an ankle, a skirt's hem), investing this replacement with libidinal energy, but denying the sexual difference his gaze has discovered.

What film theory discredited, however, Hollywood skilfully employed. In fact, the development of classical narrative cinema finds its exact parallel in the etymology of the word 'fetish'. As William Pietz (1985) has shown, the problem of fetishism first arose in a specific historical context: the trading conducted by Portuguese merchants along the coast of West Africa in the sixteenth and seventeenth centuries. Renaissance businessmen, the Portuguese were looking for straightforward economic transactions. Almost immediately, they were frustrated by what Pietz (1985: 7–9) evocatively calls 'the mystery of value'. For the Africans, material objects could embody—'simultaneously and sequentially—religious, commercial, aesthetic, and sexual' worth, and the balance among these categories seemed, at least to the Europeans, a matter of caprice. Especially troubling was the Africans' unpredictable estimate of not only their own objects, but also those of the European traders, which the merchants themselves regarded as 'trifles'.

Like the Portuguese traders, commercial filmmakers began naïvely by proposing an uncomplicated deal: a story in exchange for the price of a ticket. But they were quickly surprised by their viewers' fascination with individual players. For a brief moment, the industry resisted this unintended consequence of the movies, this admiration for actors which seemed an 'overestimation of value', a fetishism. Preserving the players' anonymity, after all, had minimized their power and kept them cheap. Inevitably, however, Hollywood came to recognize this fetishism as a means of making money, and the star system deliberately set out to encourage it. In fact, although continuity cinema's insistence on story often reduced the immediate attraction of its components ('while an image could be beautiful,' one cameraman recalls, 'it wasn't to be so beautiful as to draw attention to itself'), inadvertently, as the Impressionists and Surrealists saw, the movies glamorized everything: faces, clothes, furniture, trains. A dining-car's white, starched linen (*North by Northwest*, USA, 1959), a woman's voice (Margaret Sullavan's in *Three Comrades*, USA, 1938), a cigarette lighter (*The Maltese Falcon*, USA, 1941)—even the most ordinary objects could become, as Sam Spade put it in a rare literary allusion, 'the stuff that dreams are made of' (Ray 1995).

It is hard to know whether this effect was always intended. Constant economic pressures, the conversion to sound, and the absolute pre-eminence of narrative all encouraged Hollywood's tendency towards Fordist procedures and laconic filmmaking. The American cinema's functionalism, in other words, abetted the rationalist theoretical tradition descending from Eisenstein. In this context, Thalberg's more complicated approach seems especially significant. For

An impressionist moment, Greta Garbo in *Grand Hotel* (1932)

despite MGM's production quotas, strict regimentation, and highly developed division of labour, Thalberg often encouraged, or at least allowed, moments of the kind so admired by the Impressionists and Surrealists. In *Grand Hotel* (USA, 1932), for example, whose production he closely supervised, the camera cut suddenly to an unmotivated overhead shot of Garbo in her ballerina costume, alone for the first time, opening like a flower as she settled wearily to the floor. The narrative idled, enabling this instance of *photogénie* to unfold because, as Thalberg knew, the movie would be the better for it. The plot could wait.

Path dependence

One of the most decisive moments in the history of film theory occurred during a span of twelve months from late 1952 to early 1953. Having emerged from the Second World War alive, but with the teaching career for which he had trained foreclosed to him because of a stammar and poor health, André Bazin (Andrew 1978) confirmed his commitment to film criticism with 'The Evolution of the Language of Cinema' and 'The Virtues and Limitations of Montage' (Bazin 1967, 1971), essays in which, for the first time, someone suggested that the two most prestigious schools of filmmaking (Soviet montage and German Expressionism) were wrong. The movies' possibilities, Bazin insisted, were more radical than those ways of working had suggested.

Bazin, of course, is famous for arguing that film's true destiny is the objective representation of reality. 'The guiding myth . . . inspiring the invention of cinema', he had argued a few years earlier, 'is the accomplishment of that which dominated in a more or less vague fashion all the techniques of the mechanical reproduction of reality in the nineteenth century, from photography to the phonograph, namely an integral realism, a recreation of the world in its own image, an image unburdened by the freedom of interpretation of the artist or the irreversibility of time' (Bazin 1967: 21). The Soviets and Germans, according to Bazin (24), had betrayed this sacred purpose by 'putting their faith in the image' instead of in reality, convulsing the camera's objectivity with abstracting montages and grotesque *mise-en-scène*.

Since about 1970 this position has been represented as fantastically naïve, another version of Western culture's longing for what philosopher Jacques Derrida calls 'unmediated presence'. In a passage often singled out for critique, Bazin (1971: 60), had apparently earned this attack praising *Bicycle Thieves* (Italy, 1948) as 'one of the first examples of pure cinema': 'No more actors, no more story, no more sets, which is to say that in the perfect aesthetic illusion of reality there is no more cinema.' In fact, however, behind Bazin's realist aesthetic lay an intuition about the cinema's most profoundly radical aspect: its automatism. With photography, Bazin kept insisting, an absolutely accurate representation of the world could be produced, for the first time in history, *by accident*. This miraculous revelatory power made the Soviet or Expressionist imposition of subjective meanings seem a kind of misguided vanity.

This argument, of course, amounted to a displacement of Bazin's unrequited religious impulse. But it also involved a revival of the Impressionists' *photogénie* and the Surrealists' automatism. In his own proposed dictionary entry, Breton (1972: 26) had designated this feature of modern technology as Surrealism's defining activity:

SURREALISM, n. Psychic automatism in its pure state, by which one proposes to express—verbally, by means of the written word, or in any other manner—the actual functioning of thought. Dictated by thought, in the absence of any control by reason, exempt from any aesthetic or moral concern.

Breton had also made explicit the metaphoric connection between technology and the Surrealists' favourite game, describing automatic writing as 'a true photography of thought' (Ernst 1948: 177). For the Impressionists, *photogénie* was untranslatable but intentional, the product of particularly talented filmmakers. For the Surrealists, on the other hand, it was often accidental, and thus capable of appearing anywhere. Man Ray made the point provocatively: 'The worst films I've ever seen, the ones that send me to sleep, contain ten or fifteen marvelous minutes. The best films I've ever seen only contain 10 or 15 valid minutes' (Hammond 1978: 84).

Like the Surrealists, Bazin could occasionally find what he valued in forgettable movies. He devoted, for example, a page-long footnote in 'The Virtues and Limitations of Montage' to what he called 'an otherwise mediocre English film', *Where no Vultures Fly* (GB, 1951), praising a single moment that abandoned a 'tricky' and 'banal montage' to show parents, child, and a stalking lioness 'all in the same full shot' (1967: 49–50). In general, however, Bazin preferred to associate his cinematic ideal with a particular set of strategies deliberately employed by an elect group of filmmakers. Jean Renoir, Vittorio De Sica, F. W. Murnau, Robert Flaherty, William Wyler, and Orson Welles were great because in relying on long takes and deep focus, they had modestly permitted reality to speak for itself.

> **At the heart of the *Cahiers* position lay a privileged term that evoked both *photogénie*'s ineffability and the Surrealists' 'objective chance'. That term was 'mise-en-scène'.**

With this argument, Bazin was retreating from his thought's most radical implication, his sense of the fundamental difference between previous representational technologies and the new 'random generators' like the camera. In the hands of his followers, the *Cahiers* critics, Bazin's attitude towards intentionality became even more ambivalent. *La politique des auteurs* seemed to renounce altogether the Surrealist faith in chance, celebrating even Bazin's beloved 'reality' less than the filmmaking geniuses who could consciously summon its charms. But at the heart of the *Cahiers* position lay a privileged term that evoked both *photogénie*'s ineffability and the Surrealists' 'objective chance'.

That term was 'mise-en-scène'. As the *Cahiers* critics used it, mise-en-scène' quickly left behind its conventional meaning ('setting') to become a sacred word, shared by friends who could invoke it knowing the others would understand. (This point, and other important contributions to this chapter, come from Christian Keathley.) At first, it appeared to be simply another version of *photogénie*, a way of talking again about the untranslatable 'essence of the cinema'. Hence, Jacques Rivette on Otto Preminger's *Angel Face* (USA, 1953): 'What tempts [Preminger] if not . . . the rendering audible of particular chords unheard and rare, in which the inexplicable beauty of the modulation suddenly justifies the ensemble of the phrase? This is probably the definition of something precious . . . its enigma—the door to something beyond intellect, opening out onto the unknown. Such are the contingencies of *mise-en-scène*' (Hiller 1985: 134). Auteurism's basic problem, however, involved just this kind of attribution. More than even most theoretical groups, the *Cahiers* critics had a sense of themselves as a visionary, well-educated, sensitive elect. As long as they were associating the delights of mise-en-scène with filmmakers like Jean Renoir, they could continue to insist on the conscious aspect of a director's decisions. Renoir, after all, was aesthetically well-bred, politically liberal, and personally sympathetic. But the auteurist position increasingly prompted them to celebrate directors who had often made bad films, and who sometimes seemed neither particularly smart nor especially nice. Directors, for example, like Otto Preminger. Faced with this situation, the *Cahiers* writers revised their praise, directing it less at individual filmmakers than at the medium itself. Thus, the *Cahiers*'s American operative Andrew Sarris (1965: 13) could explicitly modulate *la politique des auteurs* into a revival of Surrealism's praise of automatism:

> For me, *mise-en-scène* is not merely the gap between what we see and feel on the screen and what we can express in words, but is also the gap between the intention of the director and his effect upon the spectator. . . . To read all sorts of poignant profundities in Preminger's inscrutable urbanity would seem to be the last word in idiocy, and yet there are moments in his films when the evidence on the screen is inconsistent with one's deepest instincts about the director as a man. It is during those moments that one feels the magical powers of *mise-en-scène* to get more out of a picture than is put there by a director.

The roots of this move lay in Bazin's tacit renewal of the Impressionist–Surrealist branch of film theory. This achievement usually goes unnoticed, since Bazin, after all, remains famous for so many other things: his championing of realism and the Italian post-war cinema, his editorship of the *Cahiers*, his spiritual fathering of the *Nouvelle Vague*. Nevertheless, Bazin's ability to reroute film theory, at least temporarily, amounted to a rare instance of a discipline escaping from what economic historians call 'path dependence' (David 1985; Passell 1996).

Path dependence developed as a way of explaining why the free market's invisible hand does not always choose the best products. Beta and Macintosh lose to inferior alternatives, while a clumsy arrangement of keyboard symbols (known as QWERTY, for the first six letters on a typewriter's upper left) becomes the international standard. Although an initial choice often occurs for reasons whose triviality eventually becomes evident (momentary production convenience, fleeting cost advantages), that decision establishes a path dependence almost impossible to break. Superior keyboard layouts have repeatedly been designed, but with every typist in the world using QWERTY, they have no chance.

Bazin recognized that film theory was especially prone to path dependence. The vagaries of film preservation, the industry's encouragement of amnesia (before television, only a handful of films were regularly and widely revived), the small size of the intellectual film community—these factors all encouraged theoretical consensus. While the Impressionist and Surrealist films, with a few exceptions, had disappeared from sight, Eisenstein's had remained in wide circulation, serving as advertisements for his position. (And vice versa: Jean-Marie Straub once observed that everyone thinks that Eisenstein was great at editing because he had so many *theories* about it; Rosenbaum 1982.) As a result, Eisenstein's rationalist, critical branch of film theory had triumphed, establishing a path dependence that Bazin challenged with all his energy.

Bazin attacked on two fronts. First, he challenged the Eisenstein tradition's basic equation of art with anti-realism. Second, he encouraged, without practising himself, a different kind of film criticism: the lyrical, discontinuous, epigrammatic flashes of subjectivity-cum-analysis that appeared in the *Cahiers du cinéma*. A few now famous examples from Godard (1972: 64, 66) suggest this form's tone:

There was theatre (Griffith), poetry (Murnau), painting (Rossellini), dance (Eisenstein), music (Renoir). Henceforth there is cinema. And the cinema is Nicholas Ray.

Never before have the characters in a film [Ray's *Bitter Victory*, France, 1957] seemed so close and yet so far away. Faced by the deserted streets of Benghazi or the sand-dunes, we suddenly think for the space of a second of something else—the snack-bars on the Champs-Elysées, a girl one liked, everything and anything, lies, the treachery of women, the shallowness, of men, playing the slot-machines. . . .

How can one talk of such a film? What is the point of saying that the meeting between Richard Burton and Ruth Roman while Curt Jurgens watches is edited with fantastic brio? Maybe this was a scene during which we had closed our eyes.

In many cases, this different critical strategy evolved into filmmaking itself, with Godard (1972: 171) again providing the explanation:

As a critic, I thought of myself as a filmmaker. Today, I still think of myself as a critic, and in a sense I am, more than before. Instead of writing criticism, I make a film, but the critical dimension is subsumed. I think of myself as an essayist, producing essays in novel form or novels in essay form: only instead of writing, I film them.

The film theory sponsored by Bazin would receive its best explanation only after its own moment had passed. Writing in 1973, Roland Barthes (1973/1981: 44) proclaimed, 'Let the commentary be itself a text. . . . There are no more critics, only writers.'

Bazin's moment lasted only fifteen years. The events of May 1968 discredited both his ideas and the critical practice he had fostered, stimulating different questions about the cinema's relationship to ideology and power. The post-1968 period coincided with the development of academic film study, and although auteurism briefly persisted as a way of doing film criticism (aided by its explicit analogy to literary authorship), its apolitical concern with aesthetics suddenly seemed reactionary. Comolli and Narboni's 1969 *Cahiers* editorial 'Cinema/Ideology/Criticism' (Nichols, 1976) represented the transition, an attempt to preserve the old auteurist heroes (Ford, Capra, *et al.*) in terms of the new political criteria. But as film studies spread through the universities, it organized itself around a theoretical approach having more to do with Eisenstein than with Bazin.

That approach has come to be known as 'semiotic', using that term as a shorthand way of summarizing the structuralist, ideological, psychoanalytic, and gender theory it encompassed. Committed largely to a species of critique defined by the Frankfurt School, this paradigm accomplished wonderful things, above all alerting us to popular culture's complicities with the most destructive, enslaving, and ignoble myths. It taught us to see the implications of those invisible operations that Brecht had called 'the apparatus', the relation, for example, between Hollywood's continuity system, apparently only a set of filmmaking protocols, and a world-view eager to conceal the necessity of choice (see Ray 1985).

These gains did not come free of charge. The Impressionist–Surrealist half of film theory fell into obscurity, banished for its political irrelevance. Indeed, 'impressionistic' became one of the new paradigm's most frequently evoked pejoratives, designating a theoretical position that was either 'untheorized' or too interested in the wrong questions. The wrong questions, however, frequently turned on the reasons why people went to the movies in the first place, the problem so vital to the Impressionists. In 1921 Jean Epstein had announced that 'The cinema is essentially supernatural. Everything is transformed. . . . The universe is on edge. The philosopher's light. The atmosphere is heavy with love. I am looking' (Abel 1988: 246). In the new dispensation, occasional film theoretician Fredric Jameson (Jameson and Kavanagh 1984: 3–4) would acknowledge that the appeal of beautiful and exciting storytelling is precisely the problem: 'Nothing can be more satisfying to a Marxist teacher', he admitted, 'than to "break" this fascination for students'. Also rendered suspect was formally experimental criticism, deemed irresponsible by rationalist critique. The Cahiers-inspired auteurist essay receded, as did the New Wave film, that hybrid of research and spectacle, Lumière and Méliès.

> ## Can the rational, politically sensitive Eisenstein tradition reunite with the Impressionist–Surrealist interest in *photogénie* and automatism?

Twenty-five years ago, Roland Barthes recognized what was happening to criticism. The semiotic paradigm that he himself had done so much to establish—'it too', Barthes (1977: 166) lamented, 'has become in some sort mythical: any student can and does denounce the bourgeois or petit-bourgeois character of such and such a form (of life, of thought, of consumption). In other words, a mythological doxa has been created: denunciation, demystification (or demythification), has itself become discourse, stock of phrases, catechistic declaration.' The problem, Barthes (1977a: 71) wrote four years later, is 'Where to go next?' In the next decade, the most important debates in film theory will turn on the extreme path dependence Barthes saw constraining the humanities. At stake will be our disciplines' ability to pro-

duce information, defined by information theory as a function of *unpredictability*. (The more predictable the message, the less information it contains; Ray 1995: 10–12). Film studies, in particular, should ask these questions: (1) Can the rational, politically sensitive Eisenstein tradition reunite with the Impressionist–Surrealist interest in *photogénie* and automatism? Can film theory, in other words, imitate filmmaking and recognize that, at its best, the cinema requires, as Thalberg understood, a subtle mixture of logical structure and untranslatable allure? (2) Can film theory revive the *Cahiers*–Nouvelle Vague experiment, learning to write differently, to stage its research in the form of a spectacle? American theoretician Gregory Ulmer (1994) has specified that this new writing practice would provide a complement to critique. It will not be hermeneutics, the science of interpretation. It will look to photography, the cinema, television, and the computer as the source of ideas about invention. It is called 'heuretics'.

A heuretic film studies might begin where *photogénie*, third meanings, and fetishism intersect: with the cinematic detail whose insistent appeal eludes precise explanation. Barthes maintained that third meanings, while resisting obvious connotations, compel 'an interrogative reading'. In doing so, he was implicitly suggesting how Impressionist reverie could prompt an active research method resembling the Surrealists' 'Irrational Enlargement', a game in which players generate chains of associations from a given object (Jean 1980: 298–301; Hammond 1978: 74–80). Here would be the instructions for such a project: *Select a detail from a movie, one that interests you without your knowing why. Follow this detail wherever it leads and report your findings.*

Here is an example of what this Impressionist–Surrealist model might produce. Studying MGM's Andy Hardy movies, I was struck by the occasional presence of a Yale pennant on Andy's wall. Following Barthes's 'instructions', I 'interrogated' this object, producing the following response:

In Andy's bedroom, only two pennants appear: *Carvel High* and *Yale*. In the 1930s, when the best of the Hardy films were made, Yale's two most famous alumni were probably Cole Porter (author of the college's football cheer) and Rudy Vallee (popularizer of 'The Whiffenpoof Song'). *Andy Hardy's Private Secretary* [USA, 1941] gives Porter's 'I've Got My Eyes on You' to Kathryn Grayson, who uses it to satisfy Andy's request (and the audience's) for something besides opera. But with his urbanity, dandyism, aristocratic wit, and cosmopolitan allusiveness, Porter is the Hardy series's antonym. Vallee's deportment, on the other hand—a studied juvenescence deployed to conceal a prima donna's ego—seems more like Rooney's own. In bursts of manic exuberance, Andy is given to expressions of self-satisfaction addressed to his bedroom mirror, pep talks descended from Franklin's *Autobiography*. Although the Hardy films unquestioningly accept Poor Richard's vulgarized legacy (chambers of commerce, boosterism, faith in 'Progress'), those values will eventually be satirized by even popular culture, especially in 1961's *How to Succeed in Business Without Really Trying*, whose hero-on-the-make serenades his own mirror image with the show's hit, 'I Believe in You.' Making a Mickey-Rooney style comeback, that play's costar, in the part of corporation president J. B. Biggley, was Rudy Vallee.

And yet: with the series making no other mention of it, the choice of the Yale pennant seems particularly arbitrary. Andy, after all, eventually follows his father's footsteps to 'Wainwright College,' whose plentiful coeds, accessible teachers, and intimate size represent the Ivy League's opposite. Obvious answers, of course, present themselves: 'Yale' as the best known college name, 'Yale' as a signifier of 'class.' Then why not 'Harvard' or 'Princeton'? If we acknowledge instead another logic (more visual, more cinematic), we might begin to see 'Yale' as an unusually valuable *design*—bold (the rare capital Y), concise (the shortest college name), memorable (the locks), available for multiple rhymes (including *hale*, the inevitable companion of *Hardy*'s near-homonym 'hearty'). From this perspective, the Yale pennant signals a relaxation of filmmaking's referential drive, a turn toward the possibilities inherent in shapes, movements, and sounds. In the Hardy series, 'Yale' suggests the cinema's revision of Mallarmé's famous warning to Degas—movies are not made with words, but with *images*. (Ray 1995: 173–4)

BIBLIOGRAPHY

*Abel, Richard (ed.) (1988), *French Film Theory and Criticism, i: 1907–1929* (Princeton: Princeton University Press).

Adorno, Theodor (1938/1980), Letter to Walter Benjamin, trans. Harry Zohn, in Fredric Jameson (ed.), *Aesthetics and Politics* (London: Verso).

Andrew, Dudley (1978), *André Bazin* (New York: Oxford University Press).

Barthes, Roland (1973/1981), 'Theory of the Text', trans. Geoff Bennington, in Robert Young (ed.), *Untying the Text: A Post-Structuralist Reader* (Boston: Routledge & Kegan Paul).

—— (1977a), *Image–Music–Text*, trans. Stephen Heath (New York: Hill & Wang).

—— (1977b), *Roland Barthes*, trans. Richard Howard (New York: Hill & Wang).

Batchelor, Ray (1994), *Henry Ford: Mass Production, Modernism and Design* (Manchester: Manchester University Press).

*Bazin, André (1967), *What is Cinema?*, 2 vols., trans. Hugh Gray, i (Berkeley, Calif.: University of California Press).

*—— (1971), *What is Cinema?*, 2 vols., trans. Hugh Gray, ii (Berkeley: University of California Press).

Benjamin, Walter (1979), *One-Way Street*, trans. Edmund Jephcott and Kingsley Shorter (London: New Left Books).

Breton, André (1972), *Manifestos of Surrealism*, trans. Richard Seaver and Helen R. Lane (Ann Arbor: University of Michigan Press).

Burch, Noël (1990), *Life to those Shadows* (Berkeley: University of California Press).

David, Paul A. (1985), 'Clio and the Economics of QWERTY', *American Economic Review*, 75/2: 332–7.

Ernst, Max (1948), *Beyond Painting and Other Writings by the Artist and his Friends* (New York: Wittenborn Schultz).

Godard, Jean-Luc (1972), *Godard on Godard*, trans. Tom Milne (New York: Viking Press).

*Hammond, Paul (ed.) (1978), *The Shadow and its Shadow: Surrealist Writings on the Cinema* (London: British Film Institute).

Hillier, Jim (ed.) (1985), *Cahiers du Cinéma. The 1950s: Neo-Realism, Hollywood, New Wave* (Cambridge, Mass.: Harvard University Press).

Jameson, Fredric, and **James Kavanagh** (1984), 'The Weakest Link: Marxism in Literary Studies', in *The Left Academy II* (New York: Praeger).

Jean, Marcel (ed.) (1980), *The Autobiography of Surrealism* (New York: Viking).

MacCabe, Colin (1980), *Godard: Image, Sounds, Politics* (Bloomington: Indiana University Press).

Nichols, Bill (ed.) (1976), *Movies and Methods* (Berkeley: University of California Press).

Passell, Peter (1996), 'Why the Best doesn't always Win', *New York Times Magazine*, 5 May: 60–1.

Pietz, William (1985), 'The Problem of the Fetish', part 1, *Res*, 9: 5–17.

—— (1987), 'The Problem of the Fetish', part 2, *Res*, 13: 23–45.

—— (1988), 'The Problem of the Fetish', part 3, *Res*, 16: 105–23.

*Ray, Robert B. (1985), *A Certain Tendency of the Hollywood Cinema 1930–1980* (Princeton: Princeton University Press).

—— (1995), *The Avant-Garde Finds Andy Hardy* (Cambridge, Mass.: Harvard University Press).

Rosenbaum, Jonathan (1982), 'The Films of Jean-Marie Straub and Danielle Huillet', in *Film at the Public*, Programme for a film series (New York: Public Theater).

CRITICAL APPROACHES

Sarris, Andrew (1965), 'Preminger's Two Periods: Studio and Solo', *Film Comment*, 3/3: 12–17.

Schatz, Thomas (1988), *The Genius of the System: Hollywood Filmmaking in the Studio Era* (New York: Pantheon Books).

Ulmer, Gregory L. (1994), *Heuretics: The Logic of Invention* (Baltimore: Johns Hopkins University Press).

Willemen, Paul (1994), *Looks and Frictions: Essays in Cultural Studies and Film Theory* (Bloomington: Indiana University Press; London: British Film Institute).

Wollen, Peter (1993), *Raiding the Icebox: Reflections on Twentieth-Century Culture* (Bloomington: Indiana University Press).

9 Film and psychoanalysis

Barbara Creed

Psychoanalysis and the cinema were born at the end of the nineteenth century. They share a common historical, social, and cultural background shaped by the forces of modernity. Theorists commonly explore how psychoanalysis, with its emphasis on the importance of desire in the life of the individual, has influenced the cinema. But the reverse is also true—the cinema may well have influenced psychoanalysis. Not only did Freud draw on cinematic terms to describe his theories, as in 'screen memories', but a number of his key ideas were developed in visual terms—particularly the theory of castration, which is dependent upon the shock registered by a close-up image of the female genitals. Further, as Freud (who loved Sherlock Holmes) was aware, his case histories unfold very much like popular mystery novels of the kind that were also adopted by the cinema from its inception.

The history of psychoanalytic film criticism is extremely complex—partly because it is long and uneven, partly because the theories are difficult, and partly because the evolution of psychoanalytic film theory after the 1970s cannot be understood without recourse to developments in separate, but related areas, such as Althusser's theory of ideology, semiotics, and feminist film theory. In the 1970s psychoanalysis became the key discipline called upon to explain a series of diverse concepts, from the way the cinema functioned as an apparatus to the nature of the screen–

spectator relationship. Despite a critical reaction against psychoanalysis, in some quarters, in the 1980s and 1990s, it exerted such a profound influence that the nature and direction of film theory and criticism has been changed in irrevocable and fundamental ways.

Pre-1970s psychoanalytic film theory

One of the first artistic movements to draw on psychoanalysis was the Surrealist movement of the 1920s and 1930s. In their quest for new modes of experience that transgressed the boundaries between dream and reality, the Surrealists extolled the potential of the cinema. They were deeply influenced by Freud's theory of dreams and his concept of the unconscious. To them, the cinema, with its special techniques such as the dissolve, superimposition, and slow motion, correspond to the nature of dreaming.

André Breton, the founder of the movement, saw cinema as a way of entering the marvellous, that realm of love and liberation. Recent studies by writers such as Hal Foster (1993) argue that Surrealism was also bound up with darker forces—explicated by Freud—such as the death drive, the compulsion to repeat, and the uncanny. Certainly, the films of the greatest exponent of cinematic Surrealism, Luis Buñel (*Un chien andalou*, France, 1928; *The Exterminating Angel*, Mexico, 1962; and *That Obscure Object of Desire*, France, 1977), explore the unconscious from this perspective.

Not all theorists used Freud. Others drew on the ideas of Carl Gustav Jung, and particularly his theory of archetypes, to understand film. The archetype is an idea or image that has been central to human existence and inherited psychically from the species by the individual. Archetypes include: the shadow or the underside of consciousness; the anima, that is the feminine aspect in men; and the animus, or the masculine aspect in women. But generally, Jungian theory has never been widely applied to the cinema. Apart from Clark Branson's *Howard Hawks: A Jungian Study* (1987) and John Izod's *The Films of Nicolas Roeg: Myth and Mind* (1992), critical works consist mainly of articles, by authors such as Albert Benderson (1979), Royal S. Brown (1980), and Don Fredericksen (1980), which analyse archetypes in the film text. Writers of the 1970s who turned to Freud and Lacan—the two most influential psychoanalysts—were critical, however, of what they perceived to be an underlying essentialism in Jungian theory, that is a tendency to explain subjectivity in unchanging, universal terms.

Many of Freud's theories have been used in film theory: the unconscious; the return of the repressed; Oedipal drama; narcissism; castration; and hysteria. Possibly his most important contributions were his accounts of the unconscious, subjectivity, and sexuality. According to Freud, large parts of human thought remain unconscious; that is, the subject does not know about the content of certain troubling ideas and often much effort is needed to make them conscious. Undesirable thoughts will be repressed or kept from consciousness by the ego under the command of the super-ego, or conscience. In Freud's view, repression is the key to understanding the neuroses. Repressed thoughts can manifest themselves in dreams, nightmares, slips of the tongue, and forms of artistic activity. These ideas have also influenced film study and some psychoanalytic critics explore the 'unconscious' of the film text—referred to as the 'subtext'—analysing it for repressed contents, perverse utterances, and evidence of the workings of desire.

Freud's notion of the formation of subjectivity is more complex. Two concepts are central: division and sexuality. The infantile ego is a divided entity. The ego refers to the child's sense of self; however, because the child, in its narcissistic phase, also takes itself, invests in itself, as the object of its own libidinal drives, the ego is both subject and object. The narcis-

sistic ego is formed in its relationship to others. One of the earliest works influenced by Freud's theory of the double was Otto's Rank's 1925 classic *The Double* which was directly influenced by a famous movie of the day, *The Student of Prague* (Germany, 1913). In his later rewriting of Freud, Lacan took Freud's notion of the divided self as the basis of his theory of the formation of subjectivity in the mirror phase (see below), which was to exert a profound influence on film theory in the 1970s.

Sexuality becomes crucial during the child's Oedipus complex. Initially, the child exists in a two-way, or dyadic, relationship with the mother. But eventually, the child must leave the maternal haven and enter the domain of law and language. As a result of the appearance of a third figure—the father—in the child's life, the child gives up its love–desire for the mother. The dyadic relationship becomes triadic. This is the moment of the Oedipal crisis. The boy represses his feelings for the mother because he fears the father will punish him, possibly even castrate him—that is, make him like his mother, whom he now realizes is not phallic. Prior to this moment the boy imagined the mother was just like himself. On the understanding that one day he will inherit a woman of his own, the boy represses his desire for the mother. This is what Freud describes as the moment of 'primal repression'; it ushers in the formation of the unconscious.

The girl gives up her love for the mother, not because she fears castration (she has nothing to lose) but because she blames the mother for not giving her a penis–phallus. She realizes that only those who possess the phallus have power. Henceforth, she transfers her love to her father, and later to the man she will marry. But, as with the boy, her repressed desire can, at any time, surface, bringing with it a problematic relationship with the mother. The individual who is unable to come to terms with his or her proper gender role (activity for boys, passivity for girls) may become an hysteric; that is, repressed desires will manifest themselves as bodily or mental symptoms such as paralysis or amnesia. Alfred Hitchcock's *Psycho* (USA, 1960) and *Marnie* (USA, 1964) present powerful examples of what might happen to the boy and girl respectively if they fail to resolve the Oedipus complex.

Freud's theories were discussed most systematically in relation to the cinema after the post-structuralist revolution in theory during the 1970s. In particular, writers applied the Oedipal trajectory to the narrative structures of classical film texts. They pointed to the fact that all narratives appeared to exhibit an Oedipal trajectory; that is, the (male) hero was confronted with a crisis in which he had to assert himself over another man (often a father figure) in order to achieve social recognition and win the woman. In this way, film was seen to represent the workings of patriarchal ideology.

In an early two-part article, 'Monsters from the ID' (1970, 1971), which pre-dates the influences of post-structuralist criticism, Margaret Tarratt analysed the science fiction film. She argued that previous writers, apart from French critics, all view science fiction films as 'reflections of society's anxiety about its increasing technological prowess and its responsibility to control the gigantic forces of destruction it possesses' (Tarratt 1970: 38). Her aim was to demonstrate that the genre was 'deeply involved with concepts of Freudian psychoanalysis and seen in many cases to derive their structure from it' (38). In particular, science fiction explores the individual's repressed sexual desires, viewed as incompatible with civilized morality. Utilizing Freud's argument that whatever is repressed will return, Tarratt discusses Oedipal desire, castration anxiety, and violent sadistic male desire.

1970s psychoanalytic theory and after

One of the major differences between pre- and post-1970s psychoanalytic theory was that the latter saw the cinema as an institution or an apparatus. Whereas early approaches, such as those of Tarratt, concentrated on the film text in relation to its hidden or repressed meanings, 1970s theory, as formulated by Jean-Louis Baudry, Christian Metz, and Laura Mulvey, emphasized the crucial importance of the cinema as an apparatus and as a signifying practice of ideology, the viewer–screen relationship, and the way in which the viewer was 'constructed' as transcendental during the spectatorial process.

Psychoanalytic film theory from the 1970s to the 1990s has travelled in at least four different, but related, directions. These should not be seen as linear progressions as they frequently overlap:

The first stage was influenced by apparatus theory as proposed by Baudry and Metz. In an attempt to avoid the totalizing imperative of the structuralist approach, they drew on psychoanalysis as a way of widening their theoretical base.

The second development was instituted by the feminist film theorist Laura Mulvey, who contested aspects of the work of Baudry and Metz by rebutting the naturalization of the filmic protagonist as an Oedipal hero, and the view of the screen–spectator relationship as a one-way process.

The third stage involved a number of feminist responses to Mulvey's work. These did not all follow the same direction. In general, they included critical studies of the female Oedipal trajectory, masculinity and masochism, fantasy theory and spectatorship, and woman as active, sadistic monster.

The fourth stage involves theorists who use psychoanalytic theory in conjunction with other critical approaches to the cinema as in post-colonial theory, queer theory, and body theory.

Apparatus theory: Baudry and Metz

The notion of the cinema as an institution or apparatus is central to 1970s theory. However, it is crucial to understand that Baudry, Metz, and Mulvey did not simply mean that the cinema was like a machine. As Metz explained, 'The cinematic institution is not just the cinema industry . . . it is also the mental machinery—another industry—which spectators "accustomed to the cinema" have internalized historically and which has adapted them to the consumption of films' (1975/1982: 2). Thus the term 'cinematic apparatus' refers to both an industrial machine as well as a mental or psychic apparatus.

Jean-Louis Baudry was the first to draw on psychoanalytic theory to analyse the cinema as an institution. According to D. N. Rodowick, one 'cannot overestimate the impact of Baudry's work in this period' (1988: 89). Baudry's pioneering ideas were later developed by Metz, who, although critical of aspects of Baudry's theories, was in agreement with his main arguments.

Baudry explored his ideas about the cinematic apparatus in two key essays. In the first, 'Ideological Effects of the Basic Cinematographic Apparatus' (1970), he argued that the cinema is ideological in that it creates an ideal, transcendental viewing subject. By this he meant that the cinema places the spectator, the 'eye-subject' (1986a: 290), at the centre of vision. Identification with the camera–projector, the seamless flow of images, narratives which restore equilibrium—all of these things give the spectator a sense of unity and control. The apparatus ensures 'the setting up of the "subject" as the active centre and origin of meaning'

(1986*a*: 286). Further, according to Baudry, by hiding the way in which it creates an impression of realism, the cinema enables the viewer to feel that events are simply unfolding—effortlessly—before his eyes. The 'reality effect' also helps to create a viewer who is at the centre of representation.

To explain the processes of identification at work in the viewing context, Baudry turned increasingly to the theories of Jacques Lacan. Baudry argued that the screen–spectator relationship activates a return to the Lacanian Imaginary, the period when the child experiences its first sense of a unified self during the mirror stage. 'The arrangement of the different elements—projector, darkened hall, screen—in addition to reproducing in a striking way the mise-en-scène of Plato's cave . . . reconstructs the situation necessary to the release of the "mirror stage" discovered by Lacan' (1986*a*: 294).

According to Lacan, there are three orders in the history of human development: the Imaginary, the Symbolic, and the Real. It is this area of Lacanian theory, particularly the Imaginary and the Symbolic, that is central to 1970s film theory. Drawing on Freud's theories of narcissism and the divided subject, Lacan proposed his theory of subjectivity. The mirror stage, which occurs during the period of the Imaginary, refers to that moment when the infant first experiences the joy of seeing itself as complete, and imagines itself to be more adult, more fully formed, perfect, than it really is. The self is constructed in a moment of recognition and misrecognition. Thus, the self is split.

Similarly, the spectator in the cinema identifies with the larger-than-life, or idealized, characters on the screen. Thus, as Mulvey (1975) later argued, the viewing experience, in which the spectator identifies with the glamorous star, is not unlike a re-enactment of the moment when the child acquires its first sense of selfhood or subjectivity through identificaton with an ideal self. But, as Lacan pointed out, this is also a moment of misrecognition—the child is not really a fully formed subject. He will only see himself in this idealized way when his image is reflected back through the eyes of others. Thus, identity is always dependent on mediation.

For the moment, the spectator in the cinema is transported back to a time when he or she experienced a sense of transcendence. But in reality, the spectator is not the point of origin, the centre of representation. Baudry argued that the comforting sense of a unified self which the viewing experience re-enacts does not emanate from the spectator but is constructed by the apparatus. Thus, the cinematic institution is complicit with ideology—and other institutions such as State and Church—whose aim is to instil in the subject a misrecognition of itself as transcendental.

In his 1975 essay 'The Apparatus', Baudry drew further parallels between Plato's cave and the cinematic apparatus. The spectators in both are in a state of 'immobility', 'shackled to the screen', staring at 'images and shadows of reality' that are not real but 'a simulacrum of it' (1986*b*: 303–4). Like spectators in the cinema, they mistake the shadowy figures for the real thing. According to Baudry, what Plato's prisoners–human beings desire—and what the cinema offers—is a return to a kind of psychic unity in which the boundary between subject and object is obliterated.

Baudry then drew connections between Plato's cave, the cinematic apparatus, and the 'maternal womb' (1986*b*: 306). He argued that 'the cinematographic apparatus brings about a state of artificial regression' which leads the spectator 'back to an anterior phase of his development'. The subject's desire to return to this phase is 'an early state of development with its own forms of satisfaction which may play a determining role in his desire for cinema and the pleasure he finds in it' (1986*b*: 313). What Baudry had in mind by this 'anterior phase' was an 'archaic moment of fusion' prior to the Lacanian mirror stage, 'a mode of identification, which has to do with the lack of differentiation between the subject and his environment, a dream-scene model which we find in the baby/breast relationship' (1986*b*: 313).

After discussing the actual differences between dream and the cinema, Baudry suggested that another wish lies behind the cinema—complementary to the one at work in Plato's cave. Without necessarily being aware of it, the subject is led to construct machines like the cinema which 'represent his own overall functioning to him . . . unaware of the fact that he is representing to himself the very scene of the unconscious where he is' (1986*b*: 316–17).

In 1975 Christian Metz published *Psychoanalysis and Cinema: The Imaginary Signifier* (translated in 1982), which was the first systematic book-length attempt to apply psychoanalytic theory to the cinema. Like Baudry, Metz also supported the analogy between screen and mirror and held that the spectator was positioned by the cinema machine in a moment that reactivated the pre-Oedipal moment of identification—that is, the moment of imaginary unity in which the infant first perceives itself as complete.

However, Metz also argued that the cinema–mirror analogy was flawed. Whereas a mirror reflects back the spectator's own image, the cinema does not. Metz also pointed out that, whereas the cinema is essentially a symbolic system, a signifying practice that mediates between the spectator and the outside world, the theory of the mirror stage refers to the pre-symbolic, the period when the infant is without language.

Nevertheless, Metz advocated the crucial importance of Lacanian psychoanalytic theory for the cinema and stressed the need to theorize the screen–spectator relationship—not just in the context of the Imaginary, but also in relation to the Symbolic. To address this issue, Metz introduced the notion of voyeurism. He argued that the viewing process is voyeuristic in that there is always a distance maintained, in the cinema, between the viewing subject and its object. The cinematic scene cannot return the spectator's gaze.

Metz also introduced a further notion which became the subtitle of his book: the imaginary signifier. The cinema, he argued, makes present what is absent. The screen might offer images that suggest completeness, but this is purely imaginary. Because the spectator is aware that the offer of unity is only imaginary, he is forced to deal with a sense of lack that is an inescapable part of the viewing process.

Metz drew an analogy between this process and the experience of the (male) child in the mirror phase. (Metz assumes the spectator is male.) When the boy looks in the mirror and identifies for the first time with himself as a unified being he is also made aware of his difference from the mother. She lacks the penis he once thought she possessed. Entry into the Symbolic also involves repression of desire for the mother and the constitution of the unconscious in response to that repression. (Here, Lacan reworks Freud's theories of the phallus and castration.) Along with repression of desire for the mother comes the birth of desire: for the speaking subject now begins a lifelong search for the lost object—the other, the little 'o' of the Imaginary, the mother he relinquished in order to acquire a social identity.

As the child enters the Symbolic it acquires language. However, it must also succumb to the 'law of the father' (the laws of society) which governs the Symbolic order. Entry into the Symbolic is entry into law, language, and loss—concepts which are inextricably bound together. Thus, entry into the Symbolic entails an awareness of sexual difference and of the 'self' as fragmented. The very concept of 'I' entails lack and loss.

When the boy mistakenly imagines his mother (sisters, woman) is castrated, his immediate response is to disavow what he has seen; he thinks she has been castrated, but he simultaneously knows that this is not true. Two courses of action are open to the boy. He can accept her difference and repress his desire for unification with the mother on the understanding that one day he will inherit a woman of his own. He can refuse to accept her difference and continue to believe that the mother is phallic. Rather than think of her lack, the fetishist will conjure up a reassuring image of another part of her body such as her breasts or her legs. He will also phallicize her body, imagining it in conjunction with phallic images such as long spiky high heels. Hence, film theorists have drawn on the theory of the phallic woman to explain the femme fatale of film noir (*Double Indemnity*, USA, 1944; *Body Heat*, USA, 1981; *The Last Seduction*, USA, 1994), who is depicted as dangerously phallic. E. Anne Kaplan's edited collection *Women in Film Noir* (1978) proved extremely influential in this context.

The Oedipal trajectory, Metz argued, is re-enacted in the cinema in relation not only to the Oedipal nature of narrative, but, most importantly, within the spectator–screen relationship. Narrative is characteristically Oedipal in that it almost always contains a male protagonist who, after resolving a crisis and overcoming a 'lack', then comes to identify with the law of the father, while successfully containing or controlling the female figure, demystifying her threat, or achieving union with her.

The concept of 'lack' is crucial to narrative in another context. According to the Russian Formalist Tzvetan Todorov, the aim of all narratives is to solve a riddle, to find an answer to an enigma, to fill a lack. All stories begin with a situation in which the status quo is upset and the hero or heroine must—in general terms—solve a problem in order for equilibrium to be restored. This approach sees the structures of narrative as being in the service of the subject's desire to overcome lack.

Furthermore, the processes of disavowal and fetishism which mark the Oedipal crisis are—according to Metz—also replayed in the cinema. In terms of disavowal, the spectator both believes in the existence of what was represented on the screen yet also knows that it does not actually exist. Conscious that the cinema only signifies what is absent, the (male) spectator is aware that his sense of identification with the image is only an illusion and that his sense of self is based on lack. Knowing full well that the original events, the profilmic diegetic drama, is missing, the spectator makes up for this absence by fetishizing his love of the cinema itself. Metz sees this structure of disavowal and fetishism as crucial to the cinema's representation of reality.

> **Apparatus theory emphasizes the way the cinema compensates for what the viewing subject lacks; the cinema offers an imaginary unity to smooth over the fragmentation at the heart of subjectivity. Narrative structures take up this process in the way they construct stories in which the 'lost object' (almost always represented by union with a woman) is recovered by the male protagonist.**

Thus, apparatus theory emphasizes the way the cinema compensates for what the viewing subject lacks; the cinema offers an imaginary unity to smooth over the fragmentation at the heart of subjectivity. Narrative structures take up this process in the way they construct stories in which the 'lost object' (almost always represented by union with a woman) is recovered by the male protagonist. In her 1985 essay 'Feminism, Film Theory and the Bachelor Machines', in which she critically assessed apparatus theory as theorized by Baudry and Metz, Constance Penley made the telling point that Metz's 'imaginary signifier' is itself a 'bachelor apparatus'—a compensatory structure designed for male pleasure.

As *The Imaginary Signifier* began to exert a profound influence on film studies in many American and British universities, problems emerged. Critics attacked on a number of fronts: they argued that apparatus theory was profoundly ahistorical; that, in its valorization of the image, it ignored the non-visual aspects of the viewing experience such as sound; and that the application of Lacanian psychoanalytic theory was not always accurate. The most sustained

criticism came from feminist critics, who argued correctly that apparatus theory completely ignored gender.

Psychoanalysis, feminism, and film: Mulvey

Psychoanalytic film theorists, particularly feminists, were interested in the construction of the viewer in relation to questions of gender and sexual desire. Apparatus theory did not address gender at all. In assuming that the spectator was male, Metz examined desire in the context of the male Oedipal trajectory.

In 1975 Laura Mulvey published a daring essay, 'Visual Pleasure and Narrative Cinema', which put female spectatorship on the agenda for all time. As Mulvey later admitted, the essay was deliberately and provocatively polemical. It established the psychoanalytic basis for a feminist theory of spectatorship which is still being debated. What Mulvey did was to redefine, in terms of gender, Metz's account of the cinema as an activity of disavowal and fetishization. Drawing on Freudian theories of scopophilia, castration, and fetishism, and Lacanian theories of the formation of subjectivity, Mulvey introduced gender into apparatus theory.

In her essay, Mulvey argued that in a world ordered by sexual imbalance the role of making things happen usually fell to the male protagonist, while the female star occupied a more passive position, functioning as an erotic object for the desiring look of the male. Woman signified image, a figure to be looked at, while man controlled the look. In other words, cinematic spectatorship is divided along gender lines. The cinema addressed itself to an ideal male spectator, and pleasure in looking was split in terms of an active male gaze and a passive female image.

> **Mulvey argued that in a world ordered by sexual imbalance the role of making things happen usually fell to the male protagonist, while the female star occupied a more passive position, functioning as an erotic object for the desiring look of the male. Woman signified image, a figure to be looked at, while man controlled the look.**

Marlene Dietrich (here admired by Cary Grant) as fetishised spectacle (*Blonde Venus*, 1932)

She argued that, although the form and figure of woman was displayed for the enjoyment of the male protagonist, and, by extension, the male spectator in the cinema, the female form was also threatening because it invoked man's unconscious anxieties about sexual difference and castration. Either the male protagonist could deal with this threat (as in the films of Hitchcock) by subjecting woman to his sadistic gaze and punishing her for being different or he could deny her difference (as in the films of Joseph von Sternberg and Marlene Dietrich) and fetishize her body by overvaluing a part of her body such as her legs or breasts. The narrative endings of films, which almost always punished the threatening woman, reinforced Mulvey's argument about the voyeuristic gaze, while the deployment of the close-up shot, which almost always fragmented parts of the female form for erotic contem-

plation, reinforced Mulvey's argument about the fetishistic look.

Whereas Freudian and Lacanian theory argued that the castration complex was a universal formation that explained the origins and perpetuation of patriarchy, Mulvey demonstrated in specific terms how the unconscious of patriarchal society organized its own signifying practices, such as film, to reinforce myths about women and to offer the male viewer pleasure. Within this system there is no place for woman. Her difference represents—to use what was fast becoming a notorious term—'lack'. However, Mulvey did not hold up this system as universal and unchangeable. If, in order to represent a new language of desire, the filmmaker found it necessary to destroy pleasure, then this was the price that must be paid.

What of the female spectator? In a second article,

'Afterthoughts on "Visual Pleasure and Narrative Cinema" Inspired by King Vidor's *Duel in the Sun* (1946)' (1981), Mulvey took up the issue of the female spectator. Since the classic Hollywood text is so dependent upon the male Oedipal trajectory and male fantasies about woman to generate pleasure, how does the female spectator experience visual pleasure? To answer this question, Mulvey drew on Freud's theory of the libido, in which he asserted that 'there is only one libido, which performs both the masculine and feminine functions' (1981: 13). Thus, when the heroine on the screen is strong, resourceful, and phallic, it is because she has reverted to the pre-Oedipal phase. According to Freud, in the lives of some women, 'there is a repeated alternation between periods in which femininity and masculinity gain the upper hand' (quoted in Mulvey 1971: 15). Mulvey concluded that the female spectator either identifies with woman as object of the narrative and (male) gaze or may adopt a 'masculine' position. But, the female spectator's 'phantasy of masculinisation is always to some extent at cross-purposes with itself, restless in its transvestite clothes' (in Mulvey 1981: 15).

It is this aspect of her work that became most controversial amongst critics, such as D. N. Rodowick (1982), who argued that her approach was too reductive and that her analysis of the female character on the screen and female spectator in the auditorium did not allow for the possibility of female desire outside a phallocentric context.

Developments in psychoanalysis, feminism, and film

Mulvey's use of psychoanalytic theory to examine the way in which the patriarchal unconscious influenced film form led to heated debates and a plethora of articles from post-structuralist feminists. Theorists such as Joan Copjec (1982), Jacqueline Rose (1980), and Constance Penley (1985) argued that apparatus theory, regardless of whether or not it took questions of gender into account, was part of a long tradition in Western thought whereby masculinity is positioned as the norm, thus denying the possibility of a place for woman. They argued that there was no space for the discussion of female spectatorship in apparatus-based theories of the cinema. Responses to Mulvey's theory of spectatorship followed four main lines: one approach was to examine the female Oedipal trajectory; another approach, known as fantasy theory, drew

on Freud's theory of the primal scene to explore the possibility of a fluid, mobile or bisexual gaze; a third concentrated on the representation of masculinity and masochism; and a fourth approach, based on Julia Kristeva's (1986) theory of the 'abject maternal figure' and on Freud's theory of castration, argued that the image of the terrifying, overpowering woman in the horror film and suspense thriller unsettles prior notions of woman as the passive object of a castrating male gaze.

The Oedipal heroine

Drawing on Freud's theory of the libido and the female Oedipal trajectory, feminists extended Mulvey's application of the theory to argue for a bisexual gaze. Perhaps the spectator did not identify in a monolithic, rigid manner with his or her gender counterpart, but actually alternated between masculine–active and feminine–passive positions, depending on the codes of identification at work in the film text.

In a reading of Hitchcock's *Rebecca* (USA, 1940), Tania Modleski (1982) argued that when the daughter goes through the Oedipus complex—although she gives up her original desire for her mother, whom she blames for not giving her a penis, and turns to the father as her love object—she never fully relinquishes her first love. Freud also argued that the girl child, unlike the boy, is predisposed towards bisexuality. The girl's love for the mother, although repressed, still exists. In *Rebecca* the unnamed heroine experiences great difficulty in moulding herself to appeal to the man's desire. When she most imagines she has achieved this aim, the narrative reveals that she is 'still attached to the "mother", still acting out the desire for the mother's approbation' (1982: 38). Recently, the notion of the female Oedipal trajectory has been invoked in a series of articles published in *Screen* (1995) on Jane Campion's *The Piano* (New Zealand, 1993), which suggests that these debates are still of great relevance to film theory.

Other work raised related issues. In *The Desire to Desire* (1987), Mary Ann Doane turned her attention to the 'woman's film' and the issue of female spectatorship. Janet Bergstrom, in 'Enunciation and Sexual Difference' (1979), questioned the premise that the spectator was male, while Annette Kuhn, in *The Power of the Image* (1985), explored cross-dressing, bisexuality, and the spectator in relation to the film *Some Like it Hot* (USA, 1959).

Fantasy theory and the mobile gaze

The concept of a more mobile gaze was explored by Elizabeth Cowie in her article 'Fantasia' (1984), in which she drew on Laplanche and Pontalis's influential essay of 1964, 'Fantasy and the Origins of Sexuality'. Laplanche and Pontalis established three original fantasies—original in that each fantasy explains an aspect of the 'origin' of the subject. The 'primal scene pictures the origin of the individual; fantasies of seduction, the origin and upsurge of sexuality; fantasies of castration, the origin of the difference between the sexes' (1964/1986: 19). These fantasies—entertained by the child—explain or provide answers to three crucial questions: 'Who am I?' 'Why do I desire?' 'Why am I different?' The concept of primal fantasies is also much more fluid than the notion of fantasy permitted by apparatus theory, which inevitably and mechanistically returns to the Oedipal fantasy. The primal fantasies run through the individual's waking and sleeping life, through conscious and unconscious desires. Laplanche and Pontalis also argued that fantasy is a staging of desire, a form of mise-en-scène. Further, the position of the subject is not static in that positions of sexual identification are not fixed. The subject engaged in the activity of fantasizing can adopt multiple positions, identifying across gender, time, and space.

Cowie argued that the importance of fantasy as a setting, a scene, is crucial because it enables film to be viewed as fantasy, as representing the mise-en-scène of desire. Similarly, the film spectator is free to assume mobile, shifting modes of identification—as Cowie demonstrated in her analysis of *Now Voyager* (USA, 1942) and *The Reckless Moment* (USA, 1949). Fantasy theory has also been used productively in relation to science fiction and horror—genres in which evidence of the fantastic is particularly strong.

Masculinity and masochism

Richard Dyer (1982) and Steve Neale (1983) both wrote articles in which they argued against Mulvey's assertion that the male body could not 'bear the burden of sexual objectification' (1975: 28). Both examined the conditions under which the eroticization of the male body is permitted and the conditions under which the female spectator is encouraged to look. Neale explored three main structures examined by Mulvey: identification, voyeurism, and fetishism. He concluded that, while the male body is eroticized and objectified, the viewer is denied a look of direct access. The male is objectified, but only in scenes of action such as boxing. Mainstream cinema cannot afford to acknowledge the possibility that the male spectator might take the male protagonist as an object of his erotic desire.

In her book *In The Realm of Pleasure* (1988), Gaylyn Studlar, however, offers a completely different interpretation of spectatorship and pleasure from the voyeuristic–sadistic model. In a revision of existing feminist psychoanalytic theories, she argues for a (male) masochistic aesthetic in film. Studlar's original study was extremely important as it was one of the first sustained attempts to break with Lacanian and Freudian theory. Instead, Studlar drew on the psychoanalytic-literary work of Gilles Deleuze, and the object-relations school of psychoanalytic theory.

Object-relations theory, derived from the work of Melanie Klein and, more recently, D. W. Winnicott, is a post-Freudian branch of psychoanalysis that places crucial importance on the relationship between the infant and its mother in the first year. Klein placed the mother at the centre of the Oedipal drama and argued for a primary phase in which both sexes identified with the feminine. She argued for womb-envy in boys as a counterpart to Freud's penis-envy in girls. In particular, she explored destructive impulses the infant might experience in its relationship with the mother and other objects (parts of the body) in the environment. During this early formative phase, the father is virtually absent.

Focusing on the pre-Oedipal and the close relationship formed during the oral phase between the infant and the dominant maternal figure, Studlar demonstrates the relevance of her theory in relation to the films of Marlene Dietrich and Joseph von Sternberg. In these Dietrich plays a dominant woman, a beautiful, often cold tyrant, with whom men fall hopelessly and helplessly in love. Titles such as *The Devil is a Woman* (USA, 1935) indicate the kinds of pleasure on offer. Studlar argues that the masochistic aesthetic has so many structures in common with the Baudry–Metz concept of the cinematic apparatus, in its archaic dimension, that it cannot be ignored and constitutes a central form of cinematic pleasure which had been previously overlooked.

Kaja Silverman also developed a theory of male masochism in *Male Subjectivity at the Margins* (1992). Silverman's aim was to explore what she describes as 'deviant' masculinities, which she sees as representing 'perverse' alternatives to phallic masculinity. Drawing on Freudian and Lacanian theory, and concentrating on the films of Rainer Werner Fassbinder, she examined the misleading alignment of the penis with the phallus and the inadequate theorization of male subjectivity in film studies. Silverman explored a number of different forms of male masochism, from passive to active. Her analysis of 'male lack' is particularly powerful, and her book, in which she argued that the spectator can derive pleasure through passivity and submission, made an important contribution to growing debates around psychoanalytic interpretations of spectatorial pleasure.

The monstrous woman

Perhaps it was inevitable, given analyses of the masochistic male, that attention would turn towards the monstrous, castrating woman. Feminist theorists argued that the representation of woman in film does not necessarily position her as a passive object of the narrative or of viewing structures. Mary Russo's essay 'Female Grotesques' (1986), which drew on the Freudian notion of repression, was very influential. So, too, was the Kristevan notion of the abject as a structure which precedes the subject–object split. Drawing on psychoanalytic theories of woman—particularly the mother—as an abject monster, writers such as Modleski (1988), Lurie (1981–2), and Creed (1993) adopted a very different approach to the representation of woman in film, by arguing that woman could be represented as an active, terrifying fury, a powerfully abject figure, and a castrating monster. This was a far cry from Freud's image of woman as 'castrated other'.

Criticisms of psychoanalytic film theory

Psychoanalysis exerted a powerful influence on models of spectatorship theory that emerged during the 1970s and early 1980s. One of the dominant criticisms of the apparatus theory was that, in all of its forms, it invariably constructed a monolithic spectator. In the Baudry model the spectator is male and passive; in the Mulvey model the spectator is male and active. Psychoanalytic criticism was accused of becoming totalizing and repetitive. Film after film was seen as always representing the male character as in control of the gaze, and woman as its object. Or woman was

invariably described as 'without a voice', or as standing outside the Symbolic order.

Rejecting the role of ideology in the formation of subjectivity, some critics were more interested in the actual details of how viewers responded to what they saw on the screen. Given that 1970s theory developed partly in reaction to this kind of empiricism, it is significant that, in recent years, there has been a renewal of interest in the area. This is evident in the work of David Bordwell and Noel Carroll, whose edited volume *Post-Theory* (1996) sets out to challenge the dominance of 1970s theory and to provide alternative approaches to spectatorship based on the use of cognitive psychology. Their interest is the role played by knowledge and viewing practices in relation to spectatorship. According to Carroll, 'Cognitivism is not a unified theory. Its name derives from its tendency to look for alternative answers to many of the questions addressed by or raised by psychoanalytic film theories, especially with respect to film reception, in terms of cognitive and rational processes rather than irrational or unconscious ones' (1996: 62). Judith Mayne argues that, while cognitivists have formulated a number of important criticisms of psychoanalytic film theory, 'the "spectator" envisaged by cognitivism is entirely different from the one conceptualized by 1970s film theory' (1993: 7). The latter addressed itself to the 'ideal spectator' of the cinematic process, while cognitivism speaks to the 'real viewer', the individual in the cinema. Mayne argues that all too often cognitivists, such as Bordwell, ignore the 'attempts that have been made to separate the subject and the viewer' (1993: 56) and recommends the writings of Teresa de Lauretis in *Alice Doesn't* (1984) as 'illustrating that the appeal to perception studies and cognitivism is not necessarily in radical contradistinction from the theories of the apparatus (as in the case with Bordwell and others), but can be instead a revision of them' (1993: 57).

Second, psychoanalytic theory was charged with ahistoricality. As early as 1975 Claire Johnston warned that 'there is a real danger that psychoanalysis can be used to blur any serious engagement with political–cultural issues'. The grand narratives of psychoanalysis, such as the Oedipus complex and castration anxiety, dominated critical activity in the 1970s and early 1980s, running the real danger of sacrificing historical issues in favour of those related to the formation of subjectivity and its relation to ideology. These critics proposed the importance, not of the grand narratives of subjectivity, but of 'micro-narratives' of social change such as those moments when cultural conflict might reveal weaknesses in the dominant culture. They argued that film should be studied more in its relationship to history and society than to the unconscious and subjectivity.

Third, some attacked the centrality of spectatorship theory and its apparently exclusive interest in the ideal spectator rather than the actual viewer. Spectatorship theory did not take into account other factors such as class, colour, race, age, or sexual preference. Nor did it consider the possibility that some viewers might be more resistant to the film's ideological workings than others. Political activists argued that psychoanalytic criticism did not provide any guide-lines on how the individual might resist the workings of an ideology that appeared to dictate completely the formation of subjectivity as split and fractured. Furthermore, they argued, not all individuals are locked into roles determined by the way subjectivity is formed.

Cultural studies has developed partly in response to these problems. It sees culture as a site of struggle. It places emphasis, not on unconscious processes, but on the history of the spectator (as shaped by class, colour, ethnicity, and so on) as well as on examining ways in which the viewer might struggle against the dominant ideology. Whereas the cognitivists have clearly rejected psychoanalysis, the latter's status within cultural studies is not so clear as cultural critics frequently utilize areas of psychoanalytic theory.

Fourth, empirical researchers argue that the major problem with psychoanalysis is that it is not a science, that psychoanalytic theories are not based on reliable data which can be scientifically measured, and that other researchers do not have access to the information pertaining to the case-studies on which the theories have been formulated.

Psychoanalytic theories reply that by its very nature theoretical abstraction cannot be verified by 'proof'. Furthermore, the entire thrust of 1970s psychoanalytic film theory was based on the fact that there is no clear or straightforward relation between the conscious and the unconscious, that what is manifested on the surface may bear no direct relation to what lies beneath, that there is no cause-and-effect relation, which manifests itself in appearance, between what the subject desires to achieve and what takes place in reality. Only via psychoanalytic readings can one explore such things as displacement, disguise, and transformation.

> **The entire thrust of 1970s psychoanalytic film theory was based on the fact that there is no clear or straightforward relation between the conscious and the unconscious, that what is manifested on the surface may bear no direct relation to what lies beneath, that there is no cause-and-effect relation, which manifests itself in appearance, between what the subject desires to achieve and what takes place in reality. Only via psychoanalytic readings can one explore such things as displacement, disguise, and transformation.**

Recent developments

Although psychoanalytic film theory has been subject to many forms of criticism over the past twenty years, it continues to expand both within and outside the academy. This is evident, not only in the work of cultural theorists such as Stuart Hall, but also in the relatively new areas of post-colonialism and queer theory, and in writings on the body. Scholars working in these areas do not use psychoanalytic theory in the totalizing way in which it was invoked in the 1970s. Rather, they draw on aspects of psychoanalytic theory to illuminate areas of their own special study. The aim in doing so is often to bring together the social and the psychic.

Post-colonial theorists such as Homi K. Bhabha and Rey Chow have drawn on psychoanalytic theories in their work. Whereas earlier writers on racism in the cinema tended to concentrate on questions of stereotyping, narrative credibility, and positive images, the focus of post-colonial theorists is on the process of subjectification, the representation of 'otherness', spectatorship, and the deployment of cinematic codes. In short, the shift is away from a study of 'flawed' or 'negative' images ('positive' images can be as demeaning as negative ones) to an understanding of the filmic construction of the relationship between colonizer and colonized, the flow of power between the two, the part played by gender differences and the positioning of the spectator in relation to such representations. In order to facilitate such analyses, theorists frequently draw on aspects of psychoanalytic theory.

In 'The Other Question', Homi K. Bhabha uses Freud's theory of castration and fetishism to analyse the stereotypes of black and white which are crucial to the colonial discourse. He argues that the fetishized stereotype in film and other cultural practices works to reactivate in the colonial subject the imaginary fantasy of 'an ideal ego that is white and whole' (1992: 322). Drawing on these concepts, he presents a new interpretation of Orson Welles's *A Touch of Evil* (USA, 1958). In his writings on the nation, Bhabha draws on Freud's 1919 essay 'The Uncanny', in which Freud refers to the 'cultural' unconscious as a state in which archaic forms find expression in the margins of modernity. Bhabha also uses Freud's theory of doubling, as elaborated in 'The Uncanny', to examine the way in which colonial cultures have been coerced by their colonizers to mimic 'white' culture—but only up to a point. Difference—and hence oppression—must always be maintained. Throughout his writings, Bhabha uses many of Freud's key theories, reinterpreting them in order to theorize the colonial discourse.

This approach has been adopted by other critics. In *Romance and the 'Yellow Peril'* (1993), Gina Marchetti focuses on Hollywood films about Asians and interracial sexuality. Adopting a position informed by postcolonial theory, Marchetti draws on psychoanalytic theories of spectatorship and feminine masquerade, refiguring these concepts for her own work on race.

In a similar vein, film critics, drawing on queer reading strategies, have carefully selected aspects of psychoanalytic theory to analyse film texts 'against the grain'. As in post-colonial theory, queer theory represents a methodological shift. It, too, rejects an earlier critical emphasis on praising 'positive' and decrying 'negative' images of homosexual men and lesbians in film. Instead, queer theory sees sexual practices—whether heterosexual, homosexual, bisexual, autosexual, transsexual—as fluid, diverse, and heterogeneous. For instance, the practices of masochism, sadism, or coprophilia may be adopted by homosexual and heterosexual alike: the belief that only heterosexual relationships (or any other type of relationship, for that matter) are somehow 'normal' is patently incorrect.

As a critical practice, queer theory seeks to analyse film texts in order to determine the way in which desire, in its many diverse forms, is constructed, and how cinematic pleasures are instituted and offered to the spectator. Previously reviled films such as *The Killing of Sister George* (GB, 1968), have been re-examined, and the history of the representation of gays and lesbians in film is being rewritten. In some films the homosexual and/or lesbian subtext, previously ignored, has been reinscribed.

Judith Butler's *Gender Trouble* (1990), which presents a queer critique of the psychoanalytic concept of fixed gender identities, has exerted a strong influence on film theorists seeking to analyse the representation of gays and lesbians in film. Wary of the 1970s approach to psychoanalytic theory, because it largely ignored the question of the gay and lesbian spectatorship, film theorists have turned to the work of writers such as Butler, Diane Fuss, Teresa de Lauretis, and Lee Edelman (see Smelik and Doty, Chapters 14 and 15).

A number of essays in *How do I Look? Queer Film and Video* (Bad Object-Choices 1991) discuss the fact that psychoanalytic approaches to the cinema have avoided discussions of lesbian sexual desire. In her article 'Lesbian Looks' Judith Mayne criticizes the way in which feminist film theory has employed psychoanalysis while also drawing on, and reinterpreting, aspects of psychoanalytic theory in her own analysis. Valerie Traub's article 'The Ambiguities of "Lesbian" Viewing Pleasure' (1991), on lesbian spectatorship and the film *Black Widow* (USA, 1987), provides a good example of a queer reading.

Another area in which film theorists have drawn on a rereading of psychoanalytic theory is that of the body. Contemporary interpretations of the horror film have generally favoured a psychoanalytic reading with emphasis on the workings of repression. Since the mid-1980s writers have paid particular attention to the representation of the body in horror—the grotesque body of the monster. Based on psychoanalytic theories of abjection, hysteria, castration, and the uncanny, such an approach sees the monstrous body as intended partly to horrify the spectator and partly to make meaning at a more general level, pointing to the abject state of the social, political, and familial body.

Other approaches to the body take up the issue of the actual body as well as the cinematic body. Steven Shaviro's *The Cinematic Body* (1993) presents a thorough attack on apparatus theory, arguing instead for 'an active and affirmative reading of the masochism of cinematic experience' (1993: 60). Drawing on the early work of Gilles Deleuze, he suggests that what 'inspires the cinematic spectator is a passion for that very loss of control, that abjection, fragmentation and subversion of self-identity that psychoanalytic theory so dubiously classifies under the rubrics of lack and castration' (1993: 57). Shaviro is highly critical of what he sees as the conventional use of psychoanalysis to construct a distance between spectator and image; he wants to use psychoanalysis to affirm and celebrate the power of the image, and of the visceral, to move and affect the viewer.

I have referred briefly to aspects of post-colonial, queer, and body theory to demonstrate that film theory, in its current use of psychoanalysis, has become more selective and nuanced. While no one would suggest a return to the totalizing approach of the 1970s, it would be misleading to argue that application of psychoanalysis to the cinema is a thing of the past. If anything, the interest in psychoanalytic film theory is as strong as ever. And the debates continue.

BIBLIOGRAPHY

Bad Object-Choices (ed.) (1991), *How do I Look? Queer Film and Video* (Seattle: Bay Press).

*****Baudry, Jean-Louis** (1970/1986*a*), 'Ideological Effects of the Basic Cinematographic Apparatus', in P. Rosen (ed.), *Narrative, Apparatus, Ideology* (New York: Columbia University Press).

—— (1975/1986*b*), 'The Apparatus: Metaphysical Approaches to Ideology', in P. Rosen (ed.), *Narrative, Apparatus, Ideology,* (New York: Columbia University Press).

Benderson, Albert (1979), 'An Archetypal Reading of *Juliet of the Spirits*', *Quarterly Review of Film Studies,* 4/2: 193–206.

Bergstrom, Janet (1979), 'Enunciation and Sexual Difference', *Camera Obscura,* 3–4: 33–70.

Bhabha, Homi K. (1992), 'The Other Question: The Stereotype and the Colonial Discourse', in *The Sexual Subject: A Screen Reader in Sexuality* (London: Routledge).

Bordwell, David, and **Noel Caroll** (eds.) (1996), *Post-Theory: Reconstructing Film Studies* (Wisconsin: University of Wisconsin Press).

Branson, Clark (1987), *Howard Hawks: A Jungian Study* (Santa Barbara, Calif.: Capra Press).

Brown, Royal S. (1980), 'Hitchcock's *Spellbound*: Jung versus Freud', *Film/Psychology Review,* 4/1: 35–58.

Butler, Judith (1990), *Gender Trouble: Feminism and the Subversion of Identity* (New York: Routledge).

Copjec, Joan (1982), 'The Anxiety of the Influencing Machine', *October,* 23.

Cowie, Elizabeth (1984), 'Fantasia', *m/f,* 9: 71–105.

Creed, Barbara (1993), *The Monstrous-Feminine: Film, Feminism and Psychoanalysis* (New York: Routledge).

de Lauretis, Teresa (1984), *Alice Doesn't: Feminism, Semiotics, Cinema* (Bloomington: Indiana University Press).

Doane, Mary Ann (1987), *The Desire to Desire: The Woman's Film of the 1940s* (Bloomington: Indiana University Press).

Donald, James (ed.) (1990), *Psychoanalysis and Cultural Theory: Thresholds* (London: Macmillan).

Dyer, Richard (1982), 'Don't Look Now: The Male Pin-Up', *Screen,* 23/3–4: 61–73.

Foster, Hal (1993), *Compulsive Beauty* (London: MIT Press).

Fredericksen, Don (1980), 'Jung/Sign/Symbol/Film', *Quarterly Review of Film Studies,* 5/4: 459–79.

Freud, Sigmund (1919/1953–66), 'The Uncanny', in *The Standard Edition of the Complete Psychological Works of Sigmund Freud,* 24 vols., trans. James Strachey (London: Hogarth), xxi.

Izod, John (1992), *The Films of Nicholas Roeg: Myth and Mind* (London: St Martin's Press).

Johnston, C. (1975), 'Femininity and Masquerade: *Anne of the Indies*', in Claire Johnston and Paul Willemen (eds.), *Jacques Tourneur* (Edinburgh: Edinburgh Film Festival).

Kaplan, E. Ann (ed.) (1978), *Women in Film Noir* (London: British Film Institute).

*—— (ed.) (1990), *Psychoanalysis and the Cinema* (New York: Routledge).

Kristeva, Julia (1986), *Powers of Horror: An Essay in Abjection,* trans. Leon S. Roudiez (New York: Columbia University Press).

Kuhn, Annette (1985), *The Power of the Image: Essays on Representation and Sexuality* (London: Routledge & Kegan Paul).

Laplanche, J., and **J.-B. Pontalis** (1964/1986), 'Fantasy and the Origins of Sexuality', in Victor Burgin, James Donald, and Cora Kaplan (eds.), *Formations of Fantasy* (London: Methuen).

Lebeau, Vicky (1995), *Lost Angels: Psychoanalysis and the Cinema* (New York: Routledge).

Lurie, Susan (1981–2), 'The Construction of the "Castrated Woman" in Psychoanalysis and Cinema', *Discourse,* 4: 52–74.

Marchetti, Gina (1993), *Romance and the 'Yellow Peril': Race, Sex and Discursive Strategies in Hollywood Fiction* (Berkeley and Los Angeles: University of California Press).

Mayne, Judith (1991), 'Lesbian Looks: Dorothy Arzner and Female Authorship', in Bad Object-Choices (1991).

—— (1993), *Cinema and Spectatorship* (London: Routledge).

*****Metz, Christian** (1975/1982), *Psychoanalysis and Cinema: The Imaginary Signifier* (London: Macmillan).

Modleski, Tania (1982), 'Never to be Thirty-Six Years Old', *Wide Angle,* 5/1: 34–41.

Modelski, Tania (1988), *The Women who Knew too Much: Hitchcock and Feminist Theory* (New York: Methuen).

*Mulvey, Laura (1975), 'Visual Pleasure and Narrative Cinema', *Screen*, 16/3: 6–18.

—— (1981), 'Afterthoughts on "Visual Pleasure and Narrative Cinema" inspired by *Duel in the Sun*', *Framework*, 15–17: 12–15.

Neale, Steve (1983), 'Masculinity as Spectacle', *Screen*, 24/6: 2–16.

Penley, Constance (1985), 'Feminism, Film Theory and the Bachelor Machines', *m/f*, 10: 39–59.

Rank, Otto (1925/1971), *The Double: A Psychoanalytic Study* (Chapel Hill: University of North Carolina Press).

Rodowick, D. N. (1982), 'The Difficulty of Difference', *Wide Angle*, 5/1: 4–15.

—— (1988), *The Crisis of Political Modernism: Criticism and Ideology on Contemporary Film Theory* (Berkeley: University of California Press).

Rose, Jacqueline (1980), 'The Cinematic Apparatus: Problems in Current Theory', in Teresa de Lauretis and Stephen Heath (eds.), *The Cinematic Apparatus* (New York: St Martin's Press).

Russo, Mary (1986), 'Female Grotesques: Carnival and Theory', in Teresa de Lauretis (ed.), *Feminist Studies/Critical Studies* (Bloomington: Indiana University Press).

Screen (1995), 36/3: 257–87. Articles on *The Piano*.

Shaviro, Steven (1993), *The Cinematic Body* (Minneapolis: University of Minnesota Press).

Silverman, Kaja (1981), 'Masochism and Subjectivity', *Framework*, 12: 2–9.

—— (1992), *Male Subjectivity at the Margins* (New York: Routledge).

Sobchack, Vivian (1992), *The Address of the Eye: A Phenomenology of Film Experience* (Princeton: Princeton University Press).

Studlar, Gaylyn (1988), *In the Realm of Pleasure: Von Sternberg, Dietrich, and the Masochistic Aesthetic* (Urbana: University of Illinois Press).

Tarratt, Margaret (1970), 'Monsters from the Id', part 1, *Films and Filming* (Nov.–Dec.), 38–42.

—— (1971), 'Monsters from the Id', part 2, *Films and Filming* (Jan.–Feb), 40–2.

Traub, Valerie (1991), 'The Ambiguities of "Lesbian" Viewing Pleasure: The (Dis)articulations of *Black Widow*', in Julia Epstein and Kristina Straub (eds.), *BodyGuards: The Cultural Politics of Gender Ambiguity* (New York: Routledge).

Williams, Linda (ed.) (1995), *Viewing Positions: Ways of Seeing Film* (New Brunswick, NJ: Rutgers University Press).

10 Post-structuralism and deconstruction

Peter Brunette

Post-structuralism is a rather vague generic name for a host of disparate theoretical developments that have followed in the wake of structuralism and semiotics. The term has been applied occasionally to the work of Michel Foucault and the later Roland Barthes, but most especially to the challenging and innovative revision of Freud propounded by the French psychoanalyst Jacques Lacan, and to the work of Jacques Derrida, a kind of 'anti-philosophy' that has come to be known as deconstruction. Since the Guide contains a separate article (by Barbara Creed, Part 1, Chapter 9) detailing the crucial influence of Lacanian psychoanalysis on film studies, this chapter will concentrate on the application of Derridean thought to the cinema.

Deconstruction is not a discipline or, even less, a methodology, but rather a questioning stance taken towards the most basic aspects of the production of knowledge. Like Lacanian psychoanalysis, it tends to concentrate on the slippages in meaning, the gaps and inconsistencies, that inevitably mark all understanding.

If the mission and focus of film studies is seen as the formal and thematic interpretation of individual films, deconstruction has little to offer. Deconstruction is not a discipline or, even less, a methodology, but rather a questioning stance taken towards the most basic aspects of the production of knowledge. Like Lacanian psychoanalysis, it tends to concentrate on the slippages in meaning, the gaps and inconsistencies, that inevitably mark all understanding. As such, deconstruction has been seen by its critics as part of the 'hermeneutics of suspicion' that has developed out of the anti-foundationalist investigations of Freud and Nietzsche.

The specific application of deconstruction to film has been far less evident than that of Lacanian psychoanalysis, but Derrida's influence on such thinkers as (to name but two) Judith Butler, a gender theorist, and Homi Bhabha, a specialist in post-colonial studies, has been profound. These theorists have in turn had a tremendous impact on recent writing on film, and thus, in this sense, it is probably correct to say that the application of Derridean thought to film has been important but largely indirect. A further complication is that some on the left have denounced deconstruction because it tends to call *all* thinking into question, even that which presents itself as progressive and liberatory. In fact, Derrida's writings can be seen as thoroughly political in nature when they are properly understood as a critique of the outmoded 'logocentric' thinking that has led to numerous political impasses now and in the past.

Nevertheless, several key deconstructive notions have been applied directly to film by a number of theorists in France and elsewhere. For example, a deconstructive perspective can challenge the historiographical assumptions that allow us conveniently to divide film history into specific, self-identical movements such as German Expressionism, Italian Neo-Realism, and so on. The notion of film genre as well is vulnerable to a deconstructive analysis, as is auteurism, and authorial intentionality, already much challenged anyway. Most importantly, perhaps, deconstruction challenges the very basis of interpretation itself, revealing the institutional and contextual constraints that necessarily accompany all attempts at reading.

Deconstruction can be approached from any number of different directions, but perhaps it can be most easily seen as a radicalization of the basic insights, developed around the turn of the century, of Swiss linguist Ferdinand de Saussure. Saussure, considered the father of structuralism and semiotics, argued that there are 'no positive terms' in language; in other words, that meanings do not stem from something inherent in the words and sounds themselves, but rather from their *difference* from other words and sounds. Thus, all alone, the sound 'p' could never be functional, nor could the word 'truth' carry any meaning, but only in so far as they differed from 't' or 'r' or 's' on the one hand, or 'error', say, on the other. If this is the case, it becomes clear that 'error' is, in some strange way that defies traditional Western logic (which, Derrida claims, is based upon a 'metaphysics of presence'), part and parcel of the meaning of its supposed opposite, truth. Paradoxically, in other words, truth cannot be thought, and thus cannot even exist, without error. Error is thus both there and not there 'within' truth, both present and absent, thus casting doubt upon the principle of non-contradiction (the very basis of Western logic), that a thing cannot be A and not-A at the same time.

It can easily be seen that Western thought has, since the beginning, relied upon a set of self-identical concepts that align themselves as binary oppositions, such as truth–error, good–evil, spirit–body, nature–culture, man–woman, and so on. In each case, one term is favoured or seen as primary or original; the second term is regarded as a (later) perversion of the first, or in some way inferior to it. The principal work of decon-

struction has been to reverse and—since a mere reversal would not disturb the underlying binary logic—to displace these ostensible oppositions as well.

Since deconstruction builds upon the insights and terminology of semiotics, one of the first binary oppositions that is called into question is that founding distinction between signifier and signified. From a post-structuralist perspective, it is easy to see the latter as a transcendent, almost spiritual entity that is privileged over the 'merely' material signifier, which is usually seen as a dispensable container with no effect on the contained. Derridean thought tends rather to focus on the 'free play' between signifier and signified that constitutes all meaning, and to show that the marks of the material signifier never really disappear in the face of the signified.

> **Derridean thought tends rather to focus on the 'free play' between signifier and signified that constitutes all meaning, and to show that the marks of the material signifier never really disappear in the face of the signified.**

Furthermore, deconstruction, like Lacanian psychoanalysis, points out that meaning effects occur as a result of the sliding within chains of signifiers, rather than because a signifier leads inevitably to a signified. After all, when one looks up a word in the dictionary, what is found is not a fixed signified, but rather more signifiers, which must be looked up in turn. Despite this similarity in viewpoint, Derrida has criticized Lacan for the impermissible originary grounding that he seems to offer in his founding triad of the Imaginary, the Symbolic, and the Real. (For deconstructionists, there can be no fixed ground or origin, since such concepts, once again, are symptoms of the metaphysics of presence.) For the same reason, deconstructive theorists have also tended to agree with the feminist critique of Lacanian film theory concerning its privileging of the phallus as the primary signifier from which all meaning arises.

In his early work, especially in *Of Grammatology* (1967), Derrida concentrates on deconstructing the symptomatic binary opposition that privileges, throughout the history of Western philosophy, speech over writing. In this book, Derrida shows that as far back as Plato and as recently as Saussure and Claude Lévi-Strauss, speech has been associated with the living breath and the speaker's 'true' meaning, guaranteed by her presence, whereas writing has been seen as dead, misleading, always the sign of an absence. This is largely the result of the curious biological fact that when we speak (and listen), meaning seems to be an unproblematic, 'natural' event with no intermediary. Signifier and signified merge effortlessly, whereas in writing their relationshiop is always more problematic. Naïvely we seem to feel that if we could only have a writer speaking to us in person, in other words, *present*, we would know exactly what she meant. Derrida shows in this book that the supposed immediacy and direct-ness of speech is a fiction, and that all the negative features associated with writing are characteristic of speech as well. In a familiar move, he reverses the hierarchy, putting writing before speech, and then dis-places the hierarchy altogether by rewriting the term 'writing', as 'Writing', with an expanded, purposely contradictory meaning that encompasses *both* writing (in the conventional sense) and speech. As such, the term joins a host of other key terms that Derrida has developed over the last thirty years, including trace, hinge, hymen, supplement, and *différance* (he purpo-sely misspells this French word to highlight its differ-ence from itself, a difference that is reflected in writing but not in speech)—terms which attempt to name an impossible 'space', to express presence and absence simultaneously, without, however, becoming a new ground. In a (to some extent quixotic) attempt to circumvent the metaphysics of presence, Derrida declares that these terms are neither 'words nor con-cepts'.

This newly expanded sense of Writing can be easily applied to film, since, after all, the word cinematogra-*phy* clearly points to its 'written' nature. Like written words, whose meanings, according to Derrida, are always 'disseminated' in multiple directions rather than being strictly linear, the image can never be con-strained to a single set of meanings. In fact, meanings that are located/constructed will inevitably be contra-dictory. Nor can authorial intentionality, already notor-iously weak in film, be said to anchor meaning, for intention will always be divided, never a unity. In fact, film itself is fundamentally split between a visual track and an audio track, which actually occupy different physical locations on the strip of celluloid, but which are artificially brought together to achieve an effect of wholeness and presence. In all these senses, it can be

said that the image is thus fundamentally 'incoherent', since any attempt to make it cohere will always neces-sitate a more or less violent epistemological effort of repression of 'secondary' meanings.

Thinking of film as a kind of writing also comple-ments the anti-realist bias of recent film theory, for it works against the idea that film can ever be a 'copy' of its referent. André Bazin and other realist theorists insisted upon the intrinsic relationship or similarity between reality and its filmic representation, but from a deconstructive perspective, once it is admitted that reality and its representation must always be *different* from each other (as well as similar), then difference has just as much a claim as similarity to being the 'essential' relation between the two.

More generally, deconstructive thinking can lead us away from a conventional idea of cinema, and its rela-tion to reality, as an *analogical* one based on similarity, to an idea of cinema, as Brunette and Wills (1989: 88) have put it, as 'an *anagram* of the real', a place of writing filled with non-natural conventions that allow us to understand it as a representation of reality.

Broadly speaking, cinema itself is, as a medium, clearly produced through negation, contradiction, and absence. It depends for its effect on the absence of what it represents, which is also paradoxically pre-sent at the same time in the form of a 'trace' (which in the original French also means 'footprint', thus carrying the simultaneous sense of absence and presence). Similarly, the photographic process is based on a nega-tion which is reversed in a positive print. And through the application of the (now partially discredited) notion of the persistence of vision, we can understand that we literally could not even *see* the cinematic image unless it were, through the operation of the shutter, just as often *not* there. (One film theorist has pointed out that the screen is completely dark about half the time we are watching a film.) The screen itself, as a material of support of the image, must also be there and not there at the same time, for if we can actually see it, we can see nothing else.

Deconstruction also calls into question the 'natural' relation between original and copy (for example, we never speak of an 'original' of a document, unless there is also a 'copy' in question; thus, in a sense, the copy can be said to create the original), and this has a pro-found effect on a mimetic or imitative theory of artistic representation. It is clear, for example, that a documen-tary, though it ostensibly 'copies' the reality it focuses upon, also helps to individuate that aspect of reality, to bring it specifically to our attention, and thus to 'create' it.

This is closely related to another idea that Derrida has explored at great length, the notion of iterability (repeatability). Here, he has pointed out that each repetition of the 'same' must, by definition, also be different (otherwise, it could not be individuated). Similarly, each time something is quoted, it has a different meaning depending on its context, something that Derrida has shown is never fully specifiable. Here the idea of the 'graft', which is closely related to Roland Barthes's notion of intertextuality, is also important. All texts are seen as being made up of innumerable grafts of other texts in ways that are never ultimately traceable. For example, when we see an actor in a film, our response is inevitably conditioned by his or her appearances in other films; yet in a conventional, logocentric form of criticism such meanings would not be considered part of the film, properly speaking, and thus 'improper'.

This leads to another crucial binary distinction that deconstruction challenges, that between the inside and the outside. During the heyday of formalist literary analysis, Marxist and Freudian critics were chastised for 'importing' discourses that were seen as 'extrinsic' into a poem or novel. In regard to film, we might ask, for example, whether the opening or closing credits are 'in' the film, thus a part of it, or 'outside' the film proper, external to it. (Is a book's preface—usually written last—part of the book proper or not?) Similarly, one wonders whether Alfred Hitchcock's famous cameo appearances in his films mean that he is a character in them. Our inability to answer these questions points precisely to a problem in the logic of inside–outside binary thinking itself.

The larger question here, one that is explored at great length in Derrida's book *The Truth in Painting* (1978), is the question of the *frame*. In Derrida's famous formulation in that book, 'there is framing, but the frame does not exist' (1978/1987 81; translation modified). This means that the location of the frame (both a physical frame, say, of a painting, or an interpretive frame or context, or any sort of boundary marker) can never be precisely determined, though its effects can be seen. In film, the cut is similarly a function with clear effects, but no physical existence. Because it is a kind of relational absence rather than an explicitly present entity, it too serves to call into question the metaphysics of presence. With this ambiguity in mind, some deconstructive film theorists have suggested that, in

fact, it makes as much sense to base a film aesthetics on the cut (absence) as on the individual image (presence).

In any case, this idea of the frame is obviously paramount in film as well, and, though focused in a somewhat different manner, just as ambiguous. What is curious about this word in its cinematic usage is that it means two opposite things at the same time (and thus can be added to Derrida's list of key words): it is both the 'outside' boundary (one speaks of the 'frameline'), and the entire *inside* of the image as well (Godard said that cinema is 'truth twenty-four frames per second'). More widely, the film frame can also be seen as that set of understandings of genre, or of the so-called 'real world', or of cinematic conventions, and so on, that we bring to a film—in other words, that *context*, ever changeable, that both allows and constrains meaning.

This frame, this image that is framed, can, furthermore, be seen both as heterogenous (think of how many discrete elements within it must be repressed in order to 'interpret' it) and graphic (again, in the sense that it is *written*), as well as pictorial. Much of Derrida's later work has been involved with exploring the pictorial nature of writing (in the conventional sense) and, conversely, the graphic nature of the image, and these investigations are directly applicable to a study of how meaning is created in film. (See especially *The Truth in Painting* and Ulmer 1985, 1989).

The most important work done thus far in relating Derrida and film has been that undertaken by the French theoretician Marie-Claire Ropars-Wuilleumier, notably in her book *Le Texte divisé* (1981). There, *inter alia*, she brilliantly compares Derrida's discussion of the hybrid form of the hieroglyph (which is made up of phonetic, that is, graphic marks that represent speech, as well as pictorial elements) with Eisenstein's development of montage theory. In both, meaning is seen as a complicated operation that comes about partially through representation, but also through the very disruption of the image itself in the form of juxtaposition. (For a provocative application of Derrida to television, see Dienst 1994.)

Perhaps the most far-reaching consequence of a deconstructive perspective on film concerns the act of interpretation. Ultimately, deconstruction shows that it is, strictly speaking, impossible to specify what a 'valid' interpretation would look like. (See Conley 1991 for the most adventurous application of this principle to the interpretation of individual films.) In this sense, it might be said that deconstruction's most important work has been the investigation of the institutions that both allow and restrict reading, or meaning-making of any sort. It is important to note, however, that Derrida himself is no propounder of an 'anything goes' theory of reading, despite the impression given by his detractors and some of his more enthusiastic followers. Instead, he has always insisted upon the double nature of his work: to push beyond the bounds of conventional logic, all the while remaining rigorously logical.

> It might be said that deconstruction's most important work has been the investigation of the institutions that both allow and restrict reading, or meaning-making of any sort.

As film studies evolves more fully into cultural studies, deconstruction will provide a corrective by revealing the ultimately metaphoric nature of much of the terminology that surrounds the relating of cultural artefacts to an economic or social 'base'. As such, its influence will continue to be powerful, if subterranean.

BIBLIOGRAPHY

*Brunette, Peter, and David Wills (1989), *Screen/Play: Derrida and Film Theory* (Princeton: Princeton University Press).

Conley, Tom (1991), *Film Hieroglyphs: Ruptures in Classical Cinema* (Minneapolis: University of Minnesota Press).

Derrida, Jacques (1967/1976), *Of Grammatology*, trans. Gayatri Spivak (Baltimore: Johns Hopkins University Press).

—— (1978/1987), *The Truth in Painting*, trans. Geoff Bennington and Ian McLeod (Chicago: University of Chicago Press).

Dienst, Richard (1994), *Still Life in Real Time: Theory after Television* (Durham, NC: Duke University Press).

Ropars-Wuilleumier, Marie-Claire (1981), *Le Texte divisé* (Paris: Presses Universitaires de France).

Ulmer, Gregory (1985), *Applied Grammatology* (Baltimore: Johns Hopkins University Press).

—— (1989), *Teletheory: Grammatology in the Age of Video* (London: Routledge).

11

Film and postmodernism

John Hill

The concept of 'postmodernism' is a notoriously problematic one, given the diverse ways (in both academia and popular discourse) in which it has been used. The term itself has been applied to an almost bewilderingly wide range of economic, social, and cultural phenomena, with the result that many commentators on postmodernism are not necessarily referring to, or focusing upon, the same things. Moreover, the epithet 'postmodern' is used not only to identify particular socio-cultural and aesthetic features of contemporary life, but also to designate new forms of theorization which are held to be appropriate to making sense of the new 'postmodern' condition. So, while postmodern theory and the analysis of postmodernism may go hand in hand, it is not necessary that they do so. Fredric Jameson, for example, is one of the most influential analysts of postmodernism; but he himself is not a postmodern theorist, given his commitment to conventional forms of social analysis and explanation (especially Marxism).

It is also fair to say that in relation to film, postmodernism has not led to a theoretical approach or body of critical writings in the way that other theoretical perspectives, such as psychoanalysis of feminism, may be seen to have. This is because it is in the character of postmodernism to be suspicious of unified theoretical frameworks and, if postmodern ideas have had an influence on film study, it has often been through unsettling the knowledge claims or ontological assumptions of earlier theory (as in the theory of 'the subject' which has underpinned much psychoanalytic and feminist film theory). Moreover, the interest in postmodernism as an object of study has often been directed towards cultural shifts which go beyond a narrow attention to film, and if film has commonly been linked with the experience of modernity, then it is generally television, rather than film, which is seen to embody the postmodern.

In order to locate some of the ways in which ideas about the postmodern have influenced the study of film, it is therefore helpful to distinguish three main strands of thinking about postmodernism. Hence, the term can be seen to have been used in philosophical debates concerned with the scope and groundings of knowledge; in socio-cultural debates concerned to assess the significance of economic and social shifts in contemporary life; and in aesthetic debates concerned with the changing character of artistic practices in the wake of the 'decline' of modernism. These three sets of debates are not, of course, unconnected, but they are sufficiently distinct to make it useful to consider them separately.

Philosophical debates

In philosophy, debates about postmodernism may be seen to demonstrate a growing suspicion towards 'universal' or all-embracing systems of thought and explanation. An influential source, in this respect, has been Jean-François Lyotard's *The Postmodern Condition* (1979). For Lyotard 'the postmodern condition' may be defined in terms of a growing 'incredulity' towards what he calls 'les grands récits' or 'metanarratives' of Western thought (1979/1984, p. xxiv). In this respect, the 'modern' which the 'postmodern' is seen to be superseding is not the artistic modernism of the late nineteenth and early twentieth century but the 'modern' system of thought associated with the Enlightenment (and philosophers such as Voltaire, Locke, and Hume) and its association with a project of 'scientific' explanation and mastery of the natural and social world. For Lyotard, the idea of progress characteristic of Enlightenment thought is no longer tenable, and he argues that it is now impossible to believe in either the progressive advancement of thought—the emancipation of reason—or the social and political emancipation to which it was once believed such reason might contribute. 'What kind of thought', Lyotard asks, 'is able to sublate Auschwitz in a general . . . process towards a universal emancipation?' (1986: 6).

Lyotard's work, in this respect, may be linked to more general strains of post-structuralist thinking and to share with them a number of features. In general terms, these may be seen to include a suspicion of totalizing theories and explanations which attempt to offer comprehensive and all-embracing accounts of social and cultural phenomena; an anti-foundationalism that rejects claims to 'absolute' or 'universal' foundations for knowledge; a rejection of the 'false universalism' of ethnocentric or Eurocentric systems of thought; and an anti-essentialism that rejects both 'depth' epistemologies which seek to lay bare 'hidden' or 'essential' realities as well as ideas of a fixed notion of identity or human 'essence'. In this last respect, a critique of Enlightenment reason is likened to a critique of the unified self which was assumed to underpin it and provide it with its foundations. Thus Stuart Hall draws a distinction between 'the Enlightenment subject', which is based upon 'a conception of the human person as a fully centred, unified individual, endowed with the capacities of reason, consciousness and action', and 'the postmodern subject', which is conceptualized as having 'no fixed, essential or permanent identity' but rather as assuming 'different identities at different times' (Hall 1992: 277).

Postmodern theory, in this regard, lays stress on the heterogeneity and fragmented character of social and cultural 'realities' and identities as well as the impossibility of any unified, or comprehensive, account of them. As such, postmodernism is often seen as, and criticized for, embracing both a relativism which accepts the impossibility of adjudicating amongst different accounts of, or knowledge claims about, reality and an 'idealism' or 'conventionalism' which accepts the impossibility of gaining access to 'reality' other than via the 'discourses' through which 'realities' are constructed. Moreover, it has also been a tendency of many postmodern arguments apparently to belie their own precepts and 'universalize' their claims concerning the 'postmodern condition' or erect precisely the 'grand narratives' of the transition from 'modernity' to 'postmodernity' which it is otherwise argued are no longer possible. As Gregor McLennan suggests, 'the progressive decline of the grand narratives' is itself 'an alternative grand narrative' (1989: 177). In this respect, it may be helpful to distinguish the scepticism towards grand theory which is a feature of postmodern philosophy from the more substantive sociological and cultural claims which have been made concerning the character of postmodernity and postmodern culture, even though these are often interlinked (as in Lyotard's work, which is both an investigation into the status of knowledge in post-industrial society and a polemic against totalizing theory).

Socio-cultural debates

Thus, in sociological debates, postmodernism has been used to identify the emergence of what is often believed to be a new economic and social order. This is sometimes linked to the idea of 'post-industrialism' (Rose 1991) and designated as either 'postmodernity' (Lyon 1994) or 'postmodernization' (Crook *et al.* 1992). 'Postmodernism' (or 'postmodernity') is, in this respect, seen to be following a period of 'modernity'. However, this is a term which is itself disputed and whose periodization is not always agreed. Thus, while 'modernity' may be seen to have emerged with the break with 'tradition' (and feudalism) represented by the advent of capitalism in the fifteenth and sixteenth centuries, it is more commonly identified with the economic and social changes characteristic of the nineteenth and early twentieth centuries, and especially those ushered in by industrialization, urbanization, and the emergence of mass social movements. Accordingly, the main features of the emerging 'postmodern' social order are usually identified in terms of a transition from an old industrial order to a new 'post-industrial' one which is, in turn, characterized by a number of features: a decline in manufacturing and the increased importance of service industries (be they business and financial or heritage and tourism); the replacement of old models of standardized, or 'Fordist', mass production by new flexible and geographically mobile forms of 'post-Fordist' production involving batch production and the targeting of specific consumer groups, or market segments; a decline in the traditional working class and the growth of white-collar workers and a 'service class' (whose attitudes and tastes, some accounts claim, postmodernist culture expresses); and therefore a diminution of the significance of class identities and divisions and an increased importance of other forms of social identity such as those related to age, gender, sexual orientation, ethnicity, and region. In this respect, the shift away from the politics of mass movements towards a 'politics of difference' may be seen to link with postmodern arguments concerning the increasing contingency and fluidity of social identities in the contemporary era.

Such shifts are also identified with the growing importance (and convergence) of the new computing and communications technologies to the changing economic and social order. Media output and information services not only provide a major 'force of production' of the 'post-industrial' economy, but also increasingly exemplify 'post-Fordist' economic practices (Lash and Urry 1994). Even more importantly, the media and the new technologies are seen to be significantly reshaping social experience and subjectivity. Two main themes can be identified. First, the speeding up of the circulation of information and images through computer-linked systems and satellites, for example, has been seen as responsible for an increasing compression of time and space, a 'deterritorialization' of culture and the construction of forms of identity which are no longer strongly identified with place (Harvey 1989; Meyrowitz 1985). These processes may in turn be linked to arguments about 'globalization' and the mixing, and pluralization, of cultural perspectives and influences which the accelerated flow of people, goods, services, images, ideas, and information is presumed to permit (albeit that this is still characterized by acute imbalances of power). A second theme emerging from the analysis of postmodernism concerns how the media, and media images and signs, are increasingly identified as a key, if not *the*

key, reality for the modern citizen. The controversial French theorist Jean Baudrillard is particularly associated with this position.

In common with post-industrial theorists, Baudrillard identifies a transition from an old industrial order based upon labour and the production of goods to a new social reproductive order based upon communication and the circulation of signs (Baudrillard 1975). However, for Baudrillard, this change also provides the basis of a new cultural condition. It is not simply that we live in a world increasingly dominated by images and signs, but that these have become our primary reality. We now live, he suggests, in a world of *simulations*, or hyperreality, which has no reality beyond itself. Indeed, for Baudrillard (1983: 41), it is 'now impossible to isolate the process of the real, or to prove the real': all that we have access to are signs and simulations. This provocative line of argument was pushed to extremes when, in 1991, Baudrillard examined the representation of the Gulf War as a 'virtual' event and declared that 'the Gulf War did not take place'. Although it is possible to read this as an argument about the changed character of contemporary warfare in the postmodern era, it also suggests some of the weaknesses of a postmodern perspective that both displays an indifference to the actuality of events beyond the 'simulacrum' and, under the guise of radicalism, simply joins a lengthy tradition of social commentary in attributing an exaggerated power and effectivity to media imagery.

Although the Baudrillardian vision of a media world of simulations is undoubtedly overstated, it does none the less direct our attention to the omnipresence within contemporary culture of media signs and images and their increasing detachment from exterior realities. However, it is television—given its continuous availability and presence within contemporary culture—that is most commonly associated with the postmodern condition rather than film. Thus, for Kroker and Cook it is television that is 'in a very literal sense, the real world . . . of *postmodern* culture, society and economy' (1986/1988: 268). This is not, of course, to say that arguments about film have not been informed by postmodern ideas. However, they have tended to be applied to individual films rather than, in the case of television, to the medium as a whole (albeit that this has then led to gross generalizations about the functioning of television 'in general'). At this point, it is therefore appropriate to look at the artistic context in which debates about postmodern film have occurred.

Aesthetic debates

If postmodern philosophy may be linked to a failing confidence in 'universal reason' and ideas of progress, it is also possible to see certain kinds of cultural practice—designated as 'postmodern'—emerging as a response to a growing lack of confidence in the value or progressiveness of modernism in the arts and design. Much of the early debate about postmodernism was linked to a consideration of architecture, and it is in relation to architecture that some of these ideas emerge most clearly.

Putting it in general terms, modernism in architecture (as, for example, in the work of Le Corbusier, the Bauhaus group, Mies van der Rohe, and the International Style) has placed a particular emphasis on function and social utility. Modern architecture, in this respect, may be seen to have demanded a 'truth to function', involving a rejection of ornament and decoration in favour of a laying bare of the materials employed and clear display of their purpose. These architectural principles were also linked to 'modern' social objectives such as the provision of mass housing (even if they were not always implemented by politicians and planners with the appropriate degree of financial investment) and seen, as in the International Style, to be 'universal' in application. For Charles Jencks, postmodernist architecture should be seen as a response to the failure of this modernist project. Indeed, he associates the 'death' of modern architecture with such events as the collapse of the Ronan Point tower block in 1969 and the blowing up of high-rise blocks in St Louis in 1972. Such events, he argues, not only signalled the failure of modern architecture as 'mass housing', but also its failure to appeal to, or communicate with, its inhabitants (Jencks 1986: 19). Thus, for Jencks, postmodernist architecture seeks to reconnect with its occupants by rejecting the functionalism of modernism, making use of decoration and ornamentation and mixing styles from different periods and places (including the vernacular). As such, Jencks defines postmodernism in terms of the concept of 'double coding', involving 'the combination of modern techniques with something else (usually traditional building) in order to communicate with the public and a concerned minority, usually other architects' (14).

Jencks acknowledges that while 'double coding' may be a feature of postmodern culture more generally, the 'failure' of modern architecture is not directly analogous to other arts. Andreas Huyssen (1986), however, suggests that the emergence of postmodern art, especially in the United States, may be linked to a certain kind of failure, or 'exhaustion', of modernism (or, more specifically, the version of modernism which became institutionalized in the United States in the 1950s). Postmodernism in this regard may be seen as a response to what Russell Berman (1984–5: 41) describes as the 'obsolescence of shock' and the corresponding loss of modernism's transgressive power. Due to its incorporation into the art market and its institutionalization as 'high art', modern art, it is argued, has lost its capacity to challenge and provoke as well as its capacity to communicate to a public beyond a small élite.

For Huyssen, the origins of this challenge may be found in pop art of the 1960s with its reaction against the dominant aesthetic of abstract expressionism and challenging of conventional notions of art through the incorporation of elements from popular culture. As such, pop art may be seen to embody a number of features which are now commonly associated with postmodern cultural practice. These may, loosely, be identified as eclecticism, an erosion of aesthetic boundaries, and a declining emphasis upon originality. Thus, just as postmodern philosophy and postmodern culture have been associated with pluralism, so the most commonly identified feature of postmodernism has been its eclecticism—its drawing upon and mixing of different styles, genres, and artistic conventions, including those of modernism. Postmodernism, in this regard, is to be understood as a movement beyond modernism which is none the less able to make use of modernist techniques and conventions as one set of stylistic choices amongst others. It is in this sense that Featherstone describes postmodernism as demonstrating 'a stylistic promiscuity' (1988: 203), while other critics have placed an emphasis upon its strategies of 'appropriation' and 'hybridization' (e.g. Wollen 1981: 168; Hassan 1986: 505).

A central component of this process has been a mixing of elements from both 'high' and 'low' culture (which may in turn be seen as an example of 'de-differentiation', or the breaking down of boundaries, which has been identified as a feature of postmodernism more generally). As Jameson has argued, artists of the 'postmodern' period have displayed a fascination with popular forms of culture such as advertising, the B movie, science fiction, and crime-writing. He suggests, however, that postmodern art does not simply 'quote' popular culture in the way that modernist art once did, but that this quotation is incorporated into the works to the point where older distinctions between 'modernist and mass culture' no longer seem to apply (Jameson 1988: 113). It is worth noting, again, that the 'break' between modernism and postmodernism is in this sense relative rather than absolute. Thus, as a number of commentators have noted, many of the features associated with postmodernism (such as the appropriation and juxtaposition of diverse materials) were also a characteristic of modernism even if they did not possess quite the same significance for the work as a whole (e.g. Callinicos 1989: 12–16; Wolff 1990: 98–9).

Finally, the borrowing of styles and techniques characteristic of postmodern art may be linked to a declining premium upon originality and the personal imprint of the 'author' (who, in parallel with the 'Enlightenment subject', is seen to have undergone something of a 'death'). Thus, for Dick Hebdige, the postmodern use of 'parody, simulation, pastiche and allegory' may be seen 'to deny the primacy or originary power of the "author"', who is no longer required to 'invent' but simply 'rework the antecedent' or rearrange the 'already-said' (Hebdige 1988: 191). However, the opposition between modernist originality and postmodernist appropriation and replication is not as clear-cut as it is sometimes argued and, even in popular culture, the 'author' has remained curiously resilient. Thus, while a film like *Blue Velvet* (USA 1986) clearly exemplifies such postmodern features as eclecticism, the mixing of avant-garde and popular conventions, and an ironic play with surface signifiers, it has still been very much in terms of the presumed 'author', David Lynch, that the film has been put into circulation, discussed, and interpreted.

Postmodernism and film

However, while individual films such as *Blue Velvet* and *Blade Runner* (Ridley Scott, 1982) have figured prominently in debates about postmodernism and film, the identification of what constitutes postmodern cinema has not been straightforward. Three main kinds of concern have been in evidence. First, the organization of the film industry itself has often been taken to exemplify 'postmodern' features. Thus, it has been argued that Hollywood has undergone a transition from 'For-

dist' mass production (the studio system) to the more 'flexible' forms of independent production (the 'New Hollywood' and after) characteristic of 'postmodern' economies, while the incorporation of Hollywood into media conglomerates with multiple entertainment interests has been seen to exemplify a 'postmodern' blurring of boundaries between (or 'de-differentiation' of) industrial practices, technologies, and cultural forms (Storper and Christopherson 1987; Tasker 1996). Second, films have, in various ways, been seen to exemplify postmodern themes or to offer 'images of postmodern society' (Harvey 1989: 308–23; Denzin 1991). Thus, the dystopian character of the contemporary science fiction film might be seen to be connected with a 'postmodern' loss of faith in the idea of progress or the changing film representations of men with a breakdown of confidence in the 'grand narratives' surrounding masculinity and patriarchal authority (Kuhn 1990; Modleski 1991). Finally, films have been seen to display the aesthetic features (such as eclecticism and the collapse of traditional artistic hierarchies) that are characteristically associated with postmodernist cultural practice. However, the identification and assessment of such aesthetic features has not been without its complications.

This is partly to do with the diversity of films to which the label has been attached (including both mainstream Hollywood films as well as 'independent' or 'experimental' film and video) and partly to do with the difficulty of clearly differentiating a 'postmodern' filmmaking practice in relation to an earlier 'modern' one (especially in the case of Hollywood). These problems have been further compounded by the differing interests that have conventionally underpinned the concern to identify postmodernist film. On the one hand, the idea of postmodernism has been used to carry on a tradition of ideological criticism which has sought to identify the social conservatism of the aesthetic conventions employed by postmodern cinema. On the other, it has been used to discuss films which may be seen to continue the 'oppositional' or 'transgressive' tradition of 'political modernism' but through a deployment of what is regarded as more culturally appropriate (i.e. postmodern) means. In this respect, discussion of postmodern cinema may be seen to follow in the wake of earlier distinctions between a 'reactionary postmodernism' and a 'postmodernism of resistance' (Foster 1983: p. xii) or between a socially conservative 'affirmative postmodernism' and an 'alternative postmodernism in which resistance, critique and negation of the status quo were redefined in non-modernist and non-avantgardist terms' (Huyssen 1984: 16).

These tensions can be seen at work in the ways in which Hollywood films since the 1970s have been addressed. Since the emergence of the New Hollywood in the late 1960s it has been common to note in Hollywood films an increasing stylistic self-consciousness, use of references to film history, and quotation from other styles (e.g. Carroll 1982). The significance of this development is, however, contested. For Fredric Jameson, in his ground-breaking essay 'Postmodernism; or, The Cultural Logic of Late Capitalism' (1984), it is clearly to be read negatively. Jameson defines postmodern culture in terms of a 'depthlessness' representative of 'a new culture of the image or the simulacrum'; a new kind of spatialized temporality and consequent 'weakening of historicity'; and the creation of a 'new type of emotional ground tone' which he describes as 'a waning of affect' (1984: 58–61). In seeking to substantiate these points, Jameson points to the 'nostalgia film' of the 1970s (such as *Chinatown* (USA, 1974) and *Body Heat* (USA, 1981)). He argues that, as a result of their use of pastiche and 'intertextual' reference, such films may be seen to exemplify a characteristically postmodern loss of historical depth. Such films, he claims, are unable to re-create a 'real' past but only a simulation of the past based upon pre-existing representations and styles (67).

In this respect, Jameson's analysis links with other critiques of recent Hollywood cinema for both its 'emptiness' and ideological conservatism. Thus, it has been common to see the formal invention and social questioning of the New Hollywood films of the late 1960s and 1970s as giving way to a more conventional and conservative Hollywood cinema from the mid-1970s onwards, especially in the wake of the success of *Star Wars* (USA, 1977) (e.g. Ryan and Kellner 1988). This has in turn been associated with a decline in what Kolker has referred to as 'the modernist project' of New Hollywood filmmaking and its replacement by the 'postmodern American film' which 'has done its best to erase the traces of sixties and seventies experimentation' (Kolker 1988: pp. x–xi). In this respect, Kolker may be seen to link postmodernism with a kind of anti-modernism (or 'reactionary postmodernism') involving a return to the 'classical' conventions or 'a linear illusionist style' (p. xi). However, it is not entirely clear whether the distinction he draws is so clear-cut. For, clearly, the New Hollywood films may themselves be plausibly identified as 'postmodern', given their self-consciousness about film history and film technique, extensive use of reference and quotation, and mixing of 'high' and 'low' art conventions (such as those of the European 'art' film and the Hollywood genre film). Similarly, although there has been an undoubted return to the 'classical' conventions of narrative and character in many post-New Hollywood films, this has also been accompanied by a continued (and, indeed, growing) use of quotation and mixing of genre elements.

Fredric Jameson's distinction between parody and pastiche may be helpful in this regard. Although both parody and pastiche are conventionally associated with postmodernism, Jameson argues that, within postmodern culture, it is pastiche which is dominant. For Jameson, while parody involves a sense of criticism or mockery of the text or texts which are being parodied, pastiche simply consists of 'blank parody': a 'neutral mimicry without parody's ulterior motives' (1984: 64–5). Although it is not an unproblematic distinction, it does have some heuristic value in discriminating between the films of the New Hollywood and after. Thus, while a New Hollywood film such as Robert Altman's *The Long Goodbye* (1973) quotes from film history and reworks genre conventions with obvious parodic intent—to debunk the myth of the private eye and the values he represents—the use of film quotations and references in a 1980s 'event' film such as *The Untouchables* (Brian De Palma, 1987) is largely characterized by the use of pastiche (as in the clever, but politically and emotionally 'blank', reconstruction of the Odessa steps sequence from the revolutionary Russian film *Battleship Potemkin*, 1925). As such, the film's use of pastiche offers less a critique of the male hero (as *the Long Goodbye* does) than an 'alibi' for the film's ideological conservatism by inoculating the film against being read too straight (in much the same way as the more recent *Independence Day* (1996) also invests its conservative militarism with a measure of tongue-in-cheek knowingness).

What this suggests is that the use of 'postmodern' conventions in Hollywood cannot simply be read off as ideologically uniform (or, indeed, that Hollywood films are *all* usefully labelled as 'postmodern' given the degree of aesthetic diversity which characterizes contemporary Hollywood filmmaking). Thus, for Linda Hutcheon, Jameson's 'blanket condemnation of Hollywood' is overstated and fails to take into account the 'oppositional and contestatory' potential of postmod-

**Hollywood postmodernism—
David Lynch's *Blue Velvet*
(1986)**

ernism which may be found in certain Hollywood films (Hutcheon 1989: 114). Unlike Jameson, she holds out the possibility of Hollywood films making use of irony and parody both to address history (as in Woody Allen's *Zelig*, 1983) and to 'subvert' Hollywood from within by their challenge to audience expectations concerning narrative and visual representation (even in such a 'light' film as De Palma's *Phantom of the Paradise*, 1974). Nevertheless, Hutcheon also acknowledges that postmodernist films are not always 'challenging in mode', that they are often likely to be 'compromised', and that, as a result of their reliance upon irony, they may also be 'ideologically ambivalent or contradictory' (1989: 107). Hence, most of her examples are actually films which are outside the mainstream of Hollywood production (*Zelig, The Purple Rose of Cairo*, (1985), *The French Lieutenant's Woman* (1981)) or not Hollywood films at all (Suzanne Osten's *The Mozart Brothers*, Sweden, 1986), Maximilian Schell's *Marlene* (West Germany, 1983), and Peter Greenaway's *A Zed and Two Noughts* (UK/Netherlands, 1985)). Indeed, more generally it is typical of writing concerned to identify a 'critical' strain of postmodernism within Hollywood that it focuses on films which tend to be unusual in Hollywood's terms (e.g. *Blade Runner, Blue Velvet, Thelma and Louise* (1991)) rather than ones which can be seen as typical.

Accordingly, it has often been outside of Hollywood that the 'adversarial' qualities of postmodern cinema

have been most firmly located. Despite its extensive use of 'allusion', Noel Carroll (1982) argues against the application of the 'postmodern' label to Hollywood filmmaking and, in a subsequent essay, identifies 'postmodern' film with the avant-garde, and specifically with various reactions against structural filmmaking, such as 'deconstructionism, the new talkie, punk film the new psychodrama, and the new symbolism' (1985: 103). In this 'alternative' tradition of filmmaking, the reworking of old materials and representations by postmodernism is interpreted not simply as a kind of surface play (or 'depthlessness'), but as part of a critical project to 'deconstruct' and subvert old meanings as well as 'construct' new ones through the repositioning of artistic and cultural discourses. Thus, Laura Kipnis explains postmodernism in terms of a cultural practice of 're-functioning' (1986: 34), while Jim Collins argues it involves the use of 'juxtaposition' as a mode of 'interrogation' (1989: 138). Thus, for Collins, the bringing together of different discursive modes in a film such as Hans-Jürgen Syberberg's *Parsifal* (1984) consists of more than just pastiche, or the aimless plundering of past styles, but both a questioning of earlier traditions of representation and 'a way of making sense of life in decentered cultures' (1989: 140).

In this respect, the critical engagement with prior representations has been seen as especially attractive to filmmakers who wish to challenge the traditional ways in which particular social groups or 'others' (such as blacks, indigenous peoples, women, and gays) have been represented and to do justice to the complexities of identity in the postmodern era. Thus, for Janet Wolff, the 'promise of postmodernism' for feminism is that, by employing the tactics of 'pastiche, irony, quotation, and juxtaposition', feminist cultural practice may engage directly with 'current images, forms, and ideas, subverting their intent and (re)appropriating their meanings' (1990: 88). Similarly, Kobena Mercer identifies the work of black British filmmakers in the 1980s as constituting 'a kind of counter-practice that contests and critiques the predominant forms in which black subjects become socially visible in different forms of cultural representation' (1988: 8). Despite the use of the term 'counter-practice' by Mercer, such filmmaking should, nevertheless, be differentiated from the Godardian model of 'counter-cinema' (or 'political modernism') and its apparent prescription of one 'correct' way of making political cinema which is universally applicable. Rather, Mercer argues that such films as *Territories* (1984) and *Handsworth Songs* (1987) employ a postmodern strategy of 'appropriation' which, through a reworking of pre-existing documentary footage, found sound, quotations, and the like, involves both a 'dis-articulation' and a 're-articulation' of 'given signifying elements of hegemonic racial discourse' (1988: 11). In doing so, he also indicates how such work represents a 'syncretism' or 'hybridity' which, he argues, is appropriate to the 'diasporean conditions' of the black communities in Britain (11).

In this respect, Mercer's work interlinks with postmodern and post-colonial emphases on the 'anti-essentialist' nature of social and cultural identities and what Ella Shohat describes as 'the mutual imbrication of "central" and "peripheral" cultures' in both the 'First' and 'Third Worlds' (1992/1996: 329). Although Shohat warns against any simple celebration of post-colonial hybridity, which she argues assumes diverse and ideological varied forms, she also suggests how hybridity can be used 'as part of resistant critique' (331). Thus, she and her collaborator Robert Stam echo a number of postmodern themes (such as the breakdown of confidence in 'grand narratives' and the problemization of representation) in their discussion of how the 'post-Third Worldist' films has moved 'beyond' the anti-colonial nationalism and political modernism of films such as *Battle of Algiers* (Algeria/Italy, 1966) and *Hour of the Furnaces* (Argentina, 1968) to interrogate nationalist discourse from the perspectives of class, gender, sex-

ual orientation, and diasporic identity, and embrace what they call 'anthropophagic, parodic-carnival-esque, and media-jujitsu strategies' (Shohat and Stam 1994: 10). In all of these cases, filmmakers in the Third World are seen to make use of First World techniques and conventions but for politically subversive ends. Thus, it is argued that, 'in their respect for difference and plurality, and in their self-consciousness about their own status as simulacra, and as texts that engage with a contemporary, mass-mediated sensibility without losing their sense of activism', the 'jujitsu' strategies of such films as the Aboriginal *Babakiueria* (Don Featherstone, Australia, 1988) and the Philippine *Mababangong Bangungot* ('Perfumed Nightmare', Kidlat Tahimik, 1977) exemplify Foster's notion of a 'resistance postmodernism' (1994: 332). However, the appropriateness of the conceptualization and periodization of postmodernism in relation to non-Western cultures remains controversial, as does its relationship to the concept of the 'post-colonial', the debate around which has now effectively overshadowed earlier arguments about the postmodern.

Conclusion: postmodernism and film studies

Although the debates about postmodernism have led to various discussions about the usefulness of the term in relation to film, it is less easy to identify a distinctive postmodern film theory. Postmodern ideas, in this respect, have tended to inform other film theories, rather than develop as a body of theory in their own right. In this respect, postmodern polemicizing against 'universalizing' and 'totalizing' theory has led to a certain refocusing of interest on the local and the specific which may be detected in the turn away from '*Screen* theory' of the 1970s towards historical research, cultural studies, and an interest in the social and cultural specificities of non-Euro-American cinemas (and a more 'multicultural' and 'dialogistic' approach to their study). One illustration of this may be found in feminist film theory.

Although feminist film theory was crucially important in the mid-1970s in introducing questions of gender into the previously sex-blind 'apparatus theory' (see Creed, Chapter 9), it itself became criticized for an 'essentializing' conceptualization of the 'female spectator' which failed to do justice to 'the multiple and fluid nature' of the female spectator who 'may be, and/or be constructed as, simultaneously female and black and gay' (Kuhn 1994: 202). As a result, Kuhn argues that 'the future for feminist work on film would appear to lie in micronarratives and microhistories of the fragmented female spectator rather than in any totalizing metapsychology of the subject of the cinematic apparatus' (202). In this respect, the convergence of feminism and cultural studies around the question of audiences has already moved in that direction. However, as Nancy Fraser and Linda Nicholson (1988) have argued in their discussion of the relations between feminism and postmodernism, while postmodern feminism may share a 'postmodernist incredulity towards metanarratives', it 'must remain theoretical' and hold on to some 'large narratives' if 'the social-critical power of feminism' is to be maintained. In this respect, their recommendation that postmodern feminist theory should be 'explicitly historical' and 'attuned to the cultural specificity of different societies and periods and to that of different groups within societies and periods' (1988/1990: 34) would seem to be a good recipe for 'postmodern' analysis more generally.

BIBLIOGRAPHY

Baudrillard, Jean (1975), *The Mirror of Production* (St Louis: Telos Press).
—— (1983), *Simulations*, trans. Paul Foss, Paul Patton, and Philip Beitchman (New York: Semiotext(e)).
—— (1991/1995), *The Gulf War did not Take Place*, trans. Paul Patton (Sydney: Power).
Berman, Russell A. (1984–5), 'Modern Art and Desublimation', *Telos*, 62: 31–57.
Callinicos, Alex (1989), *Against Postmodernism: A Marxist Critique* (Cambridge: Polity Press).
Carroll, Noel (1982), 'The Future of Allusion: Hollywood in the Seventies (and Beyond)', *October*, 20: 51–81.
—— (1985), 'Film', in Stanley Trachtenberg (ed.), *The Postmodern Moment* (Westport, Conn.: Greenwood Press).
*Collins, Jim (1989), *Uncommon Cultures: Popular Culture and Post-Modernism* (London: Routledge).
Connor, Steven (1989), *Postmodernist Culture: An Introduction to Theories of the Contemporary* (Oxford: Blackwell).
Crook, Stephen, Jan Pakulski, and Malcolm Waters (1992), *Postmodernization* (London: Routledge).
Denzin, Norman (1991), *Images of Postmodern Society: Social Theory and Contemporary Cinema* (London: Sage).

*Featherstone, Mike (1988), 'In Pursuit of the Postmodern: An Introduction', *Theory, Culture and Society*, 5/2–3: 195–215.
*Foster, Hal (1983/1985), 'Postmodernism: A Preface', in Foster (ed.), *The Anti-Aesthetic: Essays on Postmodern Culture* (Port Townshend: Bay Press); repr. as *Postmodern Culture* (London: Pluto).
Fraser, Nancy, and Linda J. Nicholson (1988/1990), 'Social Criticism without Philosophy: An Encounter between Feminism and Postmodernism', in Nicholson (ed.) *Feminism/Postmodernism* (London: Routledge).
Hall, Stuart (1992), 'The Question of Cultural Identity', in Stuart Hall and Tony McGrew (eds.), *Modernity and its Futures* (Cambridge: Polity Press).
Harvey, David (1989), *The Condition of Postmodernity* (Oxford: Blackwell).
Hassan, Ihab (1986/1987), 'Pluralism in Postmodern Perspective', *Critical Inquiry*, 12/3 (Spring), 503–20; repr. in *The Postmodern Turn: Essays in Postmodern Theory and Culture* (Ohio: Ohio State University Press).
Hebdige, Dick (1988), *Hiding in the Light: On Images and Things* (London: Routledge).
Hutcheon, Linda (1989), *The Politics of Postmodernism* (London: Routledge).
Huyssen, Andreas (1984), 'Mapping the Postmodern', *New German Critique*, 33: 5–52; repr. in *After the Great Divide: Modernism, Mass Culture and Postmodernism* (London: Macmillan).
*Jameson, Fredric (1984/1991), 'Postmodernism, Or, The Cultural Logic of Late Capitalism', *New Left Review*, 146: 53–92; repr. in *Postmodernism: Of the Cultural Logic of Late Capitalism* (London: Verso).
—— (1988), 'The Politics of Theory: Ideological Positions in the Postmodernism Debate', in *The Ideologies of Theory, ii: The Syntax of History* (London: Routledge).
Jencks, Charles (1986), *What is Post-Modernism?* (London: St Martin's Press).
Kipnis, Laura (1986), '"Refunctioning" Reconsidered: Towards a Left Popular Culture', in Colin MacCabe (ed.), *High Theory/Low Culture: Analysing Popular Film and Television* (Manchester: Manchester University Press).
Kolker, Robert Phillip (1988), *A Cinema of Loneliness: Penn, Kubrick, Scorsese, Spielberg, Altman*, 2nd edn. (Oxford: Oxford University Press).
Kroker, Arthur, and David Cook (1986/1988), *The Postmodern Scene: Excremental Culture and Hyper-Aesthetics* (New York: St Martin's Press; Basingstoke: Macmillan).
Kuhn, Annette (ed.) (1990), *Alien Zone: Cultural Theory and Contemporary Science Fiction Cinema* (London: Verso).
—— (1994), *Women's Pictures: Feminism and Cinema*, 2nd edn. (London: Verso).

Lash, Scott, and **John Urry** (1994), *Economics of Signs and Space* (London: Sage).

Lyon, David (1994), *Postmodernity* (Buckingham: Open University Press).

Lyotard, Jean-François (1979/1984), *The Postmodern Condition: A Report on Knowledge*, trans. Geoff Bennington and Brian Massumi (Minneapolis: University of Minnesota Press).

—— (1986), 'Defining the Postmodern', in Lisa Appignanesi (ed.), *Postmodernism* (London: ICA).

McClennan, Gregor (1989), *Marxism, Pluralism and Beyond: Classic Debates and New Departures* (Cambridge: Polity Press).

Mercer, Kobena (1988), 'Recoding Narratives of Race and Nation', in Mercer (ed.), *Black Film British Cinema* (London: ICA).

Meyrowitz, Joshua (1985), *No Sense of Place: The Impact of Electronic Media on Social Behavior* (Oxford: Oxford University Press).

Modleski, Tania (1991), *Feminism without Women: Culture and Criticism in a 'Postfeminist' Age* (London: Routledge).

Rodowick, D. N. (1988), *The Crisis of Political Modernism: Criticism and Ideology in Contemporary Film Theory* (Urbana: University of Illinois Press).

Rose, Margaret A. (1991), *The Post-Modern and the Post-Industrial* (Cambridge: Cambridge University Press).

Ryan, Michael, and **Douglas Kellner** (1988), *Camera Politica: The Politics and Ideology of Contemporary Hollywood Film* (Bloomington, Indiana University Press).

Shohat, Ella (1992/1996), 'Notes on the "Post-Colonial"', in Padmini Monga (ed.), *Contemporary Postcolonial Theory* (London: Arnold).

*—— and **Robert Stam** (1994), *Unthinking Eurocentrism: Multiculturalism and the Media* (London: Routledge).

Storper, Michael, and **Susan Christopherson** (1987), 'Flexible Specialization and Regional Industrial Agglomerations: The Case of the US Picture Industry', *Annals of the Association of American Geographers*, 77/1: 104–17.

Tasker, Yvonne (1996), 'Approaches to the New Hollywood', in James Curran, David Morley, and Valerie Walkerdine (eds.), *Cultural Studies and Communications* (London: Arnold).

Wolff, Janet (1990), *Feminine Sentences: Essays on Women and Culture* (Cambridge: Polity Press).

Wollen, Peter (1972), 'Counter Cinema: *Vent d'est*', *Afterimage*, 4: 6–16.

—— (1981), 'Ways of Thinking about Music Video (and Post-Modernism), *Critical Quarterly*, 28/1–2: 167–70.

Film text and context: gender, ideology, and identities

12   Marxism and film

Chuck Kleinhans

Although Marx never went to the movies, Marxism has significantly affected filmmaking by politically committed directors such as Sergei Eisenstein and Tomás Gutiérrez Alea, as well as shaped the critical and historical analysis of film in aesthetic, institutional, social, and political terms. Fundamental Marxist concepts such as ideology profoundly inform most contemporary theories of and approaches to the analysis of individual films as well as to cinema as a social institution.

Marxism fuses several different sources and types of concern. From English political economy, Marx developed his understanding of the economic foundation as fundamentally shaping (though not immutably determining) the social superstructure. From German philosophy, by inverting Hegelian idealism into a materialism that saw the world as historical and dynamically changing, Marx studied capitalism and capitalist societies as always in process. From French socialism, Marx drew his analysis of class-divided society with an active working class struggling for economic and social justice against the ruling capitalist class. Although internally divided by different movements, schools, and tendencies, and sometimes deformed into dogmatism in theory and dictatorship in practice, in its comprehensiveness, and at its best, Marxism provides a remarkably supple method for analysis. It combines practical progressive and democratic political goals with a social examination that centres on historical development and the dialectical potential for change. For this reason, Marxist analysis is an essential part of much contemporary gender, race/ ethnicity, and post-colonial thinking in film studies, even when not explicitly underlined.

Marx and Engels did not write a full-fledged aesthetics, but their comments on art (almost exclusively on literature) can be synthesized into a view which validates the Western classics and upholds a broadly construed realism in representation and narration (Morawski 1973; Solomon 1973). Marx recognized Balzac as personally a royalist in politics, but viewed his novels as narratives that accurately portrayed the complex social fabric of their time. Similarly, Lenin saw Tolstoy as a political reactionary but the author of novels which mirrored the social/political tensions of Russia. Such was the orthodoxy until the Bolshevik revolution, when Marxism shaped cinema and the other arts. With Marxists holding state power, questions of entertainment versus instruction, traditional versus radical form, drama versus documentary, literary versus visual communication, native versus foreign (especially Hollywood) models, ethnic nationalisms versus national culture, religious versus secular culture, urban versus rural, and popular audience versus intellectual creators, were raised as practical as well as theoretical matters. Intellectuals experienced and vigorously argued over both the economics of constructing a socialist film industry relying on box-office receipts and the relation of creative output to party doctrines and priorities. Sergei Eisenstein, Dziga Vertov, Lev Kuleshov, Vsevolod Pudovkin, and others wrote as filmmakers while intellectuals from different tendencies participated in the highly political and polemical debates (Taylor and Christie 1988).

The crucible of the Soviet Union of the 1920s first played out issues still important in later times and other places. In the USSR a national mass culture emerged, itself industrialized in production and partly responsive to market conditions in consumption. The state/party took control of information and journalism, as radio, the newsreel, and educational film developed. And, given limited print literacy, print journalism was complemented and, in many cases, superseded by audio and visual journalism. A comprehensive understanding of Soviet film demands an understanding of this larger context. Within the narrower realm of film aesthetics, the period dramatized several key issues. Because many artistic innovators joined the early years of the revolution, film experimentalism appeared in radical forms ranging from Alexander Dovzhenko's lyrical poeticism to Vertov's rigorous montage of images (and later sound–image) and Eisenstein's epic and operatic work. The intellectual studies of the Russian Formalists contributed to the question of innovative forms matching a revolutionary content (see Christie, Chapter 7). Traditional forms were viewed as compromised, and the possibility of developing intellectual content through the means of film form and expressive stylistics was asserted.

At the same time in the West, particularly Germany, a heightened awareness of capitalism's encroachment on the fields of culture and leisure developed with the rise of an urban mass culture audience and new means of mass-produced and disseminated culture and journalism: cinema, recorded music, the radio, the picture newspaper, and so on. Kracauer (1995), Brecht (1964), and Benjamin (1936) witnessed the expansion of the mass audience, fearing for its passivity but also identifying the liberating potential of the new media. As with the Russians, these thinkers saw cinema as changing perception and cognition as society moved from a written literacy to a visual dominance. New understandings of space and time, heralded in Cubist painting, seemed inherent to film. Informed by Freudian psychology, left-wing intellectuals hoped that new art forms could stimulate new forms of politicized thinking. Bertolt Brecht argued against the narcotic effects of dominant dramatic forms, seeing the realist/naturalist tradition since Ibsen as conforming to the Aristotelian model of catharsis: raising political issues only to send the audience away purged of any fervour for change. He championed disruptive forms which provoked viewers to new thought.

The rise of German fascism offered a new challenge to Marxist theories, and produced a series of exchanges that marked important differences within Marxist analysis of mass culture. These differences continued in the debate after the Second World War, and in film studies after 1968. The philosopher Georg Lukács advocated what amounted to a continuation of nineteenth-century realism in literature, while Brecht argued for modernist artistic innovation. Walter Benjamin agreed with Brecht and optimistically projected an inherently radical nature to film, while Marxist-influenced Frankfurt School thinkers Theodor Adorno and Max Horkheimer pessimistically concluded that fascist and US capitalist media were fundamentally alike in producing a passive public (Horkheimer and Adorno 1947).

While Soviet creative innovation and theoretical variety declined in the 1930s with Stalin's prescriptive doctrine of socialist realism in all the arts, in the West some new activities expanded the field of issues for Marxist aesthetics: examples include the development of partisan documentary and grass-roots newsreel in the United States with the Film and Photo League (Alexander 1981; Campbell 1982) and propaganda films for the Spanish Civil War. In the mid-1930s the abrupt shift in international communist politics to build a broad anti-fascist Popular Front raised new issues of producing films with and for sympathizers and liberals, such as Jean Renior's *La Vie est à nous* 'Life is Ours', (1936) (see Buchsbaum 1988). Western communist parties encouraged working with and recruiting people in the dominant capitalist media industries, including Hollywood (which created a pretext for the notorious post-war Red scare and blacklist).

The post-Second World War era saw the development of new aspects of Marxism and film. Hollywood emerged stronger than ever, dominating more of the world market. New socialist nations were established in Eastern Europe and China with attendant national cinemas, and Marxists were active in many national liberation movements in the developing world. Italian Neo-Realism provided a model of a humanistic socially committed film practice that eschewed the expensive entertainment and star system of Hollywood while validating matters of social justice, a sympathetic depiction of the lower classes, and vernacular expression in a thrifty mode. Neo-Realism influenced independent efforts in the capitalist world, and inspired directors in the developing world, particularly in Latin America and India. Critics, too, validated Neo-Realism. André Bazin, as a liberal Catholic, could find moral seriousness, while Siegfried Kracauer, from a critique of mass culture and German Expressionist film, found an alternative to frivolity and emotional manipulation (Kracauer 1947, 1960). Both posited an ontological basis for film in the replication of the physical world (see Easthope, Chapter 6). In general, in the post-war era, Marxists favoured an aesthetic of progressive realism which stood against the superficiality of entertainment and allowed for social criticism. Auteurists with progressive credentials such as Luchino Visconti and Jean Renoir, Bimal Roy and Mrinal Sen, Stanley Kubrick and Orson Welles, were esteemed. After Stalin, alternatives to Soviet models gained attention, and new militancy provoked new thinking. In Poland, Hungary, Czechoslovakia, Yugoslavia, and Cuba, significant directors and films appeared veering away from socialist realist orthodoxy.

In the 1960s a complex set of changes brought about a new stage in Marxist film analysis. Most of the intellectuals involved in developing this stage of film studies were outside, or on the border of, academia, coming from journalism, publishing, and arts and education administration, or they were students and junior faculty in higher education, often in interdisciplinary or marginalized fields since academic film studies was still being established. Thus many were self-

taught in the pertinent issues, and living through the process of discovering what a New Left could be, or learning Marxist concepts after beginning political activism. At the same time, local conditions and traditions heavily inflected the reception and diffusion of these ideas. What 'Marxist' meant in each place was distinctly different because of these contexts. And the local situation uniquely shaped the fusion of Marxism with other intellectual trends as well as the emergence of radical cultural analysis. This history played out in diverse radical film magazines. In France *Positif*, *Cinéthique*, and *Cahiers du cinéma*; in the UK *Screen* and *Framework*; in Canada *Ciné-Tracts* and *CineAction*; and in the United States *Cinéaste* and *Jump Cut*.

By the early 1970s the centre of gravity of Marxist film analysis shifted. Concepts of ideology and realism were drastically reoriented. The analysis of the dominant Hollywood cinema and European art film as 'illusionist', and that illusion having an ideological effect, evolved from several developments. The optimism of nineteenth-century Marxism in assuming that revolution would take place in the most industrialized nations as trade union and electoral politics heightened workers' consciousness and capacity for revolutionary change was severely damaged by the nationalist division during the First World War, the appearance of revolution in Russia (the most backward of the capitalist nations with an overwhelming peasant base), and the acceptance of fascism by much of the masses in Italy and Germany. As a result, Western Marxists sought deeper explanations. For some, insights from Freudian psychology showed the persistence of deep patterns in the conscious/unconscious mind. For others, the insights of Lenin's contemporary, the Italian Antonio Gramsci were helpful, particularly in his emphasis that people were not simply coercively forced by the state's police authority, but also manipulated by the hegemony or dominance of ruling-class cultural and social structures to stay in place, and to accept the existing order as 'natural'.

In classical Marxism, ideology was generally understood as the propagation of false ideas by the capitalist class, producing a 'false consciousness' in the masses which could then be countered by revolutionary 'correct ideas'. In the 1960s ideology was increasingly understood as a structural condition operating like myth in traditional societies described by Claude Lévi-Strauss: fairly complex patterns which embodied narratives and contradictions, which functioned to

'Shallow and glossy melodramas' or a 'fundamental critique of social institutions'? The films of Douglas Sirk—here, *Imitations of Life* (1959)

maintain order. In modern cultures the mass media could be seen as promulgating similar myths (Barthes 1957). French philosopher Louis Althusser drew from Mao, Gramsci, and Lacanian psychoanalysis to posit a concept of ideology which stressed that people are socially positioned in power relationships and internalize this in their unconscious: a concept given further elaboration by Foucault, who emphasized the social basis of ideology by considering institutions and history. Such an understanding of ideology meshed well with developments in semiotics and long-standing analogies between film and dreams, daydreams, and hypnotic and other liminal mental states, although it tended to produce a pessimistic, deterministic view of the potential for change. Althusser argued that revolutionary theory could move beyond ideology: a notion that (few noticed) reproduced the Leninist model with Marxist theories occupying the position formerly held by vanguard party activists in relation to the proletariat (Althusser 1965, 1970).

This view led in one direction to a position virtually identical with the Frankfurt School's pessimistic denunciation of mainstream film as narcotic, or circus-like distraction, validating only rigorous high modernist art (Arnold Schoenberg, James Joyce) as truly revolutionary. Althusser also inspired arguments that, by resisting the illusionary cinema of 'bourgeois' realism, a radical modernist form could be wedded to a politically radical content, leading some critics to validate directors such as Nagisa Oshima and Jean-Marie Straub. With translations and new critical attention, Benjamin's 'work of art' essay and other writings gained new attention, while the revived Brecht–Lukács debate became the theoretical ground for an endorsement of formal innovation and explicit politics over traditional realism. Simultaneously, Eisenstein's films and writings were recast as aesthetic experiments, and Vertov's self-reflexive *Chelovek s kinoapparatom* ('Man with the Movie Camera', USSR, 1929) was rediscovered as an avant-garde work which explored the epistemology of film. Meanwhile, in the developing world, Solanas and Getino (1969) called for a militant Third Cinema poised apart from Hollywood and auteurist art cinema and García Espinosa (1967) defended Cuban cinema as necessarily 'imperfect' compared to high production value Hollywood, but to be valued for its political content. Complemented by a wave of militant and innovative films in Latin America (and later Africa and South Asia), such arguments strengthened the case for a militant aesthetics.

It is a truism that around 1970 contemporary film studies came into being through the weaving together of Marxism, structuralism, Saussurean linguistics, psychoanalysis, and semiotics, and then was further elaborated in post-structuralist terms. In some cases, the changes amounted to complete reversals. The tradition of social documentary was called into question because of its unreflective realism. A European auteur such as Ingmar Bergman, previously praised for his high moral seriousness, was critiqued for being too theatrical by an increasingly cinematically sophisticated audience, while *Persona* (Sweden, 1966) was validated for its complex self-referentiality. But the biggest change came in a shift in the left analysis of commercial entertainment cinema as Hollywood film was reinterpreted as fundamentally realist. Thus a normative realism, understood as identical with Hollywood's practice of illusionism, was seen as producing a coherent imaginary subject position. Audience pleasure was seen as originating in the cinematic apparatus (the ensemble of physical and social conventions that govern the cinema institution, including the subject's psychology) and its illusionism, rather than contingent narrative practices, performance, and spectacle (see Creed, Chapter 9). In contrast, a self-reflexive modernism and avant-garde practices can be read as themselves producing a dispersal of meaning and deconstructing the subject position, thus calling into question both illusionism and the dominant ideology. As a result, some interpreted an extreme formalism as sufficient to establish a work as politically radical, irrespective of content, as, for example, with *Cahiers du cinéma*'s validation of Jerry Lewis's *The Bellboy* (USA, 1960), and in Gidal's advocacy of 'structural–materialist' films, while others critiqued the idea that self-reflexivity alone was political (Gidal 1978; Polan 1985).

While the overall change can be summed up as the 'politicizing of form', the precise working out varied from individual to individual, by nation, and with uneven access to ideas and films in translation. It also produced logical inconsistencies. For example, in line with their then Maoist politics, *Cahiers du cinéma* in 1972 enthusiastically validated the Godard–Gorin 'Groupe Dziga Vertov' films (1968–72)—intensely radical in form and content—as well as formally conventional Chinese documentaries. Given the investment in auteurist approaches to Hollywood prevalent in the 1960s, French and anglophone critics who were pushed in the direction of Marxist thought and politics by the heated political climate of the times tended to justify the auteurist canon using the new insights of Marxist thought. *Cahiers du cinéma* put forth a broad agenda for criticism in 1969, Comolli and Narboni's 'Cinema/Ideology/Criticism', which granted considerably leeway for considering films which appeared to be under the dominant ideology, but which escaped through formal 'cracks and fissures'. The classic demonstration was their analysis of John Ford's *Young Mr Lincoln* (USA, 1939), which argued that the director's 'inscription' of a unique 'writing' opened gaps in the text which were evidence of an escape from ideology (*Cahiers du cinéma* 1976). Left authorship analysis promoted various figures such as Nicholas Ray and Douglas Sirk who could be read as offering a fundamental critique of social institutions. The critics' motivation can be understood as stemming both from a desire to validate popular film and from the persistence of an aesthetic centred on creators. Following Bazin's dictum that 'style creates meaning', and repeating the argument of conservative auteurist Andrew Sarris, left critics asserted that Sirk's formal manipulations called his ostensibly shallow and glossy melodramas into question. Paul Willemen, for example, concluded that, 'by altering the rhetoric of bourgeois melodrama, through stylization and parody, Sirk's films distanciate themselves from the bourgeois ideology' (Willemen 1971: 67). Essentially these positions attributed class politics to cinema style. In the same vein, Jean-Luc Godard's *Week-end* (France, 1967) was interpreted by Henderson (1972, 1976) as having 'a non-bourgeois camera style' without further specifying whether that was then a working-class style.

The problems of this type of analysis derived from two false assumptions: that ideology directly reflects class identity, and that the film was the sole source of meaning. As further consideration (including critiques of some ludicrous case-studies) occurred, positions were modified and ideology was understood in a much more flexible way. While the critique of simple reflectionist concepts of 'realism' in cinematography and as an aesthetic was maintained, and the ideological nature of the apparatus was understood, increasingly theory turned to examining the meaning of a film as produced by an interaction between a text and a spectator who was understood not as an ahistorical 'subject' but as a historical person with social attributes of gender, race, class, age, nationality, and so on—all of which shaped the interpretive context. With history readmitted to the analytic frame, institutional analyses, including economic issues, were considered.

Marxism contributes to contemporary film studies in the form of historical, economic, and ideological analysis, as well as media activism. Drawing on its founders' own interests and methods, Marxism emphasizes historical analysis which aims at providing a broad context stressing multiple interacting factors including social, economic, and political connections. The revival of historical analysis reminds us that in an earlier period many film historians were Marxists: Georges Sadoul, Siegfried Kracauer, Jay Leyda, and Lewis Jacobs. Contemporary counterparts include Noël Burch, Michael Chanan, Thomas Elsaesser, David James, Klaus Kreimeier, and Janet Staiger. Studies of the class composition of cinema's past audiences, the representation of class in film, and the labour history of the cinema industry obviously interest Marxists. Wary of simple reflectionist models of film and society, Marxists remain committed to understanding the relation of film art and social–political activity. Two persistent themes are the historical film (a staple of Marxist filmmaking) and the analysis of current history in terms of the proliferation and combination of new media technologies.

Because of its inherent interest in industrial and global economics, Marxism is the primary methodology of most economic analysis of film and mass communications in general. Such studies involve not only questions of finance, production, and marketing, but also state policies (Pendakur 1990; Wasko 1982). In the past such analyses have often made sweeping generalizations about actual films and their reception, but a younger generation of researchers combines political economy with textual and reception analysis and avoids simplistic assertions of economic determination of cultural production. Increasingly issues of transnational capital, globalization of the market, capitalist ownership and control of national film cultures, and intellectual property rights focus the analysis (Mattelart and Mattelart 1992).

Marxism has had a long-standing relation to questions of political action and media. This has tended to be expressed in terms of films for propaganda and agitation, and especially in terms of a class or anti-imperialist analysis. The validation of new films and videos and the promotion of documentary has been at stake (Waugh 1984; Steven 1993). The development of a more sophisticated Marxist media theory has affected makers since the 1960s, especially with the postmodernist increase in self-conscious analytical/ expository strategies combined with the social documentary tradition. Such work often discusses social/ political issues such as race, nationalism, and AIDS, and critiques the dominant media representation of those concerns.

Today Marxism seems most dynamic when it combines its analysis of class with an analysis of gender, race, national, post-colonial, and other issues raised by progressive social–political movements. Some claim that the fall of the Soviet Union made Marxism obsolete. However, as a critical analysis of capitalist societies, at a time when the gap between rich and poor nations and between capitalist and working classes within those nations is growing, its relevance is assured.

BIBLIOGRAPHY

Adorno, Theodor, and **Walter Benjamin, Ernst Bloch, Bertolt Brecht, Georg Lukács,** and **Fredric Jameson** (1977), *Aesthetics and Politics*, trans. Ronald Taylor (London: New Left Books).

Alexander, William (1981), *Film on the Left: American Documentary Film from 1931 to 1942* (Princeton: Princeton University Press).

Althusser, Louis (1965/1970), *For Marx*, trans. Ben Brewster (New York: Monthly Review Press).

—— (1970/1972), *Lenin and Philosophy, and Other Essays*, trans. Ben Brewster (New York: Monthly Review Press).

Barthes, Roland (1957/1972), *Mythologies*, trans. Annette Lavers (New York: Hill & Wang).

Benjamin, Walter (1936/1968), *Illuminations*, ed. Hannah Arendt and trans. Harry Zohn (New York: Harcourt, Brace, & World).

Brecht, Bertolt (1964), *Brecht on Theatre*, ed. and trans. John Willett (New York: Hill & Wang).

Browne, Nick (ed.) (1990), *Cahiers du Cinéma 1969–1972: The Politics of Representation* (Cambridge, Mass.: Harvard University Press).

Buchsbaum, Jonathan (1988), *Cinéma Engagé: Film in the Popular Front* (Urbana: University of Illinois Press).

Burch, Noël (1990), *Life to those Shadows*, trans. Ben Brewster (Berkeley: University of California Press).

Cahiers du cinéma (1976), 'John Ford's *Young Mr Lincoln*', in Bill Nichols (ed.), *Movies and Methods*, i (Berkeley: University of California Press).

Campbell, Russell (1982), *Cinema Strikes Back: Radical Filmmaking in the United States 1930–1942* (Ann Arbor: UMI Research Press).

Chanan, Michael (1996), *The Dream that Kicks: The Prehistory and Early Years of Cinema in Britain*, 2nd edn. (London: Routledge).

*****Comolli, Jean-Louis,** and **Jean Narboni** (1969/1990), 'Cinema/Ideology/Criticism', trans. Susan Bennett in Browne (1990).

Elsaesser, Thomas (1989), *New German Cinema: A History* (New Brunswick, NJ: Rutgers University Press).

García Espinosa, Julio (1967/1979), 'For an Imperfect Cinema', *Jump Cut*, 20: 24–6.

Gidal, Peter (1978), 'Theory and Definition of Structural/ Materialist Film', in Gidal (ed.), *Structural Film Anthology* (London: British Film Institute).

Gramsci, Antonio (1929–35/1971), *Selections from 'The Prison Notebooks'*, ed. and trans. Quintin Hoare and Geoffrey Nowell-Smith (New York: International).

Gutiérrez Alea, Tomás (1989), 'The Viewer's Dialectic', trans. Julia Lesage (Havana: Casa de las Americas).

*****Harvey, Sylvia** (1978), *May '68 and Film Culture* (London: British Film Institute).

Henderson, Brian (1972), '*Weekend* and History', *Socialist Review*, 2/6 (no. 12): 57–92.

—— (1976), 'Toward a Non-Bourgeois Camera Style', in Bill Nichols (ed.), *Movies and Methods* (Berkeley: University of California Press).

Horkheimer, Max, and **Theodor Adorno** (1947/1972), 'The Culture Industry', trans. John Cumming in *The Dialectic of Enlightenment* (New York: Herder & Herder).

Jacobs, Lewis (1940), *The Rise of the American Film: A Critical History* (New York: Teacher's College Press).

James, David E. (1989), *Allegories of Cinema: American Film in the Sixties* (Princeton, NJ: Princeton University Press).

—— and **Rick Berg** (eds.), (1996), *The Hidden Foundation: Cinema and the Question of Class* (Minneapolis: University of Minnesota Press).

Kracauer, Siegfried (1947), *From Caligari to Hitler: A Psychological History of the German Film* (Princeton, NJ: Princeton University Press).

—— (1960), *Theory of Film: The Redemption of Physical Reality* (New York: Oxford University Press).

—— (1995), *The Mass Ornament: Weimar Essays*, ed. and trans. Thomas Y. Levin (Cambridge, Mass.: Harvard University Press).

Kreimeier, Klaus (1992), *Die Ufa-Story: Geschichte eines Filmkonzerns* (Munich: C. Hanser).

Leyda, Jay (1960), *Kino: A History of the Russian and Soviet Film* (London: George Allen & Unwin).

MacBean, James Roy (1975), *Film and Revolution* (Bloomington: Indiana University Press).

Mattelart, Armand, and **Michèle Mattelart** (1992), *Rethinking Media Theory*, trans. James A. Cohen and Urquidi (Minneapolis: University of Minnesota Press).

Morawski, Stefan (1973), 'Introduction', in Lee Baxandall and Stefan Morawski (eds.), *Marx and Engels on Literature and Art: A Selection of Writings* (St Louis: Telos Press).

Pendakur, Manjunath (1990), *Canadian Dreams and American Control: The Political Economy of the Canadian Film Industry* (Detroit: Wayne State University Press).

—— (1997), *Indian Cinema: Industry, Ideology, Consciousness* (Chicago: Lakeview Press).

Polan, Dana (1985), 'A Brechtian Cinema? Towards a Politics of Self-Reflexive Film', in Bill Nichols (ed.), *Movies and Methods* (Berkeley: University of California Press).

Richter, Hans (1986), *The Struggle for Film: Towards a Socially Responsible Cinema*, trans. Ben Brewster (Aldershot: Wildwood House).

Sadoul, Georges (1946–54), *Histoire générale du cinéma*, 5 vols. (Paris: Éditions Denoël).

Shohat, Ella, and **Robert Stam** (1994), *Unthinking Eurocentrism: Multiculturalism and the Media* (London: Routledge).

Solanas, Fernando, and **Octavio Getino** (1969/1976), 'Towards a Third Cinema', in Bill Nichols (ed.), *Movies and Methods* (Berkeley: University of California Press).

Solomon, Maynard (ed.) (1973), *Marxism and Art: Essays Classic and Contemporary* (New York: Vintage).

Staiger, Janet (1992), *Interpreting Films: Studies in the Historical Reception of American Cinema* (Princeton, NJ: Princeton University Press).

*Steven, Peter (ed.) (1985), *Jump Cut: Hollywood, Politics, and Counter-Cinema* (New York: Praeger).

—— (1993), *Brink of Reality: New Canadian Documentary Film and Video* (Toronto: Between the Lines).

Taylor, Richard, and Ian Christie (eds.) (1988), *The Film Factory: Russian and Soviet Cinema in Documents 1896–1939* (Cambridge, Mass.: Harvard University Press).

Walsh, Martin (1981), *The Brechtian Aspect of Radical Cinema* (London: British Film Institute).

Wasko, Janet (1982), *Movies and Money: Financing the American Film Industry* (Norwood, NJ: Ablex).

Waugh, Thomas (ed.) (1984), *'Show Us Life!': Toward a History and Aesthetics of the Committed Documentary* (Metuchen, NJ: Scarecrow Press).

Willemen, Paul (1971), 'Distanciation and Douglas Sirk', *Screen*, 12/2: 63–7.

The political thriller debate

John Hill from John Hill, 'Finding a Form: Politics and Aesthetics in *Fatherland, Hidden Agenda* and *Riff-Raff'*, in George McKnight (ed.), *Agent of Challenge and Defiance: The Films of Ken Loach* (Trowbridge: Flicks Books, 1997).

The background to 'the Costa-Gavras debate' was the world-wide social and political upheavals of the 1960s, when it was only to be expected that questions regarding what political role films could perform would come to the forefront. In common with the realism debate with which it was associated, the central issue concerned the possibility of making a radical film employing conventional cinematic forms. Two directors, in particular, seemed to crystallize the choices at hand. On the one hand, the films of Jean-Luc Godard, especially from *La Chinoise* (1967) onwards, demonstrated an insistence on the need for revolutionary messages (or content) to be accompanied by an appropriate revolutionary form, and were characterized by a deliberate abandonment of the traditional Hollywood conventions of linear narrative, individual, psychologically rounded characters, and a convincing dramatic illusion (or 'classic realism'). On the other hand, the films of Costa-Gavras, beginning with his exposé of political assassination, *Z* (1968), exemplified a model of political filmmaking which sought to bend mainstream Hollywood conventions to radical political ends. In doing so, they attempted to sugar the pill of radical politics with the 'entertainment' provided by the conventions of the thriller. For supporters of political thrillers, their great strength was their ability both to reach and to maintain the interest of an audience who would normally be turned off by politics; for their detractors, the weakness of such films was that their use of popular forms inevitably diluted or compromised their capacity to be genuinely politically radical and to stimulate active political thought. From this point of view, radical political purposes were more likely to be bent to the ends of mainstream Hollywood than vice versa.

What critics of political thrillers highlighted was how the use of the general conventions of narrative and realism characteristic of classical Hollywood, and of the specific conventions characteristic of the crime story or thriller, would, by their nature, encourage certain types of political perspective and discourage others. Hollywood's narrative conventions characteristically encourage explanations of social realities in individual and psychological terms, rather than economic and political ones, while the conventions of realism, with their requirement of a convincing (or 'realistic') dramatic illusion, not only highlight observable, surface realities at the expense of possibly more fundamental underlying ones, but also attach a greater significance to interpersonal relations than to social, economic, and political structures. Moreover, it is because of these tendencies, implicit in the conventions of Hollywood's narrative realism,

that political thrillers so often gravitate towards conspiracy theory or, as Kim Newman drolly observes of US thrillers of the 1970s, the view that society and government are run according to 'the same principles as the coven in *Rosemary's Baby*' (USA, 1968). Conspiratorial actions can be seen and dramatized (as in *Hidden Agenda*, GB, 1990 when a senior Tory politician and senior member of MI5 are brought together to admit what they have done) in a way that underlying social and economic forces cannot within the conventions of narrative and realism. As a result, conspiracy becomes the preferred form of explanation for how power is exercised in society, and how events are to be accounted for. In *Days of Hope* (GB, 1975). Ken Loach and Jim Allen presented the failure of the British 1926 General Strike as simply the result of individual treachery on the part of Labour and trade union leaders; in *Hidden Agenda* no less than two conspiracies are unveiled—both the conspiracy to pervert the course of justice by the security services in Northern Ireland in the early 1980s, and the conspiracy on the part of a small group of businessmen, security personnel, and politicians (led by a thinly disguised Airey Neave) to overthrow a Labour government and replace Edward Heath with Margaret Thatcher as leader of the Conservatives in Britain in the 1970s.

To be fair to the makers of the film, they appear to be convinced of the evidence for conspiracy in 1970s Britain. Moreover, there is undoubtedly a case to be answered. Conspiracy, nevertheless, provides a singularly problematic basis for political analysis and explanation, and is certainly of little value in helping us to understand the crisis of social democracy and labourism which occurred during the 1970s, and the subsequent rise to power of the New Right. The rise of the New Right was not simply willed or manufactured, but grew out of a complex set of economic, political, and ideological circumstances. Conspiracy would, at most, have been a response to these circumstances, just as the likelihood of its success would have depended upon them. In this respect, conspiracy theory has the virtue of neatness, but its cost is the loss of genuine social and political complexity.

The tendency towards personalization which is encouraged by the conventions of narrative realism is reinforced by the specific properties of the crime thriller, especially when it is structured around the investigation of an individual detective and his quest to reveal, or make visible, the truth behind a crime or enigma. Moreover, as a number of critics have suggested, the detective story formula is also characteristic-

The political thriller debate continued

ally a conservative one. It depends upon the superior powers (either intellectual or physical) of an individual investigator (who is often a loner) and, in doing so, tends to prefer the values of individualism to those of the community. In addition, the conventional narrative movement towards a solution of the crime will encourage both an identification with the forces of 'law and order' (even when the investigator is not actually a member of the police), and a general confidence in the ability of the current social set-up to triumph over injustice and right wrongs (which are then characteristically identified as the responsibility of an isolated or atypical individual, rather than of social institutions or political regimes). It is partly in recognition of these problems that political thrillers have attempted to blunt the affirmative and socially conservative impulses of the crime story by stressing the limitations of the individual detective hero and the difficulties of actually getting to the truth. Thus, the investigator may prove unable to solve the crime due to the complexity and deviousness of the forces confronting him, or he may indeed succeed in solving the mystery but then find himself unable to do anything about it—the most paranoid example of which is undoubtedly *The Parallax View* (USA, 1974), in which Warren Beatty's reporter uncovers the inevitable political conspiracy, but is then himself assassinated. *Hidden Agenda* adopts a similar, if less dramatic, strategy. CID inspector Kerrigan (Brian Cox), loosely modelled on John Stalker, is brought from England to Northern Ireland to investigate the murder of Paul Sullivan (Brad Dourif), an American lawyer who had been working for the League of Civil Liberties. He uncovers evidence of both a shoot-to-kill policy and a conspiracy to overthrow a democratically elected Labour government, but is unable to do anything about it, having been effectively silenced by the military and political forces arraigned against him. Admittedly, Ingrid (Frances McDormand), Paul's widow, is still in possession, at the film's end, of an incriminating tape which Harris (Maurice Roëves), the renegade Special Branch officer, has provided. However, given that the film has already made clear that the tape will lack credibility without Harris (whom we now know to be dead at the hands of the security services), the film's ending remains resolutely pessimistic.

While such an ending avoids glib optimism about the prospect of social reform, the film's negative inflexion of the thriller format has its limitations, not only projecting the paranoia characteristic of the political thriller genre, but also engendering a sense of powerlessness about the possibilities for social and political changes ('You can't win against these people', Kerrigan informs Ingrid).

Concern about the absence of any perspective for political

change is linked to the final criticism which has traditionally been directed at the political thriller. For, whatever the strengths and weaknesses of the actual message which the political thriller succeeds in communicating, it is still one that is, so to speak, 'pre-digested'. That is to say, opponents of the political thriller have argued that, by virtue of a reliance upon individual characters and stars with whom we identify, and upon the tightly structured patterns of narrative suspense which engage us emotionally rather than intellectually, the political thriller 'makes up our minds for us'. It may challenge, as *Hidden Agenda* does, the prevailing ideologies of society, but it does so by employing the same emotional patterns of involvement as films which offer the contrary view, and hence fails to encourage audiences to engage critically with political ideas.

In revisiting some of the criticisms of realism and the political thriller, it should be clear that I am doing so from a changed political context, and that I am not therefore advocating any return to the Godardian or 'counter-cinema' model of political filmmaking. Indeed, two major shortcomings of the traditional critique of realism was its characteristic reliance on crude binary oppositions (*either* narrative realism *or* the revolutionary avant-garde; *either* Costa-Gavras *or* Godard) and general tendency to assume that certain aesthetic strategies (primarily Brechtian) would almost necessarily deliver a radical politics. It is evident that the unitary model of political cinema which underpinned such formulations is inadequate, and that changed political circumstances now require more diverse forms of political filmmaking. It is for this reason that the revival of the concept of 'Third Cinema' has also been helpful.

The concept of Third Cinema was initially employed by the Argentinian filmmakers Fernando Solanas and Octavio Getino, to identify an emergent political cinema which was distinct from both mainstream Hollywood (First Cinema) and European 'art' cinema (Second Cinema). Current usage of the term has continued to emphasize Third Cinema's original commitment to political explanation and dialogue, but has also recognized that this commitment cannot be fulfilled by any pre-given artistic recipes. As Paul Willemen has stated, Third Cinema is not only engaged in the creation of 'new, politically . . . and cinematically illuminating types of filmic discourse', but also is aware of 'the historical variability of the necessary aesthetic strategies to be adopted'. What artistic means are appropriate to Third Cinema, therefore, will vary according to the social, political, and cultural contexts in which it is produced and to which it is addressed. The virtue of Third Cinema in this respect, is that, unlike models of counter-cinema, it does not prescribe one 'correct' way of making political cinema which is universally applicable, but

The political thriller debate continued

recognizes the need for aesthetic diversity and a sensitivity to place, and to social and cultural specifics. In doing so, it also insists upon the importance of constantly rethinking and reworking (but not necessarily overthrowing) traditional artistic models (including those of both Hollywood and the avant-garde) if cinema is to continue to be critically lucid and politically relevant.

13

Feminism and film

Patricia White

Feminism is among the social movements and cultural–critical discourses that most definitively shaped the rise of Anglo-American film studies in the 1970s; in turn, film studies, a relatively young and politicized field, provided fertile ground for feminist theory to take root in the academy. Feminist film studies, emerging from this juncture, has been both highly specialized in its theoretical debates on representation, spectatorship, and sexual difference, and broad in its cultural reach and influence. It has also involved a dual focus on critique and cultural production.

As a critical methodology, feminism makes salient the category of gender and gender hierarchy in all forms of knowledge and areas of inquiry. The female image—the female as image—has been a central feature of film and related visual media; in film criticism and theory, making gender the axis of analysis has entailed a thoroughgoing reconsideration of films for, by, and about women, and a consequent transformation of the canons of film studies. Bringing into focus the overlooked contributions of women to film history has been a key objective of feminist film studies as well as an organizing principle of women's film festivals and journalism. A concern with representation, in both a political sense (of giving voice to or speaking on behalf of women) and an aesthetic sense, has also united the activist and theoretical projects of women's film culture.

Over the past two decades, in the context of feminist politics and women's studies in the academy, feminist film studies has extended its analysis of gender in film to interrogate the representation of race, class, sexuality, and nation; encompassed media such as television and video into its paradigms; and contributed to the rethinking of film historiography, most notably in relation to consumer culture. The feminist interest in popular culture's relation to the socially disenfranchised has influenced film studies' shift from textual analysis and subject positioning to broader cultural studies of institutions and audiences. A postmodern, globalized, technologically saturated social reality has set new questions for feminist theory and methodology as for the whole of film studies.

> **In film criticism and theory, making gender the axis of analysis has entailed a thoroughgoing reconsideration of films for, by, and about women, and a consequent transformation of the canons of film studies.**

An account of principal issues, texts, and debates that have established feminist critical studies of film as a unique area of inquiry will be followed by a discussion of some of the diverse women's film production practices with which the field has engaged.

Feminist film criticism and theory

Most histories of the field of feminist film studies find a starting-point in the appearance of several book-length popular studies of women in film in the United States in the early 1970s (e.g. Rosen 1973; Haskell 1974; Mellen 1974). Their focus on 'images of women' was immediately critiqued by 'cinefeminists' interested in theorizing the structure of representation. As a result, an opposition—rhetorical in part—arose between 'American' sociological approaches and 'British' theory, of 'cinefeminism', which was based upon a critique of realism.

Reflection theory

Molly Haskell and Marjorie Rosen's studies are usually considered exemplars of 'reflection theories' of women and film: they assume that film 'reflects' social reality, that depictions of women in film mirror how society treats women, that these depictions are distortions of how women 'really are' and what they 'really want', and that 'progress' can be made (see Petro 1994). Such accounts are related to powerful feminist critiques of the effects of mainstream media, pornography, and advertising on body-image, sex roles, and violence against women, which, in turn, fuelled advocacy for women's intervention in image-making. Typically, such studies present and critique a typology of images of women—an array of virgins, vamps, victims, suffering mothers, child women, and sex kittens. The emerging film criticism of lesbians, as well as African American and Asian American women, and other women of colour, also tends to identify and reject stereotypes—such as the homicidal, man-hating lesbian, the African American mammy, the tragic mulatto, and the Asian dragon lady—and advocates more complex representations. These are categories, however, which tend to limit consideration of the social function of stereotypes and frequently lead to simplistic 'good'–'bad' readings of individual films. The identification of types and generic conventions is an important step, but simply replacing stereotypes with positive images does not transform the system that produced them.

Haskell narrativizes the history of film as an arc from 'reverence' (the silent era) to 'rape' (Hollywood in the 1960s and 1970s); the high point is represented by the strong, independent heroines of the 1940s, which reached its apotheosis in stars such as Katharine Hepburn. Presenting herself as a maverick critic, Haskell frequently distances herself from feminism, neglects to consider non-white women, and betrays a profound heterosexism (Hepburn and Tracy are for her the romantic ideal of complementarity of the sexes). Yet she makes several useful contributions, and criticism of the reductionism of her study can itself be reductive. She diagnoses violence against, and marginalization of, women in acclaimed 'New Hollywood' films, as reactions to the emergence of feminism and the threat posed by women's autonomy, and she is wary of the mystifications of European art cinema, which would appear to place women and their sexuality more centrally in their stories, while offering only a new version of the 'eternal feminine'. Finally, Haskell's comments on the woman's picture, or 'weepie'—a production category denigrated by the industry and most critics—suggest that such films actually did represent the contradictions of women's lives in patriarchal capitalism and inaugurated one of the most fruitful areas of feminist film studies.

Semiotics and ideology critique

Reviewing Haskell and Rosen's books, Claire Johnston (1975b) notes the inadequacies of the 'images of women' approach: while it grasps the ideological implications of cinema, images are seen as too easily detached from the texts and psychic structures through which they function, as well as the institutional and historical contexts that determine their form and their reception. For Johnston, film must be seen as a language and woman as a sign—not simply a transparent rendering of the real (see also Pollock 1992). In perhaps the most influential statement of this position, 'Women's Cinema as Counter Cinema', Johnston (1973) combines Roland Barthes's concept of myth as the rendering natural of ideology with auteur theory to decode the function of women in Hollywood films by Howard Hawks and John Ford, as well as women auteurs Dorothy Arzner and Ida Lupino. This, in turn, set a pattern for subsequent feminist studies of Hollywood genres such as film noir, the musical, and the western, which showed how woman as signifier performed precise iconographic and ideological functions, either constituting a genre's structural dimensions (woman = home in the western) or exposing its ideological contradictions (the femme fatale figure in film noir; see Kaplan 1978).

In this latter case, as Janet Bergstrom (1979) points out, Johnston and others were influenced by the concept of the 'progressive text' derived from the French journal *Cahiers du cinéma*. Indeed, the progressive text, or popular film which 'displayed the ideology to which it belonged' (Comolli and Narboni 1969), was the chief inheritance of feminist film studies from Marxist cultural theory (through the Russian Formalist notion of 'making strange', to Brechtian 'distanciation' and Althusserian 'contradiction') and shaped the ongoing interest in Hollywood film. *Cahiers'* methodology was also assimilated by the British journal *Screen*, which emerged as the dominant venue of work combining structuralism, semiotics, Marxism, and psychoanalysis and the touchstone for developments in feminist film theory.

Psychoanalysis

The most thoroughgoing and explicit introduction of neo-Freudian psychoanalytic theory to feminist film studies, and the single most inescapable reference in the field (and arguably in contemporary English-language film theory as a whole), is Laura Mulvey's 'Visual Pleasure and Narrative Cinema', published in *Screen* in 1975. Recommending 'a political use of psychoanalysis', this essay, like Johnston's 'Women's Cinema as Counter Cinema', was polemical both in tone and in its advocacy of theoretical rigour and a new, materialist feminist cinematic practice. However, whereas Johnston had argued that 'in order to counter our objectification in the cinema, women's collective fantasy must be released . . . [and] demands the use of the entertainment film', Mulvey insisted on a break with dominant cinema (in the form of a modernist cinematic practices which would provoke conscious reflection on the part of the spectator) and the 'rejection of pleasure as a radial weapon'. This position derived from her account of the gendered processes of spectatorial desire and identification orchestrated by classical narrative cinema and is summed up in one of her piece's headings: 'woman as image/man as bearer of the look'.

Mulvey argued that the institution of cinema is characterized by a sexual imbalance of power, and psychoanalysis may be used to explain this. Because psychoanalysis makes sexual difference its central category, feminist thinking can use it to understand women's exclusion from the realms of language, law, and desire—from, in short, what Jacques Lacan called the symbolic register. Freud's description of scopophilia—pleasure in looking—was Mulvey's starting-point. Dominant cinema deploys unconscious mechanisms in which the image of woman functions as signifier of sexual difference, confirming man as subject and maker of meaning. These mechanisms are built into the structure of the gaze and narrative itself through the manipulation of time and space by point of view, framing, editing, and other codes.

> This position derived from her account of the gendered processes of spectatorial desire and identification orchestrated by classical narrative cinema and is summed up in one of her piece's headings: 'woman as image/man as bearer of the look'.

Centred around the spectator's and the camera's look, cinema offers identificatory pleasure with one's on-screen likeness, or ego ideal (understood in terms of the Lacanian mirror stage), and libidinal gratification from the object of the gaze. The male *spectator* is doubly supported by these mechanisms of visual gratification as the gaze is relayed from the male surrogate within the diegesis to the male spectator in the audience. The woman, on the other hand, is defined in terms of *spectacle*, or what Mulvey described as 'to-be-looked-at-ness'. As Mulvey observed, 'In a world ordered by sexual imbalance, pleasure in looking has been split between active/male and passive/female'. Mulvey excluded from consideration the possible pleasures afforded a female spectator by narrative cinema through her provocative use of the male pronoun to designate the spectator. As she explained later, her essay explored 'the relationship between the image of woman on screen and the "masculinization" of the spectator position, regardless of actual sex (or possible deviance) of any real live movie-goer' (Mulvey 1981/1988: 69).

Yet if the image of woman is to be 'looked at', it also, according to the Freudian account, connotes sexual difference and a threat of castration that must be contained. According to Mulvey, narrative cinema has developed two ways to neutralize this threat, which she correlates with the filmic practices of two of film theory's most privileged auteurs: Josef von Sternberg and Alfred Hitchcock. Von Sternberg's baroque compositions, centred around the impossibly stylized image of Marlene Dietrich, are seen as exemplary of a fetishistic disavowal of the threat of sexual difference. In the Freudian scenario, the fetish stands in for the missing penis, and the fetishist disavows his knowledge of lack with belief in the compensatory object. The oblique narratives and iconic, layered compositions in von Sternberg's films exemplify, therefore, what Mulvey called fetishistic scopophilia.

In another oft-quoted formula, Mulvey described the second avenue of mastering castration anxiety as voyeurism gratified by investigation and punishment or redemption of the 'guilty' (that is, different, female) object: 'sadism demands a story', she wrote. For example, the angst-ridden, illogical world of film noir is stabilized by pinning guilt on the femme fatale. Mulvey argued that Alfred Hitchcock's films (*Vertigo* USA, 1958; and *Rear Window* USA, 1954) brilliantly fuse the fetishistic and voyeuristic–sadistic solutions to the threat posed by the image of women, and her reading inaugurated a rich strain of feminist work on the director.

Prior to Mulvey, psychoanalytic film theory had tended to confirm the hegemony and homogeneity of the patriarchal unconscious in cinema. Christian Metz extrapolated the mechanism of fetishism (considered an exclusively male perversion) to define the spectator's belief in the cinematic illusion itself; Jean-Louis Baudry argued that the 'cinematic apparatus' (defined technologically, institutionally, and ideologically) extended Western representation systems to position an ideal, transcendental subject; and the theory of suture demonstrated how cinematic syntax, for example the point-of-view construction so often used in establishing the woman as image, confirmed the coherence of the viewing subject over and against lack (see Creed, Chapter 9, for a fuller exposition of these arguments).

Feminist work in the wake of Mulvey's essay highlighted how all of these metapsychological accounts implicitly posited a male viewer—however illusory his mastery and unity might prove to be—and went on to elaborate the effects of the cinema's seemingly necessary and massive exclusion of the female subject position. However, in articulating the problem of dominant cinema so very exactly, the feminist psychoanalytic paradigm risked being trapped within the monolith. As Raymond Bellour, whose meticulous textual analyses traced and confirmed the male Oedipal trajectory

of Hollywood films from the micro-codes of editing to the macro-codes of narrative structure, candidly stated in an interview with *Camera Obscura*: 'To put it a bit hastily . . . I think a woman can love, accept, and give a positive value to these films only from her own masochism' (quoted in Bergstrom 1988: 195).

Needless to say, Bellour's was not the last word on the subject, and a number of responses to the totalization of the apparatus model soon evolved. For some theorists, if the woman's 'visual presence tends to work against the development of a story line' (Mulvey 1975: 33), then it could be argued that spectacle itself could be understood as a weak link in the totalizing patriarchal regime Mulvey delineated and used as a way of interrupting narrative closure and its presumed confirmation of spectatorial mastery. The spectacularized woman—for example, the female star, whose iconicity is also constructed intertextually and thus may exceed narrative placement—can demonstrate or defy the logic of the system that would subordinate her to the gaze of the male. Similarly, the musical genre's subordination of narrative codes to performance and spectacle might resist ideological containment, and this is possibly one source of its appeal to female and gay audiences. Other responses to and extensions of Mulvey's paradigm suggested that the male spectator's relation to the image signifying sexual difference might be masochistic, rather than necessarily sadistic. Gaylyn Studlar (1988), for example, argues that this is the effect—and the subversiveness—of the von Sternberg–Dietrich films, and Carol Clover (1992) suggests that contemporary horror films encourage their young male spectators to identify with the female victim. Finally, it was argued that cases of the spectacularization of masculinity or ethnicity, while not contradicting the association of femininity with to-be-looked-at-ness, permitted an interrogation of the wider cultural logic determining the power and hierarchy of the gaze.

Mulvey herself addressed two key omissions in her argument in her own 'Afterthoughts' on the issue: what she called 'the "woman in the audience" issue' and 'the "melodrama" issue' (Mulvey 1981/1988: 69). Both concerns stemmed from her 'own love of Hollywood melodrama' and demonstrated the irony of her earlier essay's conclusion that 'Women . . . cannot view the decline of the traditional film form with anything much more than sentimental regret' (1975: 39). Much like the choice faced by the melodrama's heroine between pursuing her desire or accepting 'correct femininity',

Mulvey argued that female spectatorship entails a tension or oscillation between psychical positions of masculinity and femininity which are legacies of the female Oedipal complex and socialization under patriarchy confirmed in dominant narrative patterns. Making a 'trans-sex identification' with the agent of desire and narrative is habitual for women. Mulvey's account of female spectatorship as it is engaged in narrativity suggests that gender identification, and hence identity, is a *process*, and this point has been picked up by Teresa de Lauretis. 'The real task', she argued, 'is to enact the contradiction of female desire, and of women as social subjects, in the terms of narrative; to perform its figures of movement and closure, image and gaze, with the constant awareness that spectators are historically engendered in social practices, in the real world, and in cinema too' (1984: 156).

In other words, the 'woman in the audience' cannot be reduced to that single term in the polarity: 'woman as image'. Her identification with that position must continually be solicited by narrative, visual, and wider cultural codes. Moreover, not every 'woman in the audience' is the same. The idea that formalist intervention is the only way of interrupting mimetic spectator–text relations ignores the fact that the socio-historical location of many audience members presents a difficult 'fit' with the textually ordained position. Lesbian spectatorship has posed a particularly revealing challenge to pscyhoanalytic theory's seeming equation of 'sexual difference' with heterosexual complementarity—the presumption that women cannot desire the image because they *are* the image (Doane 1982). As Jackie Stacey points out: 'psychoanalytic accounts which theorize identification and object choice within a framework of linked binary oppositions (masculinity/ femininity: activity/passivity) necessarily masculinize female homosexuality' (1987: 370). She then goes on to stress the inherent homoerotic components of female spectatorship. Attempts to address lesbians precisely as social subjects, as viewers, have therefore side-stepped the psychoanalytic paradigm to consider how lesbian viewers might appropriate dominant, heterosexist representations (Ellsworth 1990). Other challenges to Mulvey's paradigm from within psychoanalysis, such as the theory of film's homology with fantasy as the 'mise-en-scène of desire' (Cowie 1984), suggest that spectators do not necessarily take up predetermined or unitary positions of identification. However, while making room for identifications across gender and sexuality, such accounts tend to overestimate fantasmatic mobility, downplaying the constraints of social–sexual identity on spectatorship.

Critiques of the field's largely unexamined ethnocentrism also became more and more insistent (see Gaines 1990). In so far as sexual difference is the organizing axis of subjectivity in psychoanalysis, Lacanian feminist film theory was ill equipped to theorize the intersection of gender with racial, ethnic, class, national, or other differences—whether in visual and narrative codes or in spectatorial response. The institutionalization of the field reinforced this structuring omission. Although psychoanalytic concepts of the gaze, disavowal, and fetishism have been used to account for the racialized image (notably in work drawing on the writings of Frantz Fanon), the discourse is generally seen as too ahistorical and individualistic to be useful to an anti-racist film theory. In 'The Oppositional Gaze' (1992), bell hooks argues that black female spectators cannot help but view Hollywood films from an oppositional standpoint as the fetishized woman in film is white. Such glaring blind spots in feminist film theory called for concrete readings and new methodologies—drawn from feminist and anti-racist politics, and historical and cultural studies—to explicate the relationships of diverse women in the audience to dominant representations of femininity.

The woman's film

Mulvey's own linkage of 'the woman in the audience issue' with 'the melodrama issue' sets up an important contest of textual and contextual models. Cinema has inherited a great deal from theatrical and literary melodrama; however, the association of melodrama with femininity can be detected in the pejorative attitude with which it is often regarded. Studies of silent melodrama in various national contexts, the Hollywood 'family melodrama' of the 1950s, television genres such as soap operas, and particularly that subset of melodrama known as 'the woman's film' offer the opportunity to compare feminist methodologies and epistemologies concerned with historical context and actual viewers with those focused on textually constructed spectator positions.

The woman's film flourished in Hollywood in the 1930s, 1940s, and 1950s, but is found in most industries and survives today, notably in the made-for-TV movie. It is centred around a female star–heroine, frequently written by or adapted from the work of women, often fairly inexpensively made, and explicitly marketed to and consumed by female audiences. Typically, such films are concerned with evoking emotional responses to such 'women's issues' as heterosexual romance, domesticity, and motherhood. While some feminists have rejected such traditional associations, particularly their survival in contemporary popular culture, others have found in them an expression, however mediated, of women's contradictory experience in the patriarchal family. Indeed, the films have seemed to offer the opportunity to decode the mother as an ideological construct and to come to terms with the pre-feminist generation of 'mothers'. From the perspective of genre theory, the woman's film could be seen as performing 'cultural work'—speaking to, if displacing, genuine social conflicts—between women's economic dependence and desire for autonomy, between heterosexual and maternal ideology and sexual self-definition. The woman's film thus links the focus on 'depictions of women' in sociological criticism with cinefeminists' concern with 'the figure of the woman'. Their methodologies and evaluations, even their organizing questions, differ, however.

> **The woman's film could be seen as performing 'cultural work'—speaking to, if displacing, genuine social conflicts—between women's economic dependence and desire for autonomy, between heterosexual and maternal ideology and sexual self-definition.**

In her influential study *The Desire to Desire* (1987), Mary Ann Doane develops a theory of female spectatorship through intricate textual analyses of films produced for a female audience in wartime Hollywood. Identifying 'maternal', 'medical', and 'paranoid' subgenres of the woman's film, Doane demonstrates the frequency of overt thematizations of psychoanalysis in their depictions of family, romantic, and doctor–patient relationships; and her readings uncover scenarios of masochism and hysteria that confirm Lacanian psychoanalysis's definition of femininity as deficiency or lack. Analysing the designation 'woman's film' in terms of both possession and address, Doane con-

cludes that such films ultimately position the women they address as subject *to*, rather than *of*, the discourse of desire. Like the Joan Crawford character in the woman's film *Possessed* (USA, 1947), the female spectator is dispossessed of what appears to be her own story.

In a crucial contribution to spectatorship theory, 'Film and the Masquerade' (1982), Doane argues that the visual economy and affective intensity of the woman's film encourages the female spectator to over-identify with the image. According to the psychoanalytic model of sexual difference, the distance upon which fetishism, desire, and even criticism depend is simply not available to her: the woman is deficient in relation to the gaze. The title and plot conceit of *Dark Victory* (USA, 1939), in which the heroine must mime being able to see so that the hero (but not the audience) will leave her to suffer and die alone, serves as a hyperbolic illustration. When Doane acknowledges that it is 'quite tempting to foreclose entirely the possibility of female spectatorship', her statement must be seen in the context of feminist anti-essentialism: 'the woman' of 'the woman's film' does not exist—she is a discursive category produced within a phallocentric representational regime. Doane proposes a new trope for female spectatorship: masquerade, defined by Freudian analyst Joan Rivière as indistinguishable from 'genuine womanliness', and which can provide a means of 'flaunting' femininity's lack.

Unwilling to reject films that historically have given women solace and pleasure, other feminist theorists argue that female spectatorship encompasses more than narcissism or masochism. Although, as Ann Kaplan argues (1983a), *Stella Dallas* (USA, 1937) does indeed end with an extravagant scene of female abjection (anonymous among the crowd, the title character watches from afar the wedding of the daughter she gave up), Linda Williams argues that in it women recognize contradictory points of view: that they engage their 'multiple identificatory power' and their critical reading skills (1984/1990: 154). Not simply glorifying female sacrifice, such films allow women to mourn loss and reject its necessity.

These contrasting emphases in feminist film theory can be illustrated by two strikingly different interpretations of Alfred Hitchcock's 'woman's picture' *Rebecca* (USA, 1940), based on the 1938 novel by Daphne du Maurier. While Doane (1987) sees the anonymity of the film's heroine and the absence of the eponymous character (the hero's dead first wife Rebecca) as a negation of female subjectivity, Tania Modleski (1988) sees a compelling version of the female Oedipal drama in which the object of desire and identification is another woman—a drama all the more compelling because the power that that woman exerts over the heroine (and in turn the spectator) comes from outside the visual field (indeed from beyond the grave). Relating the woman's film to traditions in women's fiction and to popular genres such as soap operas and Gothic and romance fiction, Modleski views such highly codified narratives as responses to women's social and psychological conditions, utopian 'resolutions' of real conflicts through aesthetic means, fantasies of omnipotence and outlets for rage and desire.

If Doane is careful to specify that she speaks only of the discursively constructed female subject, who is not to be conflated with actual members of the audience, and Modleski seeks to *theorize* the position and pleasure of real women, still other feminist film scholars have challenged psychoanalytic explanations by emphasizing historical and audience studies in their work on the woman's film (see Stacey 1987). This is part of a wider movement in film studies away from the homogeneity of the cinematic institution presumed in apparatus theory, and from the centrality and determinism of the film text, towards the heterogeneity of what Stuart Hall (1980) calls encoding and decoding practices. Many signifying systems intersect in any given spectatorial situation, and spectators bring diverse identities, histories, cultural competences, and responses—both conscious and unconscious—to the movies. The tension between the plurality and diversity of actual viewers and responses and that textual and theoretical construction conceived in the singular as 'the female spectator' can be related to what Teresa de Lauretis (1984) identifies as one of the central, necessary contradictions in feminism—between woman, a philosophical or aesthetic construct, and women, materially and historically located beings who are gendered female. Work on the woman's film seeks not to resolve this tension but to explore its productivity.

Stars, reception studies, and consumer culture

It is a defining feature of the 'woman's film' that it showcases popular female stars as its suffering or transgressive heroines. Despite its central tenet that woman is a constructed image, psychoanalytically informed feminist analyses had little to say about the signifying effects of a star image in a particular textual system—let alone about how the interaction between text and spectator might be determined by foreknowledge and anticipation of the star; by, in short, intertextuality. This careful avoidance was in part a reaction to work such as Haskell's which followed journalistic conventions of writing about characters and stars, and in part a logical extension of the theory of the image of woman as male fetish and its identification with ideological complicity.

The increasing influence of cultural studies (identified with the work of the Birmingham Centre for Contemporary Cultural Studies), which looks beyond the film text for the social meaning of cinematic practices, as well as of approaches in film history that include institutional and promotional discourses and reception studies, invigorated work on film stars. As Judith Mayne (1993: 124) notes, the consequences of this shift in perspective are immediate: taking stars into account makes it hard to accept that the fascination of the movies inheres in the regressive pleasure of the projection situation, as apparatus theory argued. This approach is of particular interest to feminists, not only because female stars are the most powerful women in the film industry and represent ideologically significant versions of femininity throughout the culture, but because it is as 'fans' that women are addressed as the prototypical moviegoers. This demands reconsideration of the pronouncement that women are excluded from the spectator position and from the articulation of desire. At the very least, stars, like genre films, are offered as particular imaginary solutions to women's unfulfilled desires.

Following the methodology set out in Richard Dyer's book *Stars* (1979), critics read the inflexions of particular star images across the body of films in which the star appears as well as in promotional, publicity, and critical texts such as fan magazines and testimonials, commodity tie-ins, public appearances, tributes, and cultural citations. Dyer sees 'independent women stars' such as Katharine Hepburn and Bette Davis, or, to give a contemporary example, Susan Sarandon, as potentially oppositional types—at least at the basic level of embodying the category of the individual *as female*. Maria Laplace (1987) traces the roots of Davis's public persona and her roles in her star vehicles to the heroines of women's fiction, and reads her association with work, as well as with consumption, as particularly appealing to female spectators. Dyer also analyses Davis's restless performance style, her 'bitch' and camp roles and their reception and imitation in gay male culture. This 'structured polysemy' of a star image allows the figure to be claimed by diverse audiences and generates unpredictable effects in a range of reception contexts over time.

For example, the 'mystery' and self-sufficiency of Dietrich and Garbo (evident in their visual presentation as well as the plots of their films), the former's cruelty to men and the latter's tragic relation to love, as well as costuming codes and their on-screen flirtations with women, have been understood not only as open to appropriation by lesbian spectators today, but as drawing on the visual codes of lesbian self-representation in the 1930s. Black or ethnically coded star-images, such as those of Lena Horne or Carmen Miranda, have been decoded in relation to fantasies of racialized sexuality and the construction of American national identity and as figures of oppositional identification for non-white spectators (see Roberts 1993), and studies of national cinemas have increasingly mined the semiotic riches of popular star images.

The analysis of stars entails both sociological and psychoanalytic approaches and touches on several important directions in contemporary feminist film studies: placing the cinema within consumer culture, historicizing film exhibition and reception, and understanding active spectatorship as a process of 'negotiation'. Historically, cinema emerges within the culture of consumption. Once again it is not unreasonable to suggest that women are not marginalized as spectators, with no access except through disempowering identification with femininity-as-commodity in the figure of the star, but energetically addressed as consumers. Miriam Hansen (1991) looks at the Valentino craze in the 1920s as a definitive moment in locating female sexuality in modernity and the public sphere. Fan culture involves a range of concrete practices of consumption, purveyed by magazines, fashions, and commodity tie-ins. Jane Gaines and Charlotte Herzog (1987) demonstrate that costuming is a crucial dimension of the personae of 'women's' stars such as Joan Crawford. Consumerist discourse works *in* as well as through the woman's film, often as a potent allegory of women's attempt to define herself or satisfy her desire. Consumer goods and the surfaces of costume, skin, and hair also offer non-narrative, tactile, and visual pleasures to women. Television, which addresses consumers in the home, extends such dimensions of women's viewing practice; arguably, the television 'apparatus' itself is feminized. Television

audience studies, and feminist television scholarship in general, have been increasingly important to developments in film studies. Finally, work on consumerism can restore the question of gender to the now dominant concept of postmodernism. Many of the characteristics of postmodern society—fragmentation over coherence, style over history, surface over depth, and consumption over production—have traditionally been associated with women's condition, as Anne Friedberg (1994) demonstrates by linking the visual culture of modernity to contemporary spectatorial practices of the shopping-mall, cineplex, and home video. Friedberg suggests that there is at least some potential for mobilizing such associations on women's behalf—even as postmodernism threatens identity categories upon which feminism and other oppositional politics would seem to depend.

Indeed the traditional left's rejection of popular culture as capitalist manipulation, a position commonly associated with the Frankfurt School, frequently betrays the equation of consumption with feminine passivity. On the other hand, an unproblematic celebration of consumerism in the name of women's pleasure does not constitute 'resistance'. Generally speaking, feminist cultural studies rejects the view of female viewers as victims of 'false consciousness', but without then attributing inherently subversive powers to them. Stuart Hall's (1980) term 'negotiation' (itself a market-place metaphor, as Mayne (1993) points out) describes viewers' strategies of decoding media messages—from television news to film endings—as not wholly in conformity with, nor in complete opposition to, dominant ideology. A negotiated reading is inflected by viewers' socio-historical location and the discourses available to them. Jacqueline Bobo, in *Black Women as Cultural Readers* (1995), analyses her ethnographic research among black women viewers of Steven Spielberg's film *The Color Purple* (USA, 1985). She finds that their familiarity with Alice Walker's novel, the opportunity to see a high-budget film with a black female protagonist, and the community in which they viewed and discussed the film contributed to a more nuanced and positive reception of the film than that of many liberal reviewers, both black and white.

As the preceding account demonstrates, after more than twenty years feminist film studies has become an established academic discipline, with the critique of dominant media a primary preoccupation. But while recent work stressing the agency of the film or television viewer is an important challenge to the hierarchies

> It has been women's film *production*,
> rather than reception, that has been the
> most prominent model of resistance
> and opposition to the status quo.

presumed in Laura Mulvey's influential model, it has been women's film *production*, rather than reception, that has been the most prominent model of resistance and opposition to the status quo. Not simply an important parallel sector of 'feminism in film', women's filmmaking practice has been a constant reference and dynamic ground for theoretical work. Reclaiming women filmmakers' work within mainstream industries and in national and alternative film movements entails the re-evaluation of concepts of film authorship and criteria of film historiography and raises interesting methodological questions, such as the role of the critic in the definition of a 'feminist' film and the problem of essentialism (the notion that all women or all women's films share inherent qualities). The next sections look at areas of women's production that have raised particularly generative issues for feminist film studies.

Women's filmmaking

One of the most important discoveries of women's film festivals was of the pioneering role women played in the emergence of film. Alice Guy-Blaché is widely credited with directing the very first fiction film in 1896. She made hundreds of short films in France and later in the United States, and more than twenty feature films through her film company, Solax. The work of another prolific early woman writer-director-producer, Lois Weber, helps illuminate links between early twentieth-century middle-class feminism and the emerging cultural role of cinema. Her 'quality' dramas depicted women's agency and their favourable moral influence, addressing social issues, such as birth control (*The Hand that Rocks the Cradle*, 1917) and abortion (*Where are my Children?*, 1916), within the framework of melodrama. Well known at the time, Weber, like Guy-Blaché, was all but forgotten until feminist rediscovery in the 1970s made possible an acknowledgement of the role her work played in the contest for the respectability of cinema in the United States, and its place in hierarchies of class and taste. Film

preservation movements and new interpretations of early film history emerging in the 1980s have assisted feminist efforts to restore women's contributions to silent cinema. The role of women in the public sphere—in political and social movements, labour, leisure, and the culture of consumption—and in the formation of national identities in the first decades of the twentieth century, have been illuminated by recent studies of Neapolitan filmmaker Elvira Notari (Bruno 1995) and of Nell Shipman, the Canadian-born director of outdoor adventure films (Armatage 1995).

Feminist film scholars' questioning of established film canons draws on the retrieval of women authors and influences in feminist literary criticism. But cinema not only presents a much more limited history and scope than literature; it raises the difficulty of *defining* authorship, given the capital and technology-intensive, commercial and collaborative nature of film production, especially in Hollywood.

Women in Hollywood

Independent women directors and producers who flourished in the first decades of filmmaking were quickly marginalized by the entrenchment of the Hollywood studio system and its eventual dominance of world-wide markets. Studies of women who exercised creative control in sound-era Hollywood such as screenwriters (see Francke, 1994) or stars represent a challenge to the conflation of the idea of cinematic authorship with the figure of the director. But the few women who did work as directors in the heyday of Hollywood—Dorothy Arzner, who directed her first feature at Paramount, where she had been an editor, in 1927, and made sixteen more films before retiring from the movies in 1943, and Ida Lupino, a leading actress at Warners who turned independent producer-director in 1949 and later directed for television—have played a central role in feminist film historiography and criticism.

Claire Johnston's and Pam Cook's contributions to *The Work of Dorothy Arzner* (Johnston 1975a) combined the work of recovery with the critical model developed in Johnston's 'Women's Cinema as Counter Cinema'. The authors looked not for coherent feminist expression in Arzner's work, but for traces of 'the woman's discourse', readable in the 'gaps and fissures' of the classic text. One such moment in Arzner's 1940 film *Dance, Girl, Dance*, in which the female character 'returns the look' of the burlesque audience that would objectify her, has become a canonical example of a textual 'rupture' within patriarchal ideology. In *Directed by Dorothy Arzner* (1994), Judith Mayne reintroduced biographical information and evaluated the significance of the director's lesbianism—not only to readings of her films (her 'authorial signature' decipherable in the highlighting of relationships between women and marginal women characters in her films) but to her public profile when she was an active woman director and to her status and stature in feminist film studies as a figure of fascination.

Contemporary with the emergence of such feminist criticism, women directors were finding greater opportunities in the New Hollywood. The genre-film work of such directors as Stephanie Rothman (*Student Nurses*, 1970) or Amy Heckerling (*Fast Times at Ridgemont High*, 1982) were similarly read 'against the grain' for their feminist inflexions. The cross-over successes of a number of women first active in feminist documentary, such as Claudia Weill's *Girlfriends* (1978), Joyce Chopra's *Smooth Talk* (1985), and Donna Deitch's lesbian romance *Desert Hearts* (1985), received particular scrutiny and anticipated the emergence of contemporary figures such as Mira Nair (*Mississippi Masala*, 1992) and Kathryn Bigelow (*Strange Days*, 1995) from feminist production sectors to Hollywood.

Art film, new national cinemas, third cinema

The European 'art film' has produced a number of indisputable female 'auteurs'. Although they might make fewer compromises to commerce or popular taste than women working within the mainstream industries, their work is even less easily assimilable to the feminist rubric. This does not, however, make them uninteresting to feminist critics. The paradigmatic case is Leni Riefenstahl, documentarian to the Third Reich. Susan Sontag's influential study (1972) of a consistent fascist aesthetic in Riefenstahl's work from *Triumph of the Will* (Germany, 1935) and *Olympia* (Germany, 1938) to her African photography of the 1960s, also lays the groundwork for decoding the Riefenstahl persona. Her celebration as 'female artist' works to place her outside history (and politics), subjecting her to the same codes governing the representation of woman in film. Johnston (1973) critiqued the films of French New

Wave director Agnes Varda for perpetuating the mythology of woman as essentially unknowable and childlike, signifier of nature and sexuality *for men*. The male protagonists and fraught sexual politics of the Italian director Liliana Cavani, initially regarded as evidence that women directors could indeed make anti-feminist films, have been read more subtly by Kaja Silverman (1988) as authorial projections that unsettle patriarchal power hierarchies. Hungarian director Márta Mészáros in Hungary has built up a body of feature films unusual for a woman director, permitting auteurist analysis while expanding West European concepts of feminism and film. However, these directors' achievements must be seen not as exceptional, but inside history, politics, and national contexts. Thus, feminist critical interest has foregrounded the work of women within the New German Cinema, too often identified only with its male proponents and in Australian cinema.

In the case of 'Third Cinema' which explicitly opposed commercially controlled 'First' cinemas and auteurist 'art', or 'Second', cinema, several women's films have been seen as definitive. The single feature Afro-Cuban director Sara Gomez completed before her untimely death, *One Way or Another* ('De cierta manera', Cuba, 1977) has been widely hailed as Brechtian post-colonial feminist cinema. Its dialectical structure of romance plot and 'documentary' analysis of economic conditions stresses the necessity of consciousness-raising around sexual politics as an essential part of the transformation of the social order. Caribbean-born Sarah Maldoror depicted revolutionary women's struggle in Angola in *Sambizanga*, (1972) and women's film collectives formed in Columbia, Brazil, and Peru, and on the Indian sub-continent. The introduction of the films of Third-world women into the canon of Eurocentric feminist criticism, however, should not homogenize the struggles and conditions within which they intervened: feminist, Marxist, and anti-imperialist paradigms have not always overlapped.

Avant-Garde and counter-cinema

Despite vast disparities in resources, conditions of production, and audience, most of the work discussed so far shares the general qualities of feature-length, narrative form, produced with some division of labour, and aimed for theatrical exhibition. Avant-garde work conceived outside that model has historically been an important venue for women; the various avant-garde movements offer feminist critics examples of 'auteurs' in the truest sense, as well as grounding for theories of alternative film language. Germaine Dulac claims the title of first feminist filmmaker; she played a prominent role in the French avant-garde as an educator and theorist, as well as the maker of abstract, narrative, and documentary films. In her most important film, *The Smiling Mme Beudet* (France, 1923), Dulac infused the conventional narrative about a provincial wife with experimental techniques rendering the protagonist's frustration and fantasy. For Sandy Flitterman-Lewis (1989), Dulac's career exemplified 'a search for a new cinematic language capable of expressing female desire'.

> **While feminist film theory has consistently championed formal experimentation, the avant-garde's ethos of personal expression can be seen to foreclose consistent socio-political critique and, frequently, significant engagement with audiences.**

In the poetically rendered subjective space of *Meshes of the Afternoon* (USA, 1943) and subsequent works, Russian-born Maya Deren could be said to be conducting a similar search. Beyond the general influence that earned her the rather dubious appellation 'mother of the American avant-garde', Deren's aesthetic innovations were paid homage in the explicitly feminist work of experimental filmmakers in the 1970s such as Joyce Wieland in Canada and lesbian feminist Barbara Hammer in the United States. Economically accessible and institutionally alternative, avant-garde film has given a significant place to American women since at least the 1950s; yet the movement has been pervaded by a male heroic modernism. In an article arguing for the political importance of *naming* women's media practices, B. Ruby Rich calls the avant-garde 'the Cinema of the Sons', a cinema of rebellion against the dominant 'Cinema of the Fathers' (Rich 1990: 269). While feminist film theory has consistently championed formal experimentation, the avant-garde's ethos of personal expression can be seen to foreclose consistent socio-political critique and, frequently, significant engagement with audiences.

The women's films most privileged in the corpus of feminist film theory have tended to be forms of 'counter-cinema' which question the centrality of the image of women to representational regimes: cinematic signifying systems such as editing or the synchronization of sound and image, narrative logic, the structure of the look, processes of voyeurism and identification. These films have also been linked to the concerns of writers such as Hélène Cixous, Julia Kristeva, and Luce Irigaray with the concept of feminine writing (*écriture féminine*). Perhaps the most commented-upon text was Belgian director Chantal Akerman's minimalist three-hour portrait of a middle-class housewife-prostitute: *Jeanne Dielmann: 23 Quai du Commerce, 1080 Bruxelles* (Belgium and France, 1975) which depicted traditional femininity from a feminist stance. Laura Mulvey and Peter Wollen's exploration of Lacanian and Freudian theory from the mother's point of view in *Riddles of the Sphinx* (GB, 1975), Sally Potter's experimental short *Thriller* (GB, 1979), and American dancer-choreographer-filmmaker Yvonne Rainer's *Film about a Woman Who . . .* (USA, 1974) and *The Man who Envied Women* (USA, 1985) have also generated considerable debate (see Kuhn 1994; Kaplan 1983). For Mary Ann Doane, these filmmakers have attempted 'the elaboration of a special syntax for the female body' (1988: 227) and their concerns with language, desire, and identity have found an important critical venue in the US feminist film journal *Camera Obscura*.

Documentary

Although generally under-represented in academic criticism, the mode of filmmaking in which women's intervention has been most extensive and influential, which feminists first entered, and which remains most accessible to emerging artists, including women and people of colour, is documentary. In 1974 the National Film Board of Canada set up Studio D, a women's documentary unit, and more than 100 films, of whose style Bonnie Klein's indictment of the sex industry *Not a Love Story* (1981) is characteristic, have been made and distributed within that favourable institutional climate. Cinema verité and 'talking heads', interview-based formats allowed women to speak for themselves and to narrate history—exemplifying the feminist slogan 'the personal is the political'. Such films were meant to raise consciousness and to effect social

Unexpected framings and
discontinuous editing in
Trinh T. Min-ha's
Reassemblage (1982)

New subject positions—Sian
Martin in Ngozi Onwurah's
The Body Beautiful (1991)

change, addressing viewers in an accessible style and encouraging an active response. Hence, the form is particularly effective in constructing a community. In the heyday of 'ideological criticism', these documentary practices tended to be charged with a 'naïve realism'. Barbara Kopple's important feature-length documentary *Harlan County USA* (1976), for example, was critiqued for effacing the choices made in filming and editing that built narrative suspense. However, Julia Lesage makes a convincing case for 'the political aesthetics of feminist documentary film' in her essay of that title (1990)—arguing that such films construct, among other things, an iconography of everyday women completely absent from mainstream media— and the radical film magazine *Jump Cut*, of which Lesage is a founding editor, maintains a critical and aesthetic engagement with political films.

In the influential film *Daughter Rite* (1978), Michelle Citron, a contributor to *Jump Cut*, drew upon the immediacy and identificatory appeal of documentary while questioning its form. The film juxtaposed a cinéma verité interview with a pair of sisters with journal entries and home movie footage in order to explore the fraught connection between mother and daughter. Only by reading the credits does the viewer learn that the 'interviews' are scripted, but the film's emotional resonance, achieved through the autobiographical voice and the shared experience of being a daughter, is not diminished thereby. More recent work such as Mona Hatoum's *Measures of Distance* (1988) and Ngozi Onwurah's *The Body Beautiful* (1991) inscribe new subject positions—those of the diasporan daughter, the black daughter, and the mother herself—within the hybrid documentary 'genre' *Daughter Rite* might be credited with founding (see Kuhn 1994).

Such polyphony—of voices, points of view, and filmic idioms—increasingly characterizes feminist documentaries, particularly the self-representations of women of colour. This has, in turn, revitalized critical approaches to the form. In particular, an emerging body of theory takes on ethnographic film's traditional gaze at the 'Other', foregrounding questions of authenticity, authority, and testimony in the work of indigenous media-makers and critical anthropologists. No figure has been more crucial to this revision in feminist film studies than Vietnamese American filmmaker and theorist Trinh T. Min-ha (1991). In *Reassemblage* (1982) the filmmaker's voice-over states her intention not to speak about the Senegalese women the image track depicts in unexpected framings and discontinuous editing, but to 'speak nearby'.

With the widespread availability of the relatively inexpensive medium of video, women's media genres, exhibition venues, and critical paradigms have also proliferated. Lightweight and unobtrusive, the camcorder rejuvenated activist documentary, enabled the production of erotic videos by and for women, and reflected the 'identity politics' of the 1980s in an expanding body of independent work by women of colour and lesbians. Television commissions, women's film festivals, and the institutionalization of women's studies and film studies ensure that women's media culture remains a meeting-place of makers, users, and critics, although the symbiotic relationship that existed in the early 1980s between a certain kind of filmmaking practice and feminist film theory seems to have passed. This is due in part to the fact that the corpus is so much larger, in part to the maturation and hence diversification of feminist film studies as a discipline, and in part to larger cultural fragmentation of various kinds. Feminist filmmakers' interventions in cinematic language fit well with the 1970s and early 1980s focus in film theory on textual analysis—whether of dominant or modernist films. However, postmodernism, multiculturalism, and cultural studies has demanded a shift to contextual and local analysis, in which the boundaries between dominant and alternative, resistance and appropriation, production and reception, are significantly remapped. 'Diasporan', black, gay and lesbian, and other independent cinemas, and the cultural contexts in which they have circulated, have all required the refashioning of critical frameworks. As Teresa de Lauretis writes: 'If we rethink the problem of a specificity of women's cinema and aesthetic forms . . . in terms of address—who is making films for whom, who is looking and speaking, how, where, and to whom—then what has been seen as . . . an ideological split within feminist film culture between theory and practice, or between formalism and activism, may appear to be the very strength, the drive and productive heterogeneity of feminism' (de Lauretis 1985/1990: 296).

Conclusion

Pam Cook wrote in 1975 that 'from the outset, the Women's Movement has assumed without question the importance of mobilizing the media for women's struggle, at the same time subjecting them to a process of interrogation' (1975: 36). While carrying out that two-pronged strategy, feminist film studies has established itself as an academic field. If the terms of once-heated arguments—around the usefulness of psychoanalysis, the privileged status of Hollywood, the primacy of sexual difference—appear to have been superseded, contemporary debates are clearly founded upon them. Feminist cultural studies of popular cinema understand 'progressive texts' in social contexts: films such as *Fatal Attraction* (USA, 1987), *Aliens* (USA, 1986), and *Thelma and Louise* (USA, 1991) have therefore been analysed in terms of social anxieties about feminism, genre-mixing, popular reviews, and feminist appropriations. Queer theory has introduced the concept of gender performativity to studies of filmic representation and spectatorial response, drawing on psychoanalytic feminist theory's understanding of sexual identity as unstable, while critiquing heterosexist presumptions and giving voice to a new cultural politics. Transnational exhibition practices confirm that hypotheses of the film text as a bounded object and the spectator as fixed and unitary (Western and male) are untenable. Viewers, critics, and media practitioners mobilize 'the politics of location' to counter new forms of Hollywood hegemony with strategic new voices (see Shohat and Stam 1994). Such diverse and often contradictory methods, objects, and affiliations constitute the productive heterogeneity of contemporary feminist film culture.

BIBLIOGRAPHY

Armatage, Kay (1995), 'Nell Shipman: A Case of Heroic Femininity', in Pietropaolo and Testaferri (1995).

Bergstrom, Janet (1979), 'Rereading the Work of Claire Johnston', in Penley 1988.

—— (1988), 'Alternation, Segmentation, Hypnosis: Interview with Raymond Bellour', in Penley (1988).

Bobo, Jacqueline (1995), *Black Women as Cultural Readers* (New York: Columbia University Press).

Bruno, Giuliana (1995), 'Streetwalking around Plato's Cave', in Pietropaolo and Testaferri (1995).

*Carson, Diane, Linda Dittmar, and Janice Welsch (eds.) (1994), *Multiple Voices in Feminist Film Criticism* (Minneapolis: University of Minnesota Press).

Clover, Carol J. (1992), *Men, Women, and Chain Saws* (Princeton: Princeton University Press).

Comolli, Jean-Louis, and Jean Narboni (1969/1971), 'Cinema/Criticism/Ideology', *Screen*, 12/1: 27–35.

Cook, Pam (1975), 'Dorothy Arzner: Critical Strategies', in Johnston (1975b).

Cowie, Elizabeth (1984), 'Fantasia', *m/f*, 9: 76–105.

de Lauretis, Teresa (1984), *Alice Doesn't: Feminism, Semiotics, Cinema* (Bloomington: Indiana University Press).

—— (1985/1990), 'Rethinking Women's Cinema: Aesthetic and Feminist Theory', in Erens (1990).

Doane, Mary Ann (1982/1990), 'Film and the Masquerade: Theorizing the Female Spectator', in Erens (1990).

—— (1987), *The Desire to Desire: The Woman's Film of the 1940s* (Bloomington: Indiana University Press).

—— (1988), 'Woman's Stake: Filming the Female Body', in Penley (1988).

Dyer, Richard (1979) *Stars* (London: British Film Institute).

Ellsworth, Elizabeth (1990), 'Illicit Pleasures: Feminist Spectators and Personal Best', in Erens (1990).

*Erens, Patricia (ed.) (1990), *Issues in Feminist Film Criticism* (Bloomington: Indiana University Press).

Flitterman-Lewis, Sandy (1989), *To Desire Differently: Feminism and the French Cinema* (Urbana: University of Illinois Press).

Francke, Lizzie (1994), *Script Girls: Women Screenwriters in Hollywood* (London: British Film Institute).

Friedberg, Anne (1994), *Window Shopping: Cinema and the Postmodern* (Berkeley: University of California Press).

Gaines, Jane (1990), 'White Privilege and Looking Relations: Race and Gender in Feminist Film Theory', in Erens (1990).

—— and Charlotte Herzog (eds.) (1990), *Fabrications: Costume and the Female Body* (New York: Routledge).

Gledhill, Christine (1987), *Home is where the Heart Is: Studies in Melodrama and the Woman's Film* (London: British Film Institute).

Hall, Stuart (1980), 'Encoding/Decoding', in Stuart Hall et al. (eds.), *Culture, Media, Language* (London: Hutchinson).

Hansen, Miriam (1991), *Babel and Babylon: Spectatorship in American Silent Film* (Cambridge, Mass.: Harvard University Press).

Haskell, Molly (1974/1987), *From Reverence to Rape: The Treatment of Women in the Movies* (New York: Holt, Rinehart & Winston; 2nd edn. Chicago: University of Chicago Press).

hooks, bell (1992), 'The Oppositional Gaze', in *Black Looks* (Boston: South End Press).

Johnston, Claire (1973), 'Women's Cinema as Counter Cinema', in Claire Johnston (ed.), *Notes on Women's Cinema* (London: Society for Education in Film and Television); in Bill Nichols (ed.), *Movies and Methods*, ii (Berkeley: University of California Press).

—— (1975a), *The Work of Dorothy Arzner: Towards a Feminist Cinema* (London: British Film Institute).

—— (1975b), 'Feminist Politics and Film History', *Screen*, 16/3: 115–24.

*Kaplan, E. Ann (ed.) (1978), *Women in Film Noir* (London: British Film Institute).

—— (1983a), 'The Case of the Missing Mother: Maternal Issues in Vidor's *Stella Dallas*', *Heresies*, 16: 81–5.

—— (1983b), *Women and Film* (New York: Methuen).

*Kuhn, Annette (1994), *Women's Pictures: Feminism and Cinema*, 2nd edn. (London: Verso).

Laplace, Maria (1987), 'Producing and Consuming the Woman's Film: Discursive Struggle in *Now, Voyager*', in Gledhill (1987).

Lesage, Julia (1990), 'The Political Aesthetics of the Feminist Documentary Film', in Erens (1990).

Mayne, Judith (1990), *Woman at the Keyhole: Feminism and Women's Cinema* (Bloomington: Indiana University Press).

—— (1993), *Cinema and Spectatorship* (London: Routledge).

—— (1995), *Directed by Dorothy Arzner* (Bloomington: Indiana University Press).

Mellen, Joan (1974), *Women and their Sexuality in the New Film* (New York: Dell).

Modleski, Tania (1988), *The Women who Knew too Much: Hitchcock and Feminist Theory* (New York: Methuen).

Mulvey, Laura (1975/1990), 'Visual Pleasure and Narrative Cinema' in Erens (1990).

—— (1981/1988), 'Afterthoughts on "Visual Pleasure and Narrative Cinema" Inspired by *Duel in the Sun*' (1947) in Penley (1988).

Penley, Constance (ed.) (1988), *Feminism and Film Theory* (New York: Routledge; London: British Film Institute).

Petro, Patrice (1994), 'Feminism and Film History', in Carson et al. (1994)

Pietropaolo, Laura, and Ada Testaferri (eds.) (1995), *Feminisms in the Cinema* (Bloomington: Indiana University Press).

Pollock, Griselda (1992), 'What's Wrong with "Images of Women"?', in *The Sexual Subject: A 'Screen' Reader in Sexuality* (London: Routledge).

Rich, B. Ruby (1984), 'From Repressive Tolerance to Erotic Liberation: *Maedchen in Uniform*', in Mary Ann Doane, Patricia Mellencamp, and Linda Williams (eds.), *Re-Visions: Essays in Feminist Film Criticism* (Frederick, Md.: University Publications of America and American Film Institute).

—— (1990), 'In the Name of Feminist Film Criticism', in Erens (1990).

Roberts, Shari (1993), 'The Lady in the Tutti Frutti Hat: Carmen Miranda, a Spectacle of Ethnicity', *Cinema Journal*, 32/3: 3–23.

Rosen, Marjorie (1973), *Popcorn Venus: Women, Movies and the American Dream* (New York: Coward McCann & Geoghegan).

Shohat, Ella, and Robert Stam (1994), *Unthinking Eurocentrism: Multiculturalism and the Media* (New York: Routledge).

Silverman, Kaja (1988), 'The Female Authorial Voice', in *The Acoustic Mirror* (Bloomington: Indiana University Press).

Sontag, Susan (1972), 'Fascinating Fascism', in *Under the Sign of Saturn* (New York: Doubleday).

Stacey, Jackie (1987/1990), 'Desperately Seeking Difference', in Erens (1990).

Studlar, Gaylyn (1988), *In the Realm of Pleasure: Von Sternberg, Dietrich and the Masochistic Aesthetic* (Urbana: University of Illinois).

Trinh T. Min-Ha (1991), *When the Moon Waxes Red: Representation, Gender and Cultural Politics* (New York: Routledge).

Williams, Linda (1984/1990), '"Something Else besides a Mother": *Stella Dallas* and the Maternal Melodrama', in Erens (1990).

Rebecca

Mary Ann Doane, from Mary Ann Doane, *The Desire to Desire: The Woman's Film of the 1940s* (Bloomington: Indiana University Press/Basingstoke: MacMillan, 1987).

Rebecca (USA, 1940) belongs to that group of films which are infused by the Gothic and defined by a plot in which the wife fears her husband is a murderer. In films like *Rebecca*, *Dragonwyck* (USA, 1946), and *Undercurrent* (USA, 1946), the woman marries, often hastily, *into* the upper class; her husband has money and a social position which she cannot match. The marriage thus constitutes a type of transgression (of class barriers) which does not remain unpunished. The woman often feels dwarfed or threatened by the house itself (*Rebecca*, *Dragonwyck*). A frequent reversal of the hierarchy of mistress and servant is symptomatic of the fact that the woman is 'out of place' in her rich surroundings. Nevertheless, in films of the same genre, such as *Suspicion* (USA, 1941), *Secret beyond the Door . . .* (USA, 1948), and *Gaslight* (USA, 1944), the economic–sexual relationship is reversed. In each of these, there is at least a hint that the man marries the woman in order to obtain her money. Hence, it is not always the case that a woman from a lower class is punished for attempting to change her social and economic standing. Rather, the mixture effected by a marriage between two different classes produces horror and paranoia.

By making sexuality extremely difficult in a rich environment, both films—*Caught* (USA, 1949) and *Rebecca*—promote the illusion of separating the issue of sexuality from that of economics. What is really repressed in this scenario is the economics of sexual exchange. This repression is most evident in *Caught*, whose explicit moral—'Don't marry for money'—constitutes a negation of the economic factor in marriage. But negation, as Freud points out, is also affirmation; in *Caught* there is an unconscious acknowledgment of the economics of marriage as an institution. In the course of the film, the woman becomes the object of exchange, from Smith Ohlrig to Dr Quinada. A by-product of this exchange is the relinquishing of the posited object of her desire—the expensive mink coat.

There is a sense, then, in which both films begin with a hypothesis of female subjectivity which is subsequently disproven by the textual project. The narrative of *Caught* is introduced by the attribution of the look at the image (the 'I' of seeing) to Leonora and her friend. The film ends by positioning Leonora as the helpless, bedridden object of the medical gaze. In the beginning of *Rebecca*, the presence of a female subjectivity as the source of the enunciation is marked. A female voice-over (belonging to the Fontaine character) accompanies a hazy, dreamlike image: 'Last night I dreamed I went to Manderley again. It seems to me I stood by the iron gate leading to the drive. For a while I could not enter.' The

voice goes on to relate how, like all dreamers, she was suddenly possessed by a supernatural power and passed through the gate. This statement is accompanied by a shot in which the camera assumes the position of the 'I' and, in a sustained subjective movement, tracks forward through the gate and along the path. Yet the voice-over subsequently disappears entirely—it is not even resuscitated at the end of the film in order to provide closure through a symmetrical frame. Nevertheless, there *is* an extremely disconcerting re-emergence of a feminine 'I' later in the film. In the cottage scene in which Maxim narrates the 'unnarratable' story of the absent Rebecca to Joan Fontaine, he insists on a continual use of direct quotes and hence the first-person pronoun referring to Rebecca. His narrative is laced with these quotes from Rebecca which parallel on the soundtrack the moving image, itself adhering to the traces of an absent Rebecca. Maxim is therefore the one who pronounces the following statements: 'I'll play the part of a devoted wife'; 'When I have a child, Max, no one will be able to say that it's not yours'; 'I'll be the perfect mother just as I've been the perfect wife'; 'Well, Max, what are you going to do about it? Aren't you going to kill me?' Just as the tracking subjective shot guarantees that the story of the woman literally culminates as the image of the man, the construction of the dialogue allows Maxim to appropriate Rebecca's 'I'.

The films thus chronicle the emergence and disappearance of female subjectivity, the articulation of an 'I' which is subsequently negated. The pressure of the demand in the woman's film for the depiction of female subjectivity is so strong, and often so contradictory, that it is not at all surprising that sections such as the projection scenes in *Caught* and *Rebecca* should dwell on the problem of female spectatorship. These scenes internalize the difficulties of the genre and, in their concentration on the issue of the woman's relation to the gaze, occupy an important place in the narrative. Paranoia is here the appropriate and logical obsession. For it effects a confusion between subjectivity and objectivity, between the internal and the external, thus disallowing the gap which separates the spectator from the image of his or her desire.

In many respects, the most disturbing images of the two films are those which evoke the absence of the woman. In both films these images follow projection scenes which delineate the impossibility of female spectatorship. It is as though each film adhered to the logic which characterizes dreamwork—establishing the image of an absent woman as the delayed mirror image of a female spectator who is herself only virtual.

Rebecca

Tania Modleski, from Tania Modleski, *The Women who Knew Too Much: Hitchcock and Feminist Theory* (New York: Methuen, 1988).

As is well known by now, Laura Mulvey considers two options open to the male for warding off castration anxiety: in the course of the film the man gains control over the woman both by subjecting her to the power of the look and by investigating and demystifying her in the narrative. In *Rebecca* (USA, 1940), however, the sexual woman is never *seen*, although her presence is strongly evoked throughout the film, and so it is impossible for any man to gain control over her in the usual classical narrative fashion. I have discussed how, in the first shot of Maxim, the system of suture is reversed. This is of utmost importance. In her discussion of the system, Kaja Silverman notes, 'Classic cinema abounds in shot/reverse shot formations in which men look at women.' Typically, a shot of a woman is followed by a shot of a man—a surrogate for the male spectator— looking at her. This editing alleviates castration anxiety in two ways: first, the threat posed by the woman is allayed because the man seems to possess her; secondly, the 'gaze within the fiction' conceals 'the controlling gaze outside the fiction'—that of the castrating Other who lurks beyond the field of vision. But in *Rebecca* the beautiful, desirable woman is not only never sutured in as object of the look, not only never made a part of the film's field of vision, she is actually posited within the diegesis as all-seeing—as for example when Mrs Danvers asks

the terrified heroine if she thinks the dead come back to watch the living and says that she sometimes thinks Rebecca comes back to watch the new couple together.

In 'Film and the Labyrinth', Pascal Bonitzer equates the labyrinth with suspense and notes the power of off-screen space or 'blind space' to terrorize the viewer:

Specular space is on-screen space; it is everything we see on the screen. Off-screen space, blind space, is everything that moves (or wriggles) outside or under the surface of things, like the shark in *Jaws*. If such films 'work,' it is because we are more or less held in the sway of these two spaces. If the shark were always on screen it would quickly become a domesticated animal. What is frightening is that it is not there! The point of horror resides in the blind space.

Similarly, Rebecca herself lurks in the blind space of the film, with the result that, like the shark and unlike the second Mrs de Winter, she never becomes 'domesticated'. Rebecca is the Ariadne in this film's labyrinth, but since she does not relinquish the thread to any Theseus, her space, Manderley, remains unconquered by man.

In one of the film's most extraordinary moments the camera pointedly dynamizes Rebecca's absence. When Maxim tells

A negation of female subjectivity or a variant on the Oedipal drama? *Rebecca* (1940)

Rebecca continued

the heroine about what happened on the night of Rebecca's death ('She got up, came towards me', etc.), the camera follows Rebecca's movements in a lengthy tracking shot. Most films, of course, would have resorted to a flashback at this moment, allaying our anxiety over an empty screen by filling the 'lack'. Here, not only is Rebecca's absence stressed, but we are made to experience it as an active force. For those under the sway of Mulvey's analysis of narrative cinema, *Rebecca* may be seen as a spoof of the system, an elaborate sort of castration joke, with its flaunting of absence and lack.

It is true, however, that in the film's *narrative*, Rebecca is subjected to a brutal devaluation and punishment. Whereas the heroine, throughout most of the film, believes Rebecca to have been loved and admired by everyone, especially by Maxim, she ultimately learns that Maxim hated his first wife. 'She was', he says, 'incapable of love or tenderness or decency.' Moreover, the film punishes her for her sexuality by substituting a cancer for the baby she thought she was expecting, cancer being that peculiar disease which, according to popular myth, preys on spinster and nymphomaniac alike. In addition, Mrs Danvers receives the usual punishment inflicted on the bad mother–witch: she is burned alive when she sets fire to the Manderley mansion.

The latter part of *Rebecca*, concerned with the investigation, can be seen as yet another version of the myth of the overthrow of matriarchy by a patriarchal order. After all, Rebecca's great crime, we learn, was her challenge to patriarchal laws of succession. The night of her death she goaded Maxim into hitting her when she told him that she was carrying a child which was not his but which would one day inherit his possessions. Even more importantly, after Rebecca's death her 'spirit' presides and its power passes chiefly down the *female* line (through Mrs Danvers). Rebecca's name itself (as well as that of the house associated with her) overshadows not only the name of the 'second Mrs de Winter' but even the formidable one of the patriarch: George Fortesquieu Maximillian de Winter.

Ultimately the male authorities must step in and lay the ghost of Rebecca to rest once and for all (and true to Hollywood form, the point of view is eventually given over to Maxim while the heroine is mostly out of the picture altogether).

Nevertheless, despite this apparent closure, the film has managed in the course of its unfolding to hint at what feminine desire might be like were it allowed greater scope. First, it points to women's playfulness, granting them the power and threat of laughter. Over and over Rebecca's refusal to take men seriously is stressed, as when Mrs Danvers tells Maxim, Jack Favell, and Frank Crawley (another victim of Rebecca's seductive arts) that 'she used to sit on her bed and rock with laughter at the lot of you'. Even after the investigation, Maxim becomes upset all over again at the memory of Rebecca on the night of her death as she 'stood there laughing', taunting him with the details of her infidelity.

Moreover, Rebecca takes malicious pleasure in her own plurality. Luce Irigaray remarks, 'the force and continuity of [woman's] desire are capable of nurturing all the "feminine" masquerades for a long time'. And further, 'a woman's (re)discovery of herself can only signify the possibility of not sacrificing any of her pleasures to another, of not identifying with any one in particular, of never being simply one'. Rebecca is an intolerable figure precisely because she revels in her own multiplicity—her remarkable capacity to play the model wife and mistress of Manderley while conducting various love affairs on the side. Even after Rebecca's death, the 'force of her desire' makes itself felt, and, most appropriately, in light of Irigaray's comments, during a *masquerade* ball, in which the heroine dresses up like Rebecca, who had dressed up as Caroline de Winter, an ancestor whose portrait hangs on the wall. And all this occurs at the instigation of Mrs Danvers, another character who is identified with Rebecca, but to whom Rebecca is not limited. The eponymous and invisible villainess, then, is far from being the typical femme fatale of Hollywood cinema brought at last into the possession of men in order to secure for them a strong sense of their identity. Occupant of patriarchy's 'blind space', Rebecca is, rather, she who appears to subvert the very notion of identity—and of the visual economy which supports it.

It is no wonder that the film is (overly) determined to get rid of Rebecca, and that the task requires massive destruction. Yet there is reason to suppose that we cannot rest secure in the film's 'happy ending'. For if death by drowning did not extinguish the woman's desire, can we be certain that death by fire has reduced it utterly to ashes?

14 Gay and lesbian criticism

Anneke Smelik

Histories

Homosexuality in cinema has been there since the movies began. Homosexual characters could be glimpsed in films—as they still can today. However, their presence has characteristically been coded while homosexual characters have been taunted, ridiculed, silenced, pathologized, and more often than not killed off in the last reel. It is this rather sad history of homosexuality in cinema that Vito Russo wittily wrote down in his pioneering study *The Celluloid Closet* (1981) and which was subsequently turned into the film *The Celluloid Closet* (Rob Epstein and Jeffrey Friedman, USA, 1996), in which the filmmakers loyally adhere to Russo's project. *The Celluloid Closet* was closely linked to the rise of the gay and lesbian movement, which prompted lesbians and gay men to look differently at film and film history. This 're-visionary' look resulted in the rediscovery of forgotten films, directors, script-writers, producers, and actors and actresses; precious findings which would often be shown on the gay and lesbian film festivals that came into existence at the time, first starting in San Francisco in 1976. Russo's book, therefore, was a timely historical survey that politicized an emerging field of film studies: gay and lesbian criticism.

Until the publication of *The Celluloid Closet* in 1981, only one other book had been dedicated to this field: Parker Tyler's *Screening the Sexes* (1973), a camp clas-

sic that makes curious reading because of its delirious language, streak of misogyny, and penchant for the avant-garde and art cinema at the expense of Holly-wood films. However, its wit and unabashed lack of 'political correctness' are quite refreshing, while its pagan-Greek relish of the libidinal pleasures of the sexed body put it peculiarly close to the interests in perverse sexualities of today's queer theory. Whereas Tyler's book is written in a highly individualistic mode, *The Celluloid Closet* is invaluable not only for the poli-tical dimension that it gives to films, but also for writing a history of a hitherto oppressed group. The key term for Russo is 'visibility'. His project is to unveil the 'big lie' that lesbians and gay men do not exist and to expose the rampant homophobia that kept homosexuality in the closet both on and off the screen. His project is, therefore, an archaeological one of uncovering and exposing those moments where homosexuality becomes visible on the screen.

The Celluloid Closet has, however, been criticized for its unproblematic view of history (Medhurst 1977/1984). While Russo's book provided the gay and lesbian move-ment with a necessary history of cinema from the gay point of view, it could only do so by projecting a linear story of the representation of homosexuality in Holly-wood cinema. Such a linear story presupposes a smooth history of progression, from taboo, censorship, and stereotypes to liberation, freedom, and positive images, only to be (temporarily?) disturbed by the backlash that the AIDS crisis has induced. This progressive narrative denies the twists and turns as well as the ambivalences and contradictions of history. It also presupposes an undifferentiated notion of homosexuality, regardless of differences of gender, race, or class; Russo, indeed, has been reproached for his neglect of lesbians, and even for his 'bitchy misogyny' (Rich 1981/1984: 129 n. 30).

Stereotypes

Russo's historical approach is akin to early feminist studies of the 1970s that describe the position of women in the movies. The feminist movement and the gay and lesbian movement share a concern with questions of gender and sexuality and both are committed to the linking of the personal and the political; indeed, most of the essays and books that I discuss in this chapter are marked by a distinctly personal tone in which the writer's homosexuality is brought to bear on cinema and theory. Like early feminist and black film criticism, early gay and lesbian criticism was mostly directed at stereotyping. Films, and especially those from Hollywood, were criticized for reproducing dominant stereotypes of homosexuals—such as the sissy, the sad young man, the gay psychopath, the seductive androgyne, the unnatural woman, or the lesbian vampire—and failing to represent 'real' gays and lesbians. For straight spectators, such stereotypes could confirm prejudice, while for gay and lesbian spectators they might encourage self-hatred. However, while anger at the unfavourable representation of homosexuality (and at the reduction of homosexuals to sexuality as the defining aspect of their character) is fully justified, a simple call for positive images is not the solution as images of gays and lesbians cannot simply be seen as 'true' or 'false'. Rather, it is necessary to understand how stereotypes function in both ideological and cinematic terms.

Richard Dyer was among the first to offer a more theoretical critique of stereotypes (1977a). Dyer argues that stereotypes have the function of ordering the world around us. Stereotyping works in society both to establish and to maintain the hegemony of the dominant group (heterosexual white men) and to marginalize and exclude other social groups (homosexuals, blacks, women, the working class). Stereotypes, then, produce sharp oppositions between social groups in order to maintain clear boundaries between them. They are also normative. Stereotypes of gays and lesbians such as the queen and the dyke reproduce norms of gendered heterosexuality because they indicate that the homosexual man or woman falls short of the heterosexual norm: that they can never be a 'real' man or woman. The fashion queen Madame Lucy in *Irene* (USA, 1926), the dresser Diggs in *It's Love I'm After* (1937), the homosexual men in *La dolce vita* (Italy, 1960) or the black queen Lindy in *Car Wash* (USA, 1976) are just a few examples of 'sissies' who fail the norm of masculinity. If the queen is characteristically a source of comedy (*La Cage aux folles*, France, 1978), the dyke is mostly associated with violence. The lesbian Nazi in *Roma, città aperta* ('Rome, Open City' Italy, 1945), the communist butch in *From Russia with Love* (GB, 1963), or George–June in *The Killing of Sister George* (GB, 1969) are all examples of the dyke stereotyped as a predatory, sadistic, castrating bitch–butch (Sheldon 1977; Hetze 1986).

> **Stereotypes of gays and lesbians such as the queen and the dyke reproduce norms of gendered heterosexuality because they indicate that the homosexual man or woman falls short of the heterosexual norm: that they can never be a 'real' man or woman.**

The stereotypes of the queen as the effeminate man and the dyke as the mannish woman are, therefore, informed by the structuring opposition of sexual difference. Within semiotics, narrative is also understood to be structured through oppositions (de Lauretis 1984), and it is easy to see how stereotypes contribute to this process. For example, stereotypes of decadent homosexuals can be used to contrast with the uncorrupted heterosexual male hero, as is the case with Peter Lorre and Humphrey Bogart respectively in *The Maltese Falcon* (USA, 1941). The implication of this is that a hero can rarely be other than heterosexual (and white) in Hollywood. Thus, in spite of biographical and historical evidence of his homosexuality, the hero Lawrence is made staunchly heterosexual in *Lawrence of Arabia* (USA, 1962), while homosexuality is delegated to the evil Turkish bey.

Stereotypes can also be introduced through iconography. Visual and aural details can be used to typify homosexuality immediately. For example, codes in dressing, certain gestures, stylistic decor, or extended looks can at a glance invoke the homosexuality of a character. As Dyer (1977a) points out, such stereotypical imagery makes homosexuality visible. In contrast to gender or ethnicity, homosexuality is not after all visible at first sight. Therefore, it has to be established visually, especially in the many films in which homosexuality remains closeted. Stereotyping through iconography, therefore, categorizes the gay or lesbian character as distinct from straight characters and maintains the boundaries between them.

The main problem with stereotypes is that they appear to be inevitable and 'natural'. Here, Barthes's notion of 'myth', introduced into film studies by Claire Johnston (1973), may explain how stereotypes become naturalized. The stereotype of the homosexual character functions as a structure, a code or convention. The sign 'homosexual' represents the ideological meaning that the homosexual has for heterosexuality, as the negative or the failure of the heterosexual norm. The realist conventions of classical cinema veil the ideological representation of the sign 'homosexual', (re)presenting the constructed images, the stereotypes, of gay men and lesbians as natural and realistic. Such a theoretical critique of stereotypes helps to explain the normative and normalizing effects of heterosexual hegemony. The question is therefore not how to get rid of stereotypes (as they are both efficient and resilient), nor how to replace them with positive images (which leave the heterosexist imperative intact), but how to achieve complexity, diversity, and self-definition (see Dyer 1977a). This has been the quest of gay and lesbian cinema, which I will discuss later.

Authorship

The shift away from a sociological examination of the ways in which homosexuals have been represented on the screen to issues of ideology and sexual politics opens up a much wider and more complex field of inquiry for lesbian and gay film criticism, including a reassessment of theoretical frameworks from a gay perspective. Thus, Robin Wood (1977) returns to his earlier auteur criticism to bring questions of ideology and sexual politics to bear on the cinema of such

'auteurs' as Jean Renoir, Ingmar Bergman, and Howard Hawks. In doing so, he now finds an ambiguity in their films which indicate both a repression of homosexuality as well as the inevitable cracks in bourgeois heterosexuality.

With the advent of post-structuralist theory, however, the notion of the auteur more or less disappeared from the theoretical agenda. Neither feminists nor homosexuals deplored this 'death of the author', who was invariably a white, heterosexual male, and a genius at that. Such heroes were better buried. Yet, for feminists it mattered a great deal whether an author was female or not, and similarly for lesbians and gay men it was of paramount importance whether a text was the work of a homosexual. Medhurst (1991a: 198) reveals a double standard at work, in this respect: 'Authorship was bad, Gay Authorship was good.' The death of the author also signified a more general death of the subject, and hence of subjectivity and identity, which was now seen to be forever dispersed and disrupted. Many feminists, however, have been suspicious of the time loop involved in the death of the subject (Braidotti 1991; hooks 1990). At the historical moment when marginalized subjects—blacks, people of colour, post-colonial subjects, women, lesbians, and gay men—claim their subjectivity, the white, middle-class, heterosexual male declares that very subject to be over and out.

> **For feminists it mattered a great deal whether an author was female or not, and similarly for lesbians and gay men it was of paramount importance whether a text was the work of a homosexual.**

Medhurst (1991a) reintroduces the question of authorship in relation to homosexuality in an article on the film *Brief Encounter* (GB, 1941). While he is aware of the pitfalls of an essentialist claim to homosexual identity in the case of a gay rereading of *Brief Encounter* (attributing that gay sensibility to the playwright Noel Coward), he still wants to maintain that marginal groups like gay people should hold on to authorship for political reasons. This does not mean a regression to a simplistic reading of authorial intentions in texts, but a construction of a

Dorothy Arzner, 'the great exception'

contradictory history of homosexual identity in a heterosexual culture.

Judith Mayne (1990) tackles the difficulties of female and lesbian authorship in classical cinema in a case-study of director Dorothy Arzner, who is generally considered as the great exception—the only woman director who made a career in Hollywood. Feminist attempts to theorize Arzner's authorship have claimed her as an auteur in the male pantheon and identified her films as a progressive critique of patriarchal cinema.

However, for Mayne, Arzner's authorial inscriptions can be situated in the problematization of (lesbian) pleasure: in the relations between and among women and in marginal lesbian gestures. She suggests that 'female authorship acquires its most significant contours in Arzner's work through relations between and among women', recognizing in the representations of those relations a complex form of irony (1990: 101). In dedicating a book to the life and work of Dorothy Arzner, Mayne (1994) therefore focuses on the issues of secrecy, visibility, and lesbian representation involved in the writing of a history of a closeted lesbian film-maker in Hollywood.

Rereadings of Hollywood and spectatorship

The lesbian appeal of female Hollywood stars has also been commonly recognized. Weiss (1992) discusses the attraction of Hollywood stars like Marlene Dietrich, Greta Garbo, and Katharine Hepburn for lesbian spectators in the 1930s. Because the silver screen was often a place where dreams could be fulfilled at a time when gays were still socially isolated, she argues that the powerful image of these stars helped to shape the white urban lesbian subculture of the time. The androgynous appearances of Dietrich in *Morocco* (USA, 1930), Garbo in *Queen Christina* (USA, 1933), and Hepburn in *Sylvia Scarlett* (USA, 1935), in particular, were embraced as an image of sexual ambiguity which served as a point of identification outside conventional gender positions.

Gay male spectators performed similar kinds of oppositional reading. The homoerotic appeal of male stars like the young Marlon Brando and James Dean has been widely commented upon. Russo discovered a gay subtext in many a Hollywood film, from the display of male bodies and competition in *Ben Hur* (USA, 1926 and the 1959 remake) to the ritualized fights in westerns, such as that between Montgomery Clift and John Wayne in *Red River* (USA, 1948). The loving looks between Richard Barthelmess and Cary Grant in *Only Angels have Wings* (USA, 1939) or Dewey Martin and Kirk Douglas in *The Big Sky* (USA, 1952) also alerted the homosexual spectator to a gay subtext in the films of Howard Hawks (Russo 1981). But as Russo never tires of pointing out, homosexuality was still very much silenced and closeted in classical Hollywood films and a gay subtext was never more than a hidden text which could only be discovered by the spectator who was sensitized to the coded messages of homosexuality.

Such rereadings of Hollywood cinema have inevitably raised the issue of gay and lesbian spectatorship. Gay and lesbian criticism took most of its lead from feminist film studies and, until at least the mid-1980s, the dominant paradigm remained focused upon the organization of the look, the male gaze and the female spectacle. Although productive for feminism, the heterosexual bias of this exclusive focus on sexual difference proved difficult for gay and lesbian studies. Indeed, feminist film theory—not unlike the Hollywood cinema it criticized so fiercely— seemed unable to conceive of representation outside heterosexuality. As Patricia White (1991) aptly remarks, the 'ghostly presence of lesbianism' haunts not only Hollywood Gothics but also feminist film theory. In its special issue *Lesbians and Film* (1981, 24–5: 17), the journal *Jump Cut* also claimed that: 'It sometimes seems to us that lesbianism is the hole in the heart of feminist film criticism.' Almost ten years later matters had apparently improved very little. Mayne (1990) complains that the denial of Arzner's lesbian identity points to a curious gap in feminist film theory, indeed to the 'structuring absence' of lesbianism (1990: 107).

The indictment that Hollywood cinema was tailored to the pleasures of the male spectator raised questions about the position of the female spectator. In spite of the increasing focus on female spectatorship in feminist scholarship, the homosexual pleasures of the female spectator were largely ignored. The difficulties in theorizing the female spectator have led Jackie Stacey (1987) to exclaim that feminist film critics have written the darkest scenario possible for the female look as being male, masochistic, or marginal. In breaking open the restrictive dichotomies of feminist film theory, Stacey tries to create a space for the homosexual pleasures of spectatorship. A more complex model of cinematic spectatorship is needed in order to avoid a facile binarism that maps homosexuality onto an opposition of masculinity and femininity. Stacey suggests the need 'to separate gender identification from sexuality' which are 'too often conflated in the name of sexual difference' (1987: 53). When difference is no longer reduced to sexual difference but is also understood as difference among women, representation of an active female desire becomes possible, even in Hollywood films. In films like *All about Eve* (USA, 1950) or *Desperately Seeking Susan* (USA, 1984), narrative desire is produced by the difference between two women; by women wanting to become the idealized other. An interplay of difference and otherness prevents the collapse of that desire into identification, prompting Stacey to conclude that the rigid psychoanalytic distinction between desire and identification fails to address different constructions of desire.

De Lauretis (1988) has also drawn attention to the difficulties of imagining lesbian desire within a psycho-analytic discourse that predicates sexual difference on sexual *indifference*. She here follows Luce Irigaray's notion of the symbolic law representing only one and not two sexes: patriarchy is deeply 'hommo-sexual' as it erects the masculine to the one and only norm. Discussing the same problematic in a later essay, de Lauretis (1991: 252) observes that the institution of heterosexuality defines all sexuality to such an extent that 'the effort to represent a homosexual–lesbian desire is a subtle and difficult one'. She criticizes Stacey for conceiving of desire between women as 'woman-identified female bonding' and failing to see it as sexual. Here, and more extensively in her later book *The Practice of Love* (1994), de Lauretis returns to Freudian theory to account for the specificity of lesbian desire in terms of fetishism.

In answer to de Lauretis's criticism, Stacey (1994) argues in her study of female spectatorship that she is not concerned with a specifically lesbian audience but with a possible homoeroticism for all women in the audience. Her aim is to eroticize identification rather than de-eroticize desire. The female spectator is quite likely to encompass erotic components in her desiring look, while at the same time identifying with the woman-as-spectacle.

While these discussions of lesbian spectatorship are part of a wider movement in film studies to include the heterogeneity of the spectatorial situation, most discussions of spectatorship have been about white audiences. De Lauretis was criticized for not taking into account racial dynamics in the lesbian film *She must be Seeing Things* (USA, 1987) (see the discussion following de Lauretis's 1991 article). Little research is available about black audiences, although some critics have examined black female spectatorship in popular culture (e.g. Bobo 1995). The issue of black lesbian spectatorship, however, has hardly been raised.

On masculinity

Male gay criticism has also been concerned to assess the implications of the binary ideology of sexual difference which gay and lesbian criticism inherited from feminist film theory. Just as the dominant paradigm of feminist film theory raised questions about the male look and the female spectacle, it also raised questions about the eroticization of the male body. What, it was

asked, if the male body is the object of the female gaze or of another male gaze; and how exactly does the male body become the signifier of the phallus? (*Screen* 1992). The discussion of the representation of masculinity in cinema took off in the early 1980s and almost immediately raised the issue of homosexual desire in two programmatic articles (Dyer 1982; Neale 1983).

The image of the male body as object of a look is fraught with ambivalences, repressions, and denials. Like the masquerade, the notion of spectacle has such strong feminine connotations that for a male performer to be put on display or to don a mask threatens his very masculinity. Because the phallus is a symbol and a signifier, no man can fully symbolize it. Although the patriarchal male subject has a privileged relation to the phallus, he will always fall short of the phallic ideal. Lacan notices this effect in his essay on the meaning of the phallus: 'the curious consequence of making virile display in the human being itself seems feminine' (1977: 291). Male spectacle, then, entails being put in a feminine position. The immanent feminization of male spectacle then brings about two possible dangers for the performing male: functioning as an object of desire he can easily become the object of ridicule, and within a heterosexist culture accusations of homosexuality can be launched against him (Neale 1983; Tasker 1993).

Most critics agree that the spectatorial look in mainstream cinema is implicitly male. While for Dyer this means that images of men do not automatically 'work' for women, according to Neale the erotic element in looking at the male body has to be repressed and disavowed so as to avoid any implications of male homosexuality. Yet, male homosexuality is always present as an undercurrent; it is Hollywood's symptom. The denial of the homoeroticism of looking at images of men constantly involves sado-masochistic themes, scenes, and fantasies; hence the highly ritualized scenes of male struggle which deflect the look away from the male body to the scene of the spectacular fight. Richard Meyer (1991) explores the more homely representations of Rock Hudson's body, which made him available as an object of erotic contemplation. Meyer argues that Hudson's image was produced for the female spectator, which was only possible as long as his homosexuality remained unspoken. With the public disclosure of Hudson as an AIDS victim in 1985, his now homosexualized body was imaged as the signifier of illness and death.

Kobena Mercer (1991a) problematizes the gay male look in his exploration of aesthetic ambivalence in visual representations of the black male nude. While Robert Mapplethorpe's photographs of black males can be seen as an objectification and fetishization of the nude male body, Mercer also sees a homoerotic subversive dimension to the pictures. The identification and involvement of Mapplethorpe with his models undermine a voyeuristic gaze. Here Mercer argues that the gay identity of the author and of the spectator are important to the process of interpretation. The context of a homosexual subculture enables Mercer to read the pictures as humorous and sensitive deconstructions of race and sexuality. By replacing the object of the conventional nude in Western culture, the white woman, by the black gay male, Mapplethorpe creates a subversive ambivalence. For Mercer, Mapplethorpe problematizes the white male subject in his visual work and he ends his essay with a call for a study of the construction of whiteness within gay and lesbian criticism.

Many studies on visual representations of masculinity refer to the homoeroticism of popular figures like Batman (Medhurst 1991b) or Pee-Wee Hermann (Camera Obscura 1988; Doty 1993). Most studies of masculinity point to the crisis in which the white male heterosexual subject finds himself, a crisis in which his masculinity is fragmented and denaturalized, in which the signifiers of 'man' and 'manly' seem to have lost all of their meaning and which makes Hollywood desperate to find a 'few good white men' (Easthope 1986; Kirkham and Thumin 1993; Tasker 1993; Jeffords 1994). Yet, what is a crisis to one (the dominant subject) may well mean a liberation, or at least an opening, to the other (the marginalized subjects). Therefore, the crisis in masculinity is welcomed by gay critics. In his book on male impersonators, Mark Simpson takes great pleasure in celebrating the deconstruction of 'masculinity's claim to authenticity, to naturalness, to coherence—to dominate' (1994: 7). He hopes that the crisis of masculinity signifies a desegregation of homosexuality and heterosexuality in popular culture, transforming both in the process.

Camp

Gay studies of masculinity often border on camp readings of the male spectacle (Medhurst 1991b; Simpson 1994). Dyer (1986) addresses a different kind of homosexual spectator identification in his discussion of Judy Garland's appeal for gay men. He suggests that the star image of Garland played a role in white urban male subculture because of two of her qualities: authenticity and theatricality. Garland embodied an intensity of emotional life which was recognized as truthful by gay men who themselves lived a life on the edge as homosexuals in a straight world. Yet, Garland's deep passion was inflected with an equally deep irony, which can be seen as a characteristic of gay sensibility. Like Garland, gay sensibility holds together the antithetical qualities of authenticity and theatricality, or, in the words of Dyer, 'a fierce assertion of extreme feeling with a deprecating sense of its absurdity' (1986: 154). Of course, we enter here the notion of camp and its relation to male gay subculture. Garland was experienced as being camp. She was over-the-top, ironic, excessive, and thus a grateful object of drag acts (for example, Craig Russell in Outrageous!, Canada, 1977). Camp, however, is not merely humour but also inflected with pathos. Dyer draws attention to the 'knife edge between camp and hurt' (1986: 180) in Garland's public pain and suffering, an edge that resonated deeply with her male gay audience.

> **Camp can be seen as an oppositional reading of popular culture which offers identifications and pleasures that dominant culture denies to homosexuals.**

I do not want to discuss camp here as a phenomenon in itself. Rather than running the risk of being dead serious about something as quixotic as camp, I propose to discuss camp as a reading strategy for gay people. Camp can be seen as an oppositional reading of popular culture which offers identifications and pleasures that dominant culture denies to homosexuals. Jack Babuscio (1977) discusses camp as an expression of gay sensibility, by which he means a heightened awareness of one's social condition outside the mainstream. In this sense, camp is experiential and resists analytical discourse (Medhurst 1991b). According to Babuscio, the 'bitter-wit' of camp points to the transformation of pain into laughter, the chosen way of dealing with the incongruous situation of gays in society.

As an oppositional reading, camp can be subversive for bringing out the cultural ambiguities and contradictions that usually remain sealed over by dominant ideology. This characteristic brings camp into the realm of postmodernism, which also celebrates ambivalence and heterogeneity. Subcultural camp and postmodern theory share a penchant for irony, play, and parody, for artificiality and performance, as well as for transgressing conventional meanings of gender. This queer alliance between camp and postmodernism has often been noted. Medhurst even claims provocatively that 'postmodernism is only heterosexuals catching up with camp' (1991a: 206). It is indeed an easy leap from Babuscio's understanding of camp as signifying performance rather than existence, to Judith Butler's notion of gender signifying performance rather than identity. Just as Babuscio claims that the emphasis on style, surface, and the spectacle results in incongruities between 'what a thing or person *is* to what it *looks* like' (1977/1984: 44), Butler (1990) asserts that the stress on performativity allows us to see gender as enacting a set of discontinuous if not parodic performances. In the context of gay and lesbian criticism, it is important to realize that both camp and postmodernism denaturalize feminity and masculinity.

Camp is very much the prerogative of gay male, mostly white, subculture (although Mercer (1991b) points to the camp element in the soul tradition of black musicians, long before white pop stars began to exploit such imagery). In its deconstruction of heterosexual male authority and its expression of a displaced subjectivity within dominant culture, camp might be considered an attractive framework for lesbians. Paula Graham (1995), however, expresses her doubts about camp as a possible paradigm for lesbian readings. She argues that camp allows gay men to identify with feminine excess, that is with the phallic female star, precisely as a threat to or parody of male authority (Judy Garland, Joan Crawford, Bette Davis). For lesbians, such an identification with femininity would 'mark a subordination to masculine authority, and not a form of resistance to it' (1995: 178). This does not mean that lesbians do not enjoy camp films or the spectacle of sexual excess, but rather that gay men and lesbians do not share the same 'canon' of camp. Lesbians characteristically prefer a display of strong, masculinized, active female stars such as

Sigourney Weaver as Ripley in the first *Alien* movie (USA, 1979), Linda Hamilton in *Terminator 2: Judgement Day* (USA, 1991), and, yes, even Sharon Stone in *Basic Instinct* (USA, 1991). Such a lesbian appropriation of subject positions may be disruptive and transgressive, but not camp.

It is significant that in the 1990s the notion of 'camp' is often replaced by the term 'queer'. Camp is historically more associated with the closeted homosexuality of the 1950s and only came to the surface in the 1960s and 1970s. Postmodernism of the 1980s and 1990s brought campy strategies into the mainstream. Now, lesbians and gay men identify their oppositional reading strategies as 'queer'. Away from the notions of oppression and liberation of earlier gay and lesbian criticism, queerness is associated with the playful self-definition of a homosexuality in non-essentialist terms. Not unlike camp, but more self-assertive, queer readings are fully inflected with irony, transgressive gender parody, and deconstructed subjectivities.

Gay and lesbian filmmaking

Alongside rereadings of Hollywood films, gay and lesbian criticism has also turned to the few films made by lesbians and gay men and with gay subject-matter, although these critical explorations are relatively few and did not appear until the late 1980s (see Gever *et al.* 1993). European art cinema has provided a tradition in which the representation of gay and lesbian subject-matter is not a priori foreclosed. *Mädchen in Uniform* ('Girls in Uniform', Germany, 1931) was one of the earliest films to be rediscovered from a lesbian perspective. The film had always been praised for its stylistic qualities, as well as for its anti-fascism, but its explicit theme of lesbianism was long subject to silence and censorship. Rich (1981) argues that the anti-fascist politics of *Mädchen in Uniform* is interconnected with its lesbian theme and its struggle against authoritarian structures and sexual repression. Rich places the film in the historical context of Weimar with its vibrant lesbian subculture, especially in Berlin. Dyer (1990) too discusses the film within the German context of Weimar culture, its general openness about sexuality, and its public discussions of the notion of a third sex as introduced by Max Hirschfeld and his Institute of Sexual Science. The open lesbianism, the plea for sexual freedom, and the revolt against patriarchy have made

Mädchen in Uniform
(1931)—'open lesbianism'
and a 'plea for sexual
freedom'

Mädchen in Uniform a popular classic that still moves and delights lesbian audiences today.

Mädchen in Uniform, however, does not stand alone, but is part of a tradition of gay and lesbian filmmaking within early cinema (see Dyer 1990; Weiss 1992). Some films are explicitly gay, like *Anders als die Andern* ('Different from the Others', Germany, 1919), an ambivalent film in which the gay main character commits suicide despite the affirmative lectures given by Hirschfeld himself within the film. Other films were made by gay or lesbian filmmakers, like the surrealist shorts of Germaine Dulac which have been read as critiques of heterosexuality. Fantasy plays an important role in these experimental films. In *La Souriante Madame Beudet* ('The Smiling Mme Beudet', France, 1923) a woman fantasizes murdering her bully of a husband and escaping from her bourgeois marriage, and *La Coquille et le clergyman* ('The Seashell and the Clergyman', France, 1927) exposes Oedipal male fantasies about the mystery of 'woman'. Yet other films featured lesbian or gay characters, like the Countess Geschwitz in *Die Büchse der Pandora* ('Pandora's Box', Germany, 1928) or the male prisoner in *Geslecht in Fesseln* ('Sex in Bondage', Germany, 1928).

Jean Genet's prison film *Un chant d'amour* ('A Song of Love', France, 1950) is another classic which

has become enormously popular with gay audiences until today and which also has influenced gay filmmakers. Dyer (1990) places this short erotic fantasy in the prestigious tradition of French literature by the 'poètes maudits', the 'accursed poets' like de Sade, Baudelaire, Rimbaud, Verlaine, and Cocteau; a literature which intertwines the elements of evil, criminality, and (homo)sexuality. In his detailed analysis of the narrative structure, imagery, and ways of looking in *Un chant d'amour*, Dyer discusses the film's eroticism in terms of the tension between politics and pleasure. While some gay critics have reprimanded the film for its 'oppression' of gay men or were disturbed by its 'homophobic' representation of erotic pleasures, others took a more permissive or even celebratory attitude to the sado-masochism of the film. Dyer argues that the renewed political interest in perverse sexualities opened a Foucauldian reading of the film's eroticism in terms of the social and historical relation between sexuality and power.

The play of power and desire has become the theme of some gay and lesbian films in the 1980s, which Dyer calls a 'Genetesque' tradition. The high artificiality of Fassbinder's last film, *Querelle* (Germany, 1982, based on Genet's 1947 novel), places the story firmly within the realm of fantasy and desire. For Dyer (1990: 91), the film is 'an abstraction of the erotics of power'. The same ritualization of desire and power can be found in the sadean theatre of *Verführung: Die grausame Frau* ('Seduction: The Cruel Woman', Germany, 1985) by Elfi Mikesch and Monika Treut. This highly formalized and aestheticized exploration of sado-masochism was one of the first films to bring female desire and lesbian sexuality within the domain of power and violence. Similarly, the fantasmatic films of Ulrike Ottinger—from *Madame X—eine absolute Herrscherin* ('Madame X—an Absolute Ruler', Germany, 1977) to *Johanna D'Arc of Mongolia* (Germany, 1989)—humorously deconstruct traditional femininity and celebrate nomadic lesbian subjectivities (White 1987; Longfellow 1993).

Gay activism and identity politics

The art-house tradition of filmmaking, with its investment in fantasy as well as in the exploration of 'perverse' sexualities, is obviously related to gay and lesbian subcultures, but could not be further removed from the activist movies which came out of the gay and lesbian movement. The difference lies not so much in style (some activist movies have also used experimental forms, like the films of Barbara Hammer) as in the emphasis on the affirmation of gay identity. This kind of identity politics is quite adverse to the subversion and deconstruction of gay identity found in art-house films. Diana Fuss describes identity politics as 'the tendency to base one's politics on a sense of personal identity—as gay, as Jewish, as Black, as female' (1989: 97). In order to be able to build a political community, gay men and lesbians felt the need to consolidate a unified and visible identity. Strategies of consciousness-raising and coming out helped them to stimulate personal awareness and political action. Film was an excellent medium to lend visibility to gays and lesbians. Between 1970 and 1980 alone, the movement produced over forty affirmative documentaries, of which *Word is Out* (USA, 1977) is no doubt the most famous (see Dyer 1990). Documentary was the privileged genre, because it was considered to record reality, i.e. to document the so far unwritten and invisible history of gays and lesbians.

Identity politics, however, runs the risk of essentialism: of seeing identity as the hidden essence of one's being. Although gay activism needed this view of iden-

tity for its organization and politics, this very notion of sexual identity as eternal, ahistorical, and unchanging is paradoxically at odds with the demands for political transformation. The debate here is between essentialism and constructionism. In this respect, the influence of Foucault's discourse theory on gay and lesbian studies cannot be overestimated (although Foucault was more influential in gay studies than in lesbian studies; see Fuss 1989). His efforts to de-essentialize sexuality and to historicize homosexuality dealt a blow to any simplistic notion of homosexuality as a unified, coherent, and fixed category as well as to any claim to an unproblematic authenticity and truth. From a constructionist point of view, sexuality is not a given of nature but a construct of culture. Thus, the debate shifts from realizing a shared essence to understanding homosexuality as a product of social forces. (Dyer 1990: 275). The question then becomes how homosexuality has been shaped, defined, and regulated by dominant culture throughout history.

> **From a constructionist point of view, sexuality is not a given of nature but a construct of culture. Thus, the debate shifts from realizing a shared essence to understanding homosexuality as a product of social forces.**

Psychoanalytic theories have also added to a more complex understanding of identity. Especially within Lacanian psychoanalysis, identity is seen as fundamentally unstable and fictitious. The unconscious workings of the psyche constantly destabilize a coherent identity. Identity is therefore never a finished product, but rather always in process (see de Lauretis 1984, 1994). Such an understanding of identity does not mean that there is no identity at all; as Fuss points out 'fictions of identity, importantly, are no less powerful for being fictions' (1989: 104). Nevertheless, the Foucauldian and psychoanalytic views of identity and sexuality have together created a post-structuralist climate in which assertions of an uncomplicated gay and lesbian identity have become rather suspect.

Essentialist identity politics seeks to smooth over differences. If homosexual identity is understood as a homogeneous and shared essence, both differences *within* identity as well as differences *between* identities are ignored. As a result, gay activism had difficulties dealing with differences between gay men and lesbians, let alone accounting for differences of class and ethnicity. However, if post-structuralist theory opened up questions of identity and difference within gay and lesbian criticism (Doan 1994), it presented the problem of how different kinds of social identity relate to one another. Adding age to class to sexuality to ethnicity and so on simply results in divisive and mutually exclusive categories which fight for a position within a hierarchy of oppressions. As Kobena Mercer has argued, the rhetorical invocation of the 'race, class, gender mantra' obscures the way in which these social categories intersect (1993: 239). Mercer pleads for a hybridized understanding of identity. A hybrid identity negotiates between a plurality of different positions, which opens up the recognition of 'unity-in-diversity' (240).

The films *Looking for Langston* by Isaac Julien (GB, 1989) and *Tongues Untied* by Marlon Riggs (USA, 1990) are examples of hybridized cultural practice by black gay filmmakers. For Mercer, the foregrounding of autobiographical voices in *Tongues Untied* produces a multilayered 'dialogic voicing', which is fully aware of the multidimensional character of politics. The dialogic strategy becomes subversive in its use of playfulness and parody. These two elements, the dialogic voicing and the humour, are embedded in the oral tradition of African American culture.

Mercer reads the stylistic formalism of *Looking for Langston* as a deconstructive appropriation and re-articulation of dominant signifiers of racial and sexual representation. While the film offers an archaeology of black modernism in its 'promiscuous intertextuality' (1993: 251), it is also an allegory of black gay desire. Through the key motif of looks and looking the film explores the role of fantasy within desire. Mercer concludes his analysis of the two films with a brief discussion of authorship. The notion of hybridized identity does not foreclose the importance of an authorial signature. As Mercer argues, in so far as 'identity is not what you are so much as what you do' (240), he can claim that 'these rich, provocative, and important works do indeed "make a difference" not because of who or what the filmmakers are, but because of what they do, and above all because of the freaky way they do it' (255). It is also this proliferation of multiple voices within gay and lesbian filmmaking and criticism which testifies to the liveliness of this political field within the study of film and popular culture.

BIBLIOGRAPHY

Babuscio, Jack (1977/1984), 'Camp and Gay Sensibility', in Richard Dyer (ed.), *Gays and Film* (rev. edn. New York: Zoetrope).

Bobo, Jacqueline (1995), *Black Women as Cultural Readers* (New York: Columbia University Press).

Braidotti, Rosi (1991), *Patterns of Dissonance: A Study of Women in Contemporary Philosophy* (Cambridge: Polity Press).

Butler, Judith (1990), *Gender Trouble: Feminism and the Subversion of Identity* (New York: Routledge).

Camera Obscura (1988), Special Issue: *Male Trouble*, 17 May.

de Lauretis, Teresa (1984), *Alice Doesn't: Feminism, Semiotics, Cinema* (Bloomington: Indiana University Press).

—— (1988), 'Sexual Indifference and Lesbian Representation', *Theatre Journal*, 40/2: 155–77.

—— (1991), 'Film and the Visible', in Bad Object-Choices (eds.), *How do I Look? Queer Film and Video* (Washington: Bay Press).

—— (1994), *The Practice of Love: Lesbian Sexuality and Perverse Desire* (Bloomington: Indiana University Press).

Doan, Laura (1994), *The Lesbian Postmodern* (New York: Columbia University Press).

Doty, Alexander (1993), *Making Things Perfectly Queer: Interpreting Mass Culture* (Minneapolis: University of Minnesota Press).

*****Dyer, Richard** (1977*a*/1984), 'Stereotyping', in Richard Dyer (ed.), *Gays and Film* (rev. edn. New York: Zoetrope).

—— (1977*b*/1993), 'Homosexuality and Film Noir', in *The Matter of Images: Essays on Representations* (London: Routledge).

—— (1980), 'Reading Fassbinder's Sexual Politics', in Tony Rayns (ed.), *Fassbinder* (London: British Film Institute).

—— (1982/1992), 'Don't Look Now: The Male Pin-Up', in *The Sexual Subject: A 'Screen' Reader in Sexuality* (London: Routledge).

—— (1983/1993), 'Seen to be Believed: Some Problems in the Representation of Gay People as Typical', in *The Matter of Images: Essays on Representations* (London: Routledge).

—— (1986), *Heavenly Bodies: Film Stars and Society* (New York: St Martin's Press).

*—— (1990), *Now you See It: Studies on Lesbian and Gay Film* (London: Routledge).

Easthope, Anthony (1986), *What a Man's Gotta Do: The Masculine Myth in Popular Culture* (London: Paladin).

Ellsworth, Elizabeth (1990), 'Feminist Spectators and *Personal Best*', in Patricia Erens (ed.), *Issues in Feminist Film Criticism* (Bloomington: Indiana University Press).

Fuss, Diana (1989), *Essentially Speaking: Feminism, Nature and Difference* (New York: Routledge).

Galvin, Angela (1994), '*Basic Instinct*: Damning Dykes', in Diane Hamer and Belinda Budge (eds.), *The Good, the Bad and the Gorgeous: Popular Culture's Romance with Lesbianism* (London: Pandora).

Gever, Martha, John Greyson, and Pratibha Parmar (1993), *Queer Looks: Perspectives on Lesbian and Gay Film and Video* (New York: Routledge).

Graham, Paula (1995), 'Girl's Camp? The Politics of Parody', in Tamsin Wilton (ed.), *Immortal, Invisible: Lesbians and the Moving Image* (London: Routledge).

Hetze, Stefanie (1986), *Happy-End für wen? Kino und lesbische Frauen* (Frankfurt: Tende Verlag).

hooks, bell (1990), *Yearning: Race, Gender, and Cultural Politics* (Boston: South End Press).

Jeffords, Susan (1994), *Hard Bodies: Hollywood Masculinity in the Reagan Era* (New Brunswick, NJ: Rutgers University Press).

Johnston, Claire (1973/1977), 'Women's Cinema as Counter Cinema', in Claire Johnston (ed.), *Notes on Women's Cinema* (London: Society for Education in Film and Television); reprinted in Bill Nichols (ed.), *Movies and Methods*, 2 vols., ii (Berkeley: University of California Press).

Kirkham, Pat, and Janet Thumin (eds.) (1993), *You Tarzan: Masculinity, Movies and Men* (London: Lawrence & Wishart).

Lacan, Jacques (1977), 'The Signification of the Phallus', in *Écrits: A Selection* (New York: W. W. Norton).

Longfellow, Brenda (1993), 'Lesbian Phantasy and the Other Woman in Ottinger's *Johanna d'Arc of Mongolia*', *Screen*, 34/2: 124–36.

Mayne, Judith (1990), *The Woman at the Keyhole: Feminism and Women's Cinema* (Bloomington: Indiana University Press).

—— (1994), *Directed by Dorothy Arzner* (Bloomington: Indiana University Press).

Medhurst, Andy (1977/1984), 'Notes on Recent Gay Film Criticism', in Richard Dyer (ed.), *Gays and Film* (New York: Zoetrope).

—— (1991a), 'That Special Thrill: *Brief Encounter*, Homosexuality and Authorship', *Screen*, 32/2: 197–208.

—— (1991b), 'Batman, Deviance and Camp', in Roberta E. Pearson and William Uricchio (eds.), *The Many Lives of the Batman: Critical Approaches to a Superhero and his Media* (London: British Film Institute; New York: Routledge).

Mercer, Kobena (1991a), 'Skin Head Sex Thing: Racial Difference and the Homoerotic Imaginary', in Bad Object-Choices (eds.), *How do I Look? Queer Film and Video* (Seattle: Bay Press).

—— (1991b), 'Monster Metaphors: Notes on Michael Jackson's Thriller', in Christine Gledhill (ed.), *Stardom: Industry of Desire* (London: Routledge).

—— (1993), 'Dark and Lovely Too: Black Gay Men in Independent Film', in Gever et al. (1993).

Merck, Mandy (1993), *Perversions: Deviant Readings* (London: Virago).

Meyer, Richard (1991), 'Rock Hudson's Body', in Diana Fuss (ed.), *Inside/Out: Lesbian Theories, Gay Theories* (New York: Routledge).

Neale, Steve (1983/1992), 'Masculinity as Spectacle', *The Sexual Subject: A 'Screen' Reader in Sexuality* (London: Routledge).

Rich, Ruby (1981/1984), 'From Repressive Tolerance to Erotic Liberation: *Maedchen in Uniform*', in Mary Ann Doane, Patricia Mellencamp, and Linda Williams (eds.), *Re-Vision: Essays in Feminist Film Criticism* (Los Angeles: American Film Institute and University Publications of America).

*Russo, Vito (1981/1987), *The Celluloid Closet: Homosexuality in the Closet* (New York: Harper & Row).

Screen (1992), *The Sexual Subject: A 'Screen' Reader in Sexuality* (London: Routledge).

Sheldon, Caroline (1977/1984), 'Lesbians and Film: Some Thoughts', in Richard Dyer (ed.), *Gays and Film* (rev. edn. New York: Zoetrope).

Simpson, Mark (1994), *Male Impersonators: Men Performing Masculinity* (London: Cassell).

Stacey, Jackie (1987), 'Desperately Seeking Difference', *Screen* 28/1: 48–61.

—— (1994), *Star Gazing: Hollywood Cinema and Female Spectatorship* (London: Routledge).

—— (1995), '"If You Don't Play You Can't Win": *Desert Hearts* and the Lesbian Romance Film', in Tamsin Wilton (ed.), *Immortal, Invisible: Lesbians and the Moving Image* (London: Routledge).

Tasker, Yvonne (1993), *Spectacular Bodies: Gender, Genre and the Action Cinema* (London: Routledge).

Tyler, Parker (1973/1993), *Screening the Sexes: Homosexuality in the Movies* (New York: Da Capo Press).

Weiss, Andrea (1992), *Vampires and Violets: Lesbians in the Cinema* (London: Jonathan Cape).

White, Patricia (1987), 'Madam X of the China Seas', *Screen*, 28/4: 80–95.

—— (1991), 'Female Spectator, Lesbian Specter: *The Haunting*', in Diana Fuss (ed.), *Inside/Out: Lesbian Theories, Gay Theories* (New York: Routledge).

Williams, Linda (1986), ' "Personal Best": Women in Love', in Charlotte Brunsdon (ed.), *Films for Women* (London: British Film Institute).

Wood, Robin (1977), 'Responsibilities of a Gay Film Critic', in Bill Nichols (ed.), *Movies and Methods* 2 vols., ii (Berkeley: University of California Press).

—— (1986), *Hollywood from Vietnam to Reagan* (New York: Columbia University Press).

Zimmerman, Bonnie (1981), 'Lesbian Vampires', *Jump Cut*, 24–5: 23–4.

15

Queer Theory

Alexander Doty

Queer theory shares with feminism an interest in non-normative expressions of gender and with lesbian, gay, and bisexual studies a concern with non-straight expressions of sexuality and gender. However, queer film and popular culture theory and criticism has developed as much as a reaction to feminism and to lesbian and gay work as it has been an expansion of this work.

The questioning of essentialist identity politics, the rise of AIDS activism, and the debates surrounding 'political correctness' laid the groundwork for reappropriating the term 'queer' inside and outside the academy beginning in the mid-1980s. However, in the decade that followed, 'queer' and 'queerness' has been used and understood a number of ways in film and popular culture theory, criticism, and practice. Some use 'queer' as a hipper synonym for 'gay male', or, less frequently, 'lesbian', or as a new umbrella term for gay and lesbian (and bisexual sometimes). In relation to film and popular culture theory and criticism, perhaps this use of 'queer' can be connected to the beginning of what has been called 'New Queer Cinema' or the 'Queer New Wave'. As a result of certain high-profile screenings and awards at the Sundance and Toronto film festivals of 1991 and 1992, critics and distributors heralded a new film movement that included such works as *Paris is Burning* (Jennie Livingstone, 1990), *Tongues Untied* (Marlon Riggs, 1990), *Poison* (Todd Haynes, 1991), *My Own Private Idaho* (Gus van Sant, 1991), *Young Soul Rebels*

(Isaac Julien, 1991), *Edward II* (Derek Jarman, 1991), *The Hour and the Times* (Christopher Munch, 1992), *The Living End* (Gregg Araki, 1992), and *Swoon* (Tom Kalin, 1992). For many critics, what tied these films and videos together and set them apart from others, aside from their independent production status, was how they directly addressed a non-straight audience, as well as how they presented material that was sexually explicit, unconcerned with 'positive images', and more generally 'politically incorrect'. Some saw these characteristics, in part, as responses to the AIDS crisis, pornography, and anti-censorship debates, and in-your-face AIDS and gay and lesbian activism (ACT UP!, Outrage, Queer Nation).

However, a number of commentators at the time, including B. Ruby Rich (1993), Cherry Smyth (1992), and Pratibha Parmar (Gever *et al.* 1993), noted that 'New Queer Cinema' was used most often to describe and market independent films and videos by or about gay men, and largely white middle-class gay men at that. But adding work by women to the roll-call of New Queer Cinema—Pratibha Parmar (*Kush*, 1991), Sadie Benning (*It wasn't Love*, 1992), Su Friedrich (*First Comes Love*, 1991), Cecilia Dougherty (*Coal Miner's Granddaughter*, 1991), *Flaming Ears* (1991) still wasn't enough to justify the use of 'queer' for some. Smyth (1992) was among those who felt that most of what was called New Queer Cinema (and video) in the early 1990s was really only repackaged lesbian, gay, or 'les-

The Queer New Wave, Gus van Sant's *My Own Private Idaho* (1991)

bian and gay' work, because these films and videos do not seriously challenge or transgress established straight *or* gay and lesbian understandings of gender and sexuality. Beyond this, some commentators and film- and videomakers feel that expressing and representing queerness—as opposed to gayness, lesbianism, and bisexuality—is most (or only) possible within non-mainstream production and formal contexts, that is within avant-garde, documentary, and other independently produced alternative-to-traditional narrative forms.

Much of the queer film and popular culture theory and criticism developed in the 1990s was fuelled by the examples of New Queer Cinema, its critics, and the work of cultural critics like Judith Butler (*Gender Trouble*, 1990), Eve Kosofsky Sedgwick (*Between Men*, 1985; *Epistemology of the Closet*, 1991), Michael Warner (*Fear of a Queer Planet*, 1993), Diana Fuss (*Essentially Speaking*, 1989), Teresa de Lauretis ('Queer Theory' issue of *differences*, 1991), Sue-Ellen Case ('Tracking the Vampire', 1991), and Smyth (*Lesbians*

Talk Queer Notions, 1992). Of course, as suggested earlier, queer film and popular culture theory and criticism has also developed in relation or in response to earlier lesbian and gay film and popular culture theory and criticism, represented by the work of Richard Dyer, Robin Wood, B. Ruby Rich, Teresa de Lauretis, Jack Babuscio, and special sections in *Jump Cut* (1977, 1981) (see also Smelik, Chapter 14). But just how, or even if, queer theory and criticism is connected to lesbian and gay approaches is an issue that is still being negotiated and debated.

Aside from its uses as a synonym for gay or lesbian or bisexual, certain uses of 'queer' and 'queerness' as new umbrella terms have most strongly suggested how it might work with(in) established lesbian, gay, and bisexual film and popular culture theory and criticism. In these uses, 'queer' might be used to describe the intersection or combination of more than one established 'non-straight' sexuality or gender position in a spectator, a text, or a personality. For example, when a text like *Gentlemen Prefer Blondes* (1953) or *All about Eve* (1950) accumulates lesbian, gay, and bisexual cultural readings, it could be deemed a queer text, rather than, say, only a gay or a lesbian or a bisexual text. In a similar way, Marlene Dietrich and Bette Davis could be said to have queer star images as they have inspired lesbian, gay, and bisexual cultural appreciations. By this meaning, the text or the performer's star image does not have to have obvious (so-called 'denotative') non-straight elements to be termed 'queer'; it just needs to have gathered about it a number of non-straight cultural readings. Indeed, some queer critics contend that many popular culture texts that do contain visible gay, lesbian, bisexual, or otherwise non-straight characters and content—like *Silence of the Lambs* (1991)—aren't necessarily queer texts as they work to oppress and eliminate queerness rather than to express it. The uses of 'queer' outlined above are generally careful not to replace specifically lesbian, gay, and bisexual critical positions, readings, and pleasures. The goal here is to collect and juxtapose these positions, readings, and pleasures in order to construct a range of 'non-straight' (that is, queer) approaches to film and popular culture.

A slight variation on the approaches described above would be using queer to describe the non-straight work, positions, pleasures, and readings of people who don't share the same 'sexual orientation' as that articulated in the text they are producing or responding to. A gay man would take queer pleasure in a lesbian film, for example. Or a lesbian or straight women might be said to do queer work when she directs a film with gay content, or writes an essay discussing the erotics of, say, Kenneth Anger's films. Certain feminist critics and theorists have also begun using the term 'queer' to describe any non-normative expressions of gender by or about straight women (and, sometimes, straight men) in film and popular culture production and representation. But whether connected to feminism or not, this understanding of 'queer' can describe any work by straight-identifying film and popular culture theorists, critics, or producers that is concerned with non-normative straightness.

As with many of the films and videos of the New Queer Cinema movement, the critical and theoretical uses of 'queer' outlined above largely maintain gender difference and the orthodoxies about sexuality developed within liberal feminist theories and gay and lesbian 'identity politics' approaches. However, another variety of queer film theory and criticism has followed the more radical programmes outlined by Smyth,

Case, and others as it concentrates upon those aspects of spectatorship, cultural readership, and textual codes that suggest or establish spaces that are not quite contained within established gender and sexuality categories. By this definition, 'queer' would be reserved for those films and popular culture texts, spectator positions, pleasures, and readings that articulate spaces outside gender binaries and sexuality categories, whether these are outside normative straight understandings of gender and sexuality or outside orthodox lesbian and gay understandings of these things. This type of queer film and popular culture theory and criticism is concerned with that which does not seem to fall within either current definitions of straightness, nor within those of lesbianism or gayness—and perhaps even those of bisexuality, although this area has been given precious little attention thus far in film and popular culture theory and criticism (but see below).

> **Ultimately, the theories, criticism, and film and popular culture texts produced within this definition of 'queer' would seek to examine, challenge, and confuse sexual and gender categories.**

Ultimately, the theories, criticism, and film and popular culture texts produced within this definition of 'queer' would seek to examine, challenge, and confuse sexual and gender categories. Some film and popular culture work in this area seeks to bring established sexuality and gender categories to a crisis point by exposing their limitations as accurate descriptive terms for what happens in a lot of film and popular culture production and consumption and reading practices. For example, together or separately, 'masculine', 'feminine', 'straight', 'lesbian', and 'gay' (or, to use a term more in keeping with the period, 'homosexual') don't quite describe the image of, or the spectator responses to, Katharine Hepburn dressed as a young man within the narrative of *Sylvia Scarlett* (1936). I have deliberately left the terms 'bisexual' and 'androgynous' off the list above, as some theorists and critics working with queer–queerness feel that among established gender and sexuality concepts bisexuality and androgyny offer two of the best starting-points from which to develop theoretical and critical positions that

Katharine Hepburn dressed as a young man in *Sylvia Scarlett* (1936)

will move film and popular culture criticism and theory beyond gender difference and orthodox sexual categories. Perhaps this is because bisexuality and androgyny are often understood as being positioned both 'between' and outside gender and sexuality binaries. In a similar manner, some writers are examining transvestism and transsexuality–transgenderism as potential sites for developing queer theoretical and critical approaches to film and popular culture that are founded upon potentially more radical transgressions of gender and sexuality orthodoxies.

Given the existing range of understandings, uses, and approaches to queerness in film and popular culture theory and criticism, it is not possible to establish one 'politics' of queerness. While some would like to reserve the term 'queer' only for those films, videos, articles, and books that take up progressive or radical political positions on gender and sexuality, the fact remains that at present 'queer' and 'queerness' have been, and are being, used in film and popular culture theory and criticism in relation to a wide range of political and ideological positions, from conservative to radical.

But in one or another of their many definitional and political forms, there are signs that established theoretical and critical areas in film and popular culture are being queered. Take, for example, textual coding and

spectatorship. Certain queer film and popular culture theorists have already profoundly challenged what has come before by asserting that the concepts of subtexting and connotation are most often used as heterocentrist paradigms to undermine, subordinate, or deny a range of non- (normative) straight readings that are as 'denotative' as any others. So queer readings (decodings) of texts are not 'alternative readings' or 'subcultural readings', but readings to stand alongside normatively straight ones. Taking up certain feminist work with spectatorship and gender, queer work with spectatorship has suggested that viewers, no matter what their stated gender and sexuality identities, often position themselves 'queerly'—that is, position themselves within gender and sexuality spaces other than those with which they publicly identify. Most radically, this ever-shifting gender and sexuality positioning in relation to film and popular culture would obliterate for the spectator the sense of functioning within any particular gender and sexuality categories.

Historical studies, semiotics and structuralism, Marxist and ideological criticism, auteurism, genre studies, reception theory, and psychoanalytic, feminist, gay, lesbian, and bisexual approaches have all begun to be scrutinized, critiqued, supplemented, revised, or, in certain cases, rejected by queer film and popular culture theorists and critics. They are either seeking ways to form 'coalitions' between non- (normative) straight approaches, or wanting to examine more accurately and complexly those spaces and places in film and popular culture that fall outside existing gender and sexuality categories.

BIBLIOGRAPHY

*Bad Object-Choices (ed.) (1991), How do I Look?: Queer Film and Video (Seattle: Bay Press).

Bornstein, Kate (1994), Gender Outlaw: Of Men, Women, and the Rest of Us (New York: Routledge).

Butler, Judith (1993), 'Critically Queer', GLQ: Journal of Lesbian and Gay Studies, 1/1: 17–32; repr. in Bodies that Matter: On the Discursive Limits of 'Sex' (New York: Routledge.

—— (1990), Gender Trouble: Feminism and the Subversion of Identity (New York: Routledge).

Case, Sue-Ellen (1991), 'Tracking the Vampire', differences: A Journal of Feminist Cultural Studies, 3/2 (Summer), 1–20.

*Creekmur, Corey, K., and Alexander Doty (eds.) (1995), Out in Culture: Gay, Lesbian and Queer Essays on Popular Culture (Durham, NC: Duke University Press).

de Lauretis, Teresa (1991), Introduction, differences: A Journal of Feminist Cultural Studies, 3/2 (Summer), Special Issue: Queer Theory, pp. iii–xviii.

Doty, Alexander (1993), Making Things Perfectly Queer: Interpreting Mass Culture (Minneapolis: University of Minnesota Press).

Fuss, Diana (1989), Essentially Speaking: Feminism, Nature and Difference (New York: Routledge).

Garber, Marjorie (1992), Vested Interests: Cross-Dressing and Cultural Anxiety (New York: Routledge).

*Gever, Martha, John Greyson, and Pratibha Parmar (eds.) (1993), Queer Looks: Perspectives on Gay and Lesbian Film and Video (New York: Routledge).

The Independent Film and Video Monthly (1995), 18/5 (June), Special Issue: Queer Media.

Jump Cut (1977), 16, Special Section: Gays and Film 13–28.

—— (1981), 24–5, Special Section: Lesbians and Film 17–51.

Martin, Biddy (1994), 'Sexuality without Gender and Other Queer Utopias', Diacritics, 24/2–3: 104–21.

—— and Judith Butler (eds.) (1994), differences: A Journal of Feminist Cultural Studies 6/2–3 (Summer–Fall), Special Issue: Feminism Meets Queer Theory.

'New Queer Cinema' (1992), Sight and Sound, 2/5 (Sept.), 30–41.

Pramaggiore, Maria, and Donald E. Hall (1995), Representing Bisexualities: Subjects and Cultures of Fluid Desire (New York: New York University Press).

Rich, B. Ruby (1993), 'Reflections on a Queer Screen', GLQ: A Journal of Lesbian and Gay Studies, 1/1: 83–91.

Sedgwick, Eve Kosofsky (1985), Between Men: English Literature and Male Homosocial Desire (New York: Columbia University Press).

—— (1991), Epistemology of the Closet (Hemel Hempstead: Harvester Wheatsheaf).

—— (1993), 'Queer and Now', in Tendencies (Durham: Duke University Press).

Smyth, Cherry (1992), Lesbians Talk Queer Notions (London: Scarlet Press).

Straayer, Chris (1990), 'The She-Man: Postmodern Bi-Sexed Performance in Film and Video', Screen, 31/3 (Autumn), 262–80.

—— (1992), 'Redressing the "Natural": The Temporary Transvestite Film', Wide Angle, 14/1 (Jan.), 36–55.

Warner, Michael (1993), Introduction, in Fear of a Queer Planet: Queer Politics and Social Theory (Minneapolis: University of Minnesota Press).

Wilton, Tamsin (1995), Immortal Invisible: Lesbians and the Moving Image (New York: Routledge).

16 Pornography

Laura Kipnis

Pornography doesn't appear to be going away anytime soon, so I suggest we take this opportunity to study it. However, the question of pornography as an area of academic study or as an aspect of a film studies curriculum is invariably political and controversial. Feminism—of both popular and academic varieties—has successfully overhauled the previously prevailing definition of pornography and brought about something of an epistemic shift in thinking on the subject. Whereas pornography was once viewed as a medium simply devoted to sexual explicitness (and to whatever corresponding feelings of sexual arousal such explicitness might occasion in the—typically male--viewer), feminists have largely redefined and complicated the genre as one whose concern is not simply sex and sexual expression, but rather gender relations and power: specifically, patriarchal power and the continuing disempowerment and oppression of women.

Pornography has become a rallying-point for many feminists, the most onerous form of the 'objectification of women'—a phrase that has achieved wide currency both in and outside the academy. It has been widely seen as something of a model for degrading treatment of women in other media, from album covers to advertising to mainstream film and television. But pornography has also been regarded by some feminists as the dominant cause of female oppression, and held responsible for a vast range of effects in the world. The case against it begins with the personal discomfort it causes some (but certainly not all) women, creating a 'hostile environment' for women encountering pornographic explicitness on news-stands or in the workplace. This charge begs a question that goes largely unasked in these discussions: *why* is pornography more offensive to women than to the men who buy it or display it? If displaying pornography is considered a hostile act to women at large, what guarantees its success in achieving that aim? In other words, why don't women have the choice of being indifferent to pornography? It might seem that the question of comfort or discomfort around sexual explicitness is central to the very constitution of gendered subjectivity, a point that Freud makes about the acquisition of femininity: originally girls and boys are equally interested in sexual facts, but Oedipalization for the female entails an increasing inhibition about sexuality (Freud 1965).

The focus for anti-porn feminists, however, is not on sexual difference or on the intrapsychic realm, but on the effects it is charged pornography has in the world—from 'keeping women in their place' to violence, rape, and murder. Anti-porn feminists have charged that men are incited to re-enact the scenes that they view in pornography, that pornography is not merely fantasy, or speech, but a call to action (see Mackinnon 1993; Dworkin 1981, 1987; Gubar and Hoff 1989). Anti-porn feminists often cite controversial effects research in which men are shown pornography and pornographic films in experimental settings, and then queried about their feelings towards women and sex. In some of these studies it appears that men self-report increased violent or callous feelings toward women after viewing pornography, or increased cavalier attitudes about rape. But at the same time, much of this research suffers from quite simplistic assumptions about the nature of its content. Edward Donnerstein and Daniel Linz, leading pornography effects researchers, routinely screen the notorious sexploitation movie *I Spit on your Grave* (Meir Zarchi, USA, 1977) as an example of sexual violence against women, then measure male audiences for mood, hostility, and desensitization to rape (Donnerstein and Linz 1986). But as anyone who's actually seen this movie knows, it's no simple testimonial to rape. This is a rape-*revenge* film, in which a woman rape victim wreaks violent reprisal against her rapists, systematically and imaginatively killing all three—and one mentally challenged onlooker—by decapitation, hanging, shooting, and castration. Film theorist Carol Clover points out that even during the rape sequence, the camera angles force the viewer into identification with the female victim (1992: 139). If male college students are hostile after watching this movie (with its grisly castration scene), it's far from clear what it is they're actually reacting to.

Feminists who have desired to contest the anti-porn movement's positions have often returned to a pre-feminist position that pornography really is about sex, but that with feminism under their belts, so to speak, now women too can enjoy its forbidden fruits. The insistence by anti-porn feminists that there is no distinction between thought and deed in the pornography viewer, and that the image dictates the viewer's

> **Whereas pornography was once viewed as a medium simply devoted to sexual explicitness (and to whatever corresponding feelings of sexual arousal such explicitness might occasion in the—typically male—viewer), feminists have largely redefined and complicated the genre as one whose concern is not simply sex and sexual expression, but rather gender relations and power.**

position—that a violent act by a male character automatically decrees a male viewer's identification with that act—has also incited pro-porn or anti-censorship feminists into a mini-stampede back to the gates of psychoanalytic theory for a more complicated model of fantasy, one which reanimates these sticky questions of identification (see Stern 1982 for an early example of this move). Aren't there gaps between identity (sexual or gendered) and identification in the film viewing experience? Is that, perhaps, what pornography is good for? This is a position also suggested by Carol Clover's (1992) work on horror—a study with much relevance to pornography studies—which maintains that male horror film viewers identify with character functions rather than character genders, and that these functions (victim, hero, monster, sadist) resonate with competing parts of the viewer's psyche. Cross-gender identification offers male viewers a chance to experience a range of emotions, fears, and conflicts, with female characters functioning as 'fronts' for those more culturally forbidden affects. Other theorists have pointed out that the implication of Laura Mulvey's work ('Sadism demands a story . . .') has been to repress the issue of masochism in the male viewing experience, and that film theory in general has had a lopsided focus on male mastery and aggressivity, excluding the 'feminine', along with the complexities of cross-gender identifications (see Mulvey 1975; Rodowick 1982; Studlar 1985).

Introducing more complicated theories of identification also counterbalances a determinist tendency in feminist film theory often known by its codename: 'the gaze'. In following Mulvey's assertion that the cinematic code is based on positioning the woman as objects of either a sadistic-voyeurism or a fetishizing scopophilia, feminist theorists have often unwittingly collapsed the 'male gaze' into something resembling the Foucauldian panoptic gaze of *Discipline and Punish*. The unfortunate result is the theoretical invention of a new, all-powerful male viewing subject: not one caught in the abject dialectic of castration and futile compensatory exercises of mastery, but one for whom 'the gaze' actually accomplishes its mission. For this monolithic male gaze, fetishization *works*: male power *can* be 'natural', and the female body *can* be contained—psychically, socially, and politically. In Joan Copjec's view, the mutually constitutive interrelationship posed between gaze, subject, and apparatus in much feminist film theory results from a tendency to misread Lacan as assimilable to Foucault, and thus to

Accessible, soft Europorn of the 1970s *Émmanuelle* **(1973)**

miss the misrecognition and radical indeterminacy that constitute the subject for Lacan, instead smuggling back in a stable self and along with it a theoretical tendency to 'court determinism' (Copjec 1989; see also Kipnis 1993: 8–11). However, for other writers who have taken up Foucault's work as a tool in approaching pornography, notably Linda Williams (1989), the inherent contradictions in pornography itself—constituted as a genre by the quest for a truth which can't be represented, namely, female sexual pleasure—undermine the stability of both the form and the positions from which it can be viewed.

More recently, the rise of gay and queer studies within the academy, as well as the use of pornography in AIDS education, have introduced other questions—and other bodies—into the equation, also contesting the feminist anti-porn monopoly on the discourse. As

activist-theorist Cindy Patton writes, 'The special vernacular of porn can be used in efforts to reconstruct a language of sex to go along with the reconstructed sexualities that resist both potentially HIV-transmitting activities and the destructive effects of attempts to silence, once again, the eloquent voice of homosexualities' (1991: 378).

These debates don't, however, exhaust the topic, and I would like to suggest another area of focus for the academic study of pornography, and suggest another reason that pornography is an invariably political issue. This has to do with pornography's position at the very bottom of the very lowest rungs of the cultural hierarchy. It would be difficult to argue that the academy is not still, to a large degree, structured by an Arnoldian relation to culture, in which the very term 'culture' signifies elevation and gentility: 'higher learning'. The study of 'lower' varieties of culture—even in the form of film and television studies, established academic disciplines at this point—can still provoke a certain degree of *frisson* within the humanities.

Studying something in the humanities necessitates taking it seriously, inventing complexity for it, building some form of intimate relationship with it. It involves proximity, and thus contamination. In contrast, the social sciences can, and, indeed by definition, do safely take on all variety of deviance and abnormality—low culture, criminality, violence, sex as object of study—because social science methodologies entail a quite different set of relations from their objects of study. The social sciences are not in danger from their low objects, because their claim to the status of 'science' gives them sufficient mastery and distance.

Yet, by contrast, there is no end of cultural fretting that the humanities are 'brought down' by the study of popular culture, and this 'lowering of standards' is blamed by conservative social critics for all manner of social ills (see e.g. Bloom 1987). The energy behind the recent canon wars, the call for a return to 'traditional values'—not only for families, but in curricula—all signal a certain anxiety about the social effects that 'low' forms of culture pose to the orderly operation of social reproduction, when the low manages to infiltrate 'higher' venues, such as college campuses. It may be that this is not an unreasonable fear, given that the social world we inhabit is certainly organized along a hierarchy that runs from high to low in terms of class, and that despite whatever movement towards democratization in higher education has taken place in the post-war years, university education is still a primary instrument of class reproduction, a mechanism for ensuring the proper distinctions and segregations between classes. My argument is that none of this is unrelated to curricular issues, to the question of what gets taught and studied on campuses. Because if the social world is organized hierarchically, it is also the case that culture is organized hierarchically, along a spectrum that also runs from high to low. That is, culture too is classed, with the lower forms of culture in something of an analogous relation to the lower tiers of the class structure. Note that this is not an argument about the demographics of viewership or cultural consumption—I'm not arguing that the upper classes consume 'higher' forms of culture, and the lower classes consume strictly 'low' culture—although given that the price of a pair of opera tickets these days runs to roughly a week's salary for a minimum-wage worker, certain forms of high culture are presumably cordoned off from the lower-paid masses.

> **The feminist anti-porn argument is that pornography is a special case, with special powers to cause effects in viewers; that unlike other genres, porn viewers are seized by overwhelming urges to act out what they see on screen, whereas no one seems to think that viewers of musicals are suddenly, irresistibly compelled to start tap-dancing.**

Rather, this is an argument about the semiotics of culture, and the symbolic valences of the study of 'lower' forms of culture within institutions of 'higher' education. Given the way that cultural forms map onto class forms, with pornography implicitly in an analogy with the bottom tiers of the social, its introduction into the academy opens onto a welter of issues around class, value, and their overstructured relation to scholarship. Thus it is no accident that film studies earned a place in the academy by fashioning itself along the lines predominant in the established academic disciplines: film as 'art', auteurs as their emanating consciousness—even if the realities of industrial production contra-indicated that model of authorship. The relationship between a discipline and its object of study is an intricate one, and there are material realities governing the institutional contexts in which these disciplines operate and their objects are studied: decisions about hiring, promotion and tenure, granting and funding, also affect whether and how pornography gets studied by academics—not to mention that the study of pornography in academic settings invariably sexualizes the setting and complicates the codes of the classroom in quite unpredictable ways (Kleinhans 1996).

Dwelling on the issue of cultural value postpones another obvious issue: that pornography's manifest content is sex. Does that change how film studies should approach it as an object of analysis? Is pornography simply another film genre—like comedy, melodrama, the western—to which film studies can bring familiar analytical tools to bear, or is pornography a special case? As indicated above, the feminist anti-porn argument is that pornography is a special case, with special powers to cause effects in viewers; that unlike other genres, porn viewers are seized by overwhelming urges to act out what they see on screen, whereas no one seems to think that viewers of musicals are suddenly, irresistibly compelled to start tap-dancing. So, for these feminists, there's no distance between representation and reality, between 'realism' and documentary, between image and 'propaganda'. For these feminists, pornography *advertises*: as if any film about divorce, say, were automatically seen as advocating broken homes, or as though all war films were incitements to bomb things.

It may be that this confusion between representation and the real is something inherent to the genre, because in pornography, or at least, in hard-core pornography in which sex acts such as penetration actually *do* take place, the act is *real*. One might argue that, at those moments, the film slips—transgresses—genre boundaries; it suddenly becomes documentary. Part of the *frisson* of pornography is the power of direct cinema: we witness actors crossing a line between performing and 'being', which may complicate the identifications and pleasures of viewing. We slip from viewers into witnesses. Of course, the question of what precisely is being witnessed is a complicated one, given the way sex functions as a vehicle for so *many* meanings and affects, not just for pleasure, but also for experiences of transgression, utopian aspirations, sadness, optimism, loss, and the most primary longings for love and plenitude. If sex can be this multivalent in its meanings—and this brief list certainly doesn't exhaust the possibilities, which are as numerous as there are humans—then pornography, too, is vast in the kinds of contents and messages it opens onto.

> **The question of what precisely is being witnessed is a complicated one, given the way sex functions as a vehicle for so *many* meanings and affects, not just for pleasure, but also for experiences of transgression, utopian aspirations, sadness, optimism, loss, and the most primary longings for love and plenitude.**

Whether the pornography experience is seen as pleasurable or profoundly displeasurable, it holds a mirror up to the culture, mapping its borders and boundaries through strategic acts of transgression. Pornography is dedicated to propriety violations of every shape, manner, and form, and proprieties have deep links to the maintenance of social order and to who we are as social subjects (see Kipnis 1996). The links between the culture, proprieties, and the deep structure of the psyche are evident in how very transfixed we are, as viewers and as a culture, before the pornographic scene, whether with pleasure or disgust, intellectually or viscerally. The intensity of the debates it has spawned are some testament to this fascination, and to the work pornography does as a genre: it distils the issues that are central to our culture and to the constitution of the self, and reiterates them through the code of sex. Unlikely as it may seem, I'd suggest that pornography contains a vast amount of social knowledge, which is another reason it demands study.

Now go do your homework.

BIBLIOGRAPHY

Bloom, Allan (1987), *The Closing of the American Mind* (New York: Simon & Schuster).

*****Church Gibson, Pamela,** and **Roma Gibson** (eds.) (1993), *Dirty looks: Women, Pornography, Power* (London: British Film Institute).

Clover, Carol (1992), *Men, Women and Chain Saws: Gender in the Modern Horror Film* (Princeton: Princeton University Press).

Copjec, Joan (1989), 'The Orthopsychic Subject', *October* (Summer), 53–71.

Donnerstein, Edward, and **Daniel Linz** (1986), 'Mass Media, Sexual Violence and Male Viewers: Current Theory and Research', *American Behavioral Scientist* 29 (May–June), 601–18.

Dworkin, Andrea (1981), *Pornography: Men Possessing Women* (New York: Perigee).

—— (1987), *Intercourse* (New York: Free Press).

Freud, Sigmund (1965), 'Femininity', in *New Introductory Lectures on Psychoanalysis* (New York: Norton).

Gubar, Susan, and **Joan Hoff** (eds.) (1989), *For Adult Users Only: The Dilemma of Violent Pornography* (Bloomington: Indiana University Press).

Kipnis, Laura (1993), *Ecstasy Unlimited: On Sex, Capital, Gender and Aesthetics* (Minneapolis: Minnesota University Press).

*—— (1999), *Bound and Gagged: Pornography and the Politics of Fantasy* (Durham, North Carolina: Duke University Press).

Kleinhans, Chuck (1996), 'Some Pragmatics in Teaching Sexual Images', *Jump Cut*, 40, Special Section: *Teaching Sexual Images*, 119–22.

MacKinnon, Catharine (1993), *Only Words* (Cambridge, Mass.: Harvard University Press).

Mulvey, Laura (1975), 'Visual Pleasure and Narrative Cinema', *Screen*, 16/3: 6–18.

Patton, Cindy (1991), 'Visualizing Safe Sex: When Pedagogy and Pornography Collide', in Diana Fuss (ed.), *Inside/Out: Lesbian Theories, Gay Theories* (New York: Routledge).

Rodowick, D. N. (1982), 'The Difficulty of Difference', *Wide Angle*, 5/1: 4–15.

Stern, Lesley (1982), 'The Body as Evidence', *Screen*, 23/5: 38–60.

Studlar, Gaylyn (1985), 'Masochism and the Perverse Pleasures of the Cinema', in Bill Nichols (ed.), *Movies and Methods* (Berkeley: California University Press).

*****Williams, Linda** (1989), *Hard Core: Power, Pleasure, and the Frenzy of the Visible* (Berkeley: California University Press).

17

Race, ethnicity, and film

Robyn Wiegman

It is rare to find a film studies scholar today who would assert that the study of race and ethnicity has little or no bearing on the discipline. Who can talk about the western, for instance, without some attention to the ideological construction of a mythic American past predicated on the wholesale binary arrangement of good white men and bad, bloodthirsty Indians? What account of the silent film era can proceed without commentary on its language of stereotype, from the Italian American gangster to the Latino greaser to the African American rapist? And how can we discuss the Hollywood industry without analysis of its workplace segregations or Motion Picture morality codes? From genre to spectator, from directorship to narration, in the ideological as well as the material realm, race and ethnicity have a foundational effect on the study of Hollywood film industry, representational practices, and spectatorial cultures.

And yet, it is difficult to speak of the study of race and ethnicity as constituting a fully formed field within film studies, at least not one definable along the lines set forth by Patricia White in 'Feminism and Film' for this volume. In that chapter, White convincingly offers a history and theoretical agenda that constitutes feminist film criticism as a coherent field within the broader disciplinary area of Anglo-American film studies. Citing the women's movement as genesis for investigations into images of women, White surveys several decades of feminist scholarship which have fundamentally

altered the way film is studied and, arguably, produced. No such overarching narrative or shared body of primary scholarship exists for the study of race and ethnicity in film.

This does not mean that political activism has not been crucial to the development of race and ethnicity in film criticism, or that the diverse categories of analysis and production organized under the rubrics of race and ethnicity bear no political or critical affinities to one another. Chicano film history, for instance, cannot be adequately discussed apart from Chicano political activity in the 1960s (Fregoso 1993), and much of the new black cinema is formed in the context of the political complexities of diasporic identities (Martin 1995). The point is simply that the study of race and ethnicity in film has taken shape according to the formation of race and ethnicity in US culture more widely, reflecting not a cross-ethnic political agenda geared to white supremacy's massive deployment, but the discrete histories and political projects of specific identity sites: African American, Asian American, Chicano–Latino, Native American, Jewish American, Italian American, and Irish American (see, respectively, Bogle 1989; Wong 1978; Garcia Berumen 1995; Bataille and Silet 1980; Friedman 1982; Lourdeaux 1990; and Curran 1989).

Focused on specific identities, and the characters, actors, writers, or directors who embody them, the large majority of film studies scholarship traces the history of representation (the images' school) and documents the discriminatory employment practices of the industry. While such analyses have been important, critics in the late 1980s began to question the implicit segregation of race and ethnicity to non-white and non-WASP others. What would it mean to think of race and ethnicity in ways that both critique and exceed the 'minority' rubric? What aspects of formal cinematic analysis might be affected by considering race and ethnicity as critical categories irreducible to bodies? And what theoretical frameworks best articulate the historical differences and schematic overlap between the two terms? These are only some of the questions being posed by film studies scholars as the twentieth century draws to a close.

In such a context, the task of defining race and ethnicity as key themes in film studies is rather daunting. Not only must we account for the cinematic histories of specific groups, but we must also address how and why the thematic approach is an inadequate critical framework for understanding the relationships of power embedded in race and ethnicity as both socio-political and critical terms. To begin to meet these needs, this chapter examines the way the study of race and ethnicity has taken shape, first as a critical concern with the stereotype and later as a conversation about the stereotype's production in the context of post-structuralism and global image cultures. The final section looks to cross-ethnic and interethnic analysis, alongside an interrogation into the racialization of whiteness, as the new directions through which race and ethnicity might coalesce as a collective critical endeavour and organized field. But first, what do scholars mean when we talk about race and ethnicity?

Defining terms

The answer to this question varies, in part because the definitions of terms are historically mobile. As Lester Friedman points out in *Unspeakable Images* (1991), 'ethnicity' is a derivative of the Greek *ethnos*, meaning nation or race. In its earliest usage, ethnicity referred to pagans, those who were not Christian or Jewish, and only later became attached to political, national, linguistic and/or physical differences. To contemporary race theorists, this mobility demonstrates that race and ethnicity are social constructions linked to the specific discursive spheres within which they are used (Goldberg 1990). In the transformation of natural history into

the human sciences, for instance, race undergoes a radical rearticulation, losing its primary tie to national identity to become a biological distinction evinced by skin, hair, and cranial shape (Wiegman 1995). In the United States, these changes were crucial to white supremacy in the aftermath of the Civil War, making possible a continued subjugation of African Americans as racially different in the context of their official entrance into a shared national identity. So powerful has the racialization of 'blackness' been in the United States that film scholarship today concerning African Americans overwhelmingly uses race and not ethnicity as its central term (see Bobo 1995; Boyd 1996; Reid 1993; Snead 1994).

> To contemporary race theorists, this mobility demonstrates that race and ethnicity are social constructions linked to the specific discursive spheres within which they are used.

Scholarship examining Jewish American filmic representation and industry participation, on the other hand, is decidely organized under the rubric of ethnicity (Erens 1984; Friedman 1982). This is the case even though early cinematic representations of Jews were predicated on nineteenth-century racialized notions of Jewish identity, notions which culminated in the genocidal catastrophe of the Second World War. In the cinematic classic, *The Jazz Singer* (USA, 1927), in which a cantor's son seeks assimilation into the American 'mainstream' through vaudeville, Jakie Rabinowitz erases his Jewishness only to put on blackface and participate in the miming of African American musical traditions (Rogin 1996). In blackface, the protagonist demonstrates his assimilable whiteness, and it is this demonstration that inaugurates the necessary compromise between a racialized difference and ethnic life in a new world.

The transformation of Jewish identity from a primarily racial to ethnic discourse is the most extreme example of a process that, in far more subtle ways, has affected other European immigrant groups, most notably the Italian and Irish. In silent film and the early talkies, images of these groups relied on certain characteristics of race discourse, featuring—through the representation of the body, its skin, hair, and facial shape—physiognomic assertions of innate and inferior differences. Edward G. Robinson's stereotype-setting role of an Italian gangster in *Little Caesar* (USA, 1930), for instance, indexes ethnic identity via the characteristics of racial physical deficiencies such as his 'swarthy' skin, and it does so in the context of an emergent generic form, the gangster film, that would criminalize Italian American identity (see Golden 1980). But while race discourse influenced the early images of immigrants from Europe and promoted certain essentializing notions of difference, their representation throughout the twentieth century has been part of an expanding whiteness. Ethnic variations within white racial identity reference, often stereotypically (but without the institutional force of national discrimination and exclusion), customs, languages, and artefacts drawn from a group's past cultural or national milieu.

Other immigrant groups in the United States have not fared as well in the popular imaginary as have those of European descent. Asians, for instance, have long sought the kind of differentiation within race categorization which would recognize specific ethnicities, but instead the popular conception melds together the disparate histories, cultures, and languages of those from East Asia (Korea, China, and Japan) and Southeast Asia (Vietnam, Cambodia, Laos, Thailand, the Philippines, and the Indonesian archipelago). In Charlie Chan, Kung Fu, the Dragon Lady, and other staple Asian figures of US film (such as the Vietcong), ethnicity is powerfully overridden by an emphasis on physical difference. Richard Feng's 'In Search of Asian American Cinema' reads the lack of specificity informing the film industry's approach to, and conversation about, Asian American ethnicities in the context of the contemporary commodification of identity. As he puts it, 'there is a market for Asian American Cinema—the problem is, it's a market that looks for Asian faces and looks no further' (Feng 1995: 34).

The illegibility of ethnic differentiations is the norm as well for those groups pre-existing the arrival of European colonialists in the Americas. Film scholarship on Native Americans, like the movies themselves, have rarely paid attention to the specificities of tribal cultures (Friar and Friar 1972). Instead the 'Indian' is represented as a homogenized figure whose cultural and highly racialized physical differences serve as background for the ideological production of the 'American' as of white European descent. Rarely are tribal languages part of the Hollywood text. *Little Big Man* (USA, 1970)

begins with Cheyenne but fails to carry it through; *Windwalker* (USA, 1980) and *Dances with Wolves* (USA, 1990) both use Lakota, but the former stars Trevor Howard in redface while the latter continues to centre the sensitive white man (Castillo 1991).

In a similar way, but with a somewhat more complicated political genealogy, scholarship on what Allen Woll (1980) first called the 'Latin image' in cinema foregrounds the complexities of immigration and colonization as the primary ways (in addition to slavery) that we organize groups within the critical terrain of race and ethnicity. While contemporary debates about immigration often highlight a 'crisis' at the Mexican–American border, the history of this border is inextricable from US colonialism, making Mexican Americans the products of two overlapping historical formations: colonialism (in the US military acquisition of the South-west and California in the mid-nineteenth century) and immigration (in the economic exploitation of Mexico in the twentieth). It is no doubt because of this tense and lengthy relationship that Hollywood films have been far more interested in Mexicans and their US descendants (Chicanos) than in any other group from the whole of Latin America. It is also the case that some of the most politicized counter-cinema in the United States has been produced under the banner of Chicano–Latino (Noriega 1992; Noriega and Lopez 1996), and much of this film production and its critical analysis stresses ethnic and not racial difference. Edward James Olmos's *American Me* (USA, 1992), for instance, makes this point through its representation of the white Chicano JD (William Forsythe).

Where ethnicity provides the means for differentiations based on culture, language, and national origins, race renders the reduction of human differences to innate, biological phenomena, phenomena that circulate culturally as the visible ledger for defining and justifying economic and political hierarchies between white and non-white groups.

What this brief, and albeit condensed, history of the deployment of race and ethnicity as critical terms in the study of US cinema indicates is twofold. First, the terms are differentially mobile. Where ethnicity provides the means for differentiations based on culture, language, and national origins, race renders the reduction of human differences to innate, biological phenomena, phenomena that circulate culturally as the visible ledger for defining and justifying economic and political hierarchies between white and non-white groups. Only when we are dealing with European immigrants and their descendants does ethnicity become the sole operative term, whether in the complex language of specific films or the critical archive. In all other instances, a racial fetishism of the corporeal is at least covertly, if not overtly, staged. Therefore (and this is the second point), race and ethnicity as terms in film criticism are themselves products of a broader and highly political discourse about power and privilege in the United States.

The stereotype

To the extent that all stereotypes of human groups are predicated on the reduction of complex cultural codes to easily consumable visual and verbal cues, the film stereotype is paradigmatically linked to racial discourse. This does not mean that all stereotypes are raced, but rather that the logic of race as visually discernible underwrites the production and circulation of the stereotype. For film studies scholars concerned with the way cinema shapes the cultural imaginary, this 'fact' has generated a large body of scholarship dedicated to cataloguing and critiquing stereotypical images (Hilger 1986; Leab 1975; Miller 1980; Pettit 1980; O'Connor 1980; Richard 1992, 1993, 1994; Woll and Miller 1987). Across the three decades that now constitute the history of the study of stereotypes, we can trace the emergence of important issues about representation and difference, the political economy of the industry, spectatorship and identification, and, most importantly, the relationship between film and culture.

Eugene Franklin Wong's *On Visual Media Racism* (1978) remains one of the earliest and best studies of the function and production of the stereotype in Hollywood film. In his specific concern with the reduction of the diverse histories and cultures of Asians in US media, Wong's analysis exemplifies the way the stereotype has been critically approached for other racialized cultural identities (African American, Chicano–Latino, and Native American) by focusing on the stereotype's rela-

tionship to (1) broad historical and political processes, (2) labour practices in the industry, (3) ideologies concerning race, sexuality, and gender, and (4) film characterization, narrative, setting, costume, and cosmetics. He thus provides a materialist analysis of the stereotype, its ideological production, and its function as an element of the symbolic structure of the filmic text.

For Wong, the stereotype is a form of representation in film that produces non-white cultures and characters as static and one-dimensional. Acting is therefore more gestural than performatively complex; more about the cliché than emotional range. For this reason, a group's stereotyped image tends to oscillate between two simple poles: good and bad, noble and savage, loyal and traitorous, kind-hearted and villainous. It is by virtue of this condensation that an image becomes a stereotype; its racialization is achieved by an implicit or explicit moral assessment concerning the group's inherent 'essence'. Silent-film images of Asians, for instance, relied on a small range of signifiers to evoke Asian difference, such as the pigtail, the slanted eye, nodding, and laundry work. The titles alone tell the story of subordinate difference: *Heathen Chinese and the Sunday School Teachers* (USA, 1904), *The Chinese Rubbernecks* (USA, 1903), and *The Yellow Peril* (USA, 1908).

> It is by virtue of this condensation that an image becomes a stereotype; its racialization is achieved by an implicit or explicit moral assessment concerning the group's inherent 'essence'.

Many of the stereotypes of non-white men that film critics have analysed—the Mexican 'greaser', the Native savage, the African American beast—can be found in the silent era, which coincides historically with widespread political conversation about immigration, racial equality, and the meaning of being 'American'. These stereotypes most often functioned to shape popular memory about slavery, the Civil War, and Anglo-American acquisition of both Native and Mexican land. The violent Mexican, for instance, justified US aggression and spawned a series of films whose titles foreground their type: *The Greaser's Gauntlet* (USA, 1908), *Tony the Greaser* (USA, 1911), *Bronco*

The Ku Klux Klan mete out their version of justice in Griffith's controversial *Birth of a Nation* (1915)

Billy and the Greaser (USA, 1914), *The Greaser's Revenge* (USA, 1914), *Guns and Greasers* (USA, 1918). When the Mexican government threatened to ban all Hollywood imports in the 1920s (Delpar 1984), the 'greaser' disappeared from the screen, only to return with a vengeance in the second half of the century in *The Wild Bunch* (USA, 1969) and *Bring me the Head of Alfredo García* (USA, 1974). A new genre form, what critics call 'gang exploitation', is the latest rendition of the theme: *Boulevard Nights* (USA, 1979), *Walk Proud* (USA, 1979), *Defiance* (USA, 1980), and *Bound by Honor* (USA, 1993).

Violent Native Americans are likewise a long-running stereotype, making their 'savage' debut in such films as *The Massacre* (USA, 1912) and D. W. Griffith's *The Battle of Elderbush Gulch* (USA, 1913), before

becoming enshrined in the western. The narrative formula is now familiar: Native tribal cultures are homogenized as bloodthirsty hordes that attack, rape, and mercilessly pillage well-meaning Anglos who are trying to bring civilization to the continent. Late-century updates of the battle for territory have fared well at the box-office with *Dances with Wolves* (USA, 1990) and *Last of the Mohicans* (USA, 1992) (Edgerton 1994).

No single film in the silent era is more important to the critical history of the stereotype than is D. W. Griffith's *The Birth of a Nation* (USA, 1915). Here, the late nineteenth-century image of the African American male as rapist turns to pure spectacle in the ideologically weighted aesthetics of black-and-white film. In Gus, played in blackface by Walter Long, we have the filmic birth of what Donald Bogle

(1989) calls the 'brutal black buck', a sexually uncontrollable figure who lusts after white women. As the repository for a host of white anger and fear in the aftermath of the Civil War, the rapist image was part of a public discourse that 'explained' lynching; it is this replication of the justification of hate crimes against blacks that spurred the National Association for the Advancement of Colored People (NAACP) to seek complete censorship of the film. It was banned in five states and nineteen cities (Bogle 1989), but, according to Cripps (1977), white liberals were so overpowered by the film's aesthetic splendour that on the whole they failed to protest against the film's rendition of black equality as a national crisis (just as film scholarship has often seen the film's discourse on race as a surface aspect of narrative and not central to its aesthetic success; see Rogin 1985).

The African American male is not the only figure for whom racial difference becomes sexualized in the repetitive logic of the stereotype, nor is violence the only formulation of racialized sexuality in the cinema. As Wong (1978) discusses in his analysis of the industry's institutional forms of racism, a double standard governs sexuality, affecting both narrative structures and casting practices. This standard, which enables white men alone to transgress the social injunction against miscegenation and all interracial sexual desire, has produced two gendered sets of stereotypes, each one containing an opposed symbolic pair. For non-white males, the image is either of a sexually aggressive masculinity that threatens white womanhood or of an effeminate and symbolically castrated male—the difference between, say, Gus and Mr Bojangles from the Shirley Temple films—or, in terms of Asian representation, Tori of *The Cheat* (USA, 1915) and Song Liling of *M Butterfly* (USA, 1993). For non-white females, the stereotype oscillates between a nurturing, de-sexualized, loyal figure and a woman of exotic, loose, and dangerous sexuality: from O-Lan in *The Good Earth* (USA, 1937) to Hue Fei in *Shanghai Express* (USA, 1932) or from Mammy in *Gone With the Wind* (USA, 1939) to Epiphany Proudfoot in *Angel Heart* (USA, 1987).

Film studies scholars have interpreted the sexualization of race in Hollywood film as evidence of a much larger anxiety in American culture concerning interracial sexuality. After all, the democratic ideal of the 'melting-pot' brings into crisis the relationship between separatist cultures, languages, and sexual activity and the full force of integration which would reconfigure the family and romance along with national identity. Since their beginning, film narratives have been obsessively drawn to this crisis, rehearsing a variety of interracial configurations and concluding, almost always, that the cost of interracial sex is much too high (*The Savage*, USA, 1953; *Imitation of Life*, USA, 1959; *A Man Called Horse*, USA, 1970; *West Side Story*, USA, 1961; and *Jungle Fever*, USA, 1991) or likely to result in tragedy. Thus, in *The Indian Squaw's Sacrifice* (USA, 1910), the title character, Noweeta, nurses a wounded white man back to health and marries him. Later he meets a white woman he had loved before, so Noweeta kills herself to allow her husband to return to the woman he loves. The same pattern occurs with minor variations in other films representing Native Americans as in *The Kentuckian* (USA, 1908) and Cecil DeMille's *The Squaw Man* (USA, 1914). Often, one of the lovers is killed at the end, thereby undoing the interracial liaison, as in *Broken Arrow* (USA, 1950) and *A Man Called Horse*.

> **Film studies scholars have interpreted the sexualization of race in Hollywood film as evidence of a much larger anxiety in American culture concerning interracial sexuality.**

Reflected in many of these narratives are industry labour practices, or what Wong (1978) calls role segregation and role stratification. Role segregation refers to the ways in which non-white actors are, by virtue of their race, ineligible for certain kinds of roles, while white actors are able to move 'horizontally' into even those roles racially defined as black, Asian, Native American, or Chicano. In the study of stereotypes, 'breakthrough' films are those in which lead roles designated as non-white are actually played by non-white actors, as in *Salt of the Earth* (USA, 1954), *The World of Suzie Wong* (USA, 1960), and *Uncle Tom's Cabin* (USA, 1927). Until the mid-1960s role segregation facilitated the anxiety around miscegenation by enabling white actors to play roles of non-white characters in stories of interracial sexuality, thereby skirting the Motion Picture Production Code (called the Hays Code), which forbade representations of miscegenation (Cortés 1993). In *Pinky* (USA, 1949), for instance, the title character, who has been passing for white, returns home, where she comes to terms with her 'blackness' and rejects the white man who loves her. Here, the scenes between Pinky and her beau, while narratively interracial, are none the less white, thereby avoiding a realist depiction of black and white sexual desire. The larger the role, the more likely it is—think of *Bordertown* (USA, 1935), *Down Argentine Way* (USA, 1940), *Viva Zapata!* (USA, 1952), *The Searchers* (USA, 1956), *Windwalker* (USA, 1980), and *Evita* (USA, 1996)—that a white actor will get the part, especially if the story entails an interracial sexual encounter (Wong 1978).

The industry's use of role segregation is part of the history of the stereotype for a number of reasons. First, it enables white actors to occupy and signify the full range of humanity in film as a body of cultural representation, which has the powerful effect of locking non-white actors into minor roles, or what Wong (1987) calls role stratification. In minor roles, character development and complexity are even harder to achieve as narrative combines with the ideology of the camera to reiterate the secondary or background nature of non-white groups and cultures. In the western, for instance, most Native Americans will be confined to minor roles, often shot in groups from long distance, and rarely individualized through spoken lines (Hilger 1995). Other genres, such as the war story, assemble groups of non-white actors as the enemy, thereby reiterating stereotyped notions of a group's inherent violence (*Full Metal Jacket*, USA, 1987; *Sands of Iwo Jima*, USA, 1949). Second, the practice of horizontal movement of whites into non-white roles has necessitated certain kinds of development in film cosmetology that are part of the stereotype's performance. In *My Geisha* (USA, 1962), make-up artists created a new procedure for actress Shirley MacLaine's transformation from Anglo to Asian by using dental plaster, clay, and wax to fashion rubber eyepieces as her epicanthic fold. This, combined with dark brown contact lenses, a black wig, and certain habits of halting speech, perform Asian racial difference for the big screen (Wong, 1978).

What scholarly analysis of the stereotype most powerfully reveals, then, is the pervasiveness of racism as an institutionalized element of Hollywood film. In filmic structure and forms of visual pleasure (narrative, setting, cosmetology, and camera technique) as well as in industry labour practices and 'morality' codes, we witness the full arsenal of the stereotype's production. Add to this other elements—the ethnicity of directors and producers, or the specificities of English-language use—and one can begin to explore how the seeming simplicity of stereotypes is the effect of complex histories and representational forms. This is not to say, however, that the scholarly archive on the stereotype has gone uncritiqued. In light of independent cinematic production and post-structuralist theorizations of both 'representation' and subjectivity, critical understandings of the stereotype have been transformed.

Textuality, spectatorship, and the 'real'

Perhaps the most important early critique of the stereotype is Steve Neale's 'The Same Old Story: Stereotypes and Difference' (1979). Neale defines four primary critical problems. First, the emphasis on stereotypes constrains critical analysis by remaining too tied to the level of character and characterization, thereby obscuring other features of a text or ignoring altogether the textual specificities of individual films. Second, the identification of a stereotype does not illuminate racism as either a representational or a social practice; it merely points to it. In doing so it relies, third, on an empirically based notion of the 'real' that both precedes and measures the accuracy of the image. And, fourth, such an approach promotes the idea that artistic production is inherently progressive when it offers positive images to counter the negativity of the stereotype. Because of these critical fallacies, Neale proposes a shift in attention from repetition (the citing of the 'same old story' in text after text) to difference (a focus on how texts construct racial meanings).

In defining what he understands as the weakness of ideological criticism, Neale draws on the theoretical traditions of formalism, psychoanalysis, and post-structuralism to foreground the text as a specific and discrete cultural production, question the forms of identification involved in spectatorship, and retrieve representation from its reduction to the 'real'. All these issues have remained central to critical conversations in the 1980s and 1990s, but Neale's emphasis on the stereotype as inherently problematic, perhaps even useless, has not been retained (Snead 1994; Shohat and Stam 1994). Instead, the impulse has been to deepen the theorization of the stereotype by elaborating its textual production—its circulation as a sign—and by exploring its function in the construction of social subjectivities and psychic identifications and disavowals.

In their editorial introduction to *Screen*'s first special issue devoted to questions of race, Robert Stam and

Louise Spence (1983) begin to elaborate a comprehensive methodology to account for the textual practices and intertextual contexts through which 'difference is transformed into "other"-ness and exploited or penalized by and for power' (1983: 3). This emphasis on power directs attention both to the use of the camera as a representational practice and to cinema as an economic and political apparatus that circulates ways of interpreting and consuming the world. Framing the concept of voyeurism around race, and tying it both to the diegesis and to the political economy of cinema (i.e. the international market), Stam and Spence cite the camera as a crucial element in the global construction of the First World as 'subject'.

In the western's repeated motif of the encircled wagon, for instance, the camera transforms Native American difference into hierarchical otherness by locating the primary point of view behind or at the level of the wagon, with sound in the ensuing battle isolating Anglo pain and death (and most often collectivizing Indian utterance in the war 'whoop'). Shot scale and duration—close-ups focusing down upon white women and children, for instance, or the wide-angle long shot taking in a horizon filled by hostile figures—wed the technical features of filmic production to ideologies of race. The racism of a text is thus an effect of its aesthetic language and formal features of production and not simply a matter of narrative or characterization. As such, 'positive images' can be as pernicious as degrading ones, depending on the comprehensive racial discourse of a text (as in *Guess Who's Coming to Dinner*, USA, 1968).

> **The racism of a text is thus an effect of its aesthetic language and formal features of production and not simply a matter of narrative or characterization.**

In demonstrating that racial discourse is more than a citation of historically racialized bodies, Stam and Spence theoretically identify a 'structuring absence' fundamental to the segregationist logic of much pre-1960s Hollywood film. For instance, Alfred Hitchcock's *The Wrong Man* (USA, 1957), in which scenes of New York City are devoid of people of colour, offers a racial discourse keyed to white visual pleasure. Critically to analyse the structuring absence of this film does not mean decrying its lack of realism in depicting New York City, but examining instead how its racial fantasy and visual pleasure are connected. In doing so, the critic will locate the question of realism within (and not outside) the text by explicating the film's mechanisms of suture—its construction of an internal 'reality'. For Stam and Spence, a comprehensive methodology for studying the stereotype thus entails an analysis of the narrative structures, genre conventions, and cinematic styles through which a discourse of race achieves its reality effect in a given film. In the analysis of dominant Hollywood cinema, this critical move has shifted the burden of the charge of racism from individuals (e.g. Hitchcock) to the broader practices of filmic production.

But what about the spectator? For Stam and Spence, the audience is not fully constituted by the film text, nor is the filmic experience limited to its individualized visual consumption. Spectators are shaped simultaneously by the ideologies of the wider culture and their specific gender, race, and class locations. Because of this, 'aberrant readings' are both possible and plausible. 'Black Americans, presumably, never took Stepin Fetchit to be an accurate representation of their race as a whole' (Stam and Spence 1983: 19). Note 'presumably'. Here, the stereotype that fixes the black image on the screen is transparent in its distortion, thereby enabling black audiences to reject and rewrite the stereotype. Homi Bhabha's essay on the stereotype, published later in the same year, begins to complicate this picture of resistant readers and their identifications, and on two counts. One, knowledge of the inaccuracy of the stereotype, he argues, does not forestall the political effect of the stereotype; indeed, the stereotype is effective on a colonialized subject precisely through its distortion. Two, spectator identifications are far more complex and ambivalent than their reduction to social identity asserts; therefore, 'the' black audience takes shape in contradictory and disparate ways (Bhabha 1983). More recently, Stuart Hall captures these issues in his title 'What is this "Black" in Black Popular Culture?' (1992).

In film studies, the critique of identity that is now nearly synonymous with post-structuralist analysis owes a great deal to the conversations about realism in the early 1980s. From these conversations the assumption that one 'reads' a film according to one's social identity, which is itself produced by one's positioning in hierarchies of power, is reframed; identity is rather an effect of discursive and material practices, not the essentialist ground for their explanations (Lubiano 1991; Snead 1994). And further, counter-reading is about historical and political oppositionality, and not essentialized difference (Fregoso 1993). This last point is forcefully made in a 1988 *Screen* volume titled *The Last 'Special Issue' on Race*. Here, guest editors Isaac Julien and Kobena Mercer assert that '*Screen* theory' has marginalized race and ethnicity not only through the 'special', segregated volume, but in its popularization of the notion of difference as 'Otherness'. Declaring this the 'last special issue', they hope to move the conversation of race and ethnicity from margin to centre by foregrounding the politics of both critical discourse and cinematic practices. In doing so, the volume sets the stage for three of the most important critical emphases in the 1990s: independent film, whiteness, and ethnicity in the context of global media culture.

The present tense

The issue of independent cinema has always gone hand in hand with the analysis of the stereotype, leading to a general assumption in the 1960s and 1970s that once those from stereotyped groups controlled the means of production, new film cultures would be born. *Zoot Suit* (USA, 1981), *Chan is Missing* (USA, 1982), *El Norte* (USA, 1983), *She's Gotta Have It* (USA, 1986), *Born in East LA* (USA, 1987), and *Pow Wow Highway* (USA, 1988) each gained recognition for their self-conscious counter to Hollywood formulations. A number of these directors—Luis Valdez, Wayne Wang, and Spike Lee—have made the 'crossover' move, with big budgets and mainstream critical acclaim (*La Bamba*, USA, 1987; *The Joy Luck Club*, USA, 1993; *Do the Right Thing*, USA, 1989).

With Hollywood seemingly willing to cash in on 'ethnic' markets, media critics and activists find themselves in the 1990s debating the 'burden of representation' that attends such widely circulated texts (Diawara 1993; Leong 1991). In a complicated analysis of Spike Lee's own claims to tell the truth of African American culture and experience, Wahneema Lubiano, for instance, emphasizes the scarcity of diverse representations within ethnic groups as part of her broader critique of Lee's political retreat into homophobic and sexist interpretations of black masculinity (Lubiano 1991). At issue in Lubiano's analysis is the relationship between representative blackness and the proliferate whiteness of US image industries.

Whiteness, of course, has long been the context and subtext of the study of stereotypes, but until Richard Dyer's 'White' in the 'last special' *Screen* issue (1988), it has lacked any careful critical analysis. Dyer's essay begins by noting how whiteness as an ethnic category seems to lack specificity, coming into focus only as emptiness, absence, denial, or death, as is the case in *Night of the Living Dead* (USA, 1968, 1990). The resistance of whiteness to specification is an effect of its construction as the unmarked category in US racial discourse. For this reason, new work in the field is geared toward explicating both the socio-historical relationship between white identity forms and cinema and the representational practices within specific films that produce and circulate whiteness as sign (Bernardi 1996). The critical project of rendering whiteness tangible in the filmic text as one of film's most powerful and reliable narrative, characterological, and signifying systems entails a methodology that attends to textuality, on the one hand, and to Hollywood film's pedagogic function in the construction of a national imaginary, on the other (Carby 1993).

> *Unthinking Eurocentrism* **elaborates an interethnic and cross-ethnic critical agenda for the study of film, one that situates difference not in a paradigm of margin and centre, but as a de-centred, polyvocal multiculturalism.**

It is this emphasis on the pedagogic that underwrites Ella Shohat and Robert Stam's important book *Unthinking Eurocentrism* (1994). Situating filmic production in the histories and formations of nations, and paying attention to the international economy of film, this text implicitly argues against the Eurocentric formulation of difference as physiological and racial. Instead, the authors want a critical analysis that examines 'ethnicities-in-relation', which means rethinking official national histories in order to link communities, histories, and identities formed across the borders of formalized nation-states. They read film culture in the context of the 'Americas' and not simply the United States, in the regions of Britain's imperial reach and not simply Europe, in the Third World, and not simply the First. In so doing, *Unthinking Eurocentrism* elaborates an interethnic and cross-ethnic critical agenda for the study of film, one that situates difference not in a paradigm of margin and centre, but as a de-centred, polyvocal multiculturalism. This text thus offers a model for the study of race, ethnicity, and film in contemporary transnational economies of production and consumption. But more than this, it stakes out a comprehensive theoretical agenda that links diverse US populations—African Americans, Asian Americans, Chicano–Latinos, Native Americans, Jews, and Anglo-Americans—to global image cultures, independent cinemas, and Third World productions. In short, it defines a new disciplinary agenda for the study of race, ethnicity, and film.

BIBLIOGRAPHY

Aleiss, Angela (1995), 'Native Americans: The Surprising Silents', *Cineaste* 21/3: 34–5.

Balibar, Étienne, and **Immanuel Wallerstein** (1991), *Race, Nation, Class: Ambiguous Identities* (London: Verso).

Bataille, Gretchen M., and **Charles L. P. Silet** (1980), *The Pretend Indians: Images of Native Americans in the Movies* (Ames: Iowa State University Press).

Bernardi, Daniel (ed.) (1996), *The Birth of Whiteness: Race and the Emergence of US Cinema* (New Brunswick, NJ: Rutgers University Press).

Bernstein, Matthew, and **Gaylyn Studlar** (eds.) (1996), *Visions of the East: Orientalism in Film* (New Brunswick, NJ: Rutgers University Press).

Bhabha, Homi (1983), 'The Other Question . . . The Stereotype and Colonial Discourse', *Screen*, 24/6: 18–36.

Bobo, Jacqueline (1995), *Black Women as Cultural Readers* (New York: Columbia University Press).

***Bogle, Donald** (1989), *Toms, Coons, Mulattoes, Mammies, and Bucks: An Interpretive History of Blacks in American Films* (New York: Continuum).

Boyd, Todd (1996), *Am I Black enough for You? Popular Culture from the Hood and Beyond* (Berkeley: University of California Press).

Carby, Hazel (1993), 'Encoding White Resentment. Grand Canyon: A Narrative for our Times', in Cameron McCarthy and Warren Crichlow (eds.), *Race, Identity, and Representation in Education* (New York: Routledge).

Castillo, Edward (1991), Review of *Dances with Wolves*, *Film Quarterly*, 44/4: 14–23.

Churchill, Ward (1992), *Fantasies of the Master Race: Literature, Cinema, and the Colonization of American Indians* (Monroe, Me.: Common Courage Press).

Cortés, Carlos E. (1993), 'Them and Us: Immigration as Societal Barometer and Social Education in American Film', in Robert Brent Toplin (ed.), *Hollywood as Mirror: Changing Views of Outsiders and Enemies in American Movies* (Westport, Conn.: Greenwood Press).

Cripps, Thomas (1977), *Slow Fade to Black: The Negro in American Film 1900–1942* (New York: Oxford University Press).

—— (1993), *Making Movies Black: The Hollywood Message Movie from World War II to the Civil Rights Era* (New York: Oxford University Press).

Curran, Joseph M. (1989), *Hibernian Green on the Silver Screen: The Irish and American Movies* (Westport, Conn.: Greenwood Press).

Delpar, Helen (1984), 'Goodbye to the Greaser': Mexico, the MPPDA, and Derogatory Films', *Journal of Popular Film and Television*, 12: 34–41.

Diawara, Manthia (ed.) (1993), *Black American Cinema* (New York: Routledge).

Dyer, Richard (1977), 'Stereotyping', in Dyer (ed.), *Gays and Film* (London: British Film Institute).

—— (1988), 'White', *Screen*, 29/4: 44–65.

Edgerton, Gary (1994), '"A Breed Apart": Hollywood, Racial Stereotyping and the Promise of Revisionism in *The Last of the Mohicans*' *Journal of American Culture*, 17/2: 1–20.

Erens, Patricia (1984), *The Jew in American Cinema* (Bloomington: Indiana University Press).

Feng, Richard (1995), 'In Search of Asian American Cinema', *Cineaste*, 21/3: 32–5.

Fregoso, Rosa Linda (1993), *The Bronze Screen: Chicana and Chicano Film Culture* (Minneapolis: University of Minnesota Press).

Friar, Ralph E., and **Natasha A. Friar** (1972), *The Only Good Indian: The Hollywood Gospel* (New York: Drama Book Specialist).

Friedman, Lester D. (1982), *Hollywood's Image of the Jew* (New York: Ungar).

—— (ed.) (1991), *Unspeakable Images: Ethnicity and the American Cinema* (Urbana: University of Illinois Press).

Gaines, Jane (1988), 'White Privilege and Looking Relations: Race and Gender in Feminist Film Theory', *Screen*, 29/4: 12–27.

Garcia Berumen, Frank Javier (1995), *The Chicano/Hispanic Image in American Film* (New York: Vantage Press).

Goldberg, Theo (ed.) (1990), *Anatomy of Racism* (Minneapolis: University of Minnesota).

Golden, Daniel Sembroff (1980), 'The Fate of La Famiglia: Italian Images in American Film', in Randall M. Miller (ed.) *The Kaleidoscopic Lens: How Hollywood Views Ethnic Groups* (Englewood, NJ: Jerome S. Ozer).

Hall, Stuart (1992), 'What is this "Black" in Black Popular Culture?', in Gina Dent (ed.), *Black Popular Culture* (Seattle: Bay Press).

Hilger, Michael (1986), *The American Indian in Film* (Metuchen, NJ: Scarecrow Press).

—— (1995), *From Savage to Nobleman: Images of Native Americans in Film* (Lanham, Md.: Scarecrow Press).

Julien, Isaac, and **Kobena Mercer** (1988), 'De Margin and De Centre', *Screen*, 29/4: 2–10.

King, John, Ana M. Lopez, and **Manuel Alvarado** (eds.) (1993), *Mediating Two Worlds: Cinematic Encounters in the Americas* (London: British Film Institute).

Leab, Daniel (1975), *From Sambo to Superspade: The Black Experience in Motion Pictures* (Boston: Houghton Mifflin).

Leong, Russell (ed.) (1991), *Moving the Image: Independent Asian Pacific American Media Arts* (Los Angeles: UCLA Asian American Studies Center and Visual Communications Publications).

Lourdeaux, Lee (1990), *Italian and Irish Filmmakers in America: Ford, Capra, Coppola, and Scorsese* (Philadelphia: Temple University Press).

Lubiano, Wahneema (1991), '"But Compared to What? Etc.": Reading Realism, Representation, and Essentialism in *School Daze*, *Do the Right Thing* and the Spike Lee Discourse', *Black American Literature Forum*, 25/2: 253–82.

Lund, Karen C. (1994), *American Indians in Silent Film: Motion Pictures in the Library of Congress* (Washington: Library of Congress).

Martin, Michael T. (ed.) (1995), *Cinemas of the Black Diaspora: Diversity, Dependence, and Oppositionality* (Detroit: Wayne State University Press).

Miller, Randall (ed.) (1980), *The Kaleidoscopic Lens: How Hollywood Views Ethnic Groups* (Englewood, NJ: Jerome S. Ozer).

Neale, Steve (1979), 'The Same Old Story: Stereotypes and Difference', *Screen Education*, 32–3: 33–7.

Noriega, Chon A. (ed.) (1992), *Chicanos and Film: Representation and Resistance* (Minneapolis: University of Minnesota Press).

—— and **Ana M. Lopez** (eds.) (1996), *The Ethnic Eye: Latino Media Arts* (Minneapolis: University of Minnesota Press).

O'Connor, John E. (1980), *The Hollywood Indian: Stereotypes of Native Americans in Films* (Trenton, NJ: New Jersey State Museum).

Pettit, Arthur G. (1980), *Images of the Mexican American in Fiction and Film* (College Station: Texas A & M University Press).

Reid, Mark (1993), *Redefining Black Film* (Berkeley: University of California Press).

Richard, Alfred Charles (1992), *The Hispanic Image on the Silver Screen: An Interpretive Filmography from Silents into Sound 1898–1935* (Westport, Conn.: Greenwood Press).

—— (1993), *Contemporary Hollywood's Negative Hispanic Image: An Interpretive Filmography 1936–1955* (Westport, Conn.: Greenwood Press).

—— (1994), *Contemporary Hollywood's Negative Hispanic Image: An Interpretive Filmography 1956–1993* (Westport, Conn.: Greenwood Press).

Rogin, Michael (1985), '"The Sword became a Flashing Vision": D. W. Griffith's *The Birth of a Nation*', *Representations*, 9/1: 150–95.

—— (1996), *Blackface, White Noise: Jewish Immigrants in the Hollywood Melting Pot* (Berkeley: University of California Press).

*****Shohat, Ella,** and **Robert Stam** (1994), *Unthinking Eurocentrism: Multiculturalism and the Media* (New York: Routledge).

Snead, James A. (1994), *White Screens, Black Images: Hollywood from the Dark Side*, ed. Colin MacCabe and Cornel West (New York: Routledge).

Sollors, Werner (1986), *Beyond Ethnicity* (New York: Oxford University Press).

Stam, Robert, and **Louise Spence** (1983), 'Colonialism, Racism and Representation', *Screen*, 24/2: 2–20.

Thi Thanh Nga (1995), 'The Long March from Wong to Woo: Asians in Hollywood', *Cineaste*, 21/4: 38–40.

Trinh T. Min-ha (1991), *When the Moon Waxes Red: Representation, Gender and Cultural Politics* (New York: Routledge).

Wiegman, Robyn (1995), *American Anatomies: Theorizing Race and Gender* (Durham, NC: Duke University Press).

Woll, Allen L. (1980), *The Latin Image in American Film* (Los Angeles: UCLA Latin American Center Publications).

—— and **Randall M. Miller** (eds.) (1987), *Ethnic and Racial Images in American Film and Television* (New York: Garland).

Wong, Eugene Franklin (1978), *On Visual Media Racism: Asians in American Motion Pictures* (New York: Arno Press).

18

Film and cultural identity

Rey Chow

A film about how film was first invented in Germany, Wim Wenders's *Die Brüder Skladanowsky* ('The Brothers Skladanowsky' Part I, 1994) offers important clues to the contentious relationship between film and cultural identity. Using the style and the shooting and editing skills of the silent era, and filming with an antique, hand-cranked camera, Wenders and students from the Munich Academy for Television and Film recast this originary moment in cinematic history as the tale of a loved one lost and found.

Disturbed by her Uncle Eugen's imminent departure on a long journey, Max Skladanowsky's 5-year-old daughter implores her father and his other brother, Emil, to bring Eugen back into her life. She gets her wish: as she waves goodbye to Uncle Eugen, the little girl is told that he is still with them, inside the box containing the film they had made of him before he left. Soon she is overjoyed to see, through the 'Bioscop' invented by her father, a life-size Uncle Eugen flickering on the screen, making funny expressions and performing acrobatic feats just as when he was still with them. Uncle Eugen has disappeared in person, but has reappeared on film—and he will be there for ever.

Elegant and moving, Wenders's film about the beginning of film reminds us of the key features of the medium of signification that was novel in the 1890s. First, film (and here I intend photography as well as cinema) is, structurally, a story about the relationship between absence and presence, between disappearance and reappearance. Filmic representation reproduces the world with a resemblance unknown to artists before its arrival. Whether what is captured is a human face, a body, an object, or a place, the illusion of presence generated is such that a new kind of realism, one that vies with life itself, aggressively asserts itself. If cultural identity is something that always finds an anchor in specific media of representation, it is easy to see why the modes of illusory presence made possible by film have become such strong contenders in the controversial negotiations for cultural identity. Second, in a manner that summarizes the essence of many early silent films, Wenders's work draws attention to the agile movements of the human body as they are captured by the equipment built by Max Skladanowsky. Because sound and dialogue were not yet available, the filmmaker had to turn the ingredients he had into so many spatial inscriptions on the screen. What could have better conveyed the liveliness of this new illusory world than the exaggerated hieroglyphic movements of the human body, coming across as a series of images-in-motion? The compelling sense of photographic realism in film is thus punctuated with an equally compelling sense of melodrama—of technologically magnified movements that highlight the presences unfolding on the screen as artificial and constructed experiments. Melodrama here is not so much the result of sentimental narration as it is the effect of a caricatured defamiliarization of a familiar form (the human body). Made possible by the innovative manœuvres of light and temporality, of exposure and speed, such defamiliarization has a direct bearing on the new modes of seeing and showing.

The coexistence of an unprecedented realism and a novel melodramatization means that, from the very earliest moments, the modes of identity construction offered by film were modes of *relativity* and *relations* rather than essences and fixities. Film techniques such as montage, close-ups, panoramic shots, long shots, jump cuts, slow motion, flashback, and so forth, which result in processes of introjection, projection, or rejection that take place between the images and narratives shown on the screen, on the one hand, and audiences' sense of self, place, history, and pleasure, on the other, confirm the predominance of such modes of relativity and relations. With film, people's identification of who they are can no longer be regarded as a mere ontological or phenomenological event. Such identification is now profoundly enmeshed with technological intervention, which ensures that even (or especially) when the camera seems the least intrusive, the permeation of the film spectacle by the apparatus is complete and unquestionable. And it is the completeness of the effect of illusion that makes the reception of film controversial.

> **With film, people's identification of who they are can no longer be regarded as a mere ontological or phenomenological event. Such identification is now profoundly enmeshed with technological intervention.**

It was the understanding of this fundamentally manipulable constitution of film—this open-ended relation between spectacle and audience due, paradoxically, to the completeness of technological permeation—that led Walter Benjamin to associate film with revolutionary production and political change (Benjamin 1936, 1969, 1986). For, as Benjamin speculated in the 1930s, film's throughly *mediated* nature makes it a cultural opportunity to be seized for political purposes. Just as for the film actor performing in front of the camera is a kind of exile from his own body because it demands the simulation of emotional con-

tinuity in what is technically a disjointed process of production, so for the audience, Benjamin writes, the new attitude of reception is distraction and manipulation. As opposed to the absorption and concentration required by the traditional novel, which has to be read in solitude and in private, film requires a mode of interaction that is public and collective, and that allows audiences to take control of their situation by adopting changing, rather than stable, positions. Film, in other words, turns the recipient potentially into a producer who plays an active rather than passive role in the shaping of his or her cultural environment.

Whereas Benjamin in his Marxist, Brechtian moments was willing to grant to a movie audience the significance of an organized mob, later generations of film critics, notably feminist critics with a training in psychoanalysis, would elaborate the agency of the viewer with much greater complexity by way of processes of subjectivity formation. Such critics would argue that fantasies, memories, and other unconscious experiences, as well as the gender roles imposed by the dominant culture at large, play important roles in mediating the impact of the spectacle (see Creed and White, Chapters 9 and 13).

The crucial theoretical concept informing psychoanalytic interpretations of identity is 'suture'. In the context of cinema, 'suture' refers to the interactions between the enunciation of the filmic apparatus, the spectacle, and the viewing subject—interactions which, by soliciting or 'interpellating' (see Althusser 1971) the viewing subject in a series of shifting positions, allow it to gain access to coherent meaning (see Heath 1981). As Kaja Silverman writes, 'The operation of suture is successful at the moment that the viewing subject says, "Yes, that's me," or "That's what I see"' (Silverman 1983: 205). As expressed through suture— literally a 'sewing-up' of gaps—cinematic identification is an eminently ideological process: subjectivity is imagined primarily as a lack, which is then exploited, through its desire to know, by the visual field enunciated by the omnipotent filmic apparatus, which withholds more than it reveals. In order to have access to the plenitude that is the basis for identity, the subject must give up something of its own in order to be 'hooked up' with the Other, the visual field, which is, none the less, for ever beyond its grasp. No matter how successful, therefore, the subject's possession of meaning is by definition compensatory and incomplete. (This process of subject formation through suture is comparable to an individual's attempt to acquire identity in certain social situations. For instance, in order to gain acceptance into a particular social group, an individual must be willing to sacrifice, to part with certain things to which he or she feels personally attached but which are not socially acceptable; such personal sacrifices, however, are not guarantees that the social identity acquired is complete or permanent because, as is often the case, the social group is capricious and arbitrary in its demands.)

Because it foregrounds processes of identification through relations of visuality, cinema is one of the most explicit systems of suturing, the operations of which can be explained effectively through the simple acts of seeing. Meanwhile, cinema also offers a homology with the dominant culture at large, in that the latter, too, may be seen as a repressive system in which individual subjects gain access to their identities only by forsaking parts of themselves, parts that are, moreover, never fully found again.

Using suture, ideology, and other related psychoanalytic concepts, feminist critics concerned with identitarian politics have, since Laura Mulvey's groundbreaking work in 1975, been steadily exposing the masculinism of mainstream cinema as well as of the dominant, heterosexist culture of the West. As a means of countering the repressive effects of dominant modes of visuality and identification, some go on to analyse in detail the ambiguities of the visual representations of women (see, for instance, Mayne 1989; Doane *et al.* 1984; Penley 1989), while others make use of the problematic of spectatorship, notably the spectatorship of women audiences, to theorize alternative ways of seeing, of constructing subjectivities and identities (see e.g. Silverman 1988; de Lauretis 1984, 1987).

Once identity is linked to spectatorship, a new spectrum of theoretical possibilities opens up. For instance, critics who have been influenced by Edward Said's *Orientalism* (1978) can now make the connection that orientalism, as the system of signification that represents non-Western cultures to Western recipients in the course of Western imperialism, operates visually as well as narratologically to subject 'the Orient' to ideological manipulation. They point out that, much like representations of women in classical narrative cinema, representations of 'the Orient' are often fetishized objects manufactured for the satiation of the masculinist gaze of the West. As a means to expose the culturally imperialist assumptions behind European and American cinemas, the spectatorship of non-Western audiences thus also takes on vital significance (see e.g. Chow 1991: 3–33).

Because it conceptualizes identity non-negotiably as the effect of a repressive but necessary closure, suture has been theoretically pre-emptive. This can be seen in the two major ways in which the relationship between film and identity is usually investigated. For both, an acceptance of the idea of suture is indispensable.

This acceptance may function negatively, when the understanding of suture is used as a way to debunk and criticize certain kinds of identity—as ideologically conditioned by patriarchy and imperialism, for instance. Or, this acceptance may function positively and *implicitly*, in the counter-critical practice of demonstrating that some types of film may serve as places for the construction of other (usually marginalized) types of identity. It is important to remember, however, that even when critics who are intent on subverting mainstream culture assert that 'alternative' cinemas give rise to 'alternative' identities, as long as they imagine identities exclusively by way of the classic interpellation of subjectivities, they are not departing theoretically from the fundamental operations of suture. In fact, one may go so far as to say that it is when critics attempt to idealize the 'other' identities claimed for 'other' cinemas that they tend to run the greatest risk of reinscribing the ideologically coercive processes of identification through suturing.

For these reasons, I would propose that any attempt to theorize film and cultural identity should try to move beyond both the criticism and the implicit reinscription of the effects of suture. In this light, it might be productive to return to aspects of film which may not immediately seem to be concerned with identity as such but which, arguably, offer alternatives to the impasses created by suture.

Let us think more closely about the implications of the modes of visuality opened up by film. To go back to the story of the Skladanowsky brothers, what does it mean for Uncle Eugen to 'appear' when he is physically absent? From an anthropocentric perspective, we would probably say that the person Eugen was the 'origin', the 'reality' that gave rise to the film which then became a document, a record of him. From the perspective of the filmic images, however, this assumption of 'origin' is no longer essential, for Eugen is now a movie which has taken on an independent, mechanically reproducible existence of its own. With

New and undreamt-of possibilities of experimentation—Ruttman's *Berlin, Symphony of a City* (1927)

the passage of time, more and more reprints can be made and every one of them will be the same. The 'original' Uncle Eugen will no longer be of relevance.

Film, precisely because it signifies the thorough permeation of reality by the mechanical apparatus and thus the production of a seamless resemblance to reality itself, displaces once and for all the sovereignty of the so-called original, which is now often an imperfect and less permanent copy of itself: Uncle Eugen's image remains long after he is dead. This obvious aspect of filmic reproduction is what underlies Benjamin's argument about the decline of the aura, the term he uses to describe the irreplaceable sense of presence that was unique to traditional works of art when such works of art were rooted in specific times and spaces (Benjamin 1969). What was alarming about the arrival of film (as it was for many poets and artists) was precisely the destruction of the aura, a destruction that is programmed into film's mode of reproduction and is part of film's 'nature' as a medium. This essential *iconoclasm* of filmic reproduction is encapsulated in Wenders's story by the phantasmagorically alive and replayable image of Uncle Eugen in his own absence. This image signifies the end of the aura and the sacredness that used to be attached to the original human figure, to the human figure as the original. It also signifies a change in terms of the agency of seeing: the realist accuracy of the image announces that a mechanical eye, the eye of the camera, has replaced the human eye altogether in its capacity to capture and reproduce the world with precision (see Comolli 1978). As the effects of mechanicity, filmic images carry with them an inhuman quality even as they are filled with human contents. This is the reason why film has been compared to a process of embalming (Bazin 1967: 9–16), to fossilization, and to death.

But what film destroys in terms of the aura, it gains in portability and transmissibility. With 'death' come new, previously undreamt-of possibilities of experimentation, as the mechanically reproduced images become sites of the elaboration of what Benedict Anderson, in a study of the emergence of nationalism in modern history, calls 'imagined communities' (Anderson 1983). We see this, for instance, in the mundane, anonymous sights of the big city that are typical of early silent films such as Walther Ruttmann's *Berlin—Die Sinfonie der Großstadt* ('Berlin: Symphony of a City', Germany 1927) and Dziga Vertov's *Man with the Movie Camera* (USSR, 1929). Scenes of workers going to work, housewives shopping, schoolchildren assembling for school,

passengers travelling by train; scenes of carriages, engines, automobiles, railway stations, typewriters, phones, gutters, street lamps, shop fronts—all such scenes testify to a certain fascination with the potentialities of seeing, of what can be made visible. The mechanically reproduced image has brought about a perception of the world as an infinite collection of objects and people permanently on display in their humdrum existence. At the same time, because film is not only reproducible but also transportable, it can be shown in different places, usually remote from the ones where they are originally made. Coinciding with upheavals of traditional populations bound to the land and with massive migrations from the countryside to metropolitan areas around the world, film ubiquitously assumes the significance of the monumental: the cinema auditorium, as Paul Virilio writes, puts order into visual chaos like a cenotaph. As the activity of moviegoing gratifies 'the wish of migrant workers for a lasting and even eternal homeland', cinema becomes the site of 'a new aboriginality in the midst of demographic anarchy' (Virilio 1989: 39).

The iconoclastic, portable imprints of filmic images and the metropolitan, migratory constitution of their audiences mean that film is always a rich means of exploring cultural crisis—of exploring culture itself as a crisis. We have seen many examples of such uses of film in various cinemas in the period following the Second World War: the suffocating existentialist portrayals of the breakdown of human communication in Italian and French avant-garde films; the sentimental middle-class family melodramas of Hollywood; the aesthetic experiments with vision and narration in Japanese cinema; the self-conscious parodies of fascism in the New German Cinema; the explosive renderings of diaspora and 'otherness' in what is called 'Third Cinema' (see Hall 1990; Pines and Willemen 1989). By the 1980s and early 1990s, with the films of the mainland Chinese Fifth Generation directors, it becomes clear that film can be used for the exploration of crises, especially in cultures whose experience of modernity is marked, as it were, by conflicts between an indigenous tradition and foreign influences, between the demands of nationalism and the demands of Westernization.

For mainland Chinese directors such as Chen Kaige, Zhang Yimou, Tian Zhuangzhuang, and Zhang Nuanxin, reflecting on 'culture' inevitably involves the rethinking of origins—the 'pasts' that give rise to the present moment; the narratives, myths, rituals, customs, and practices that account for how a people becomes what it is. Because such rethinking plays on the historical relation between what is absent and what is present, film becomes, for these directors and their counterparts elsewhere in Asia (see Dissanayake 1988), an ideal medium: its projectional mechanism means that the elaboration of the past as what is bygone, what is behind us, can simultaneously take the form of images moving, in their vivid luminosity, in front of us. The simple dialectical relationship between visual absence and visual presence that was dramatized by film from the very first thus lends itself appropriately to an articulation of the dilemmas and contradictions, the nostalgias and hopes, that characterize struggles towards modernity. In such struggles, as we see in films such as *Yellow Earth* (1984), *Sacrifice Youth* (1985), *Judou* (1990), and *Raise the Red Lantern* (1991), the definitively modernist effort to reconceptualize origins typically attributes to indigenous traditions the significance of a primitive past in all the ambiguous senses of 'primitivism'. This special intersection between film and primitivism has been described in terms of 'primitive passions' (Chow 1995).

As the viewing of film does not require literacy in the traditional sense of knowing how to read and write, film signals the transformation of word-based cultures into cultures that are increasingly dominated by the visual image, a transformation that may be understood as a special kind of translation in the postmodern, post-colonial world. Intersemiotic in nature, film-as-translation involves histories and populations hitherto excluded by the restricted sense of literacy, and challenges the class hierarchies long established by such literacy in societies, West and East (Chow 1995). And, in so far as its images are permanently inscribed, film also functions as an immense visual archive, assimilating literature, popular culture, architecture, fashion, memorabilia, and the contents of junk shops, waiting to be properly inspected for its meanings and uses (Elsaesser 1989: 322–3).

Any attempt to discuss film and cultural identity would therefore need to take into account the multiple significance of filmic visuality in modernity. This is especially so when modernity is part of post-coloniality, as in the case of many non-Western cultures, in which to become 'modern' signifies an ongoing re-visioning of indigenous cultural traditions alongside the obligatory turns towards the West or 'the world at large'. In this light, it is worth remembering that film has always been, since its inception, a *transcultural* phe-

nomenon, having as it does the capacity to transcend 'culture'—to create modes of fascination which are readily accessible and which engage audiences in ways independent of their linguistic and cultural specificities. Consider, for instance, the greatly popular versions of fairy-tale romance, sex, kitsch, and violence from Hollywood; alternatively, consider the greatly popular slapstick humour and action films of Jackie Chan from Hong Kong. To be sure, such popular films can inevitably be read as so many constructions of national, sexual, cultural identities; as so many impositions of Western, American, or other types of ideology upon the rest of the world. While I would not for a moment deny that to be the case, it seems to me equally noteworthy that the world-wide appeal of many such films has something to do, rather, with their *not* being bound by well-defined identities, so that it is their specifically *filmic*, indeed phantasmagoric, significations of masculinism, moral righteousness, love, loyalty, family, and horror that speak to audiences across the globe, regardless of their own languages and cultures. (Hitchcock is reputed to have commented while making *Psycho* (USA, 1960) that he wanted Japanese audiences to scream at the same places as Hollywood audiences.)

> **Film has always been, since its inception, a *transcultural* phenomenon, having as it does the capacity to transcend 'culture'—to create modes of fascination which are readily accessible and which engage audiences in ways independent of their linguistic and cultural specificities.**

The phantasmagoric effects of illusion on the movie screen are reminders once again of the iconoclasm, the fundamental replacement of human perception by the machine that is film's very constitution. This originary iconoclasm, this power of the technologized visual image to communicate beyond verbal language, should perhaps be beheld as a useful enigma, one that serves to unsettle any easy assumption we may have of the processes of identification generated by film as a medium, be such identification in relation to subjectivity or to differing cultural contexts. In a theoretical climate in which identities are usually imagined—far too hastily I think—as being 'sutured' with specific times, places, practices, and cultures, thinking through this problematic of film's transcultural appeal should prove to be an instructive exercise.

BIBLIOGRAPHY

Althusser, Louis (1971), 'Ideology and Ideology State Apparatuses (Notes towards an Investigation)', in *Lenin and Philosophy and Other Essays*, trans. Ben Brewster (New York: Monthly Review Press).

Anderson, Benedict (1983), *Imagined Communities: Reflections on the Origin and Spread of Nationalism* (London: Verso).

Bazin, André (1967), *What is Cinema?*, ed. and trans. Hugh Gray, i (Berkeley and Los Angeles: University of California Press).

Benjamin, Walter (1936/1969), 'The Work of Art in the Age of Mechanical Reproduction', in *Illuminations*, ed. Hannah Arendt and trans. Harry Zohn (New York: Schocken Books).

—— (1986), 'The Author as Producer', in *Reflections: Essays, Aphorisms, Autobiographical Writings*, ed. Peter Demetz and trans. Edmund Jephcott (New York: Schocken).

Chow, Rey (1991), *Woman and Chinese Modernity: The Politics of Reading between West and East* (Minneapolis: University of Minnesota Press).

—— (1995), *Primitive Passions: Visuality, Sexuality, Ethnography, and Contemporary Chinese Cinema* (New York: Columbia University Press).

Comolli, Jean-Louis (1978), 'Machines of the Visible', in Teresa de Lauretis and Stephen Heath (eds.), *The Cinematic Apparatus* (London: Macmillan).

de Lauretis, Teresa (1984), *Alice Doesn't: Feminism, Semiotics, Cinema* (Bloomington: Indiana University Press).

—— (1987), *Technologies of Gender: Essays on Theory, Film, and Fiction* (Bloomington: Indiana University Press).

*****Dissanayake, Wimal** (ed.) (1988), *Cinema and Cultural Identity: Reflections on Films from Japan, India, and China* (Lanham, Md.: University Press of America).

Doane, Mary Ann, Patricia Mellencamp, and **Linda Williams** (eds.) (1984), *Re-Vision: Essays in Feminist Film Criticism* (Frederick, Md.: University Publications of America).

Elsaesser, Thomas (1989), *New German Cinema: A History* (New Brunswick, NJ: Rutgers University Press).

Hall, Stuart (1990), 'Cultural Identity and Diaspora', in J. Rutherford (ed.), *Identity: Community, Culture, Difference* (London: Lawrence & Wishart).

Heath, Stephen (1981), *Questions of Cinema* (Bloomington: Indiana University Press).

Mayne, Judith (1989), *Kino and the Woman Question: Feminism and Soviet Silent Film* (Columbus: Ohio State University Press).

Mulvey, Laura (1975), 'Visual Pleasure and Narrative Cinema', *Screen*, 16/3: 6–18; repr. in Penley (1989).

Penley, Constance (ed.) (1989), *Feminism and Film Theory* (New York: Routledge; London: British Film Institute).

—— and **Sharon Willis** (eds.) (1993), *Male Trouble* (Minneapolis: University of Minnesota Press).

Pines, Jim, and **Paul Willemen** (eds.) (1989), *Questions of Third Cinema* (London: British Film Institute).

Said, Edward (1978), *Orientalism* (London: Routledge & Kegan Paul).

Silverman, Kaja (1983), *The Subject of Semiotics* (New York: Oxford University Press).

—— (1988), *The Acoustic Mirror: The Female Voice in Psychoanalysis and Cinema* (Bloomington: Indiana University Press).

Virilio, Paul (1989), *War and Cinema: The Logistics of Perception*, trans. Patrick Camiller (London: Verso).

19

Film and history

Dudley Andrew

Attitudes

We are concerned here with film and with history; so let's begin by calling up a film that nearly half a century ago abruptly burrowed into the past so unforgettably that it was said to inaugurate the modern cinema, thus constituting itself an event of history. *Viaggio in Italia* ('Voyage to Italy', Italy, 1953) 'burst open a breach, and all cinema on pain of death must pass through it', wrote Jacques Rivette in a famous declaration of faith. 'With the appearance of *Viaggio in Italia* all films have suddenly aged ten years', he continued (Rivette 1955/1985: 192). Like James Joyce's *Ulysses*, Rossellini's film was controversial in its own day and remains recalcitrant even now, because it minutely records a contemporary civilization that appears at once diminished and sacred in the light of its ancient counterpart. Rossellini's film defines the modern by clinically analysing

post-war European values and by inventing a form to do so. A meandering essay, a sort of 'ba(l)ade', in Deleuze's term (1983: 280), it ignores the classicism of narrative cinema and the hermeticism of the avant-garde to thrust cinematography up against a reality that is both material and spiritual. Rossellini had the audacity to name his main character Joyce and to send him and his wife Katherine (Ingrid Bergman) on a journey as full of the ordinary and the extraordinary as that of Leopold Bloom.

This voyage of a couple in domestic crisis across strange and ancient landscapes becomes a descent into a past that is both personal and public, where private ethical choices are equivalent to decisive historiographic options. Mr Joyce (George Sanders), acerbic, sceptical, and practical, will sell Uncle Homer's(!) estate, eager to convert the 'strangeness' of what he has inherited into the familiarity of negoti-

Ingrid Bergman overwhelmed by her feelings—the Pompeii sequence in *Voyage to Italy* (1953)

able currency that he can take back with him to England. His wife, by contrast, gradually allows the features of the landscape and the people she sees to break through her preoccupations and her diffidence. Slowly she opens herself to the stunning world that she is drawn to visit. We see her looking, available, though she averts her gaze when confronted by those of a pregnant woman and then of an immense Roman statue.

Two magnificent sequences analogize the historian's encounter with the past. In the first of these Katherine visits the phosphorous fields around Vesuvius guided by an old and garrulous caretaker. Annoyed by his patter of arcane lore, she is about to return to her car when he demonstrates the effect of holding a torch near any of the volcanic openings on this torn-up crust of earth. Even the warmth of a cigarette produces a startling release of smoke far across the field, an immense exhalation from inside this ancient but living and explosive mountain. Later, at Pompeii, the couple assist at the exhumation of what turns out to be another couple buried by the volcano 2000 years ago. As the archaeologists dextrously bring out the outline of a man and woman caught by sudden death in bed together, Katherine finds herself overwhelmed. She runs from the spot, followed by her estranged husband. 'I was pretty moved myself,' he confesses. She is more than moved. She recognizes to her fullest capacity the tedium and insignificance of her own existence measured against this unmistakable sign of the holiness and the brevity of life. This is the epiphany she had earlier avoided when, at the art museum, she ran from the statue of Apollo, whose gaze accused her small-mindedness.

Viaggio in Italia alerts her and us to the possibilities of exchange between past and present, through the manner by which we look and through our response to being looked at, that is, being measured by a living past. When we take time to locate the fissures on their surfaces—their breathing-holes—we allow films to exhale, to release a fine mist that is evidence of an immense power they still retain while locked away in archives or in the pages of history books. Like any history, that of the cinema is an account—even an accounting—of a former state of affairs. But as *Viaggio in Italia* continues to prove, this is a history of living matter, whose inestimable power to affect us should be found and released by our probing.

In what follows, I aim to track the tension between the sheer existence of films and our ways of making sense of their appearance and effects, that is, the tension between *films* as moments of experience and the *cinema* as a tradition and an institution. The discipline of film history tends to leave the moments of experience alone, since these are singular, whereas it strives instead to explain the system that holds them suspended.

Traditionally the primary task of the film historian has been to unearth unknown films or unknown facts and connections relating to known films, in an effort to establish, maintain, or adjust the value system by which cultures care about a cinematic past. Not long ago this seemed a simple thing, unproblematic compared to theory or criticism. Done well or badly, film history was in essence a chronicle of inventors, businessmen, directors, and, most particularly, films. Not all films naturally, just as not all directors or inventors, but the worthy ones, those that made a difference, from *A Trip to the Moon* (France, 1902) to *Wings of Desire* (West Germany and France, 1987) or *Jurassic Park* (USA, 1993). The early accounts by American Terry Ramsaye (1926) or by Frenchmen Maurice Bardèche and Robert Brasillach (1938), interrogate 'worth' hardly at all; instead they directly attribute worth to this or that movie or personality.

> **Traditionally the primary task of the film historian has been to unearth unknown films or unknown facts and connections relating to known films, in an effort to establish, maintain, or adjust the value system by which cultures care about a cinematic past.**

This attitude paved the way for the auteurism of the 1960s and 1970s, when the critic Andrew Sarris (1969) could claim to be providing film history by delivering his notorious seven-tiered ranking of film directors. Of course such a canon answers to values which are of purely aesthetic, not historical, interest. This is confirmed by the auteurist's attraction to masterpieces, films that, by definition, escape history and speak timelessly.

Lists of significant films, directors, and events may not constitute good history, but they do form the basis for the overviews of the development of film art written after the Second World War and that spawned the many histories of film available as textbooks today. Multi-volume treatises by Georges Sadoul (1975) and Jean Mitry (1968–80) in French, Ulrich Gregor and Enno Patalas (1962) in German, and Jerzy Toeplitz (1979) in Polish and German have had single-volume counterparts in English (by Arthur Knight (1957), David Robinson (1973/1981), and many others) that trace what might be thought of as the biography of cinema, from its birth through a clumsy adolescence to an increasing maturity after the Second World War. Maturity is measured less by the growth of the industry than by the subtlety and variety of techniques of expression, by the extension of themes and subjects, and by the respect accorded the medium by the culture at large.

Aesthetic film histories strive to account for all significant developments that cinema has undergone, but therein lies the problem, for a single conception of significance constrains them to think of difference in terms of the formation of identity. This is clearest in Mitry's monumental project, which traces only those cinematic rivulets and streams that feed into the current of the present. If a source dried out or went permanently underground, it was deemed unfit for study, because demonstrably unfit for life. This was the case, for instance, with the Shanghai melodramas of the early 1930s and with Brazilian *cangaços* of the 1950s, neither of which show up in Mitry or in other aesthetic overviews. Mitry's volumes can be read as a Darwinian tale of survival, that is, as the tale of 'ourselves' and 'our' cinema, since 'we' are the ones who have survived and have commanded a history. This explains his dismissal (and not his alone) of other forms of film (animated, educational, and home movies), of other peoples making films (the massive output of Egypt and Turkey, scarcely ever mentioned), and of 'others' represented in film (women and minorities in particular). The force of these less visible 'phenomena' surely carved out underground galleries and waterways, or seeped into swamps and bogs, but canonical historians abandon them there without much thought, until recently when one can note an effort to give them a place in textbooks.

Confidence in a grand, singular story of film art began to erode in the 1970s even before news of the general crisis in historiography reached the ears of film scholars. It was in order to dig beneath taste and to interlink isolated observations and judgements that 'professional' history came to insist on a more positivist approach to the study of cinema's past. All along there have been devoted individual archival researchers who know what it is to establish evidence and advance defensible (and refutable) claims about this or that aspect of film history, but only towards the end of the 1970s can one sense the emergence of an entire positivist ethos among film scholars concerned with, or suddenly turning to, historical matters. Robert Allen and Douglas Gomery in their important *Film History* (1985) coupled good film historiography with standard social history, thereby giving to film history maturity and a method its earlier phases completely lacked.

> **Confidence in a grand, singular story of film art began to erode in the 1970s even before news of the general crisis in historiography reached the ears of film scholars.**

Under positivism one can group every disciplinary approach to film, including the discipline of history itself with its tradition of balances and counterbalances. Those writing on film from historical perspectives no longer can exempt themselves from the burdens of exhaustive research and the ethics of corroboration. They have also felt the responsibility of incorporating within their historical research the gains made possible by the disciplines of sociology, anthropology, economics, and even psychology, all of which have been called upon to make cinema studies responsible to modern criteria of plausibility and of appropriate academic discourse. And, more recently, they have sought to apply these rationalized approaches to an indefinitely large corpus, recognizing that all films, not just the canonical, participate in broader systems that require systematic understanding.

The priority now accorded to discipline and system obliterates the concept of intrinsic value. The laws and rules by which events occur or by which names emerge into history are far more significant to the positivist than those events or names themselves. Most historians today are out to show the forces and conditions that produced the past and thus indicate the present, whether in a strict (determinist) or loose (conjunctural) manner.

A recent essay by one of the most prominent of such scholars, David Bordwell (1994), bears an indicative title: 'The Power of a Research Tradition: Prospects for Progress in the Study of Film Style'. Tradition and progress are precisely terms that can anchor a notion of 'positivism', since they implement regulated research protocols complete with systems of checks and balances. In this way history can become less idiosyncratic, apparently less dependent on taste, rhetoric, or ideology. And in this way scholars from utterly different perspectives and background can contribute to the project of increased understanding of the various factors at play in the cinema complex. Particular topics or problems (the emergence of film noir during and after the Second World War, the growth of the blockbuster style along with its attendant marketing strategy, the anomaly of *Viaggio in Italia* and the dispersal of neorealism) are analysed less through attention to their own properties than by a calculus of determination which brings to bear from the full complex those factors that are pertinent to the case at hand.

Bordwell's essay generously credits work from various historiographic paradigms, including those who gave us 'the standard version of the basic story'. According to Bordwell, André Bazin countered the standard version of film as a standard art by emphasizing not the development of cinema's signifying prowess but the tension between stylization and realism. Bazin's 'dialectical' view accounted for many more types of film that grew up once the sound era had overturned many original conceptions about the medium. Bordwell completes his survey of histories of film style by isolating the 'revolutionary' views of Noël Burch, the first scholar to scour the back alleys of film production for those neglected films and movements that, by the fact of their neglect, provide a particularly apt index to the technical, stylistic, and social range of possibilities for the medium. Burch studied the special cases of primitive cinema, Japanese pre-war works, and the avant-garde, isolating for analysis types of film that are seldom mentioned in either the standard version or its dialectical Bazinian counterpart.

These three versions of history, along with Bordwell's compendium that includes them all, are themselves largely determined by the moment of their own composition. All help form the zigzag pattern of knowledge about film style to which we in the university today should feel urged to contribute. The excesses of one version call for the correctives of the next. In this way, a more and more refined view takes shape under successive rhetorics and with increasingly subtle research strategies. Positivism would let nothing be lost. It was born in the university and flourishes there.

And yet in its sober procedures academic film history, history as autopsy, gives up the surprising life the movies may still retain for those who adopt the attitude of revelatory history Walter Benjamin wanted to foster. For Benjamin the past can catch up with and overwhelm the future in sudden bursts. If lived vigilantly and in high expectation, the present may suddenly illuminate shards of the broken mirror of the past scattered throughout the rubble of that catastrophe we call history. Benjamin—fetishistic book collector yet visionary Marxist—married the sacred to what he understood to be the post-historical. The cinema precociously serves both functions, for films exist not just in archives but in ciné-clubs and on video, where they can still release their power. *Viaggio in Italia* certifies this. The most modern of films, abjuring tradition, beauty, and premeditation to grasp its subject with unprecedented swiftness and immediacy, it nevertheless stands in awe of something quite ancient: the Neopolitans who coexist with statues, legends, icons, and a landscape that speaks to them incessantly and to which they respond in prayer and patter. Like Ingrid Bergman's eye, Rossellini's darting camera, indiscreet on the streets of Naples, probing caves, museums, holes in the crust of the earth, is an opening into which pours something at once ancient and of the moment, something that struck André Bazin forcefully in 1953 and can strike us anew today. We should not have been surprised when Rossellini later took up his grand project to film the history of civilization. It was meant to be a living history.

Though he claims professional allegiance to the positivist line, Pierre Sorlin recognizes the persistence of an unprofessional, unruly, and revelatory history of exceptional moments when he patronizingly observes: 'The pre-positivist attitude remains widespread, is unlikely to disappear, and if it is not taken too seriously this baroque—or even surrealist—encounter with mystical moments (Expressionism, film noir, the nouvelle vague . . .) and madonnas (Marilyn Monroe, Brigitte Bardot) . . . is not without its charm' (Sorlin 1992: 5).

Sorlin's characterization, and even his vocabulary, play into a dichotomy Robert Ray (1988) laid out some years ago in reviewing David Bordwell's work: on the one side lies the progressive, disciplined, impersonal, verifiable, classical paradigm of knowledge; on the other, the haphazard, personal, baroque, surrealist,

form (see also Ray, Chapter 8). Think of scholarship as travel. One may move into cinema's past in several different fashions. The positivist approach I have characterized as a military march that conquers ground under the direction of a general (who surveys the field from on high, plotting strategic approaches). In utter contrast, the baroque, surrealist approach remains personal, whimsical, effectively unrepeatable and nontransferable. Though best exemplified by the *flâneur*, if one sought a military model to oppose to the general it would be the 'knight errant', for this historian works by chance encounters, by erring, by finding order in error.

These two extremes, the one fully public and accountable, the other private and creatively irresponsible, do not exhaust the approaches open to anyone interested in going into the past. There lies a third approach, what Claude Lévi-Strauss in the introduction of his *Tristes tropiques* (1955) termed the 'excursion'. The historian intent on an excursion—preparing to write an 'excursus'—sets off with a goal vaguely in mind but is prepared to let the event of the journey itself and the landscape it traverses help steer or even dictate the inquiry. Such a historiography is patently hermeneutic, for it opens the vision of the historian to a different vision altogether. In our field that different vision may be provided by a powerful film or by a different culture indexed by a host of films. We may despair of understanding these in the way they were first understood, but we can 'comprehend' their significance for ourselves as well as for others (see Andrew 1984: 180–7 for an elaboration on this distinction). Let us keep this array of research attitudes in mind as we turn to historical methods in film scholarship.

Methods

The archives of films

Cinema grew to its majority just in time to participate in a serious shift in historiography towards an account of existence and away from the recounting of the triumphs and defeats of the powerful. Goaded on in the latter half of the nineteenth century by the emergence of sociology and anthropology—nascent disciplines eager to understand the micro-operations of everyday life among seldom heard 'other peoples'— a new breed of historian began to question the utility of the age-old historical enterprise of providing the pedigree for, and singing the exploits of, some ruler, ruling class, or nation. Before this century, even the most measured 'story of civilization' was inevitably one of princes and the vicissitudes of their political and military struggles. While the legacy of this tradition persists, particularly in more popular books, professional historiography since 1900 looks more often and more closely at the complex weave of the tapestry that makes up civilization rather than reading the colourful patterns that stand out as its dramatic picture.

Unquestionably, this lowering of historical goals suggests an evolution of a discipline as old as Herodotus, an evolution visible in literary mimesis as well, whereby the means of representation have increasingly taken sustenance from the everyday, the heterogeneous, the facticity of teeming life. History, like fiction, and like cinema, involves a ratio of brute material to intelligible organization. At the turn of this century, the coefficient of the material side of this ratio grew dramatically as historians took account of new sorts of archive telling of different sorts of life, telling in effect a different history.

Cinema constitutes a crucial historical archive of this sort, and in two senses. First, all films preserve visual information gathered through the lens, some parading this function, others oblivious to it. Of all film types, home movies would seem most intent to gather and preserve; next would come newsreels, since these claim merely to capture and catalogue the events they purport to address. Distant relatives of newsreels are documentaries, which rely on the veracity of the images they steal from newsreels or capture themselves, organizing these to some purpose or argument whose intent interacts with this material. Fiction films would seem to be at the far end of the archive, made to tease the imagination; nevertheless, such films can occasionally be caught napping, as they reveal to the vigilant historian (seldom to the paying customer) some raw matter undigested by the stories they tell (Ferro 1988: 30).

Cinema's second archival function derives from fiction films once again, only this time when they operate alertly, and quite properly, as fiction. Movies, especially popular ones, comprise a record of the aspirations, obsessions, and frustrations of those who spend time and money making or viewing them. Such investment guarantees and measures the value attached to fiction—value which it is the job of the historian to calculate, explain, or extend. Marc Ferro, perhaps the most notable historian to have devoted full attention to the cinematic archive, puts it thus: 'Every film has a value as a document, whatever its seeming nature. This is true even if it has been shot in the studio . . . Besides, if it is true that the not-said and the imaginary have as much historical value as History, then the cinema, and especially the fictional film, open a royal way to psycho-socio-historical zones never reached by the analysis of "documents"' (Ferro 1988: 82–3).

Given its double archival existence, films have sustained two quite different types of historical investigation: social historians raid films for the direct (audio)visual evidence they supply about social existence at a precise moment, while film historians interest themselves in the indirect testimony fiction films deliver concerning fads, prejudices, obsessions, moods, neuroses. Generally the former consult the fullest archive available for their topic (several years of a newsreel, for example, or all the home movies taken by a particular family), while the latter may focus on a few fiction films, selected as the richest examples, the most indicative source, of indirect evidence.

> **Social historians raid films for the direct (audio)visual evidence they supply about social existence at a precise moment, while film historians interest themselves in the indirect testimony fiction films deliver concerning fads, prejudices, obsessions, moods, neuroses.**

It must be said immediately that the social historian maintains no special relation to 'historical films' (*La Marseillaise*, France, 1938; *Scipione l'Africano* Italy, 1937; *October*, USSR, 1928) since these constitute merely one genre among others that may attract certain historians personally but that offer no intrinsically privileged site for professional historical investigation. On the other hand, the aesthetic and rhetorical elements and patterns of all films must at some level and at some point concern all historians. This is the case even in the most straightforward newsreels where camera placement or movement and shot juxtaposition contribute to defining the event under consideration. Ferro (1988: 30–44) proved this point by giving equal analytical attention to a series of quite different films from the Soviet silent period: newsreels, propaganda

efforts by both Reds and Whites, commissioned historical fictions made by Eisenstein and Pudovkin, and a
purportedly neutral fiction by Kuleshov (*Dura Lex*, 'By
the Law', USSR, 1926). Each film can be read for its
inclusions and exclusions, for its structure, and for what
French historians have called the 'mentalité' it
expresses. Ferro entitles another brief article 'Dissolves in *Jud Süss*', to signal that even when dealing
with explicitly social effects (anti-Semitism in the case
of this notorious piece of Nazi propaganda art) the
historian can (and often must) work directly with the
language of cinema (Ferro 1988: 139–41). Whether or
not the historian claims aptitude in this regard, it is
assumed by all that cinematic techniques reveal patterns and intentions of organization as the medium
shapes to some extent (depending on the genre) the
material in the chosen archive.

By conducting minute analyses of aspects of little-
known films, Ferro edged close to another sort of film
history, that coming from buffs, collectors, and critics.
Such people are unashamed to be concerned with
something much smaller than social history: with films,
their makers, their mutual influences, and their processes of production and reception. Film historians,
as we commonly know them and as opposed to social
historians, descend from this family tree of 'amateurs',
often those who have laboured within the cinema community and feel authorized to report upon its workings.
Today's more conscientious film students riffle through
archives of movies, studio records, private papers of
famous personalities, and journalistic criticism just to
step into the footprints of their predecessors who saun-
tered nonchalantly alongside the film industry and
culture of some earlier epoch. They understand
that they must break out of the bubble of lore
and engage the social and cultural reach of a favourite movie or personality just to explain properly its
particular resonance and fascination.

And so both types of historian, those primarily concerned with movies and those concerned with society,
find that they need to enter the other's domain simply
to do justice to their topic. The latter now must adopt a
disciplinary vocabulary and learn techniques of analysis seldom employed in the days when films were
raided unproblematically as an open archive to be
moved wholesale into the historian's discourse. And
the former must read widely in the records of a bygone
era so as to place a prized or fascinating phenomenon
in a context where it becomes significant, not just
iridescent.

The social historian and film

Partisans of one or another tradition of social
science discourse may want to claim for some forebear
the role of first pioneer to enter the unexplored domain
of films. German scholars mark the date 1914, when a
stunning dissertation on patterns of film spectatorship
appeared seemingly from nowhere (Altenloh 1914).
For a long time it had been felt that the earliest serious
writing on cinema concerned artistic issues alone, with
Hugo Munsterberg and Vachel Lindsay generally cited
in front of a phalanx of French aestheticians led by
Louis Delluc and Riccioto Canudo, all of whom were
intent to distinguish the remarkable properties of this
new medium. This dissertation, however, inaugurates a
different tradition of writing about film, a social analysis
that takes account of cinema's sharp intervention in
modern history (see Gripsrud, Part 1, Chapter 22).

The most common sociological studies consider
cinema a mirror to society, and in two senses. First,
one can tabulate the frequency with which various
social types crop up in the movies of a particular time
and place. This quantitative study is usually preliminary
to an interpretation of the way groups are depicted and
therefore valued. The very effect of interpretation
makes cinema a mirror in a second sense, for it displays
the face not just of those whom the movies are about
but of those who make and watch the movies. It may be
shocking for us today to see how a social group has
been misrepresented (see e.g. the studies of Jews
(Sorlin 1981), women (Flitterman-Lewis 1989), and
North Africans (Slavin 1996) in French pre-war movies),
but the greater shock comes from recognizing the face
of those by whom and for whom such misrepresenta-
tions were exactly what fit.

German sociology of cinema has unquestioanbly
produced the most profound work of this sort, primarily
through the Frankfurt School, which was a product of
the Weimer culture it learned to analyse. Arguably the
most celebrated of all social film histories was written
by Siegfried Kracauer, who eventually consolidated his
daily reflections on the portentous movies he watched
during the Weimar years into the magisterial *From
Caligari to Hitler* (1947). This full-blown psycho-social
analysis makes the ugly visage of a nascent Nazism
emerge from the several-score films under consideration. While his audacious thesis has inspired countless
other social historians to enlarge their ambitions *vis-à-
vis* cinema, Kracauer has been reproached for having
set up his conclusions in the very choice of films that

guide his vision. That choice rests on the conviction that the cinema gives privileged access to a national unconscious and its predispositions, equally in films whose ambitions do and don't go beyond that of simple entertainment. Kracauer here encounters a perpetual conundrum, for at one and the same time he relies on the instinctive, unthought relation of film images to the culture that produces them while he also gives priority to the most complex, resonant, and sophisticated examples—examples that have behind them a good deal of thought as well as the prestige of art. In fact, his corpus consists of the export cinema of the Weimar period, from the Expressionist masterpiece mentioned in his title to *M* (1931) and *The Blue Angel* (1930), films, it is fair to say, that extend and transmit certain literary obsessions from the Romantic era right up through the Weimar period.

Kracauer was certainly not alone in believing that the cinema had in fact become the mechanism for the massive dissemination of significant cultural values. Moreover, he paid scant attention to the popular sources of popular genres (comedies, for example, other than those of Lubitsch, or Tyrolian films). Paul Monaco (1976), on the other hand, investigating the same Weimar period, explicitly restricts himself to the films with the highest box-office success so as to exclude his own judgements, letting the audience decide what is important through their attendance. While box-office performance still serves as an important indicator of the social influence of films, clearly television has taken over cinema's mass entertainment function. Hence films engender numerous competing criteria for their importance, whereas in our day statistical head-counts (Nielsen ratings) are justified as the prime research protocol in the study of television's impact.

In short, most film histories accept the role interpretation plays from the outset, including the selection of those films that promise to respond most fully to a certain social interrogation. In his influential articles, ostensibly written to correct Kracauer, Thomas Elsaesser (1982, 1983) doesn't hesitate to name and work with a limited number of Weimar films that entwine an intricate cinematic discourse with a deeply psychoanalytic one. He argues that these privileged examples foster a particularly trenchant understanding of German culture applicable to the hundreds of films he chooses to leave by the wayside, including those where attendance may have been highest.

No matter how consistent Elsaesser's arguments

may be, by openly adopting an interpretive stance he will leave unsatisfied those historians intent on emphasizing different values. Exactly this dissatisfaction is visible in still another book on German films of the 1920s, Patrice Petro's *Joyless Streets* (1989). Petro forthrightly admires the work accomplished by Kracauer and Elsaesser, yet she senses something more to be said, another interpretation of the period accessed not by a statistical selection à la Monaco, but by a different—in this case feminist—critical insight. Petro's corpus includes only films that rather openly appeal to women, specifically melodramas of the street. Hers is not—or not yet—a reception study, although she has obviously divided national psychology into male and female subjectivity, implying that further subdivisions (according to social class, education, urbanization, profession) might provide a more refined understanding of the specific attractions and psycho-social 'work' cinema performed in this epoch. Petro remains on the side of textual analysis, however, because her impressive contextual research doesn't displace cinema, but assists her in choosing the films worth analysing and the terms of analysis that seem most warranted. The street films, she discovers, directly solicited a female audience that was larger than the male one that Kracauer inevitably speaks about. Producers must have had women in mind for these melodramas and for other genres as well. The burgeoning magazine trade aimed at women supports this supposition, especially when one learns of the business ties between the press and the cinema in late Weimar.

As Petro among others makes clear, cinema never exists in a sphere by itself but is supported by other cultural phenomena that it draws on, transforms, or transmits. And so one might categorize film histories less on the basis of the films chosen for discussion than on that of the intertexts (explicit or implied) from which those films derive their power for the historian. Petro's interest in contemporaneous journalism and fashion sets her directly against Lotte Eisner, for instance, whose influential version of Weimar cinema, *The Haunted Screen* (1969), bears its context in its subtitle: *Expressionism in the German Cinema and the Influence of Max Reinhardt*.

Having reached Eisner, we have drifted beyond social historiography and into the history of film as art, where interpretation unapologetically establishes both the corpus to be investigated and the pertinent contexts within which to read the films. But even

Eisner's comparatively rarefied art-historical attitude illustrates that all film histories bear a social dimension. When she details the persistence in key films of nightmarish metaphors or when she places Weimar masterworks alongside theatre productions of inhuman scale on the one side and of private anguish on the other, she characterizes the troubled era she writes about and the spiritual key of its social dysfunctionalism. Petro, meanwhile, though anxious to contribute to a precise understanding of a broader spectrum of society, happily makes her case through the astute analysis of films that take on importance in their difference from other films we know about, that is, in a film-historical context.

Only the pure sociologist, hoping to avoid interpretation, escapes this hermeneutic situation, but thereby risks escaping film history as well, making films no different from other cultural phenomena that could equally have been chosen as indices (or mirrors) of peoples at a given place and moment. The interests of film history lie beyond the purely social.

The film historian and culture

It has already been argued that the primary task of the film historian has traditionally been to unearth unknown films or unknown facts and connections relating to known films. First of all this has meant refining the map that displays these films and relations. Spatially, historians, after having so regularly mined Hollywood and Europe, look to other centres of production, discovering archives in distant locations. In the United States alternative production practices such as the New York avant-garde, black film companies, and studios based in Chicago have been excavated. Small in scale though these may be, they point to a cinematic potential that the dominant paradigm denies or suppresses. As for the temporal map, our lazy reliance on decades has always been questioned by historians who measure rhythms of change on more intrinsic criteria: on changes in technology, for instance, or artistic and cultural movements.

As for the content of the map, film historians are ever goaded to startle us, to upset or adjust our picture of how things have been. They do this most patently through discoveries of lost films (Oscar Micheaux's *œuvre*) or misunderstood practices (the *benshi* in Japan, the *bonimenteur* in Quebec). We are also startled by new configurations of things already known, or new ideas about the significance of these.

The surge of interest in early cinema, for instance, measures the strength of the 'cinema of attractions', a comparatively recent idea that rescued—for attention and for preservation—hundreds of films and techniques from the dustbin to which they had been assigned, a dustbin labelled 'false starts' or 'primitive'.

> **Film historians are ever goaded to startle us, to upset or adjust our picture of how things have been.**

Still another way historians upset the historical horizon that surrounds us is by changing scale. Zooming in to snoop on the minutiae of a film or a studio or a distribution agency can reverse received opinions about the standard operations of something presumably as well known as the classical Hollywood cinema. This was the case with the standard assumption that Hollywood studios of the 1930s were hothouses of self-engendered fictions. Intense examination of daily trade journals has now shown that all studios employed personnel to ferret out news stories that might be capitalized upon in both production and distribution. Far from this being an era of pure fiction, the documentary impulse was systematically exploited at all levels (Benelli 1992). Baseball movies, films about current events like the birth of the Dion quintuplets, and of course the entire gangster genre were part of a strategy that became visible when historians zeroed in on micro-operations of studios.

At the other extreme are relations exposed for the first time when a historian gambles on a very distant perspective. Jacques Aumont (1989) has studied cinema in relation to the long history of painting. Cinema participates in a relatively new function of the image that ever since the French Revolution has addressed what he dubs 'the mutable eye'. With the modern spectator in mind, he links cinema to various nineteenth-century optical phenomena (the diorama, the railroad car) and ties techniques satisfying this spectator that originated in silent movies to the most recent of Godard's inventions.

Each of these disruptions of the historical horizon provides a contrary view of the past through the assertion of a new perspective. Even more disruptive, however, and therefore in some senses more genuinely in line with critical historiography, are the efforts—increasing in recent years—to invalidate any single perspective whatever. In cinema studies, historians now take pride in describing situations wherein more than one temporal framework is at play (African cinema's laconic pace, both tied to indigenous life and to the European art film), more than one audience function (the appeal to gays and to straights of Judy Garland), more than one idea of the national (the self-conflicted Irish cinema, or the *œuvre* of Juzo Itami in relation to a Japan he references but scarcely believes in), and so on. The acknowledgement, and often the celebration, of subcultures and fragmented nations goes hand in hand with the description of hybrid genres and films. This assertion of the power of specific elements over unity and order comes at a high price. Historians risk occupying a position from which they can understand only singularities, which are by definition unrepeatable, and from which no generalizations can be drawn. Historical detail can stand in the way of the story of history.

In fact every history that treats the cinema must calculate the importance of films within a world larger than film. Culture can be said to surround each film like an atmosphere comprised of numerous layers or spheres, as numerous as we want. One may identify these as though they successively encompass one another moving from the centre (the individual film) out towards the stratosphere of national and international politics and events. Intermediate layers might include the film industry, traditions of genres, the biographies of film-makers, the status of the other arts, the institutions of culture, and the organization of social classes. The further out from the centre the historian navigates, the more difficult it is to steer research in a way that is powered by the medium and not by some other agenda or discipline. Thus a political history of Hollywood in the 1950s needs to articulate the links that connect decadent film noir, self-conscious musicals, and budding docu-dramas to the concerns of Capitol Hill and of voters comfortable with Dwight Eisenhower at their helm but uncomfortable about their own security. Of course the blacklistings and the McCarthy hearings have provided precisely this type of linkage, as do biographies of the Hollywood Ten, the agenda of the Legion of Decency, and other such factors.

The permeability of these spheres permits an event at one layer to affect elements in another layer, producing interactions that can bring individual movies or the cinema as a whole into prominence. The direction of this interactive flow is reversible, although it is usually tracked from the top down. For example, a change of government may bring in a new minister of education who promotes the expansion of literary journals. These journals may, in turn, promote an aesthetic that works its views on the legitimate theatre. Ultimately film acting, including the kinds of roles created for, or chosen by, key actors, may encourage a specific cinematic style, amounting to a significant alteration in the way the culture represents itself on the screen (see Andrew 1995, chapter 1, for an exemplification of this process).

Cultural interaction of this sort—a trickle-down process from government to popular expression—may be rare in a country like France, but occurs regularly in states exercising rigid political control. But the pervasiveness of censorship, even in democratic societies, reminds us that governments themselves can be disturbed by images bubbling up from beneath the cultural surface. Censorship bears witness to the power that films evidently deploy beyond the sphere of the strictly cinematic.

No history with aspirations of thickly representing an era's cinema can ignore this traffic among spheres. Yet every history needs to identify the most pertinent spheres within which to track the (shifting) values of cinema. Pertinence depends both on the researcher and on the topic under scrutiny. In my study of French films of the 1930s (Andrew 1995), for example, I was at pains to establish the special relevance of a particular cultural sphere containing subgroups such as the Surrealists and the novelists published by Gallimard Press. This choice challenged an earlier study, Francis Courtade's *Les Malédictions du cinéma français* (1977), which examines French films within the atmosphere of official history (political proclamations, censorship rulings) and official events in the film world (technological innovations like sound, economic developments like the fall of Gaumont). In certain revolutionary eras such as that of the Soviet Union of the 1920s, Courtade's focus seems apt; one would expect the Soviet film historian to follow very closely the major events of public life, since cinema explicitly participated in a national reawakening. But in the inter-war period of France, cinematic values were forged and debated less in the political sphere than in the cultural sphere, or rather in the nebulous zones where transactions between high and popular culture were possible. Here the effect on cinema of personalities from the established arts outweighed, from my perspective, all governmental and most economic pressures. And so the involvement in cinema of novelists and publishing houses, classical composers, painters, architects, and playwrights serve as more than anecdotes and do more than validate a popular art. Their involvement testifies to changes in the function of cinema and helps specify the direction such changes took. This cultural sphere is pertinent precisely because it identifies the site of development in a cinema that, from the perspective of the political or economic spheres, can hardly be said to have changed at all.

> **A cultural history of cinema proceeds neither through the direct appreciation of films, nor through the direct amassing of 'relevant facts' associated with the movies, but through an indirect reconstruction of the conditions of representation that permitted such films to be made, to be understood, even to be misunderstood.**

In brief, a cultural history of cinema proceeds neither through the direct appreciation of films, nor through the direct amassing of 'relevant facts' associated with the movies, but through an indirect reconstruction of the conditions of representation that permitted such films to be made, to be understood, even to be misunderstood (see King, Part 1, Chapter 23). This is a doubly hermeneutic venture, for it puts into play the reading of films for their cultural consequence and the reading of culture for the values or moods conveyed in films. Deciding which films are appropriate in relation to which spheres constitutes a founding act of interpretation.

Against interpretation: history without the historian

Aware how blind official culture has been to the presence (and the history) of women, minorities, the disfranchised, and the unrepresented, how can a film historian guard against simply repeating or varying the tastes she or he has inherited? Since interpretation selects and values, some historians work to dispense with it altogether by refusing to discriminate amongst

the objects brought in for examination. This applies to a certain sociological film history that avoids the pre-judgement involved in selecting material, through a protocol of inclusion that chooses automatically. In *The Classical Hollywood Cinema* (1985), for example, Bordwell and his co-authors developed an algorithm to select films for analysis so as to avoid the vagaries of personal or cultural preference.

In current terminology, 'histoire sérielle' counters standard interpretive history, where a 'series' is any set of homogeneous elements (such as films, or studio contracts) that can be ordered into chronological sequence and counted. Originally developed to help map the history of slow-moving factors (prices of corn across decades, for example, as opposed to a peasant rebellion cropping up in one concentrated moment), serial history has been adopted by certain film historians, who have begun to treat films as elements in a series (see Burguière 1984: 631–3). Michèle Lagny, arguing for this new form of history, reminds us that, no matter what their quality, films are produced regularly and under conditions that apply equally to neighbouring films (Lagny 1994). Instead of singling out one film or making an intelligent selection, serial history submits all films in a given corpus to an unchanging inquiry. Trends can thus be measured statistically.

Serial methods seem ideally suited to documentaries, where the distinctiveness of the individual text or auteur is seldom a significant factor. But nothing prohibits a historian from employing this method for the fiction films of a period, measuring their length, for example, or their cost, or the number of dissolves, or the number of actors they employ. In this sort of history individual films lose their 'centrality' in favour of the extended lateral series. Moreover, the series constituted by a chronology of films is not surrounded by decreasingly relevant spheres, as in the model put forth above, but coexists with other series that can be called into play by the intuition (or whim) of the historian. On the other hand, just as in the concentric model, any series becomes significant only when significantly related to something outside it, usually to other series that are parallel or that intersect it at some nodal point. Thus a series of wartime documentaries might be placed alongside a series of newspaper editorials or against the number of troops conscripted. In short, statistics never really speak for themselves. They must be articulated, that is, put into relations that form a discourse and eventually an argument.

The significance of a group of simultaneous series

suggests the existence of a pervasive and distinct approach to experience obtaining in a given culture, a *mentalité*, linked to what is often discussed as the 'sensibility', 'ideology', or 'mood' of a substantial period of time. A *mentalité* is, like a climate, something that humans have no control over, and something that usually exists before and after them; yet to establish such an entity would seem to require far more interpretation than statistics. One might track the *mentalité* of a nation by analysing the kinds of material set for baccalaureate examinations or the fields of research of professors promoted to national chairs. In our period, the vocabulary of top-forty songs over a couple of decades might be examined in conjunction with dialogue in top-grossing films, and these two series could be placed alongside various demographic studies (teenage pregnancy, suburbanism, and so on).

Few film histories have rigorously employed the methods of the history of *mentalités*. Most studies of films written in this vein aim for global characterizations of national mood. For the period of 1940s America, for example, Dana Polan's book *Power and Paranoia* (1985) samples a number of genres and styles in characterizing the prevalent mood and dominant aesthetic of the time. Obvious social conditions are mentioned as fostering this attitude (the war and its aftermath with attendant shifts in work, status, and values). Yet to what specific institutions, policies, or events can films be tied? Segregation? The bomb? Communism? These are constant sources of irritation that undoubtedly affected, or directly motivated, films from the end of the war into the 1950s, yet the terms themselves are unruly, requiring detailed analysis before we can see the issues actually affecting a specific arena such as the cinema. We are led to ask what sort of historical, as opposed to thematic, examination might reveal the connections between films and these weighty concerns. And once again interpretation seems inevitable, perhaps not at the initial point of selecting material, but at the later stage of putting it into significant relation with other material.

Participating in a gnawing debate between objectivity and interpretation, the most sophisticated kinds of historical examination (in cinema studies as elsewhere) share much with the discipline of anthropology, conceived as a dialogue between self and other, a dialogue whose rules are constantly being renegotiated. In our case, this means maintaining a dialogue between films and culture that remains open and under constant revision. Rather than becoming trapped inside a closed field of movies, yet before giving the movies over to laws that sociologists and economists have already arrived at, the film historian may interact with movies on behalf of culture. This is the middle road located somewhere between the highway of socio-economic history and the folk path of personal biography. Along this road lies the varied landscape of culture, a landscape whose ecology features the complex and contradictory interplay of institutions, expressions, and repressions, all subject to the force fields of power. The cultural historian bears, to the limit, the burden of the contested middle, by insisting on a stance between the already hermeneutic enterprises of the critic and the historian. Refusing to stop where most critics do, at the boundaries of texts, refusing as well the comfort of a direct pipeline to an era's 'imaginary' held out by certain brands of socio-economics, the cultural historian reads and weighs culture in texts and texts in culture. In this way the logic of changing values can be understood as felt.

It is no coincidence that this section on method should conclude with an affirmation of hermeneutics, exactly as did the first section, on attitude. History, as Siegfried Kracauer observed in his book on the subject, *The Last Things before the Last* (1969), hovers above the particulars of life, but not so high as theory, whose obsession with regularities and design blinds it to the contours of the landscape below. Historians can drop down low for detail, then rise to gain the perspective that seems to suit them or gives them densest significance. If those 'details' be movies playing, we might imagine, at some drive-in theatre below, the film historian can home in to watch something projected on a social landscape. Fascinated, the historian may momentarily cease thinking of the past as past, but directly view his or her own world as touched by what is shown; this is when history is projected straight through our present and into an open future.

BIBLIOGRAPHY

*Allen, Robert, and **Douglas Gomery** (1985), *Film History: Theory and Practice* (New York: Knopf).

Altenloh, Emilie (1914/1977), *Zur Sociologie des Kinos* (Jena: Eugen Diedrichs; Hamburg: Medienladen)

Andrew, Dudley (1984), *Concepts in Film Theory* (New York: Oxford University Press).

—— (1989), 'Response to Robert Ray: The Limits of Delight', *Strategies*, 2: 157–65.

Andrew, Dudley (1995), *Mists of Regret: Culture and Sensibility in Classic French Film* (Princeton: Princeton University Press).

Aumont, Jacques (1989), *L'Œil interminable* (Paris: Librarie Séguier).

—— André Gaudreault, and Michel Marie (1989), *Histoire du cinéma: nouvelles approches* (Paris: Publications de la Sorbonne).

Bardèche, Maurice, and Robert Brasillach (1938), *History of the Moving Pictures*, trans. Iris Barry (New York: Museum of Modern Art).

Bazin, André (1967/1970), *What is Cinema?*, 2 vols., trans. Hugh Gray (Berkeley: University of California Press).

Benelli, Dana (1992), 'Jungles and National Landscapes: Documentary and Hollywood Film in the 1930s' (doctoral dissertation, University of Iowa).

Benjamin, Walter (1930/1968), 'Theses on the Philosophy of History', in *Illuminations* (New York: Schocken Books).

Bordwell, David (1994), 'The Power of a Research Tradition: Prospects for Progress in the Study of Film Style', *Film History*, 6/1: (Spring), 59–79.

—— Kristin Thompson, and Janet Staiger (1985), *The Classical Hollywood Cinema* (New York: Columbia University Press).

Burch, Noël (1979), *To the Distant Observer: Form and Meaning in the Japanese Cinema* (Berkeley: University of California Press).

—— (1991), *Life to those Shadows* (London: British Film Institute).

Burguière, André (ed.) (1984), *Dictionnaire des sciences historiques* (Paris: Presses Universitaires de France).

Cinémaction (1992), no. 65, Special Issue: *Cinéma et histoire: autour de Marc Ferro*.

Courtade, Francis (1978), *Les Malédictions du cinéma français* (Paris: Alain Moreau).

Deleuze, Gilles (1983), *L'Image-Mouvement* (Paris: Éditions de Minuit).

Dyer, Richard, and Ginette Vincendeau (eds.) (1992), *Popular European Cinema* (London: Routledge).

Eisner, Lotte (1969), *The Haunted Screen: Expressionism in the German Cinema and the Influence of Max Reinhardt* (Berkeley: University of California Press).

Elsaesser, Thomas (1982), 'Social Mobility and the Fantastic: German Silent Cinema', 5/2, 14–25.

—— (1983), 'Lulu and the Meter Man: Louise Brooks, Pabst and Pandora's Box', *Screen*, 4–5 (July–Oct.), 4–36.

—— (1984), 'Film History and Visual Pleasure: Weimar Cinema' in Patricia Mellencamp and Philip Rosen (eds.), *Cinema Histories/Cinema Practices* (Frederick, Md.: University Publications of America).

*Ferro, Marc (1988), *Cinema and History*, trans. Naomi Greene (Detroit: Wayne State University Press).

Film History: An International Journal (1994), 6/1, Special Issue: *Philosophy of Film History* (Spring).

Flitterman-Lewis, Sandy (1989), *To Desire Differently: Feminism and the French Cinema* (Urbana: University of Illinois Press).

Godard, Jean-Luc (1980), *Introduction une véritable histoire du cinéma* (Paris: Albatros).

Gregor, Ulrich, and Enno Patalas (1962), *Geschichte des Films* (Gütersloh: S. Mohn).

Iris (1984), 2/2, Special Issue: *Toward a Theory of Film History*.

Knight, Arthur (1957), *The Liveliest Art* (New York: Macmillan).

Kracauer, Siegfried (1947), *From Caligari to Hitler* (Princeton: Princeton University Press).

—— (1969), *History: The Last Things before the Last* (New York: Oxford).

Lagny, Michèle (1992), *De l'histoire du cinéma* (Paris: Armand Colin).

—— (1994), 'Film History, or History Expropriated', *Film History*, 6/1 (Spring), 26–44.

Mitry, Jean (1968–80), *Histoire du cinéma*, 5 vols. (Paris: Éditions Universitaires).

Monaco, Paul (1976), *Cinema and Society* (New York: Elsevier).

Petro, Patrice (1989), *Joyless Streets: Women and Melodramatic Representation in Weimar Germany* (Princeton: Princeton University Press).

Polan, Dana (1986), *Power and Paranoia: History, Narrative and the American Cinema 1940–1950* (New York: Columbia University Press).

Prédal, René, *La Société française à travers le cinéma* (Paris: Armand Colin).

Ramsaye, Terry (1926), *A Million and One Nights* (New York: Simon & Schuster).

Ray, Robert (1988), 'The Bordwell Regime and the Stakes of Knowledge', *Strategies*, 1 (Fall), 143–81.

—— (1995), *The Avant-Garde Finds Andy Hardy* (Cambridge, Mass.: Harvard University Press).

Rivette, Jacques (1955/1985), 'Letter on Rossellini', in Jim Hillier (ed.), *Cahiers du Cinéma. The 1950s: Neo-Realism, Hollywood, New Wave* (Cambridge, Mass.: Harvard University Press).

*Robinson, David (1973/1981), *The History of World Cinema* (New York: Stein & Day).

Rotha, Paul (1949), *The Film till Now* (London: Vision Press).

Sadoul, Georges (1975), *Histoire générale du cinéma* (Paris: Denoel).

Sarris, Andrew (1969), *the American Cinema: Directors and Directions* (New York: Dutton).

Schefer, Jean-Louis (1980), *L'Homme ordinaire du cinéma* (Paris: Gallimard).

Slavin, David (1996), 'Native Sons? White Blindspots, Male Fantasies, and Imperial Myths in French *Cinéma Colonial* of the 1930s', in S. Ungar and T. Conley (eds.), *Identity Papers* (Minneapolis: University of Minnesota Press).

*Sorlin, Pierre** (1980), *The Film in History: Restaging the Past* (NJ: Barnes Noble).

—— (1981), 'Jewish Images in French Cinema of the 1930s', *Historical Journal of Film, Radio and TV*, 1/2: 140–9.

—— (1991), *European Cinemas, European Societies* (London: Routledge).

—— (1992), 'Cinema, an Undiscoverable History?', *Paragraphs*, 14/1 (Mar.), 1–18.

Toeplitz, Jerzy (1979), *Geschichte des Films*, 4 vols., trans. Lilli Kaufman from Polish (Munich: Rogner & Bernhard).

Weinberg, Herman G. (1970), *Saint Cinema* (New York: Dover).

20

Sociology and film

Andrew Tudor

The rise of sociology as an academic discipline is one of the more striking intellectual success stories of the twentieth century. From its roots in the attempt to comprehend properly the enormous changes that came with industrial capitalism, sociology has grown into a richly diverse assembly of theories, methods, and substantive studies which, however else they may differ, share a desire to examine the emergent patterns of social organization that characterize human activity. At first sight, then, it is both surprising and disappointing to discover how little the discipline has contributed to our understanding of film. After all, before the advent of television the cinema was perhaps *the* institution of large-scale cultural production, exemplifying much of what was distinctive about the twentieth century's new forms of communication. Surely such a remarkable social development should have been of vital sociological interest.

For a brief period, of course, it was, though now more than sixty years ago. Fuelled by public concern in the United States at the end of the 1920s, the Payne Fund financed a series of ambitious research projects, conducted between 1929 and 1932, exploring the impact of motion pictures upon youth: 'our movie made children' as the popularization of the Payne Fund Studies called them. The studies brought together sociologists and social psychologists to investigate a range of topics, the flavour of which may be inferred from some of the titles under which the

research was published: *Movies, Delinquency and Crime* (Blumer and Hauser 1933); *The Content of Motion Pictures* (Dale 1933); *The Social Conduct and Attitude of Movie Fans* (May and Shuttleworth 1933); *Motion Pictures and the Social Attitudes of Children* (Peterson and Thurstone 1936). These volumes shared a forthright concern about the capacity of this new and powerful medium to have an impact on the attitudes, emotions, and behaviour of the young people who, then as now, formed the majority of its audience. They also shared a commitment to the newly emergent methodologies of the social sciences, using experimental studies, survey research techniques, extended interviews, and early forms of content analysis in their attempt to demonstrate that the movies were indeed having significant effects. Summarizing their findings, Charters (1935: 43) claimed that the motion picture 'has unusual power to impart information, to influence specific attitudes toward objects of social value, to affect emotions either in gross or microscopic proportions, to affect health in minor degree through sleep disturbance, and to affect profoundly the patterns of conduct of children'.

The Payne Fund Studies, then, set the tone for subsequent sociological approaches to film. First and foremost they were concerned with the *effects* of film, and, more specifically, with the possibility of deleterious effects on those (the young) presumed to be least able to fend for themselves. Having once focused on effects, they were inevitably much concerned with method and measurement. How to measure attitude before and after exposure to a film? How to analyse content scientifically, so as to assess a film's distinctive impact? They sought variously ingenious answers to these methodological questions, and in so doing they, and their academic descendants in the mass communications research of the 1930s and 1940s, made a remarkable contribution to the general development of social research methodology. So much so, indeed, that in retrospect it is possible to see in the Payne Fund Studies an outline of methodologies of precisely the kind that would much later attract critical charges of empiricism and scientism and that, as we shall see, were important in modern film theory's distrust of sociology. In fairness, however, it should be noted that not all the studies were equally open to the charge of restrictive empiricism. Herbert Blumer's contributions, for example (Blumer 1933; Blumer and Hauser 1935), are marked by the more ethnographic concerns of his Chicago School background, and in the 1950s he was himself to campaign against widespread scientistic use of the language of 'variables' in social research. But for the most part the Payne Fund Studies did begin a tradition in the sociology of film that was to focus primarily upon the measurable effects of film on particular social categories of audience. In so doing they not only limited the kinds of question that sociology might pose about film; they also ensured that the distinctive character of cinema itself was lost within the more general rubric of 'mass communications'.

Thus it was that the dominant framework within which sociologists came to consider the cinema—if they considered it at all—was that of mass communications research. Not exclusively, of course. There were one or two social portraits of the movie industry in its heyday (e.g. Rosten 1941; Powdermaker 1950) and there was always the industry-fostered enterprise of audience research, whether predominantly statistical (Handel 1950) or more concerned with qualitative accounts of the moviegoing experience as volunteered by audience members (Mayer 1946, 1948). But these were minor tributaries to the mainstream of communications research where, in the 1950s especially, widespread concern to measure media effects dovetailed neatly into the frequent claim that modern society was typically a 'mass society'.

This is not the place to examine the detail of the mass society thesis. Sufficient here to enumerate only those elements of the thesis which were to have a formative impact on the way sociology approached the study of film. We have already seen something of that in the emphasis on effects of mass communications research. To this mass society theory added a profoundly negative evaluation of so-called 'mass culture', employing the category as something of a conceptual dustbin into which cultural critics of otherwise quite diverse persuasions could cast all the distinctive cultural products of modern society (for a useful account of the origin and development of these mass culture arguments, see Swingewood 1977). The unreflective élitism of this view is well known, whether its proponents were conventionally of the left (the Frankfurt School) or of the right (Leavis, Eliot). What is perhaps less apparent is its impact on sociological approaches to the media, film included, which often took as given the characteristic evaluations espoused by mass society theorists and led researchers to conduct their work on the assumption that mass culture was inevitably crude and unsubtle, while its consumers were little more than undiscriminating dupes. The mass society thesis, then, served to legitimize a framework for sociological analysis which effectively denied both the variability of audiences and the richness of many popular cultural texts, thereby neglecting the complexity of the cinematic institution as well as the polysemic potential of its products. Much cinema, in this view, was no more than a commercially motivated means of pandering to the lowest common denominator, its inherent crudity ensuring that little or no theoretical or methodological sophistication was necessary for its proper sociological comprehension. Any intelligent observer, it was implied, could easily see popular film for the restricted form that it was.

Of course this view is unsustainable. Yet for many years something quite like it was sustained in the received wisdom of sociological approaches to the mass media. Only a tiny proportion of sociological work resisted the mass culture argument and examined film with any commitment to the idea that processes of meaning construction might be more complex than was suggested by the traditional 'hypodermic model' of mass communication. Some of that work simply bypassed the mass culture tradition by examining those rarer forms of cinema which were by then widely recognized as approximating to 'high art' and therefore could be seen to invite and merit more elaborate treatment. One such instance was Huaco's (1965) analysis of three 'film movements' (German Expressionism, Soviet Expressive Realism, and Italian

Neo-Realism) employing a curious combination of Smelser's functionalist theory of collective behaviour and a somewhat unsophisticated base–superstructure metaphor. Revealingly, this volume claimed to deal with 'film art' rather than just film. However, as mass culture orthodoxy came under sustained attack during the course of the 1960s, sociological work developed on more than just 'film art', a process driven especially by the re-evaluation of Hollywood film by critics first in France and then in Britain, although also fed by growing dissent within sociology itself. When, later in the decade, the ideas of French structuralism began to have an impact in a range of subject areas (including both sociology and the nascent discipline of film studies) there was promise of a common framework of analysis through which a new, interdisciplinary understanding of film might be forged. By the late 1960s this had advanced to the point where the interests of the semiology and the sociology of film appeared to be converging, so much so that when the British Film Institute's Education Department published a collection of working papers emerging from its influential seminar series, four of the five contributors were academic sociologists (Wollen 1969).

Yet this positive concern with sociology was to prove short-lived, and as film theory became a central intellectual focus in English-language film studies its emergent orthodoxy systematically sidelined sociology's potential contribution. The charge most commonly made was that sociology suffered from precisely the kind of unreflective empiricism which film theory sought to combat in its own field of study. Ten years earlier that might have been true. By the late 1960s, however, such an allegation was, at best, questionable and, at worst, uninformed misrepresentation. The mass communications tradition was already under severe critical attack from within the discipline, and sociology more generally was in some ferment, shifting away from the apparent methodological and theoretical consensus that had characterized the post-war years. Whatever else it might have been, the sociology of this period was not empiricist in the traditional sense. Indeed, as a discipline it was arguably more theoretically reflexive and sophisticated than anything then envisaged in film theory.

In the event, the marginal role played by the sociology of film in the flowering of film theory in the 1970s had less to do with sociology's intrinsic empiricist failings than with the characteristic assumptions within which film theory itself developed. Here the position

that came to be associated with the journal *Screen* was extremely influential, dictating terms within which debate was conducted and hence moulding the concerns of film theory even for those who did not subscribe to the *Screen* group's position. What was it about this perspective that had the effect of excluding sociology? The answer is not straightforward. After the first wave of enthusiasm for structuralist and semiotic approaches to film, it rapidly became apparent that the very formalism of such theories, in some ways a virtue, also extracted a price. Analysis tended to focus excessively on the film text (and film language) at the expense of any systematic understanding of the context within which texts were produced and understood. In consequence, neither individual spectators nor social structures featured satisfactorily in early semiotic analyses of cinema. On the face of it, this perceived failing opened up conceptual space for a distinctive sociological contribution. Unfortunately, however, film theory developed in a different direction, undeniably seeking to incorporate a social dimension into analysis, but not by application of sociological theories or methods. Instead, it was through the concept of ideology as that had been developed in Althusser's work that film theory sought to progress, borrowing particularly from his Lacan-influenced account of the ways in which subjects are constructed by systems of discourse. In this account the subject is constituted by and through the film text and is thereby caught within ideology.

Why this particular theoretical emphasis came to the fore is a complex question of intellectual and political history which cannot be dealt with here. The net effect, though, was to turn the film-theoretical enterprise towards analyses of the textual constitution of subjects and to a method based in structural psychoanalysis, rather than towards the kind of contextual concerns which would have necessitated a more directly sociological approach (see Creed, Chapter 9). To make matters worse, the Althusserian framework offered an especially distinctive reading of the role of theory itself, a form of conventionalism within which theory was seen to constitute its object without reference to an independent 'reality'. Accordingly, any attempt to promote empirical work not cast in these terms—necessarily the case for a sociology of film—was condemned with the catch-all label 'empiricism', an allegation which was applied as indiscriminately as it was empty of intellectual force (see Lovell 1980 for an excellent critique).

Thus was sociology marginalized in subsequent film theory.

In claiming that the Althusserian and Lacanian turn in film theory effectively excluded sociological considerations I do not mean to suggest that this was a matter of wilful intellectual conspiracy. It was, rather, that the terms of film-theoretical discourse which became commonplace during the 1970s and 1980s relegated sociological considerations to the periphery. The irony is that this was precisely when sociology could have best played a positive role in contributing to an interdisciplinary understanding of film, and subsequent film theory has been less than adequate in this respect, largely persisting with a radically unsociological view of cinema. Even those later scholars dissatisfied with the prevailing dependence on psychoanalytically influenced film theory have resorted to alternative psychological approaches—for example, drawing upon cognitive psychology—rather than to sociological frameworks (e.g. Bordwell 1985; Branigan 1992). Such authors have done much to expand the concerns of modern film theory, but without making a great deal of progress in understanding the sociological workings of the cinematic apparatus.

Accordingly, sociological analyses of film have been sporadic rather than sustained over the past quarter of a century, moving from the naïve optimism of general framing texts (Jarvie 1970; Tudor 1974) to qualified applications of the sociological perspective, often in the context of other theoretical and substantive interests. In this respect the rise of cultural and media studies as legitimate academic 'disciplines' has been crucial, providing a framework within which sociologically informed researchers have contributed to further understanding of film. Although rarely explicitly labelled sociology, the work of Dyer (1979, 1986), Hill (1986), and Wright (1975), among others, will serve to suggest the variety of such indirect sociological influences. It is this kind of work that offers the constructive blurring of disciplinary boundaries that was once promised by the temporary alliance between the sociology and the semiotics of film. Today, however, the energy and promise of such interdisciplinary alliances is not to be found in film studies at all, but more generally in cultural studies, where television is understandably the single most prominent focus. And in spite of the recent efforts of, for example, Norman Denzin (1991, 1995), a sustained sociology of film is still something of a pipe-dream.

But why should we need any such enterprise? One line of argument is to suggest that during the twentieth century sociology has accumulated a good deal of empirical knowledge about the workings of the social world, as well as establishing a not inconsiderable repertoire of research methods, and that both resources could contribute significantly to our stock of knowledge about film. In this respect we have no less need now than we have ever had for specific sociological studies of particular genres, of systems of film production, or of the social character of film spectatorship. Ironically, however, in the present circumstance of film studies it is perhaps in the area of general theory and method that sociology is most immediately relevant. This is especially apparent once we recognize that the future of film studies is inextricably bound up with the fate of cultural studies, which, deeply influenced by film theory in its formative days, has now outgrown its ailing film-theoretical parent. But contemporary cultural studies, it is widely believed, is faced with what various authors have called a 'paradigm crisis'. Formerly committed to a deterministic analysis which largely equated culture with ideology and which gave analytic primacy to texts and to systems of discourse, in recent years cultural studies has retreated from this 'strong programme', turning instead to much more localized, ethnographically inclined researches into processes of cultural consumption.

In many ways this has been a welcome development, especially where it has led to detailed empirical research into people's diverse and inventive 'reading practices'. But it has also bred dissatisfaction. For all the virtues apparent in recent work, there is a growing belief that cultural studies is losing its critical and analytic edge by retreating into forms of analysis which neglect the larger social context within which culture is utilized and reproduced, or by theorizing that context only in the grossest terms. Interestingly, sociology too has experienced just such conceptual polarization, at different times expressing itself in conflicting concerns with micro- versus macro-theorizing, with social determinism versus social phenomenology, and with society versus the individual. The difference is that sociology faced these divisions significantly earlier than cultural studies and has in the course of the 1980s generated a body of new theory oriented to concepts appropriate for understanding the crucial interaction between social structure and social agency.

It is here, surely, that sociology could play a positive part in renewing theory and method in cultural studies and, thereby, foster a more sophisticated understanding of the social institution of cinema. Film, after all, is more than mere celluloid. It is socially constructed within a three-cornered association between film-makers, film spectators, and the film texts themselves, and at every point in that nexus of relationships we encounter negotiation and interaction involving active social beings and institutionalized social practices. Sociology is the intellectual resource best suited to probing that particular complex of social activity. Note, however, that this is not to propose an academically imperialist project, a sociology of cinema in a strongly reductive sense. It is, rather, to suggest that in its recent theoretical and methodological concerns sociology has begun to forge an analytic position which could help to reconcile the potentially warring opposites of modern cultural studies. In so doing, it could still contribute centrally to a multidisciplinary understanding of twentieth-century culture, a culture within which film itself played a historically crucial formative role.

BIBLIOGRAPHY

Blumer, Herbert (1933), *Movies and Conduct* (New York: Macmillan).

—— and **P. M. Hauser** (1935), *Movies, Delinquency and Crime* (New York: Macmillan).

Bordwell, David (1985), *Narration in the Fiction Film* (Madison: University of Wisconsin Press).

Branigan, Edward (1992), *Narrative Comprehension and Film* (London: Routledge).

Charters, W. W. (1935), *Motion Pictures and Youth* (New York: Macmillan).

Dale, Edgar (1933), *The Content of Motion Pictures* (New York: Macmillan).

Denzin, Norman K. (1991), *Images of the Postmodern: Social Theory and Contemporary Cinema* (London: Sage).

*—— (1995), *The Cinematic Society: The Voyeur's Gaze* (London: Sage).

Dyer, Richard (1979), *Stars* (London: British Film Institute).

—— (1986), *Heavenly Bodies: Film Stars and Society* (London: British Film Institute and Macmillan).

Handel, Leo A. (1950), *Hollywood Looks at its Audience* (Urbana: University of Illinois Press).

Hill, John (1986), *Sex, Class and Realism: British Cinema 1956–1963* (London: British Film Institute).

Huaco, George A. (1965), *The Sociology of Film Art* (New York: Basic Books).

Jarvie, I. C. (1970), *Towards a Sociology of the Cinema: A Comparative Essay on the Structure and Functioning of a Major Entertainment Industry* (London: Routledge & Kegan Paul).

Lovell, Terry (1980), *Pictures of Reality: Aesthetics, Politics, Pleasure* (London: British Film Institute).

May, Mark A., and **Frank K. Shuttleworth** (1933), *The Social Conduct and Attitudes of Movie Fans* (New York: Macmillan).

Mayer, J. P. (1946), *Sociology of Film* (London: Faber & Faber).

—— (1948), *British Cinemas and their Audiences* (London: Dobson).

Peterson, Ruth C., and **L. I. Thurstone** (1933), *Motion Pictures and the Social Attitudes of Children* (New York: Macmillan).

Powdermaker, Hortense (1950), *Hollywood: The Dream Factory* (Boston: Little Brown).

Rosten, Leo C. (1941), *Hollywood: The Movie Colony, the Movie Makers* (New York: Harcourt Brace).

Swingewood, Alan (1977), *The Myth of Mass Culture* (London: Macmillan).

Tudor, Andrew (1974), *Images and Influence: Studies in the Sociology of Film* (London: George Allen & Unwin).

Wollen, Peter (ed.) (1969), *Working Papers on the Cinema: Sociology and Semiology* (London: British Film Institute).

Wright, Will (1975), *Six Guns and Society: A Structural Study of the Western* (Berkeley: University of California Press).

21

Cultural studies and film

Graeme Turner

The development of film studies and its establishment within the academy precedes that of cultural studies, but over the last two decades there have been close parallels between the two intellectual and analytical projects. Both traditions are implicated in the turn towards the analysis of popular culture that commenced during the 1950s and 1960s in most Western countries. The spread of mass media culture, the installation of the teenager as an identifiable market category, and the various expressions of anxiety about the 'Americanization' of Western cultures as a consequence of the large-scale export of the products of the American mass entertainment industries, all assisted in raising the level of seriousness with which popular culture came to be regarded over the post-war decades. This change in the kind of attention directed towards popular culture in both the academic and the broader community resulted in significant modifications in the way popular cultural forms were examined and understood. Film studies and cultural studies have been among the participants in, and beneficiaries of, these shifts.

Film studies and cultural studies share a common interest in the textual analysis of popular forms and in the history of the cultural and industrial systems which produce these forms. However, there are limits to the commonality this might imply. Film studies is intensely interested in the individual text and retains a fundamental acknowledgement of aesthetic value; cultural studies disavowed the notion of aesthetic value from the beginning and is only now returning to see just how it might come to grips with such a fundamental gap in its account of the operation of culture (Frow 1995). Film studies is an academic discipline, with all the institutional and political considerations that entails. Cultural studies likes to think of itself as an 'undiscipline' (Clarke 1991) and, despite its galloping institutionalization, operates in an interdisciplinary fashion as a mode of critique and interrogation. The project of film studies in the academy is still primarily an interpretive one—of textual analysis—while the history of cultural studies has seen it move from a focus on the text to the analysis of the audience, and from there to mapping the discursive, economic, and regulatory contexts within which the two come together. Notwithstanding these rather fundamental differences, one can still trace important historical links between the two traditions and suggest ways in which trade between them has been, and might continue to be, useful.

These links are not uniformly distributed across the various national academies and intellectual traditions, however. Departments of film are most numerous in the United States, and the discipline is perhaps the most established and secure there. Cultural studies is, alternatively, a relatively recent addition to the humanities in the United States and is still at the very early stages of establishing its territory and its relation to cognate disciplines such as film, English, or communications. Further, and in constrast to the situation in Britain or in Australia, cultural studies in the United States seems intent on becoming a discipline itself and thus implicitly challenges film and English in ways that encourage the elaboration of points of difference rather than the pursuit of common goals. In Australia, and to a lesser extent in Canada, film studies, media studies, and cultural studies all move across similar interdisciplinary terrain, thus discouraging the kind of close identification with any single disciplinary tradition that would make comparisons especially meaningful. It is in Britain where the most explicit and productive 'trade' has occurred, and so this chapter will concentrate on the British situation.

The beginnings of cultural studies in Britain have been traced to such events as the conference of the National Union of Teachers in 1960 (Laing 1986; Turner 1990), itself embedded in the gradual development of public debates about the problem of 'discrimination' in popular culture (Hoggart 1958; Hall and Whannel 1964; Thompson 1964). Popularly framed as a problem highlighted by school pupils' enthusiastic consumption of mass culture products their teachers regarded as meretricious, its discussion led to the view that popular culture could no longer be dismissed without closer analysis. Indeed, if teachers expected their students to discriminate between 'good' and 'bad' cultural forms, they should start to exercise some discrimination themselves by resisting the temptation to see all popular culture as uniformly worthless.

At this time, most popular cultural forms were a long way from benefiting from such a view, but film was actually quite well positioned. The work of the French journal *Cahiers du cinéma* during the 1950s had recovered previously denigrated examples of mainstream Hollywood cinema for serious analysis, thus blurring the distinctions between commercial and art cinema. The development of theories of 'auteurism' in the United States during the 1960s, which appropriated the literary notion of authorship and bestowed it upon directors of (even Hollywood) films, legitimized the critical reassessment of such mainstream commercial filmmakers as John Ford and Alfred Hitchcock (Caughie 1981; Sarris 1969, 1970; Wollen 1972). A further associated enabling strategy was the renovation of conventional understandings of film genres which dispelled some of their pejorative connotations—those which placed them as merely the markers of an industrial or formula-driven system of production (Braudy 1976; Cawelti 1976; Schatz 1981; Feuer 1982).

This revised understanding of genre more realistically acknowledged the conditions within which mainstream feature films were produced, as well as the expressive or artistic potential of films produced within such conditions. Consequently, film studies established a form of analysis for a broad range of film texts which was not dissimilar to that already familiar within literary studies. It focused on the evaluation of the single film text, interested itself in the signatures of individual auteurs, and charted the trajectories of genres and film movements through variations in the patterns of their textual properties. Film, then, was probably the first of the mass communication forms to achieve respectability among critics of mass culture by establishing its validity as a textual system and as an aesthetic object—in spite, and in the full understanding, of its industrial conditions of production.

Film studies responded to this opportunity by developing a very sophisticated body of analysis of individual film texts, of individual directors, of film movements, and of film's formal signifying systems. By the middle of the 1970s, when cultural studies was still at a very early stage of development, film studies' analytical protocols were falling into place. Significantly, its interest in the workings of film 'language' had moved it towards more linguistic and systemic models of analysis: the influence of semiotics had begun to be felt, and the explanatory promise of psychoanalysis was also being explored (Metz 1974; Wollen 1972; Dayan 1974; see also Creed, Chapter 9). As a consequence of such interests, the relation between film and other signifying systems—language, dreams, culture itself—became more important (Metz 1982). Film ceased to be regarded solely as an aesthetic object and was increasingly the subject of exploration as a signifying system which had cultural, psychological, technological, even physiological, bases (Neale 1985). Into the 1980s the importance of also understanding the industrial systems of production and the principles of economic organization became a prominent consideration as well (Bordwell *et al.* 1985; Kerr 1986; Gomery 1986).

By the mid-1970s cultural studies, too, was developing systemic models to enable the close analysis of a wide range of textual forms. Cultural studies' objective was slightly different, however: its target was the nature of the political interests served by the patterns of meaning or strategies of representation such analyses uncovered (Hall 1977, 1980a, 1982). Initially moti-

> **Cultural studies' target was the nature of the political interests served by the patterns of meaning or strategies of representation such analyses uncovered.**

vated by its conviction of the importance and complexity of mass cultural forms, cultural studies from the mid-1970s to the mid-1980s was dominated by an assessment of the political function of these forms in practice—usually approached through the nomination of the ideologies they revealed and enacted through media texts (Fiske and Hartley 1978; Williamson 1978; Hall 1982). While far from celebratory of mass culture at this point in its history, cultural studies nevertheless took it very seriously as a system for making meaning.

While one might have expected the parallels between this cultural studies project and that of film studies to have encouraged some convergence of the two traditions, for most of this period they were in vigorous disputation. The form and function of the textual systems produced by mass culture became the primary subject of dispute between cultural studies and the body of film theory identified with the British journal *Screen*. What came to be known through this debate as 'Screen theory' was, of course, a simplified and perhaps unfairly homogenized digest of what had actually appeared in the pages of the journal. Nevertheless, there were certain prevailing influences on the content of *Screen* at this time: the semiotic–psychoanalytic cinema theory of Christian Metz and Althusserian explanations of ideology (Metz 1974, 1982; Althusser 1971). While these influences were also powerful in cultural studies, the shared interest did not produce much co-operation, however. When the Birmingham Centre for Contemporary Cultural Studies (BCCCS) began to investigate *Screen* theory, it was largely to contest what it regarded as *Screen*'s deterministic view of the power of the text (Hall 1980b; Morley 1980). In *Screen* theory, it was argued, texts were discussed in terms of their capacity to 'position' the viewer, telling the viewer how to 'read' the text and thus inserting him or her into a particular relationship to the narrative and into a complacent relationship to dominant ideologies. At its most extreme, suggested the BCCCS critiques, such an account saw the text as all-powerful: as if film texts always determined how

they were to be read. Morley (1980) among others, argued for a much greater recognition of 'agency', of the audience's freedom to negotiate quite resistant and even oppositional readings to those apparently structured into by the text. It was wrong, in Morley's view, to suggest that texts were read 'whole and straight' by every reader who encountered them.

This became a lengthy debate between the two theoretical traditions, one which helped shape the definition of the category of the text during the 1980s and still affects discussion of the text–reader relation today. The most celebrated exchange, perhaps, occurred around the critique of the subgenre of documentary realist television drama exemplified by the BBC's series *Days of Hope* (Ken Loach, GB, 1975), a story of British working-class experiences from before the First World War to the late 1920s which was screened in Britain in the mid-1970s. The series had a clearly oppositional agenda, setting out a left critique of contemporary British politics through its detailed and damning re-creation of the past. However, by accusing it of unwittingly offering a complacent view of history, *Screen* theorists seemed to some to be employing the most extreme application of 'textual determinism'. Colin MacCabe (1981) was the most uncompromising proponent of the *Screen* theory line, arguing that realist narratives were doomed by their narrative form and the epistemology which underpinned it. Realist narratives, MacCabe suggested, could never be critical of current political ideologies. This was because realism was a set of representational codes which must offer the viewer a comfortable position from which to see the representation even of bitter political struggles as natural or inevitable, hence defusing any potential for a critical or 'progressive' reading. By implication then, no matter what its intentions were, *Days of Hope* was defeated by its formal and ideological complicity with the politics it set out to attack. While such a critique had largely been accepted when applied to mainstream Hollywood realism, its application to projects that appeared to do something a little more radical was vigorously contested, primarily from within cultural studies but also from within film theory. Paradoxically, even though the battle lines were initially drawn around these competing formulations of the power of textual conventions, the focus on television meant that the debate moved across the boundaries between cultural studies and film studies. Under the heat of this debate, it seemed, firm distinctions between the two disciplinary traditions started to melt away. (A collection of the key essays in this debate can be found in Bennett *et al.* 1981.)

An analogous debate developed around Laura Mulvey's critique of classical Hollywood narrative (1975), which also seemed to argue that the dominant narrative form used in mainstream cinema offered only one position from which it could make sense. In this case, paraphrased crudely, Mulvey argued that if popular texts establish a position from which we find it comfortable to view and identify with them, it should not surprise us to discover that the viewing position constructed within the conventional discourses of Hollywood cinema is that of the male, not the female, viewer. The debates around what Mulvey called 'the male gaze' are of central importance to contemporary film studies and are dealt with elsewhere in this volume (see Creed and White, Chapters 9 and 13); however, it is worth noting their implication in the relation between film and cultural studies. Again, cultural studies responses to this argument have questioned the implicit proposition of a single, overly determined, reading of the text (Modleski 1988). While the original idea has been productively developed and elaborated within film studies and has its own history there, within cultural studies Mulvey's argument has been a crucial provocation to the analysis of the popularity of mass media texts aimed particularly at female consumers—soap operas and romance fiction, for instance (Hobson

1982; Radway 1984; Ang 1985). Significantly, it is the revised notion of the 'female spectator', a notion which appropriates and then complicates Mulvey's suggestion of a single, undifferentiated female response to the film text, which has been particularly enabling in cultural studies, where it has been most usefully applied to television and popular fiction (Pribram 1988; Seiter *et al.* 1991). As researchers from both traditions have pursued the shared broad objectives of feminist critiques of represenation, the line dividing the two disciplines is very thin indeed in this analytical territory. Many contemporary analyses of film texts which focus on the representation of women—through discussions of the female hero in *Aliens* (USA, 1986), or *Thelma and Louise* (USA, 1991), for instance—do so through a striking hybrid of film and cultural studies approaches (Collins *et al.* 1993).

Such hybridizing notwithstanding, the above debates emphasize a crucial difference between what cultural studies and *Screen* theory did with their texts. *Screen* theory sought its 'progressive texts', those which were both textually unconventional (anti-realist and ultimately avant-garde) and politically radical in their denial of the 'comfortable' viewing position associated with both MacCabe and Mulvey's critiques. At its most programmatic, this quest looked like an aesthetic preference for the avant-garde which almost automatically wrote off all popular cinema. On the other hand, for cultural studies, it was the popularity

Female heroes—*Thelma and Louise* (1991)

of popular cinema itself that was so interesting. If we were not to believe that this popularity was simply the result of people being duped, then we had to go further than critiques of realism or the more deterministic assessments of the relation between the reader and the text had so far taken us. Crucially, it was the processes which produced texts and audiences, not the experience of the texts themselves, that interested cultural studies.

> **Crucially, it was the processes which produced texts and audiences, not the experience of the texts themselves, that interested cultural studies.**

Such concerns were also percolating through other discussions of film—even in the pages of *Screen*. Richard Dyer's work (1982, 1986) on the social and cultural significance of 'stars' investigated the way popular cinema creates its meanings and maintains its relation with its audience. Examining stars as semiotic 'signs', Dyer explored how particular well-known actors take already encoded meanings onto the screen with them, meanings which are also part of the audience's cultural competencies (see Butler, Part 2, Chapter 9, for a fuller exposition). Dyer's work straddled the two competing traditions; while it was unashamedly evaluative in its description of the film experience, it also insisted upon the cultural origins of the processes through which texts generate their meanings, and through which these meanings circulate and establish themselves. Such work provided a clear acknowledgement of the importance of both text and context, and a respect for the agency of the spectator that has come to be typical of contemporary film studies.

It is possible to discern a number of common directions in film and cultural studies since the mid-1980s. First, the devotion to 'high-theory' (such as that identified with *Screen*) has slackened considerably. Indeed, one recent collection adopted what it clearly regarded as a novel strategy by having well-known film theorists actually write about contemporary popular film texts and place them within current social and political debates; finally, it seemed, 'film theory' could 'go to the movies' (Collins *et al.* 1993). Next, as cultural studies has moved away from texts to audiences, and thence to the social structures which situate people as audiences, so too has film studies returned to exam-

ine its constitutive cultural and economic contexts. Studies of the classical Hollywood cinema today are as likely to be industrial histories of production houses, studios, and the international trade in cinema 'product' as a review of classic film texts (Bordwell *et al.* 1985). The broad debates about globalization that have so dominated discussion of television in recent years have also informed discussions of Hollywood and its relation to other, smaller, 'national' cinemas. To deal with 'national cinema' today is to interrogate closely discourses of nationality, the enclosure of small film industries within the imperatives of international competition, and the rationale and effect of local systems of subsidy, protection, and regulation, and then to place the film texts produced by national cinemas within this complex discursive, economic, and cultural framework. The problematics of regional cinemas such as the Asian cinema (Dissanayake 1994), of small national cinemas such as the Australian cinema (O'Regan 1996), or of the broader cultural politics of representation within Third-World cinema (Chow 1995) are becoming fundamental issues within contemporary film studies. Such problematics situate film within arguments about nation formation, about post-coloniality, and about the regulation of international trade in cultural products, and in many cases will privilege such problematics over the interpretive treatment of individual film texts. At such points, cultural studies and film share common concerns and pursue very similar goals.

Where cultural studies may still have something to offer film studies is in the area of audience research. For cultural studies, the late 1980s were dominated by what came to be called 'audience studies'. Beginning with the *Nationwide* studies by Charlotte Brunsdon and David Morley (1978), and developing in sophistication (Morley 1986, 1992; Buckingham 1987), the history of cultural studies analysis of the audience begins—again—with the text. Initially, these so-called ethnographies of audience readings (primarily) of television programmes were set up as a way of authorizing the researcher's preferred readings of texts. Increasingly, however, the variety and contingency of audience readings became the focus of attention and the

> **Where cultural studies may still have something to offer film studies is in the area of audience research.**

text was left behind. Morley's later work (1986, 1992) turned up rich evidence that certain contextual factors (social determinants such as one's position within the family, whether or not one was employed, one's gender) could dramatically influence audience reading positions and encouraged the view that it was these social determinants and *their* operation that would really repay study. By broadening beyond their textual provocations, the contextualizing rhythms of audience studies have taught us a great deal about how we read television texts and how we integrate these readings with other aspects of our everyday life. So far, there are few parallels to this tradition in film studies, although there is some very interesting historiographical work which does build on feminist appropriations of audience research (Hansen 1991). Indeed, as Janet Staiger (1992) has suggested, research into the reception of film texts can differentiate itself from the cultural studies tradition by a detailed focus on the specific historical conditions within which consumption occurs. In general, however, industry audience research remains the dominant mode of audience analysis in film studies, and the possible benefits of the cultural studies ethnographies—contestable as they admittedly are—have not yet been explored.

Film studies, for its part, has something to offer cultural studies in that it has managed to provide criticism that is socially and culturally informed but which still maintains some notion of value which can help explain what it is (beyond ideology, that is) that attracts audiences over and over again to particular texts. Cultural studies has ducked this issue for most of its history and is only now returning cautiously to it. Film theory may be of some assistance in this task as the boundaries between the approaches become more permeable. There is some prospect of this. It is certainly true that disciplinary disputes between the two traditions seem to be in the past and the capacity for the attributes of each to inform the analyses of the other is very strong. The relation so far has been complicated, but the tensions I have described in this overview—disputes over territory, over the framing protocols of textual analysis, and over the appropriate conception of the culturally constructed relation between text, reader, and context—have proved to be immensely productive.

BIBLIOGRAPHY

Althusser, Louis (1971), *Lenin and Philosophy and Other Essays* (New York: Monthly Review Press).

Ang, Ien (1985), *Watching 'Dallas': Soap Opera and the Melodramatic Imagination* (London: Methuen).

*****Bennett, Tony, Susan Boyd-Bowman, Colin Mercer,** and **Janet Woollacott** (eds.) (1981), *Popular Television and Film (London: British Film Institute).*

Bordwell, David, Janet Staiger, and **Kristin Thompson** (1985), *The Classical Hollywood Cinema: Film Style and Mode of Production to 1960* (London: Routledge).

Braudy, Leo (1976), *The World in a Frame* (New York: Anchor Press).

Brunsdon, Charlotte, and **David Morley** (1978), *Everyday Television: 'Nationwide'* (London: British Film Institute).

Buckingham, David (1987), *Public Secrets: 'EastEnders' and its Audience* (London: British Film Institute).

Caughie, John (1981), *Theories of Authorship* (London: Routledge & Kegan Paul).

Cawelti, John (1976), *Adventure, Mystery and Romance: Formula Stories as Art and Popular Culture* (Chicago: University of Chicago Press).

Chow, Rey (1995), *Consuming Passions: Visuality, Sexuality, Ethnography and Contemporary Chinese Cinema* (New York: Columbia University Press).

Clarke, John (1991), *New Times and Old Enemies: Essays on Cultural Studies and America* (London, HarperCollins).

Collins, Jim, Hilary Radner, and **Ava Preacher Collins** (eds.) (1993), *Film Theory Goes to the Movies* (New York: Routledge).

Dayan, Daniel (1974), 'The Tutor Code of Classical Cinema', *Film Quarterly*, 28/1: 22–31.

Dissanayake, Wimal (ed.) (1994), *Colonialism and Nationalism in Asian Cinema* (Bloomington: Indiana University Press).

Dyer, Richard (1982), *Stars* (London: British Film Institute).

—— (1986), *Heavenly Bodies: Film Stars and Society* (London: British Film Institute).

Feuer, Jane (1982), *The Hollywood Musical* (London: British Film Institute and Macmillan).

Fiske, John, and **John Hartley** (1978), *Reading Television* (London: Methuen).

Frow, John (1995), *Cultural Studies and Cultural Value* (Oxford: Oxford University Press).

Gomery, Douglas (1986), *The Hollywood Studio System* (London: Macmillan).

Hall, Stuart (1977), 'Culture, the Media and the "Ideological Effect"', in James Curran, Michael Gurevitch, and Janet Woollacott (eds.), *Communication and Society* (London: Edward Arnold).

—— (1980*a*), 'The Determination of News Photography', in Stanley Cohen and Jock Young (eds.), *The Manufacture of News: Social Problems, Deviance and the Mass Media* (London: Constable).

—— (1980*b*), 'Recent Developments in Theories of Language and Ideology: A Critical Note', in Stuart Hall,

Dorothy Hobson, Andrew Lowe, and Janet Woollacott (eds.), *Culture, Media, Language* (London: Hutchinson).

—— (1982), 'The Rediscovery of "Ideology": The Return of the Repressed in Media Studies', in Michael Gurevitch, Tony Bennett, Andrew Lowe, and Paul Willis (eds.), *Culture, Society and the Media* (Milton Keynes: Open University Press).

—— and **Paddy Whannell** (1964), *The Popular Arts* (London: Hutchinson).

Hansen, Miriam (1991), *Babel and Babylon: Spectatorship in American Silent Film* (Cambridge, Mass.: Harvard University Press).

Hobson, Dorothy (1982), *'Crossroads': The Drama of a Soap Opera* (London: Methuen).

Hoggart, Richard (1958), *The Uses of Literacy* (London: Penguin).

Kerr, Paul (ed.) (1986), *The Hollywood Film Industry* (London: Routledge & Kegan Paul).

Laing, Stuart (1986), *Representations of Working Class Life 1957–1964* (London: Macmillan).

MacCabe, Colin (1981), 'Realism and the Cinema: Notes on Some Brechtian Theses', in Tony Bennett *et al.* (eds.), *Popular Television and Film* (London):

Metz, Christian (1974), *Film Language: A Semiotics of the Cinema*, trans. Michael Taylor (London: Oxford University Press).

—— (1982), *Psychoanalysis and the Cinema: The Imaginary Signifier*, trans. Celia Britton *et al.* (Bloomington: Indiana University Press).

Modleski, Tania (1988), *The Women Who Knew Too Much: Hitchcock and Feminist Film Theory* (New York: Methuen).

Morley, David (1980), 'Texts, Readers, Subjects', in Stuart Hall, Dorothy Hobson, Andrew Lowe, and Janet Woollacott (eds.), *Culture, Media, Language* (London: Hutchinson).

—— (1986), *Family Television: Cultural Power and Domestic Leisure* (London: Comedia).

—— (1992), *Television, Audiences and Cultural Studies* (London: Routledge).

Mulvey, Laura (1975), 'Visual Pleasure and Narrative Cinema', *Screen,* 16/3: 6–18.

Neale, Steve (1985), *Cinema and Technology: Image, Sound, Colour* (London: British Film Institute and Macmillan).

O'Regan, Tom (1996), *Australian Cinema* (London: Routledge).

Pribram, Deidre (1988), *Female Spectators: Looking at Film and Television* (London: Verso).

Radway, Janice (1984), *Reading the Romance: Women, Patriarchy and Popular Literature* (Chapel Hill: University of North Carolina Press).

Sarris, Andrew (1969), *The American Cinema: Directors and Directions 1929–1968* (New York: Dutton).

—— (1970), 'Notes on the Auteur Theory in 1970', *Film Comment* 6/3 (Fall), 1–8.

Schatz, Thomas (1981), *Hollywood Genres: Formulas, Filmmaking, and the Studio System* (New York: Random House).

Seiter, Ellen, Hans Borchers, Gabriele Kreutzner, and **Eva-Marie Warth** (eds.) (1991), *Remote Control: Television, Audiences and Cultural Power* (London: Routledge).

Staiger, Janet (1992), 'Film, Reception and Cultural Studies', *Centennial Review*, 36/1: 9–104.

Thompson, Denys (1964), *Discrimination and Popular Culture* (London: Penguin).

*Turner, Graeme (1990), *British Cultural Studies: An Introduction* (Boston: Unwin Hyman).

Wollen, Peter (1972), *Signs and Meaning in the Cinema* (Bloomington: Indiana University Press).

Williamson, Judith (1978), *Decoding Advertisements: Ideology and Meaning in Advertising* (London: Marion Boyars).

22 Film audiences

Jostein Gripsrud

Why are audiences interesting?

When the hundredth anniversary of cinema was celebrated in 1995, 'cinema' was defined as the screening of moving images for a paying audience. The presence of an audience is, in other words, an essential part of the very definition of the medium. Very different kinds of film scholarship are concerned with film audiences or relations between film and its audiences. In quantitative terms, scholarly research and writing about film audiences, or some dimension of film–audience relations, clearly outnumber (and outweigh!) publications about any other aspect of the film medium, such as film production or the aesthetics of film.

Film's early status as a paradigmatic mass medium is a major part of the explanation for this. Its colossal popularity with working-class people and women and children of most classes gave various 'responsible' people reasons to worry about the impact of the movies on the minds and behaviour of these social groups. Given the intense and pleasurable experiences that people seemed to get from the cinema, it appeared obvious that the influence on people's minds would also be intense. Modern, social-scientific mass communication research was to a considerable extent developed in response to such fears through projects launched to document and substantiate them (even though these did not necessarily deliver the expected results).

But film's enormous potential for influencing the masses was also central to seminal contributions to theories of film as a textual form. The leader of the Bolshevik revolution in Russia, V. I. Lenin, proclaimed that film was the most important of all the arts since it was the most efficient medium for propaganda, and Soviet film theory (and that of Eisenstein, in particular) was very much concerned with how to move the mass audiences of film to perceive the world in certain ways—and act accordingly. The basis for a long tradition in film theory is precisely a Marxist conception of film as a medium for changing people's way of thinking

> In quantitative terms, scholarly research and writing about film audiences, or some dimension of film–audience relations, clearly outnumber (and outweigh!) publications about any other aspect of the film medium, such as film production or the aesthetics of film. Film's early status as a paradigmatic mass medium is a major part of the explanation for this.

in 'progressive' directions, or, on the contrary, for the reproduction and dissemination of ideology in the sense of 'false consciousness'. The semiotic and psychoanalytic *Screen* theory of the 1970s represented a particular development of this tradition.

A more recent, quite heterogeneous body of work favours a more pragmatic theory of meaning, according to which determinate meaning is not inherent in the filmic signs or texts themselves but is constructed by spectators in accordance with certain context-dependent conventions. This position can take a variety of forms, drawing on diverse theoretical traditions such as hermeneutics, phenomenology, the semiotic theory of C. S. Peirce, or eclectic formations such as British cultural studies. Cognitivist approaches, focusing on the 'processing' of film in the human brain, have also gained some prominence (see King, Chapter 23).

All of the above approaches to film audiences and the encounter between audiences and films share the idea that it is through the existence of an audience that film acquires social and cultural importance. The production of a film provides a raw material which regulates the potential range of experiences and meanings to be associated with it, but it is through audiences that films become 'inputs' into larger socio-cultural processes.

> **The production of a film provides a raw material which regulates the potential range of experiences and meanings to be associated with it, but it is through audiences that films become 'inputs' into larger socio-cultural processes.**

The following overview will largely concentrate on the tradition of research on actual film audiences, as it has developed in response to the history of the medium. (For reasons of space, I have had to exclude the otherwise very interesting forms of audience studies conducted by or for the film industry. A good overview is provided in Austin 1989.) This emphasis is chosen partly because other entries in the present volume will cover the other, text-centred approaches, and partly because there has been a revived interest in empirical audience research since the early 1980s, not least in studies of film history. Much of the prehistory of such work has been little known, however. Empirical audience research has often been regarded antagonistically by scholars in text-oriented film studies—and vice versa. However, creative scholarship can only benefit from a broad knowledge of different traditions.

The movies as a social problem: the first audience studies in context

The first public complaints over the moral standards of films were heard in the 1890s both in the United States (cf. Jowett 1976: 109–10) and the United Kingdom (Kuhn 1988: 15), but public reactions against the medium did not gain momentum until after 1905. It seems reasonable to assume that it was the explosive growth in the number of more or less permanent movie theatres from about 1905 that really brought the cinema to the attention of public authorities and the social groups that actively participate in public debates. Importantly, the repertoire of the cinemas was also beginning to change at about the same time, with fiction formats such as anarchic farces, crime stories, and melodramatic love stories becoming increasingly prominent.

The introduction of censorship which occurred in a number of different forms in most Western countries in the course of just six to seven years around 1910 is an indication of how seriously the 'dangers' of the movies were perceived. All such measures were preceded by public debates which to a greater or lesser extent also involved forms of research on movie theatres and movie audiences. The first film audience research was, in other words, motivated by anxieties about the social consequences of the medium's immense popularity, especially with children and adolescents. Numerous attempts were made in many countries to estimate audience numbers and social patterns of attendance before 1910, often in methodologically crude surveys conducted by teachers' associations, school authorities, social workers, and the like (see e.g. Jowett 1976: 45–6). Such efforts characteristically sought to verify the intuitive feelings of educators, religious leaders, and many social reformers that movies were for the most part detrimental to the psychic, moral, and even physical health of those who regularly went to see them.

The themes and results of these early studies were to be repeated again and again in later, and methodologically more sophisticated, studies. A research tradition was formed in which the medium of film was (is) conceived primarily as a social problem. It was seen as an isolated, primary cause of a number of negative effects. This cause–effect (or, rather, stimulus–response) conception of the relations between movies and audiences was drawn from mechanistic and biologistic psychological theories in vogue in the early decades of this century. Seeing the movies as a social problem was also related to widespread theories of the mass as a characteristic social form in modern societies. Individuals who had moved to rapidly growing cities had been cut off from their traditional bonds, norms, and authorities and were now seen to be basically vulnerable to mass persuasion. Moreover, for the first theorist of the mass, Gustave Le Bon, writing in 1895, the mass or crowd was 'distinguished by feminine characteristics' as it tended to move very easily into emotional extremes (Huyssen 1986: 196). One might suspect, therefore, that the cinema was conceived as a social problem precisely because central parts of its *audiences* were experienced as a problem for teachers and other authorities. That the problem was in part conceived as *feminine* is highly significant: for the threat of the movies was, not least, about a loss of control and a tendency towards self-indulgence and weakness.

The cinema became a privileged sign of social and cultural changes which made élites worried. As such, it played the role of a much-needed scapegoat which rational arguments could hardly do much to change. In 1917 the British National Council of Public Morals undertook an 'independent enquiry into the physical, social, moral and educational influence of the cinema, with special reference to young people' (quoted in Richards 1984: 70). A 400-page report, based on numerous sources of information, was published, in which the general conclusion was that 'no social problem of the day demands more earnest attention', and that the cinema had 'potentialities for evil' which were 'manifold' (even though cinema could also become 'a powerful influence for good'). And on the question of links between movies and juvenile crime, the commission of inquiry concluded 'that while a connection between the cinema and crime has to a limited extent in special cases been shown, yet it certainly has not been proved that the increase in juvenile crime generally has been consequent on the cinema, or has been independent of other factors more conducive to wrongdoing' (Richards 1989: 71). Still, the issue was

not settled, and the same anxieties motivated new inquiries well into the 1930s.

The movies as social force: the Payne Fund Studies

By the 1920s the cinema was well established as the major form of entertainment for the larger part of the population in all Western countries. An 'art' cinema was developed in, for instance, Germany and France, and cinema's increasing respectability could also be seen in many countries from the emergence of film criticism in major newspapers and magazines. However, in the United States, especially, it seems that the earlier moral panics over the influence of the movies were still in evidence. Unlike many other countries, the United States had not established forms of public censorship which would have calmed the nerves of those most worried. Moreover, as the prohibition of alcohol between 1920 and 1933 indicates, the so-called 'roaring twenties' was a period when puritan morality was particularly strong, perhaps in reaction to the number of social and cultural changes then challenging traditional values, such as women's entry into the labour force and new relations between the sexes, and the emergence and spread of consumerism (involving spending rather than saving).

In this situation, the movies were still very much suspected of being a primary source of inspiration for delinquency and general moral decay. This was so even if a 1925 study of 4,000 'juvenile delinquency' cases showed that only 1 per cent of these could in some way be tied to movie influence. (The study was conducted by Healy and Brommer and referred to in Blanchard 1928: 204; cf. Jowett 1976: 216.) Alice Miller Mitchell published the first major scholarly survey entirely devoted to children and the movies in 1929, and concluded that, even if 'the delinquent does have a wider cinema experience than do the other children studied', the survey did not provide any conclusive evidence for a causal link between movies and delinquency (quoted in Jowett 1976: 219). However, such sensible reasoning was not to deter activists who perceived the movie repertoire in much more offensive and threatening terms.

The most comprehensive and also probably most influential of all empirical research projects on film audiences—the so-called Payne Fund Studies—was organized in 1928 by the Reverend William H. Short, who was executive director of something called the Motion Picture Research Council. A group of psychologists, sociologists, and educators from a number of institutions, directed by Dr W. W. Charters from the Bureau of Educational Research, Ohio State University, began work as soon as a grant of $200,000 was secured from the philanthropic foundation the Payne Fund. Investigations took place between 1929 and 1932, and the results were published in at least twelve volumes—eight books in 1933, three in 1935, and one in 1937. In addition, a journalist, Henry James Forman, wrote a popularized summary of the studies, *Our Movie Made Children* (1933). This book focused completely on results which seemed to support the view that movies had detrimental effects, and it became very influential in the public debate which preceded the much stricter enforcement of Hollywood's so-called Production Code from the summer of 1934 on. The actual studies themselves also had an undertone of anxiety or concern, but they were far more nuanced than Forman's outright attack on the movie industry suggested.

The Payne Fund Studies employed all the research methods then available to 'scientific' studies of sociological and psychological phenomena, and developed some of them further. Methods included quantitative 'content analyses', large-scale surveys, laboratory experiments, participant observation, the collection of written 'movie autobiographies' from large numbers of people, and so on. The studies can be grouped in two categories. The first consists of studies which tried to determine the size and composition of movie audiences, and to assess the 'contents' of films. The second category of studies were attempts to assess the various 'effects' of viewing.

One series of studies of this latter sort was conducted by Ruth C. Peterson and L. I. Thurstone (1933). They were interested in whether films influenced the general attitudes of children towards ethnic or racial groups and certain central social issues such as crime, the punishment of criminals, war, capital punishment, and prohibition. The results were very clear: even single films seemed to have considerable influence on children's attitudes, and the cumulative effect of several films with a similar view of groups or issues was even more striking (Lowery and DeFleur 1995). Despite their sophistication, these studies, none the less, displayed a number of severe theoretical and methodological problems. The very term 'attitude' is problematic, the methods for 'measuring' the phe-

nomenon are debatable, no so-called control groups were used—and so forth. Still, the evidence presented could well be seen as quite convincing, particularly since the children had little or no experience of, or insight into, the respective areas under investigation. Very few, if any, of these small-town kids had ever known black or Chinese people, for example. Films portraying these groups positively or negatively, therefore, could be all the more influential. It is similarly unlikely that they had given much thought to the issues of war or the treatment of criminals. What was demonstrated, then, was the impact of films in a situation where other sources of information were more or less lacking and opinions and attitudes were therefore relatively easy to influence.

The most interesting of the Payne Fund Studies, however, was methodologically very different. Herbert Blumer collected 'motion-picture autobiographies' from over 1,100 university and college students, 583 high-school students, 67 office workers, and 58 factory workers, who were instructed to 'write in as natural and truthful manner as possible accounts of their experiences with "movies" as far as they could recall them' (Blumer 1933: 4). In addition, about 150 students and schoolchildren were interviewed, and accounts of conversations ('taken nearly as verbatim as possible', 11) between students at different levels were collected. Finally, questionnaires were distributed to 1,200 children in the fifth and sixth grades of twelve public schools in different areas of Chicago, and the behaviour of children at neighbourhood cinemas and in play after these visits was observed. The voluminous material gathered in these ways was not primarily intended for sophisticated statistical treatment. Rather the point was to explore the ways in which cinema audiences themselves thought and felt about their moviegoing, the films they saw, and how they influenced them. The published report, *Movies and Conduct* (Blumer 1933), is full of vivid descriptions of movie experiences and of how young people picked up tips on anything from play, kissing, fashion, and table manners to attitudes and daydreams. Just one random example from a female high-school student's contribution:

I have imagined playing with a movie hero many times, though; that is while I'm watching the picture. I forget about it when I'm outside the theater. Buddy Rogers and Rudy Valentino have kissed me oodles of times, but they don't know it. God bless 'em!—Yes, love scenes have thrilled me and made me more receptive to love. I was going with a fellow whom I liked as a playmate, so to speak; he was a little younger than me and he liked me a great deal. We went to the movie—Billie Dove in it. Oh, I can't recall the name but Antonio Moreno was the lead, and there were some lovely scenes which just got me all hot 'n' bothered. After the movie we went for a ride 'n' parked along the lake; it was a gorgeous night. Well, I just melted (as it were) in his arms, making him believe I loved him, which I didn't. I sort of came to, but I promised to go steady with him. I went with him 'til I couldn't bear the sight of him. . . . I've wished many times that we'd never seen the movie. (Blumer 1933: 223)

Blumer's conclusions were relatively careful. However, the material had convinced him that 'the forte of motion pictures is in their emotional effect', and that 'their appeal and their success reside ultimately in the emotional agitation which they induce'. A successful production was one which managed to draw 'the observer' into the drama so that 'he loses himself' and, in such a condition, 'the observer becomes malleable to the touch of what is shown' and 'develops a readiness to certain forms of action which are foreign in some degree to his ordinary conduct' (Blumer 1933: 198). Blumer also argued that the movies were so emotionally demanding that the audience could be left 'emotionally exhausted' and, instead of ordinary emotional responses, they would experience an emotional and moral confusion: 'Insofar as one may seek to cover in a single proposition the more abiding effect of motion pictures upon the minds of movie-goers, it would be, in the judgement of the writer, in terms of a medley of vague and variable impressions—a disconnected assemblage of ideas, feelings, vagaries, and impulses' (199). Blumer's conclusion was that films could confuse people morally in various ways: for instance, by presenting immoral behaviour as attractive even if the film's overt moral 'message' was impeccable. In a methodologically similar study of inmates, ex-convicts, and young people in various reform schools and so on, he pointed to the obvious importance of social-background factors both in the choice of films and in reactions to them. But he remained convinced that movies could 'lead . . . to misconduct', and that this inevitably raised the issue of 'social control' (Blumer and Hauser 1933: 202).

The Chicago School sociologist Blumer was thus no simplistic 'hypodermic needle' theorist, even if there are clear traces of the stimulus–response model in his work, and his conclusion is that movies had a powerful influence on young people's lives. His observations of strong emotional experiences, and identification as 'losing oneself', have links to both previous and later scholarship on film (and television). Hugo Münsterberg's *The Photoplay: A Psychological Study* (1916), which Hansen (1983: 154 n. 14) describes as 'the first systematic attempt to theorize spectatorship', provided, for example, a sort of theoretical basis for ideas of film as a 'strong' medium which could be used both for better and for worse. Films could, Münsterberg argues, be an 'incomparable power for remoulding and upbuilding the national soul', even if '[t]he possibilities of psychical infection cannot be overlooked'. 'No psychologist', he continues, 'can determine exactly how much the general spirit of righteous honesty, of sexual cleanliness, may be weakened by the unbridled influence of plays which lower moral standards' (May 1983: 42). With somewhat different, and far more impressive, theoretical underpinnings, the whole theorization of 'the spectator' in cine-psychoanalytic studies from Christian Metz onwards is also centred on the persuasive ideological functions of 'identification' (see Creed, Part 1, Chapter 9). In this respect, Blumer was probably less blind to the importance of contextual factors in determining the 'effects' of cinema than some of the work in the *Screen* tradition appeared to be.

The Payne Fund Studies, however, are all quite insensitive to film as a form of *art*. They chop up filmic texts in so many 'themes' and 'content elements', with total lack of respect for a film's wholeness and the interrelations of a variety of aesthetic means and potential meanings. This provoked the neo-Aristotelian philosopher Mortimer Adler to formulate a fundamental critique of this whole approach to what he considered an art form in his *Art and Prudence* (1937), subsequently popularized in Raymond Moley's *Are we Movie Made?* (1938). Nevertheless, at least some of the Payne Fund Studies were more nuanced and theoretically reflective than much post-war research. Sociologist Paul G. Cressey (1938) summarized the experiences gained in the project as follows:

'Going to the movies' is a unified experience involving always a specific film, a specific personality, a specific social situation and a specific time and mood; therefore, any program of research which does not recognize all essential phases of the motion picture experience can offer little more than conjecture as to the cinema's net 'effect' in actual settings and communities. (Cressey 1938: 518)

It is worth wondering where such insights went in the following decades. Research along similarly intelligent lines had in fact been done almost twenty-five years earlier, in Germany. But for a number of imaginable reasons, it remained unknown to Anglo-Americans until Miriam Hansen referred to it in a 1983 article in English.

The cinema as cultural resource: Emilie Altenloh

The German sociologist Emilie Altenloh's doctoral dissertation, *Zur Soziologie des Kino* (1914), which she wrote at the age of 26, is in fact one of the most interesting contributions to empirical audience studies. This is particularly so because of her general approach. The dissertation is marked by a holistic sociological and historical perspective on the cinema and its audiences. Almost half of its 102 pages are devoted to film production, including the product itself, distribution, and the legal framework. The second half is about the audience, and their attendance at the cinema is understood in relation to both their other cultural preferences (theatre, music, and so on) and their gender, class, profession, and political interests. A historical perspective runs through the whole text; and both social developments (industrialization, modernization) and the changes in the domain of popular culture are brought into her interpretive and explanatory reasoning. What also makes it strikingly different from, say, the Payne Fund Studies is that worries over 'harmful effects' are hardly expressed at all. While the author openly distinguishes between more and less 'primitive' movies and tastes (the genre preferences of many young male workers were expressed in answers that 'smell of blood and dead bodies'; Altenloh 1914: 66), the tone is generally one of sympathy, not moralizing.

Altenloh's primary material for the audience study was movie theatre statistics and 2,400 simple questionnaires which were distributed via professional organizations, trade unions, and schools of various kinds in the city of Mannheim and, in part, in Heidelberg. The study provides a detailed picture not only of the social composition of audiences but also of the differences between various sections of the audience in terms of genre preferences and the overall context of their going to the movies, including their relations to other cultural forms and media. The survey demonstrated, for instance, that male audiences varied quite a lot in their generic preferences and general attitudes

to the cinema, in ways which clearly related to their membership of particular social groups, while female moviegoers seemed to be more homogeneous in their tastes for music, melodrama, and particular kinds of documentary material (waterfalls, waves, ice floes . . .). What was striking in all of the questionnaire material, however, was how little people could say to explain why they were so drawn to the movie experience. The reasons were as many as there were individuals in the audience; they were, however, all out for something their everyday experiences did not provide. Altenloh thought that 'the cinema succeeds in addressing just enough of those individuals' needs to provide a substitute for what could really be "better", thus assuming a powerful reality in relation to which all questions as to whether the cinema is good or evil, or has any right to exist, appear useless' (Hansen 1983: 179).

Altenloh's study suggested that the cinema functioned as a social space for experiences and forms of communication that were largely excluded from other public arenas—not least because central parts of the audience were in practice excluded from these other arenas. It was, to a degree, a public sphere for the unspeakable, where those otherwise spoken *for*, without a voice of their own, felt at least spoken *to*. And whatever else one could say about Altenloh's questionnaire methodology, it did, even if within strict limitations, allow cinema's core audiences to speak for themselves—and through a sympathetic interpreter.

British observations—and two blank decades

In Britain the early 1930s brought a series of local inquiries into the 'effects' of cinema, particularly on children and youth. Most of them sought to justify the hostility towards the movies which motivated their efforts, and were generally deficient in scholarly standards of research and argumentation. While reports like these played an important role in public debates, the more interesting work on cinema audiences was of a different nature. The statistician Simon Rowson conducted the first systematic survey of cinema attendance in 1934 (Rowson 1936), and a number of other surveys were also conducted throughout the decade. But the most fascinating of British studies of film audiences in the 1930s and 1940s were of the kind now referred to as 'ethnographic', i.e. mainly based in various forms of participant observation.

Sociological studies such as E. W. Bakke's *The Unemployed Man* (1933) and H. Llewellyn Smith *et al.*'s *The New Survey of London Life and Labour* (1935) included observations of the role of the cinema in the everyday lives of ordinary people in particular social milieux, as did a number of other books and articles with both scholarly and other kinds of authors (Richards 1989, ch. 1). The interest in an 'anthropological study of our own civilization' also lay behind the establishment of Mass-Observation in 1937. This was a unique organization devoted to the gathering of knowledge about everyday life in British society, and was based on the voluntary observational work of ordinary (if, predominantly, middle-class) people. Mass-Observation grew out of the same intellectual milieu as the documentary film movement associated with John Grierson, and cinemagoing was first studied in what was known as the 'Worktown' project—a study of Bolton, Lancashire—which was obviously inspired by Robert Lynd and Helen Merrell's *Middletown: A Study in American Culture* (1929). Survey methodology, loosely structured interviews, and participant observation were employed in this project, and the material collected provides a richly detailed picture of moviegoing in Bolton. Both before and during the war Mass-Observation continued to collect information from its volunteers all over Britain about cinemagoing (including that of the volunteers themselves), reactions to particular films during screenings (laughs, comments, etc.), favourite stars and films, and so on. Material was also gathered through popular newspapers and the film magazine *Picturegoer*, the readers of which were asked to write letters about their cinema habits and preferences (Richards and Sheridan 1987: 1–18).

This last procedure was also used by the sociologist J. P. Mayer when working on his *British Cinemas and their Audiences* (1948), which includes sixty of the letters Mayer received from readers of *Picturegoer*. This book, however, seems to be the last of its kind to arrive for decades. From the early 1950s on, television largely took over the cinema's role as the major source of popular entertainment and, as a result, became the object of very similar concerns to those previously directed at the movies. Social scientists generally lost interest in film and its 'effects', while an individualistic and consumer-oriented 'uses and gratifications' approach evolved as a new paradigm in mainstream communication research. When film studies became established as an academic discipline in the 1960s, it was as a purely aesthetic discipline, devoted to studies of films-as-texts, of masterpieces and 'auteurs'. Having film accepted as a worthy object of study entailed a qualification of it as 'Art'. Sociological studies of the audience were regarded as irrelevant—as philistine activities, which were only of interest to aesthetically insensitive social scientists, politicians, bureaucrats, and the movie business. When the audience reappeared in film theory around 1970, it was at first as a generalized textual construct only. But in 1978, at the Centre for Contemporary Cultural Studies, Tom Jeffrey published a paper entitled *Mass-Observation: A Brief History*. Mass-Observation and empirical studies of actual audiences were, in other words, 'rediscovered' in the context of the ethnographic studies of contemporary (youth) culture conducted by the so-called Birmingham School. The 1980s then brought a new wave of interest in film audiences.

From textually derived spectators to actual audiences

The politically inflected theorization of spectatorship in the 1970s can be seen, to use a psychoanalytical metaphor, as a 'return of the repressed' after a period of purely aesthetic approaches. But the political interest in film spectators may also be seen as a kind of 'displacement', in that the central audiovisual medium had for a number of decades been television. From a political point of view, it is also striking that most of the films analysed were made decades before—they were not what contemporary audiences went to the cinema to see. An interest in contemporary movie audiences is still relatively rare in film studies.

This is not at all to say that the theories in question were irrelevant and that all the efforts of *Screen* theory were a waste of time and energy. Ideas about 'spectator positions' suggested by filmic texts are in line with ancient rhetorical theory and also with more recent phenomenological and hermeneutic theories of literature. However problematic it may have been, Laura

> **An interest in contemporary movie audiences is still relatively rare in film studies.**

The position of the spectator—a film audience of the classical era

Mulvey's 1975 article about the structural gendering of mainstream film was a seminal attempt at grounding a feminist theory of film in more fundamental matters than the simple counting of stereotyped sex roles. On the whole, psychoanalytic theory in the tradition of Christian Metz is still the only significant theory which seriously approaches the 'deeper' reasons for our desires for and pleasures in film experiences. It deals with phenomena we cannot expect to explain either through direct observation or through interviews, but which still remain essential. The tradition of empirical studies of actual audiences can only, like Emilie Altenloh in 1914, conclude that people have few and hardly satisfactory answers when asked why they go to the movies again and again.

The problem of *Screen* theory was rather that the issue of *real* audiences was either dismissed as 'empiricist' or postponed indefinitely. This contrasted with developments in literary studies (which film studies for the most part grew out of), where studies of historical, concrete instances of reception were, so to speak, booming in many countries in the 1970s—inspired, in part, by German reception theorists. Film studies only took a similar turn after the cultural studies of *television* demonstrated that textual analysis and audience studies could be intelligently and fruitfully combined. Charlotte Brunsdon and Dave Morley's work on the programme *Nationwide* (Brunsdon and Morley 1978; Morley 1980) was seminal here. It was followed later by such work as Ien Ang's influential study of the Dutch reception of *Dallas* (1985), and in the late 1980s the 'ethnographic' study of television audiences was generally recognized as the 'sexiest field within the field' in the increasingly interdisciplinary area where mass communication, communication, media, cultural, and film studies converged. This convergence was also facilitated by a 'ferment in the field' of mass communication research which opened the way for so-called qualitative (as opposed to strictly quantitative and statistical) methods in both textual and audience analyses, and forms of critical theory.

It is characteristic of film studies, though, that work on film audiences is still largely of a historical kind. Present-day, actual film audiences get very little attention. Thus, there has been quite intensive research on the exhibition practices, forms of reception, and social composition of audiences between the 1890s and 1960, and research on early film (before 1917), in particular, has flourished, combining solid historical investigation of primary sources with considerable theoretical sophistication (see Elsaesser 1990 on seminal work here). Ways of theorizing 'spectatorship' in a social context that are new to Anglo-American film studies have also been introduced in this area, specifically through Miriam Hansen's use of the concept of (proletarian) public sphere(s) in her *Babel and Babylon* (1991).

The general transition in feminist film studies from an interest only in a textually constructed spectator to studies which are concerned at least as much with actual audiences was marked, for instance, by Annette Kuhn's 1984 *Screen* article 'Women's Genres', which called for a rethinking of interrelations between the two. This demand was linked to other work within feminist film theory which had severely complicated the notion of 'the spectator' by, first, distinguishing between male and female spectator positions, and then further deconstructing the apparent unity or singularity of each of these (see Modleski 1988, introduction). In anthologies such as Deidre Pribram's *Female Spectators* (1988), the relations between textual and socio-historical approaches were discussed in new, more open ways, and Patrice Petro's *Joyless Streets* (1989) took to non-filmic sources (magazines, photojournalism) in an attempt to construct historically specific female spectator positions in Weimar Germany.

The convergence between previously segregated approaches has been particularly striking in studies of film stars, previously a phenomenon reserved for fandom and sociology. Richard Dyer's book *Stars* (1979) introduced this area into academic film studies, and it rapidly became a meeting place between historical, sociological, culturalist, semiotic, and cine-psychoanalytical forms of scholarship (Gledhill 1991). In many respects Jackie Stacey's *Star Gazing* (1994) represents a coming-together of all of these, integrating (among other things) discussions of spectator theories, statistical information, and the written memories of female

moviegoers of the 1940s and 1950s. She draws on Mass-Observation material, and employs methods similar to those of both Herbert Blumer and (particularly) J. P. Mayer, thus acknowledging the value of the historical tradition of empirical, sociological studies of movie audiences (even if, significantly, neither of these two forerunners are mentioned in her book).

Stacey's book thus indicates that film studies may have reached a point where theoretical and methodological orthodoxies have given way to a more productive, critically informed rethinking of theoretical and methodological boundaries. Such reasoned eclecticism is far from unproblematic, however, for there are, in the current conjuncture, many reasons to suggest the importance of film scholarship which goes beyond empirical studies of historical or current film audiences and their experiences of the movies. Still, it seems clear that the theoretical and methodological developments over the last two decades or so have clearly contributed to making film studies a highly vital, central field within the broader area of media studies.

BIBLIOGRAPHY

Adler, Mortimer J. (1937), *Art and Prudence* (New York: Longmans, Green).

Altenloh, Emilie (1914), *Zur Soziologie des Kino: Die Kino-Unternehmung und die sozialen Schichten ihrer Besucher* (Leipzig: Spamerschen Buchdruckerei).

Ang, Ien (1985), *Watching 'Dallas': Soap Opera and the Melodramatic Imagination* (London: Methuen).

*****Austin, Bruce A.** (1989), *Immediate Seating: A Look at Movie Audiences* (Belmont, Calif.: Wadsworth).

Blanchard, Phyllis (1928), *Child and Society* (New York: Longman's, Green).

*****Blumer, Herbert** (1933), *Movies and Conduct* (New York: Macmillan).

—— and **Philip M. Hauser** (1933), *Movies, Delinquency and Crime* (New York: Macmillan).

Brunsdon, Charlotte, and **David Morley** (1978), *Everyday Television: 'Nationwide'* (London: British Film Institute).

Cressey, Paul G. (1938), 'The Motion Picture Industry as Modified by Social Background and Personality', *American Sociological Review*, 3/4: 516–25.

Dyer, Richard (1979), *Stars* (London: British Film Institute).

Elsaesser, Thomas (ed.) (1990), *Early Cinema: Space, Frame, Narrative* (London: British Film Institute).

Forman, Henry James (1933), *Our Movie Made Children* (New York: Macmillan).

Gledhill, Christine (ed.) (1991), *Stardom: Industry of Desire* (London: Routledge).

*Hansen, Miriam (1983), 'Early Silent Cinema: Whose Public Sphere?', *New German Critique*, 29 (Spring–Summer), 147–84.

*—— (1991), *Babel and Babylon: Spectatorship in American Silent Film* (Cambridge, Mass: Harvard University Press).

Huyssen, Andreas (1986), 'Mass Culture as Woman: Modernism's Other', in T. Modleski (ed.), *Studies in Entertainment: Critical Approaches to Mass Culture* (Bloomington: Indiana University Press).

Jeffrey, Tom (1978), *Mass-Observation: A Short History*, Birmingham Centre for Contemporary Cultural Studies Stencilled Occasional Papers, No. 55, (Birmingham: BCCCS).

Jowett, Garth (1976), *Film: The Democratic Art* (Boston: Little, Brown).

Kuhn, Annette (1984), 'Women's Genres', *Screen*, 25/1: 18–28.

—— (1988), *Cinema, Censorship and Sexuality 1909–1925* (London: Routledge).

Le Bon (1895/1981), *The Crowd* (Harmondsworth: Penguin).

Lowery, Shearon A., and Melvin L. DeFleur (1995), *Milestones in Mass Communication Research: Media Effects* (New York: Longman).

Lynd, Robert S., and Helen Merrell (1929), *Middletown: A Study in American Culture* (New York: Harcourt, Brace, & World).

May, Lary (1983), *Screening out the Past: The Birth of Mass Culture and the Motion Picture Industry* (Chicago: University of Chicago Press).

Mayer, J. P. (1948), *British Cinemas and their Audiences* (London: Dennis Dobson).

Mitchell, Alice Miller (1929/1971), *Children and the Movies* (Chicago: University of Chicago Press; repr. New York: Jerome S. Ozer).

Modleski, Tania (1988), *The Women who Knew too Much: Hitchcock and Feminist Theory* (New York: Methuen).

Moley, Raymond (1938), *Are we Movie Made?* (New York: Macy-Masius).

Morley, David (1980), *The 'Nationwide' Audience* (London: British Film Institute).

Mulvey, Laura (1975), 'Visual Pleasure and Narrative Cinema', *Screen*, 16/3: 6–18.

Münsterberg, Hugo (1916/1970), *The Photoplay: A Psychological Study* (New York: Dover).

National Council of Public Morals (1917), *The Cinema: Its Present Position and Future Possibilities* (London: NCPM).

Peterson, Ruth C., and L. I. Thurstone (1933), *Motion Pictures and the Social Attitudes of Children* (New York: Macmillan).

Petro, Patrice (1989), *Joyless Streets: Women and Melodramatic Representation in Weimar Germany* (Princeton: Princeton University Press).

Pribram, E. Deidre (ed.) (1988), *Female Spectators: Looking at Film and Television* (London: Verso).

Richards, Jeffrey (1989), *The Age of the Dream Palace: Cinema and Society in Britain 1930–1939* (London: Routledge).

*—— and Dorothy Sheridan (eds.) (1987), *Mass-Observation at the Movies* (London: Routledge & Kegan Paul).

Rowson, Simon (1936), 'A Statistical Survey of the Cinema Industry in Great Britain in 1934', *Journal of the Royal Statistical Society*, 99(1), 67–129.

Smith, H. Llewellyn, *et al.* (1935), *The New Survey of London Life and Labour* (London).

*Stacey, Jackie, (1994), *Star Gazing: Hollywood Cinema and Female Spectatorship* (London: Routledge).

Hermeneutics, reception aesthetics, and film interpretation

Noel King

Meaning in cinema is obvious: the average cinema film appears straightforward and can be understood immediately (with subtitles) by virtually everyone on the planet.   John Ellis 1981: 14

Very few spectators seek to read texts. They want to raid them for some relevance to their own interests. The study of movies undoubtedly has its place, but very few moviegoers want to study movies. They want to loot them.   Raymond Durgnat 1981: 77

Any interpretive practice seeks to show that texts mean more than they seem to say. But one might ask, why does a text not say what it means?
                              David Bordwell 1989a: 64–5

Between readerly respect and textual pillage falls the shadow. The gap that opens across these quotation-epigraphs indicates an enduring dilemma for film criticism's way of understanding the act of film viewing: is it to be thought of as a self-evident, communally shared activity of meaning-making ('meaning is obvious') or as an unpredictable activity in which the many individualities present in a specific cinema audience submit a particular film to many different interpretative processings ('raid', 'loot')? Once the traditions of hermeneutics and reception aesthetics are recruited to the area of film studies, they soon confront a double question: what will count as an 'appropriate' reading of a given film and to what extent

will the contingencies of the extra-textual determine the form of interpretative processing to which a particular film is subject? The central theoretical issue concerns the extent to which a text can be said to exert determinacy in the face of its many readings and uses. If reading is 'poaching', as Michel de Certeau (1984: 165–76) has suggested, if it is, 'by definition . . . rebellious and vagabond', as Roger Chartier (1994, p. viii) claims, then dispute necessarily centres on whether it is the rights of texts or of readers which are to prevail.

Interpretation

In *Interpretation and Overinterpretation* (1992), Umberto Eco intervenes in these debates on meaning, reading, and interpretation, principally by debating the 'neo-pragmatist' position that says texts have no essential coherence and that there is no difference between interpreting a text and using it. In outlining the 'dialectics between the rights of texts and the rights of their interpreters' (1992: 23), Eco side-steps debates

> **The central theoretical issue concerns the extent to which a text can be said to exert determinacy in the face of its many readings and uses.**

about authors' versus readers' intentions by introducing a third factor, the 'intention of the text' (25). In the wake of the floating of the signifier, Eco wants to establish some terms upon which interpretation might be grounded. Accordingly, he distances himself from ecstatic notions of the interpretative licence afforded by a belief in unlimited semiosis by talking about the criteria enabling one to put forward an interpretation.

While acknowledging that interpretations sometimes work by generating 'associations', Eco would prefer these associations to be at least partially evoked by the text. When Wordsworth used the word 'gay' it did not possess the meaning it would later carry, and so an interpretation of Wordsworth should respect the 'cultural and liguistic background' (69) against which his writing was produced. Concerned, as he is, to establish the interpretative criteria by which one could specify a degree of textual facticity rather than infinite elasticity or malleability, Eco argues that some version of 'the text-in-itself' exists 'between the mysterious history of a textual production' (e.g. medieval practices of textual composition) and 'the uncontrollable drift of its future readings' (e.g. what a contemporary critic 'reads into' Wordsworth). A degree of determinacy is to be found in the fact that 'the text qua text still represents a comfortable presence, the point to which we can stick' (88).

This is a view which is anathema to the neo-pragmatist Richard Rorty (1992: 93), however, who argues that 'all anybody ever does with anything is use it. Interpreting something, knowing it, penetrating to its essence, and so on are all just various ways of describing some process of putting it to work.' Textual coherence, therefore, is not internal but produced by the uses to which a text is put: 'a text just has whatever coherence it happened to acquire during the last roll of the hermeneutic wheel' (97). Rorty's example is a 'set of marks' that could variously be described as English words, hard to read, a Joyce manuscript, an early version of Ulysses, or worth a million dollars, and he argues that this coherence 'is neither internal nor external to anything, it is just a function of what has been said so far about those marks' (98).

A similar concern to weigh the relationship between formal(ist) attention to textual structure and phenomenological attention to a reader's subjectivity is also central to the accounts of interpretation provided by hermeneutics and reception aesthetics. In the case of film studies, the turn towards reception theory has been in reaction to the perceived limitations of 'textual

analysis' (and the forms of text–subject relationship which this seems to imply). Patrice Petro (1986: 11) suggests that the interest in reception has grown out of 'a general dissatisfaction with prevailing theories of subject-formation in film and literary studies', while Janet Staiger (1992: 8) argues that 'reception studies' is preferable to 'textual studies', because of its emphasis on 'the history of the interactions between real readers and texts, actual spectators and films'. According to Staiger, 'textual studies' explains an object by generating an interpretation of it, whereas 'reception studies' seeks to understand acts of interpretation as so many historically and culturally situated events: 'Reception studies is not textual interpretation but a historical explanation of the activities of interpretation' (212).

Arguing in this way, Staiger is not only distancing herself from textual analysis but questioning the whole value of 'interpretation'. As such she is a part of a debate over whether or not academic writing on film should continue to generate 'new' interpretations of texts or whether it should perform some other, non-interpretative function. From the late 1970s on, an increasing exasperation has been expressed in relation to the proliferation of acts of interpretation in film and literary studies. In 1981 Jonathan Culler claimed that the 'one thing we do not need is more interpretations of literary works' (1981: 6). David Bordwell (1989a: 18, 261) echoed Culler's sentiment. Arguing that film studies had followed 'the interpretive path . . . already laid down in the humanistic disciplines', he goes on, 'We need no more diagnoses of the subversive moment in a slasher movie, or celebrations of a "theoretical" film for its critique of mainstream cinema, or treatments of the most recent art film as a meditation on cinema and subjectivity.' The show of exasperation from these two critics in the face of ever-proliferating interpretative manœuvres testifies to the triumph of criticism-as-interpretation within university humanities courses and to its broader reach into the domains of book, journal, and magazine publication. However, for Bordwell, one particularly baleful consequence of the institutionalization of intepretation-as-criticism has been the production of a person who 'look[s] for interpretability' in relation to the films he or she encounters (32), according to a 'dominant framework' of 'revealing' 'hidden' 'levels' of meaning (2).

It is this interpretative tradition of which Bordwell is heavily critical. Echoing Wittgenstein, he argues that 'we must look beneath what critics say and examine what they—concretely, practically—do' (1989a: 144).

For him, the production of an interpretation is 'a skill, like throwing a pot' and because 'its primary product is a piece of language, it is also a rhetorical art' (251). He therefore describes the critic as:

a person who can perform particular tasks: conceive the possibility of ascribing implicit or repressed meanings to films, invoke acceptable semantic fields, map them onto texts by using conventional schemata and procedures, and produce a 'model film' that embodies the interpretation. Though acquired by each individual, these skills and knowledge structures are institutionally defined and transmitted. And though it is possible to abstract a critical 'theory' or 'method' from individual 'readings', and thus to reify that theory or method as a self-sufficient procedure of discovery or validation, employing such an apparatus will not carry any critic all the way through an interpretation. Decisions about cues, patterns, and mapping must still be made by 'just going on' as Wittgenstein puts it, and following the tacit logic of craft tradition. (202, 204)

In this respect, Bordwell's account of the institution of—and academic institutionalization of—film criticism connects him, however loosely, with such things as Stanley Fish's notion of 'interpretive communities' (presented in *Is there a Text in this Class?*, 1980) and with Fish's subsequent work on 'professionalism' and 'the literary community' (now collected in *Doing what Comes Naturally*, 1990). At the same time, Bordwell's book has similarities with some other writing that seeks to show the specific institutional limits of interpretation (Culler 1988; Frow 1986; Weber 1985). Bordwell's characterization of this situation is to say: 'To use Todorov's term, film interpretation has become almost wholly "finalistic", based upon an a priori codification of what a film must ultimately mean. "It is foreknowledge of the meaning to be discovered that guides the interpretation." Many of the film's nuances now go unremarked because the interpretive optic in force has virtually no way to register them' (1989a: 260). The critical manœuvre of deciding that the 'the driven male protagonist' and 'overall style' of Anthony Mann's *Raw Deal* (1947) would 'put it into the class of *film noir*' is an example of such an 'optic' in action. Making such an interpretative move 'will recast the film along certain lines, throwing particular cues into relief and downplaying others' (142).

In presenting this account of the dominant practices of film criticism, and in stressing that 'meanings are not found, but made', Bordwell none the less insists that film criticism is not a place where total relativism or an infinite diversity of interpretation operate. For Bordwell, meaning is constructed out of textual cues (a composition, a camera movement, a line of dialogue), and the play between the individual and the institutional is evident in the fact that 'each individual' acquires those 'skills and knowledge structures' (3) courtesy of the institution. Critics, he claims, 'typically agree upon what textual cues are "there", even if they interpret the cues in differing ways' (3). However, a stronger distinction needs to be made between applying a grid of reading—or activating a regime of reading—and producing an interpretation. One could, for example, produce very different 'interpretations' of the imagistic significance of tattoos in Charles Laughton's *The Night of the Hunter* (1946), Jonathan Demme's *The Silence of the Lambs* (1991), and Martin Scorsese's 1992 version of J. Lee Thompson's *Cape Fear* (1962) while working within an agreed system of image, motif, or theme-based reading. To ask the significance of a motif in a text is to invite a series of declarations of interpretative difference which are all generated within a shared system constituted by the act of asking about the significance of a particular motif.

One of the main strengths (and provocations) of Bordwell's position lies in his claim that the institution of film criticism encourages a drive to produce innovative acts of critical exegesis at the same time as it operates certain limits and constraints in order to determine what will count as 'innovative'. The academic institution, he suggests, regulates the production of novelty in interpretation, and a broad rule for the interpreter is said to be: 'Quit when the interpretation starts to sound like those that we supplant' (1989a: 247). The film scholar's principal authority derives from 'knowing how to make movies mean', and this is done by applying a series of rhetorical strategies. Bordwell mentions one such interpretative strategy, that of '*domestication*, the taming of the new', an activity which 'subsumes the unfamiliar to the familiar'. This is said to be an 'institutionally necessary function' since 'the unschematised film is the uninterpretable film' (256). Given the drive to produce new interpretations, and given the potential endlessness of interpretation, the question inevitably arises of when and how to stop the pursuit of interpretative novelty. Initially, says Bordwell, one finds the threshold of interpretative termination only 'by positing a meaning that is more subtle, pervasive, remote, or elusive than other meanings, particularly those already constructed by other critics' (246).

Historical poetics and cultural poetics

If Bordwell is sceptical of the value of 'interpretation', his counter-bid for a more productive form of film criticism promotes the twin notions of a 'historical poetics' and a 'neoformalism' (1989a: 263–74; 1989b: 369–98). According to Bordwell, 'neoformalist poetics' is not a methodology but 'an angle of heuristic approach, a way of asking questions' (1989b: 379). The neo-formalist critic's task is to provide a descriptive reconstruction of the options facing a filmmaker within a given historical conjuncture: 'Neoformalist poetics has been especially interested in how, against a background of conventions, a film or a director's work stands out' (1989b: 382). Bordwell says that the two main questions film criticism should ask are: 'how are particular films put together? Call this the problem of films' *composition*', and, 'what *effects* and *functions* do particular films have?' (1989a: 263). The principal virtue of a 'historical poetics' of cinema, therefore, rests in its attempt to reconstruct earlier acts of film comprehension (see e.g. Gunning 1991). Bordwell contends that a 'self-conscious historical poetics of cinema' (1989a: 266) is best placed to produce studies of particular cinematic forms, genres, and styles in such a way as would demonstrate 'how, in determinate circumstances, films are put together, serve specific functions and achieve specific effects' (266–7). The beginnings of such a critical practice are said to reside in the work of Arnheim, Russian Formalism, the early Soviet filmmakers, Bazin's (1967) writing on the evolution of cinematic language, and Noël Burch's (1979) work on the history of style in Japanese cinema. An 'open-textured historical poetics of film' would display, Bordwell argues, an 'awareness of historically existent options' (268) in cinema. The poetician's task is to analyse the 'norms, traditions, habits . . . that govern a practice and its products' (269). Such a historical poetics would study practices of reception as well as those of production, seeking to establish particular viewing conventions, 'the inferential protocols of certain historical modes of viewing' (272) or historically specific 'norms of comprehension' (274).

The neo-formalist perspective, therefore, escapes the cycle of interpretative one-upmanship described above by setting itself a different critical task, describing how innovation is achieved within a received and enabling system: 'Neoformalism balances a concern for revealing the tacit conventions governing the ordinary film with a keen interest in the bizarre film that subtly, or flagrantly, challenges them' (1989b: 382). This formulation also overlaps with points Stephen Greenblatt has been making since he invented the term 'new historicism' in the early 1980s to describe a particular orientation towards textuality and interpretation (1982: 3–6). Greenblatt uses the term interchangeably with 'cultural poetics' or a 'poetics of culture', and has recently added to his definition of what is involved (1994: 114–27). He does so, characteristically, by relating an anecdote concerning his visit to the Uffizi, in Florence, to attend an exhibition called 'A School for Piero', on the occasion of Piero's 500th anniversary. Although the exhibition sought to place Piero in context, the 'school' of the exhibition's title, Greenblatt was none the less struck by the strangeness of the Piero painting when displayed in this context:

I think the intention of the exhibit was, in a sense, the intention of the 'old historicism'. That is, to give you a sense of the context out of which Piero's work came. It would explain and help you to understand the remarkable achievement of Piero, indicating how he learned to do these things with perspective and how he learned to achieve certain effects of light and so on. But actually the effect of the exhibit on me was *exactly* the opposite of this. I was staggered by how *weird* Piero's double-portrait [of Federico de Montefeltro and his wife, Battista Sforza] was. . . . Not that the radical achievement of Piero had been normalised but rather that its true peculiarity, its unexpected, unforeseeable, surprising power, suddenly welled up. And I would say that one long-term commitment of any cultural poetics or new historicism—which is always, to some extent, an anti-historicism—would be to *intensify* and not to lose that sense of surprise. One of the problems with Marxist aesthetics was that it tended so easily to round up the usual suspects, and tended so much to collapse what looked remarkable into the predictable, the familiar, the same. But in fact one's experience of life is *precisely* of things that you can't possibly have predicted. *Afterwards* they may look inevitable or you may project back.

The anecdote demonstrates the importance of two key words for Greenblatt's formulations, 'resonance' and 'wonder'. The play between these two terms indicates the difference of the 'new historicism' from an 'old(er) historicism' and also from the 'new criticism' that was so dominant in American English departments from the 1950s to the late 1970s. Greenblatt's new historicism is not a stunningly sharp break with these earlier interpretative traditions, but it is a significant reorientation of them. Respectful of the deep historical contextualizing knowledge of the older historicism (for example, the work of Louis Martz and Stephen Orgel) new historicism is also mindful of the intense formal attention to detail contained in the new criticism. The particular reorientation contained in the new historicism rests in the extent to which it seeks to relate the 'wonder' of a particular textual artefact—the capacity for an artwork to astonish or surprise its viewer or reader in a moment of ravishing *arrest*—to a sense of the artwork's 'resonance'—the broader cultural-discursive framework which enabled it to be composed in the first place. The notion of 'resonance' directs our attention to those larger systems of cultural meaning which enable someone to write, paint, create an artistic work of some kind within the artistic or cultural conventions of a given historical period. The notion of 'wonder' describes those occasions on which the artwork escapes, exceeds, or somehow breaks away from the larger system which made it possible in the first place.

For Greenblatt, cultural poetics designates the play between the available discourses enabling cultural production in a particular time together with an acknowledgement of those occasions on which an artwork seems to move beyond the discursive or representational systems that obtain in a particular historical moment. In this respect, the parallel with Bordwell's neo-formalist interest in the 'bizarre' film is evident. However, just as Bordwell expresses an interest in 'historical modes of viewing', so Greenblatt's concern is as much with the habitual critical-theoretical ways of knowing about cultural objects as it is with the historically available representational systems enabling the composition of particular cultural artefacts in particular historical periods. In this sense, there is a double temporality to be placed on the concepts of 'resonance' and 'wonder'.

Cultural hermeneutics

Similar issues are also explored in Dudley Andrew's two books *Film in the Aura of Art* (1984) and *Mists of Regret* (1995). In *Film in the Aura of Art*, Andrew generates readings of seven film classics and offers a reconsideration of the work of Orson Welles and Kenji Mizoguchi. Discussing the relation of particular films to the systems in which they were produced, Andrew says, 'these films would be unreadable without the system whose sameness they hope to escape' (1984: 13). For Andrew, meaning 'is formed in the give and take between tradi-

tion and the encounter of the new' (14), and he later suggests, 'every film struggles to stand on its own apart from the system that confers intelligibility on it. Hollywood is only one name for the regularity of this process of differentiation endemic to the culture industry of every nation and art form' (193–4).

Andrew's critical practice unites formalism with phenomenology, and if it displays a closeness to Bordwell's position (on the side of formalism) it is also close to the phenomenological film criticism of Stanley Cavell (1981). Both Andrew and Cavell regard their film criticism as a kind of cultural conversation, and each claims to have been selected by the films they discuss rather then the other way about. So Andrew's 'close study of fertile films' is one in which 'the films have the first word and, frequently, the last' (1984, p. xi), while Cavell claims, 'I am always saying that we must let the films themselves teach us how to look at them and how to think about them' (1981: 25). Andrew's critical practice is in part calculated to discover 'what sort of films command the kind of respect I am according them?' (1984, p. xi) since, 'like all interpretation, my essays are a conversation within culture, not an argument about culture' (p. xiii).

By the time of *Mists of Regret*, Andrew has consolidated his critical stance into what he calls a 'cultural hermeneutics' (1995: 3), explaining that a cultural history of cinema seeks to establish 'an indirect reconstruction of the conditions of representation that permitted such films to be made, to be understood, even to be misunderstood, controversial, or trivial' (22). Inspired by Barthes's (1967) notion of *écriture* as outlined in *Writing Degree Zero* (rather than the different understanding later given to that term by Derrida and Kristeva), he coins the term 'optique' to designate 'the limited plurality of (cinematic) options available in any epoch' (1995: 19). 'Optique', he argues, carries 'an echo of option, of a limited set of possibilities alive at a given moment in a specific cinematic situation' and also 'involves the specification of audience expectations, needs and uses' (19).

The phenomenological side of Andrew's writing is evident when he suggests that the films with which he is concerned 'are entrances to a different way of being a spectator, not totally different . . . but different enough to tempt us to reconstruct the spectator to which they were addressed . . . As a historian, I am a spectator ready to become another spectator' (22–3). This is an argument anticipated in an earlier piece when he describes hermeneutics as 'a theory which entertains the relationship between a text worthy of respect and a consequential, historically grounded reading of that text . . . It seeks in the body of the text the significance which only that body has for it' (1982: 60). He goes on, 'The point of departure for hermeneutics couldn't be more evident: what do we have to do when we don't understand what we read?' (62). The apparent straightforwardness of his statement, however, belies the fact that 'not understanding' can take a number of quite different forms.

'Not understanding'

For example, it could indicate our lack of familiarity with the representational-compositional system within which the text was produced, thereby requiring a task of historical familiarizing. As Roger Chartier (8–9) has warned, 'A history of reading must not limit itself to the genealogy of our own contemporary manner of reading, in silence and using only our eyes; it must also (and perhaps above all) take on the task of retracing forgotten gestures and habits that have not existed for some time.' He argues against 'a purely semantic definition of the text (which inhabits not only structuralist criticism in all its variants but also the literary theories most attuned to a reconstruction of the reception of works)' in favour of a recognition of how 'a text . . . is invested with a new meaning and status when the mechanisms that make it available to interpretation change' and when 'its form is apprehended by new readers who read it in other ways than did previous readers' (3, 16). In saying this, Chartier has in mind the fact that while a text retains a certain textual structure, it also changes as the social circumstances and modes of reading that surround it undergo change. Chartier's point is the same as de Certeau's: namely, that the more distant a text becomes from the institutions that participated in its initial socio-cultural visibility, the

The more distant a text becomes from the institutions that participated in its initial socio-cultural visibility, the more likely it is that readers will exercise their capacities for forms of reading that depart from the terms within which the text initially counted on being read.

more likely it is that readers will exercise their capacities for forms of reading that depart from the terms within which the text initially counted on being read.

A second instance of 'not understanding' could involve a clash of representational systems, thereby requiring a task of cross-cultural familiarizing. Umberto Eco's discussion of the reception of Michelangelo Antonioni's China film *Chung Kuo Cina* (1972), provides evidence of this form of misunderstanding (1986: 281–8). The differences between the encoding and decoding of Antonioni's film led to a clash of representational systems which in turn generated highly politically charged encounters. Eco reports that Antonioni wanted to present a 'tender, docile picture' of China and the Chinese because 'for us, gentleness is opposed to neurotic competition'. Unfortunately, 'for the Chinese that docility decodes as resignation' (285), and so the representation was taken to be an insulting one. Eco describes a specific sequence in the film, one involving the representation of the Nanking Bridge, as a way of indicating a clash of representational systems: 'Thus we see how the now famous criticism in *Renmin Ribao* could regard the shot of the Nanking bridge as an attempt to make it appear distorted and unstable, because a culture that prizes frontal representation and symmetrical distance shots cannot accept the language of Western cinema, which, to suggest impressiveness, foreshortens and frames from below, prizing asymmetry and tension over balance.' Consequently the Chinese critic 'sees another logic . . . and becomes indignant' (287).

Finally, 'not understanding' could be the positive consequence of our familiarity with a particular *dispositif*, whereby a state of incomprehension or unknowingness is the calculatedly produced relation of reader to textual artefact. As Schlegel (quoted in Hunter 1988: 164) observed, 'A classical text must never be entirely comprehensible. But those who are cultivated and who cultivate themselves must always seem to learn more from it.' This would seem to be a good description of the kinds of things art cinema viewers do when they consume art films. Ian Hunter has used the Schlegel quotation to argue that a reader's self-doubt and a text's inscrutability are the twin outcomes of a post-Romantic aesthetic system in which the notion of the unfathomable, aesthetically inexhaustible text, far from being an essential textual attribute, is purely the artefact of the critical machinery that is put to work on a text in order to produce a sense of 'aesthetic unfathomability'. When activated in this way it produces a sense of 'ethical incompletion' in the interpreter, as one who can only ever 'imperfectly' understand the text (1988: 159–84). Tony Bennett's gloss on the system Hunter is describing refers to it as involving the 'conception of the literary text as unfathomable—as the site for an endless practice of reading which can never be wrong yet never be right' (1990: 280).

For example, Bordwell (1989: 268) responds to Teresa de Lauretis's (1984) interpretation of *Bad Timing* (Nicolas Roeg, 1980) as a film which 'undercuts the spectator's pleasure by preventing both visual and narrative identification, by making it literally as difficult to see as to understand events and their succession, their timing: and our sense of time becomes uncertain in the film, as its vision for us is blurry'. Bordwell's comment on this is: 'On the contrary: such problems of identification and such temporal uncertainties constitute fundamental art cinema conventions, and they have shaped viewing skills ever since *Hiroshima mon amour* [Alain Resnais, 1959], *The Red Desert* ['Deserto rosso', Michelangelo Antonioni, 1964], *Persona* [Ingmar Bergman, 1966] and similar films became models for ambitious directors' (1989a: 268). To stay with the example of *Bad Timing*, one can see how Bordwell's point can be linked to some aspect of Hunter's arguments. First, if we contrast the editing technique used to introduce a flashback to the techniques used in classical Hollywood cinema, we can notice the way an interpretation is produced by the viewer's

knowledge of or familiarity with a particular textual technique (here a mode of editing) *in tandem with* that viewer's performing of some ethical work on the self of the kind described by Hunter.

For a neo-formalist poetics, the flashback would be a device whose different renderings across the history of Hollywood could become the object of scrutiny (see Turim 1989). To recall some signallings of flashbacks in classical Hollywood cinema: wind blows through an open window as the camera moves in close on a table-top calendar whose leaves are 'blown' backwards until we reach the date it is necessary to reach for that point in the fiction (Douglas Sirk's *Written on the Wind*, 1957). A character has to tell another character what *really* happened in a gunfight that occurred some time earlier. He drags on a cigarette, says, 'Think back, Pilgrim,' and exhales the smoke, which momentarily defocuses the screen to enable us to make the transition back to that time (John Wayne to Jimmy Stewart in John Ford's 1962 film *The Man who Shot Liberty Valance*, although, to be more precise, this is a flashback within a flashback structure). An intense light fixes around the eyes of a character as the camera moves into close-up (typical film noir flashback).

Bad Timing, on the other hand, cuts directly, taking its viewer abruptly across different times and locations. And the controversial scenes depicting Alex's (Art Garfunkel) rape or 'ravishment' of the comatose Milena (Theresa Russell)—scenes which have provoked

Structured ambiguity—*Bad Timing* (1980)

much writing on this film—are given to the viewer by way of a cut on the look of the investigator, Netusil (Harvey Keitel). This is one of the film's modernist gestures (or, as Bordwell would put it, 'art cinema conventions')—albeit one used to troubling sexual-political effect. Its consequence is to prompt the viewer to ask him- or herself whether this event really happened or whether it is Netusil's fantasy. And this viewer also knows that the film will not provide a definitive answer (no John Wayne here). So we encounter a film which employs some of the techniques of a modernist, art-cinema practice to produce structured ambiguity or the 'ambiguity effect'. Its viewer can never know for sure, although of course many viewers might decide one way or another and have conversations and arguments accordingly.

But one of the textual points of the film is to insist on the ambiguity and undecidability of this moment. There is no equivalent of third-person omniscient narration and no first-person character confession. All we have to go on is our capacity to interpret a textual device calculated to help produce an ambiguity effect. The 'correct' reading-position to take up is one in which we are content not to be able to decide. Consequently, these features of textual openness, ambiguity, and undecidability are achieved under definite conditions. The technique of editing constitutes a formal textual convention or condition, but it is one which needs to be accompanied by the ethical-interpretive work the viewer has to do on him- or herself. For example, the viewer has to inhabit a mode of reading which says: 'Read for maximum ambiguity; interpret knowing that there will be no definite resolution and take pleasure in this circumstance.' And one of the main points to be derived from a reading of Bordwell and Hunter is that particular critical protocols need to be in place in order for a film to be said to be ineffable. This ability to entertain ineffability constitutes a specific reading competence.

Reading formation

This discussion of the relations between texts and readings returns us to the central questions concerning text–reading–context relations. What is to count as a text and a reading, and to what extent is a text to be explained in terms of the conditions of its production, its first appearance and initial social circulation, as opposed to its subsequent insertion into a range of historically varying social–cultural contexts? In recent film studies, there has been an adoption of Tony Bennett's notion of a 'reading formation' (1983a, 1984) as one way of answering these questions and rethinking what historically situated viewers and/or commentators have done with specific films (Staiger 1992; Klinger 1994). Since Bennett's notion of a 'reading formation' has become a favoured way of rethinking the idea of 'reception' in relation to popular media texts, it seems appropriate to outline the reading formation that allowed Bennett to generate his notion.

The conception most immediately derives from Bennett's reading of Brecht (on 'rewriting'), Macherey (1977, on 'textual encrustations'), Carlo Ginzburg's suggestive account in The Cheese and the Worms (1978) of Menocchio as a reader, and the then-developing notion of intertextuality. But a broader context for the development of the term was the late 1970s reconsideration of Marxist aesthetics (to which Bennett's Formalism and Marxism (1979) was a strong contribution), principally in relation to literary texts as English literary critics became more familiar with the work of Brecht, Althusser, and Pierre Macherey. A revitalized Marxism focused on the notion of 'rewriting' and 'consumptional production' by advocating critical analysis of the historically variable existence and activities of texts. It was a mode of analysis that started from the proposition that 'what the entire history of discourse on literature shows is how much, in how many different circumstances, a text can be made to signify' (Mulhern 1978: 102). For this perspective 'text' means 'not only the works themselves but all the intepretations which have been attached to them and which finally are incorporated into them' (Macherey 1977: 7).

Bennett's conception of a 'reading formation' was meant to show that meaning is always transitive rather than inherent: 'It is not a thing which texts can have, but is something that can only be produced, and always differently, within the reading formations that regulate the encounters between texts and readers' (1983a: 218). It was also calculated to help rethink questions of popular reading, where reading was understood to refer to 'the means and mechanisms whereby all texts . . . may be "productively activated" during what is traditionally, and inadequately, thought of as the process of their consumption or reception'. The conception of reading formation was thus meant to attend to the actual history of a text's social functioning rather than privileging the originating conditions of a given text's production. The notion of a productive activation was meant to replace or displace the notion of textual interpretation: it provided a means of targeting the procedures whereby 'in the course of its history, a text is constantly re-written into a variety of different material, social, institutional and ideological contexts' (223). Bennett sought to 'imply a process in which texts, readers and the relations between them are all subject to variable determinations' (223). Any notion of an auto-telically secure text-in-itself as a stable object-to-be-read, or even as a fixed unit able to be ranged alongside the many readings done of it, is dissolved into 'the reading relations and, within those, the reading forma-tions which concretely and historically structure the interaction between texts and readers' (223). Rather than conceiving of an encounter between the polar-ized entities of 'the text' (open to a formal description) and 'the reading subject' (open to a reader-response perspective) Bennett proposed an investigation of the 'interaction between the *culturally* activated text and the *culturally* activated reader, an interaction that is structured by the material, social, ideological and insti-tutional relationship in which both texts and readers are inescapably inscribed' (22).

In this way the conception of a 'reading formation' seeks to avoid both a textual formalism and an extra-textual notion of a social context that finds a particular textual expression. Texts, readers, and contexts are not conceived as 'separable elements, fixed in their rela-tion to one another' because 'different reading forma-tions . . . produce their own texts, their own readers and their own contexts' (8). Thus texts are studied 'as constituted as objects-to-be-read within the different reading formations which have modulated their exis-tence as historically active, culturally received texts' (8). The study is simultaneously of texts in the light of their readings, readings in the light of their texts. The theo-retical consequence of this, applied to 'the Bond phe-nomenon', and expressed in *Bond and Beyond* (Bennett and Woollacott 1987), is that the text that is read 'is an always-already culturally activated object', just as 'the reader is an always-already culturally acti-vated subject . . . text and reader are conceived as being co-produced within a reading formation, gridded onto one another in a determinate compact unity' (64).

Barbara Klinger's (1994) book on Douglas Sirk uses Bennett's theoretical emphases to chart the way in which Sirk's films, over the years, have been character-ized as 'subversive, adult, trash, classic, camp, and vehi-cles of gender definition' (p. xv). Her case-study of the reception of Sirk's films outlines 'how different histor-ical, cultural, and institutional contexts produced meaning and ideological significance for Douglas Sirk melodramas from the 1950s to the 1990s' (157). By examining 'the institutional, cultural, and historical conditions that enabled these different identities to emerge' the book becomes a study of how some 'habi-tats of meaning operate', and by surrendering the idea that 'a film or novel has an essence that can be cap-tured once and for all by the proper critical method' Klinger's analysis is able to attend to textual forms conceived as 'historical chameleons with shifting iden-tities' (pp. xv, xvi). Thus Klinger is able to pursue the social destiny of a filmmaker's critical reputation and explore the various interpretive grids that were acti-vated in order to make Sirk's films mean differently in different social-historical contexts. By presenting a pic-ture of 'a text continually in the throes of transforma-tion' (161), her book indicates 'the social conditions and institutions that help constitute contingent mean-ings for texts as they circulate publicly' (p. xvi). In doing this Klinger elaborates Janet Staiger's notion of a criti-cism that avoids textual interpretation in favour of a historical explanation of the event of interpreting a text.

> **Klinger is able to pursue the social destiny of a filmmaker's critical reputation and explore the various interpretive grids that were activated in order to make Sirk's films mean differently in different social-historical contexts.**

Historical case-studies of particular films 'show how, under different circumstances, films assume different identities and cultural functions' (1994, p. xvii). Klin-ger's analysis explores the way diverse regions of com-mentary seek to define the Hollywood film over a long period of time. 'Historical research helps reconstruct the semiotic environment in which the text/viewer interaction took place, showing us discourses at work in the process of reception' (p. xx). Such a theoretical orientation eschews textual interpretation, any analysis of the text's internal strategies, in favour of seeking to describe the institutions underpinning the text's social reception at various points in its social life. In a similar critical gesture, Paul Smith (1993), analysing the cultural presence of Clint Eastwood, uses the phrase 'cotextual histories' to refer to 'the ensemble of ever-shifting discursive possibilities that cohabit with any particular text in a given culture at a specific moment . . . cotextual histories implicate the processes of both the production and reception of a text or utterance' (p. xv).

'Rereading' and the category of queer

Once things take root, it is sometimes hard to remember how historically contingent, how adventitious, their emergence was. The emergence and rapid consolidation and institutionalization of 'queer theory' in the United States, United Kingdom, and Australia throughout the 1990s is a case in point. There has been an explosion of books, articles, and conferences as queer theory widens from being a localized rethinking of what to do in the already (in the United States) firmly established field of gay–lesbian studies, to engage the critical attention of other literary–film–cultural domains. A measure of the success of queer as a cultural category and an intellectual–academic commodity is evident in the way it exists both as a means of rereading cultural texts produced before the emergence of the category of queer (it enables an interpretive remapping of earlier cultural terrain) *and* it becomes an umbrella term used by current cultural producers to describe their products and activities (films, novels, plays, installations). Queer theory performs a double cultural–hermeneutic operation by rereading earlier texts and providing a self-understanding for current cultural production, whereas, say, the new historicism seems confined to the first activity of providing new ways of reading cultural texts from earlier historical periods. New historicism licenses interpretation in a new way, as does neo-pragmatism. And from a neo-pragmatist perspective two questions present themselves in relation to the category of queer: is the 'queer voice' *really* there or is it produced by an act of theoretical invention–intervention? Does this difference matter? Does queer theory become further evidence of the claims of neo-pragmatism? As a mode of reading, is it, to recall Rorty's remarks on *Ulysses*, simply something we currently are able to 'say about the marks'? Or, as Durgnat might put it, is it one more way we have of 'looting' texts?

For example, Alfred Hitchcock's film *Marnie* (1964) is found to contain a 'queer voice' (Knapp 1993). This reading was not available in 1964 because the ability to perform a queer theory analysis only became possible twenty-five years later as a result of a specific reorganization of critical protocols conducted in relation to film and literary texts. (And here it would be necessary to establish the relation of queer theory to the category of camp which had been around for thirty years (at least since Manny Farber's 1940s and 1950s film criticism) and which had attracted more concentrated critical attention from the 1960s (Sontag) on to 1970s and 1980s (Russo, Dyer, Britton) and 1990s (Ross, Robertson).)

Conclusion

The brief discussion of some issues attaching to the highly productive category of queer returns us to some of the points made at the beginning. If we accede to the notion that an appropriate interpretation is one which respects and, where necessary, reconstructs the meaning-making context into which the film first emerged, then Bordwell's 'historical poetics', Andrew's 'optique' and 'cultural hermeneutics', Greenblatt's 'cultural poetics', and Eco's respecting of lexical historicity all share a surprising amount of common ground. And yet the work of people like Bennett and Klinger alert us to the need to be aware of the many different contexts within which meanings can be produced for texts (something also supported by that aspect of Greenblatt's 'cultural poetics' which places an obligation on current acts of critical analysis to grasp and explain the 'difference' of an 'astonishing' artwork).

It is not, finally, a matter of opting for neo-pragmatism over cultural poetics or historical poetics over cultural hermeneutics. The different critical orientations explored throughout this chapter would, I think, agree with the following observation from Chartier: 'to be sure, the creators . . . always aspire to pin down their meaning and proclaim the correct interpretation, the interpretation that sets out to constrain reading (or viewing). But without fail, reception invents, shifts about, distorts' (1994, p. x). And, equally without fail, there will be generated an ongoing set of critical perspectives seeking to explain the gap that opens between textual composition and origin and textual peregrination and appropriation.

BIBLIOGRAPHY

Andrew, Dudley (1982) 'Interpretation, the Spirit in the Body', *Bulletin of the Midwest Modern Language Association*, 15/1: 57–70.

—— (1984), *Film in the Aura of Art* (Princeton: Princeton University Press).

—— (1995), *Mists of Regret: Culture and Sensibility in Classic French Film* (Princeton: Princeton University Press).

Barthes, Roland (1967) *Writing Degree Zero*, trans. Annette Lavers and Colin Smith (New York: Hill & Wang).

Bazin, André (1967), 'Evolution of the Language of Cinema', in *What is Cinema?* ed. and trans. Hugh Gray (Berkeley: University of California Press).

Bellour, Raymond (1975), 'The Unattainable Text', *Screen*, 16/3: 19–28.

Bennett, Tony (1979), *Formalism and Marxism* (London: Methuen)

—— (1983a), 'Texts, Readers and Reading Formations', *Literature and History*, 9/2: 214–27.

—— (1983b) 'The Bond Phenomenon: Theorising a Popular Hero', *Southern Review*, 16/2: 195–225.

—— (1984), 'Texts in History: The Determination of Readings and their Texts', *Australian Journal of Communication*, 5/6: 3–11.

—— (1990), *Outside Literature* (London: Routledge).

—— and Janet Woollacott (1987), *Bond and Beyond: The Political Career of a Popular Hero* (London: Macmillan).

*Bordwell, David (1989a) *Making Meaning: Inference and Rhetoric in the Interpretation of Cinema* (Cambridge, Mass.: Harvard University Press).

—— (1989b) 'Historical Poetics of Cinema', in R. Barton Palmer (ed.), *The Cinematic Text: Methods and Approaches* (New York: AMS Press).

Burch, Noël (1979), *To the Distant Observer: Form and Meaning in the Japanese Cinema* (Berkeley: University of California Press).

Cavell, Stanley (1981), *Pursuits of Happiness: Hollywood's Comedies of Remarriage* (Cambridge, Mass.: Harvard University Press).

Chartier, Roger (1994), *The Order of Books: Readers, Authors, and Libraries in Europe between the Fourteenth and Eighteenth Centuries*, trans. Lydia G. Cochrane (Stanford, Calif.: Stanford University Press).

Culler, Jonathan (1981), ·*The Pursuit of Signs: Semiotics, Literature, Deconstruction* (London: Routledge & Kegan Paul).

—— (1988), *Framing the Sign: Criticism and its Institutions* (Oxford: Basil Blackwell).

de Certeau, Michel (1984), *The Practice of Everyday Life*, trans. Steven F. Rendall (Berkeley: University of California Press).

de Lauretis, Teresa (1984), *Alice Doesn't: Feminism, Semiotics, Cinema* (Bloomington: Indiana University Press).

Durgnat, Raymond (1981), 'Nostalgia: Code and Anticode: A Review of Jonathan Rosenbaum's *Moving Places: A Life at the Movies*', *Wide Angle*, 4/4: 76–8.

Eco, Umberto (1986), 'De Interpretatione: The Difficulty of Being Marco Polo (On the Occasion of Antonioni's China Film)', in *Faith in Fakes: Essays*, trans. William Weaver (London: Secker & Warburg).

—— (1992), with Richard Rorty, Jonathan Culler, and Christine Brooke-Rose *Interpretation and Overinterpretation*, ed. Stefan Collini (Cambridge: Cambridge University Press).

Ellis, John (1981), 'Notes on the Obvious', in M. A. Abbas and Tak-Wai Wong (eds.), *Literary Theory Today* (Hong Kong: Hong Kong University Press).

Fish, Stanley (1980), *Is there a Text in this Class?: The Authority of Interpretive Communities* (Cambridge, Mass.: Harvard University Press).

—— (1990), *Doing what Comes Naturally: Change, Rhetoric, and the Practice of Theory in Literary and Legal Studies* (Durham, NC: Duke University Press).

Frow, John (1986), *Marxism and Literary History* (Oxford: Basil Blackwell).

Ginzburg, Carlo (1978), *The Cheese and the Worms: The Cosmos of a Sixteenth Century Miller*, trans. John and Ann Tedeschi (London: Routledge & Kegan Paul).

Greenblatt, Stephen J. (1982), 'Introduction', *Genre*, 13: 3–6.

—— (1990), *Learning to Curse: Essays in Early Modern Culture* (London: Routledge).

—— (1994), 'Intensifying the Surprise as well as the School', Interview with Noel King, *Textual Practice*, 8/1: 114–27.

Gunning, Tom (1991), *D. W. Griffith and the Origins of American Narrative Film: The Early Years at Biograph* (Chicago: University of Illinois Press).

Hansen, Miriam (1991), *Babel and Babylon: Spectatorship in American Silent Film* (Cambridge, Mass.: Harvard University Press).

Hunter, Ian (1988), 'The Occasion of Criticism', *Poetics*, 17/1–2: 159–84.

*Klinger, Barbara (1990), 'Digressions at the Cinema: Commodification and Reception in Mass Culture,' in James Naremore and Patrick Brantlinger (eds.), *Modernity and Mass Culture* (Bloomington: Indiana University Press).

—— (1994), *Melodrama and Meaning: History, Culture and the Films of Douglas Sirk* (Bloomington: Indiana University Press).

Knapp, Lucretia (1993/1995), 'The Queer Voice in *Marnie*', *Cinema Journal*, 32/4 (Summer), 6–23; repr. in Corey K. Creekmur and Alexander Doty (eds.), *Out in Culture: Gay, Lesbian and Queer Essays in Popular Culture* (London: Cassell).

Macherey, Pierre (1977), 'An Interview', ed. and trans. Colin Mercer and Jean Redford, *Red Letters*, 5: 3–9.

Mulhern, Francis (1978), 'Marxism in Literary Criticism', *New Left Review*, 108.

Palmer, R. Barton (ed.), *The Cinematic Text: Methods and Approaches* (New York: AMS Press).

Petro, Patrice (1986), 'Reception Theories and the Avant-Garde', *Wide-Angle*, 8/1: 11–17.

Rorty, Richard (1992), 'The Pragmatist's Progress', in Eco (1992).

Smith, Paul (1993), *Clint Eastwood: A Cultural Production* (Minneapolis: University of Minnesota Press).

*Staiger, Janet (1992), *Interpreting films: Studies in the Historical Reception of American Cinema* (Princeton: Princeton University Press).

Turim, Maureen (1989), *Flashbacks in Film: Memory and History* (New York: Routledge).

Weber, Samuel (1985), 'The Limits of Professionalism', *Oxford Literary Review*, 5/1–2: 59–79.

List of Picture and Reading Sources

PICTURES

Unless otherwise stated all photographic material was reproduced courtesy of the Kobal collection. Whilst every effort has been made to identify copyright holders that has not been possible in a few cases. We apologize for any apparent negligence and any omissions brought to our attention will be remedied in any future editions. 1.1 Courtesy of Hyphen Films etc. 1.2 Courtesy of the British Film Institute 1.3 RKO/Goldwyn 1946 1.4 Universal City Studios, Inc. a division of MCA 1956 1.6 Polygram 1.7 Paramount 1.8 Miramax 1994 1.9 Turner Entertainment Co. 1939 1.10 Courtesy of Ian Christie 1.11 Courtesy of Ian Christie 1.12 Metro Goldwyn Mayer Inc. 1932 1.13 Paramount 1.14 De Laurentis and Warner Home Video 1.15 Universal City Studios, Inc. a division of MCA 1934 1.16 and 1.17 © Women Make Movies Inc. 1.18 Universal City Studios, Inc. a division of MCA 1940 1.19 Courtesy of the British Film Institute 1.22 RKO/Goldwyn 1936 1.23 Courtesy of the British Film Institute 1.26 and 1.27 Metro Goldwyn Mayer Inc. 1991 1.29 The Rank Organization Plc 1980

READINGS

Robin Wood: 'Written on the Wind' from Robin Wood, *University Vision*, 12, 1974. Peter Wollen: 'Citizen Kane', from 'Introduction to Citizen Kane' in *Film Reader*, 1, 1975. Richard Taylor and Ian Christie: Translation of Viktor Shklovsky's 'Poetry Prose in Cinema' from Richard Taylor and Ian Christie (eds.), *The Film Factory: Russian and Soviet Cinema in Documents 1896–1939* (revised edition, London and New York: Routledge) © Richard Taylor, 1994. John Hill: 'The Political Thriller Debate' from John Hill, 'Finding a Form: Politics and Aesthetics in *Fatherland, Hidden Agenda*, and *Riff-Raff*' in George McKnight (ed.), *Agent of Challenge and Defiance: The Films of Ken Loach* (Trowbridge: Flicks Books, 1997). Mary Anne Doane: 'Rebecca' from Mary Anne Doane, *The Desire to Desire: The Woman's Film of the 1940s*, Basingstoke Macmillan Ltd/Bloomington, Indiana University Press 1987. © Mary Anne Doane. Tania Modleski: 'Rebecca' from *The Women Who Knew Too Much: Hitchcock and Feminist Theory*, Methuen, 1988.

Index of Selected Films and Names